Ralph Ellison
and the
Raft of Hope

Ralph Ellison and the Raft of Hope

A Political Companion to *Invisible Man*

Edited by
LUCAS E. MOREL

THE UNIVERSITY PRESS OF KENTUCKY

Scholarly publisher for the Commonwealth,
serving Bellarmine University, Berea College, Centre
College of Kentucky, Eastern Kentucky University,
The Filson Historical Society, Georgetown College,
Kentucky Historical Society, Kentucky State University,
Morehead State University, Murray State University,
Northern Kentucky University, Transylvania University,
University of Kentucky, University of Louisville,
and Western Kentucky University.
All rights reserved.

Editorial and Sales Offices: The University Press of Kentucky
663 South Limestone Street, Lexington, Kentucky 40508-4008

08 07 06 05 04   5 4 3 2 1

Library of Congress Cataloging-in-Publication Data
Morel, Lucas E., 1964-
    Ralph Ellison and the raft of hope : a political companion to
    Invisible man / Lucas Morel.
        p. cm.
    Includes bibliographical references and index.
    ISBN 0-8131-2312-7 (hardcover : alk. paper)
    1. Ellison, Ralph. Invisible man. 2. Politics and literature—United
States—History—20th century. 3. Political fiction, American—History
and criticism. 4. Ellison, Ralph—Political and social views.
5. African American men in literature. 6. African Americans in
literature. I. Title.
PS3555.L625I5356 2004
813'.54—dc22   2003020611

This book is printed on acid-free recycled paper meeting
the requirements of the American National Standard
for Permanence in Paper for Printed Library Materials.

Manufactured in the United States of America.

DuBOIS

To my youngest son, Ellison Charles Morel

Contents

Contributors

Danielle Allen, Professor of Classics and Political Theory at the University of Chicago; 2001 recipient of a MacArthur fellowship; and author of *The World of Prometheus: The Politics of Punishing in Democratic Athens* (Princeton University Press, 2000) and *Talking to Strangers: On Little Rock and Political Friendship* (University of Chicago, 2004).

Charles "Pete" Banner-Haley, Associate Professor of History and the former Director of the Africana-Latin American Studies Program at Colgate University and author of *The Fruits of Integration: Black Middle Class Ideology and Culture, 1960–1990* (University Press of Mississippi, 1994).

Herman Beavers, Associate Professor of English at the University of Pennsylvania; poet; and author of *Wrestling Angels into Song: The Fictions of Ernest J. Gaines and James Alan McPherson* (University of Pennsylvania Press, 1995).

Alfred L. Brophy, Professor of Law at the University of Alabama School of Law; author of *Reconstructing the Dreamland: The Tulsa Riot of 1921—Race, Reparations, and Reconciliation* (Oxford University Press, 2002); and editor of the *Oklahoma City University Law Review* symposium issue on "Ralph Ellison and the Law."

John F. Callahan, Morgan S. Odell Professor of Humanities at Lewis and Clark College, author of *In the African-American Grain: Call-and-Response in 20th Century Black Fiction* (University of Illinois Press, 1988; reprint, 2001); editor of *Juneteenth* and *The Collected Essays of Ralph Ellison;* and literary executor of Ralph Ellison's estate.

Marc C. Conner, Associate Professor of English at Washington and Lee University and editor of *The Aesthetics of Toni Morrison: Speaking the Unspeakable* (University Press of Mississippi, 2000).

Thomas S. Engeman, Associate Professor of Political Science at Loyola University Chicago; editor of *Thomas Jefferson and the Politics of Nature* (University of Notre Dame Press, 2000); author, with Raymond Tatalovich, of *The Presidency and Political Science: Two Hundred Years of Constitutional Debate* (The Johns Hopkins University Press, 2003); and editor, with Michael Zuckert, of *Protestantism and the American Founding* (University of Notre Dame Press, forthcoming).

Lucas E. Morel, Associate Professor of Politics at Washington and Lee University and author of *Lincoln's Sacred Effort: Defining Religion's Role in American Self-Government* (Lexington Books, 2000).

William R. Nash, Associate Professor of American Literature and Civilization and Director of African-American Studies at Middlebury College and author of *Charles Johnson's Fiction* (University of Illinois Press, 2002).

James Seaton, Professor of English at Michigan State University and author of *Cultural Conservatism, Political Liberalism: From Criticism to Cultural Studies* (University of Michigan Press, 1996).

Kenneth W. Warren, Associate Professor of English and the Associate Director of the Center for the Study of Race, Politics, and Culture at the University of Chicago; author of *So Black and Blue: Ralph Ellison and the Occasion of Criticism* (University of Chicago Press, 2003) and *Black and White Strangers: Race and American Literary Realism* (University of Chicago Press, 1993).

Acknowledgments

This volume of scholarly reflections on Ralph Ellison's *Invisible Man* owes a great deal to my home institution, Washington and Lee University. Special thanks go to Larry Peppers, professor of Economics and dean of the Williams School of Commerce, Economics, and Politics, and Robert Strong, the William Lyne Wilson professor and chair of the Politics Department. Their support of this book stretches back to February 2002, when Washington and Lee University hosted a symposium to commemorate the 50th anniversary of the publication of Ellison's landmark novel. Most of the essays in this collection took first flight at this symposium. Scholars from a variety of disciplines gathered to take a closer look at the political lessons and aspirations of *Invisible Man* than had been exhibited to date.

To my colleague in the English Department, Marc Conner, my heartfelt thanks for helping this student of politics negotiate the challenging terrain of the American novel and African-American studies. For assistance with the Ralph Ellison Papers at the Library of Congress, I thank Alice Birney and the literary executor of Ralph Ellison's estate, my friend John Callahan. I am also grateful to Mrs. Fanny Ellison for permission to use quotations from Ralph Ellison's published and unpublished works, and am much obliged to Nancy Kaye, whose wonderful 1982 photograph of Ralph Ellison graces the cover of this book.

Steve Wrinn, director of the University Press of Kentucky, is a gem of a man who believed in this book as soon as he heard the idea. Thanks also to Angelique Cain Galskis and Gena Henry, editors at UPK, and Mary Grivetti, production editor at Shepherd, Inc., for guiding this collection through various phases of its production.

As ever, I thank my wife, Cherie, and children, Luke, Hannah, and Ellison, for their abiding love and support. The blessing of a devoted and affectionate family is beyond measure.

The novel at its best demands a sort of complexity of vision which politics doesn't like.

—RALPH ELLISON

Recovering the Political Artistry of Invisible Man

LUCAS E. MOREL

But what kind of society will make him see me, I thought. . . .

—INVISIBLE MAN

Abraham Lincoln once said that government action in a free society follows public opinion. Therefore, whoever could change public opinion could, to that degree, change the political landscape.[1] Ralph Ellison declared his intention to shape public opinion when he received the National Book Award in 1953 for *Invisible Man*. In his acceptance speech, he commented that his own attempt to write a major novel derived from a feeling that "except for the work of William Faulkner something vital had gone out of American prose after Mark Twain." He added that American writers once assumed "a much greater responsibility for the condition of democracy and, indeed, their works were imaginative projections of the conflicts within the human heart which arose when the sacred principles of the Constitution and the Bill of Rights clashed with the practical exigencies of human greed and fear, hate and love."[2] Ellison hoped to follow in the footsteps of these great American writers not only by developing and honing his craft as they did theirs, but also by writing *Invisible Man* as a deliberate attempt "to return to the mood of personal moral responsibility for democracy."[3] The connection between literature and politics could not have been made clearer.

This led him to conclude that a person might "deliberately overemphasize and say that most prose fiction in the United States . . . is basically 'about' the values and cost of living in a democracy."[4] Born and raised in the United States, Ellison spoke "the language of the Bible and the Constitution" as a matter of course, and, thus, understood his vocation as an American writer to be a morally and politically serious endeavor. He viewed the American people as "a collectivity of politically astute citizens who, by virtue of our vaunted system of universal education and our freedom of opportunity, would be prepared to govern."[5] Accordingly, American fiction at its finest was political fieldwork of a sort. Finding in literature "a medium for transcending the divisions of our society,"[6] Ellison would aspire to nothing less as a civic-minded writer.

Ralph Ellison expressed his civic duty by writing for people free enough to learn about and aspire to more than their society allowed. Anything less—whether as novelist or critic—would undermine the challenge and moral import of his writing, and allow the reader "to evade self-scrutiny."[7] As he put it in an introduction written for *Invisible Man* 30 years after its original publication, "while fiction is but a form of symbolic action, a mere game of 'as if,' therein lies its true function and its potential for effecting change. For at its most serious, just as is true of politics at its best, it is a thrust toward a human ideal."[8] Given the "improvised character" of American society,[9] Ellison imitated the kind of freedom he found in the greatest of American and world writers, novelists who could not speak truthfully about their world and the place of humanity in it without bringing the ideal to bear upon social reality as their readers knew it. To get readers to recognize the humanity of those hidden by stereotypes was, therefore, one of Ellison's literary aims.[10] Needless to say, Ellison understood the novel as "a function of American democracy"[11] and American writing as "an ethical instrument."[12]

In *Invisible Man*, Ellison took a society everyone "knows" and reduced it "to a symbolic form" that involved "the reader's sense of life" as well as "giving expression to his, the writer's, own most deeply held values." He believed this integration of sentiments, this commingling of reader and writer, would help the reader "go below the level of racial structuring and down into those areas where we are simply men and women, human beings living on this blue orb, and not always living so well."[13] When asked to give advice to a writer just starting out, Ellison replied: "[T]he integration of American society on the level of the imagination is one of this young writer's basic tasks. It is one way in which he is able to possess his world, and in his writings help shape the values of large segments of a society which otherwise would not admit his existence, much less his right to participate or to judge."[14] In 1965, when Ellison gave this interview, integration was a highly charged political concept. Ellison deliberately used the word "integration" to illustrate how profoundly he saw the connection between what he was doing in his stories and what others were doing in the streets for the Civil Rights Movement.

Given Ellison's appreciation of the "sacred principles" of the American founding,[15] as well as his consistent observations of its failed practice, it is surprising to find so little written in the 50 years since the novel's publication that makes "visible" the politics of *Invisible Man*—especially the contradiction between ideal and practice that Ellison explores in the novel. Over 40 years would pass before Jerry Gafio Watts's *Heroism and the Black Intellectual: Ralph Ellison, Politics, and Afro-American Intellectual Life* (1994) would be published—the first and only book-length treatment of Ellison's vocation as a political artist until H. William Rice's *Ralph Ellison and the Politics of the Novel* (2003). But as Watts acknowledges, he is "less concerned with the substantive meanings of the artistic and intellectual productions of particular black artists than with the ideological contexts that helped to shape their intellectual outlooks."[16] Approaching Ellison's politics from a sociological perspective, Watts seeks to uncover "those material forces that an individual black intellectual had to face in order to engage in his or her creative activity." Moreover, preferring to look primarily at Ellison's "explicit social and political writings," Watts admits he gives little attention to *Invisible Man.* Even the short stories of Ellison receive little scrutiny. (They were published in a collection entitled *Flying Home and Other Stories* two years after Watts's book was published.)

Nevertheless, Watts views Ellison as an "apolitical artist" because he did not take direct part in the modern Civil Rights Movement, a decision that supposedly distanced him from the world of "material interests" and, hence, led to a diminished political expression.[17] Furthermore, because Ellison "rejected social deterministic theories" outright, thinking them incapable of accounting for the freedom he believed black Americans always possessed, Watts finds Ellison wanting as a political commentator: his "critique of deterministic discussions of oppression rings evasive" and his "depictions of freedom and heroic possibility were romantic" as well as "ahistorical and acontextual." Watts concludes that Ellison's bourgeois ideology "limits his ability to perceive the depth of the impact of subjugation in people's lives."[18] The political aspirations of *Invisible Man* and Ralph Ellison's literary craft, we argue, deserve a more sympathetic reading.

H. William Rice's *Ralph Ellison and the Politics of the Novel* (2003) judges what Ellison's writings teach about literature's potential to influence politics against his times and, especially, the burgeoning Civil Rights Movement. Rice offers an instructive study of the political uses of language, contrasting the advantages and disadvantages of the spoken versus the written word. However, given his emphasis on the rhetoric of Ellison's writings, as opposed to a more direct examination of the politics of *Invisible Man,* Ellison's political teachings remain veiled, if not invisible. In addition, Rice argues that "despite his attempt to be responsible for democracy, Ellison ultimately failed as so many other American writers have done" because he did not foresee the impact that black leaders like Martin Luther King, Jr. or Malcolm X would have on American society.[19] Leaving aside the question of literature's capacity for political prognostication, we argue that great writers like Ellison teach other important lessons for civic-minded readers: principal among these is the extent to which a self-governing people falls short of its highest ideals—a key theme of this collection of essays. Rice lauds Ellison for highlighting this function of the American novelist, but concludes that his fiction did not provide the national self-identity and self-correction Ellison himself expected America's greatest writers to provide.[20]

T.V. Reed presents a more sympathetic assessment of Ellison's political achievement as a writer in his essay, "Invisible Movements, Black Powers: Double Vision and Trickster Politics in *Invisible Man*," interpreting *Invisible Man* as "an important, nuanced radical democratic political analysis."[21] Where Rice faults Ellison for putting faith in novels instead of activists (and for writing a novel that argued as much), Reed praises him for showing "that there is no rhetorical strategy, no cultural symbol, no political figure or figured politics that can not abuse or be abused." Rice sees more hope for political progress in "the preachers and the rhetoricians and the photographers and those who chanced to walk among them."[22] To the contrary, Reed learns from *Invisible Man* that, even for political activists, there is "no strategy that can guarantee 'eloquence,' that formal connection between idea and audience, no form that cannot be misheard or misread."[23]

Reed's analysis of *Invisible Man* falls short, however, in its insistence upon "a kind of political trickster voice" to offer the greatest clarity to the narrator's political thinking. This voice, Reed argues, "shows the necessity of recognizing the provisionality of all liberation discourses, their corruptibility and their divisiveness, even as it acknowledges their respective value as partial truths." This plausible reading of the various and disparate voices that beckon Invisible Man tries to preserve "both integrationist and [black] nationalist" visions of a better America without a sufficient recognition of the principles of each that are diametrically opposed to the other. Reed shows what *Invisible Man* teaches readers to *avoid* in their civic capacity. What they should *pursue* in its place, as Reed renders it, depends upon a "double" vision that even Reed predicts "will fall into blurred vision before long."[24]

Julia Eichelberger's *Prophets of Recognition* (1999), as the title suggests, makes vision or sight the key metaphor to understand the political lessons of the fiction of Ralph Ellison, Toni Morrison, Saul Bellow, and Eudora Welty. Moreover, the gap between humane ideals and humane practice serves as the focus of her examination of the common theme addressed by these authors. Eichelberger argues that Ellison and the rest "offer readers a vision of an as-yet unrealized democracy in which individuals acknowledge or recognize the innate worth of one another," and gleans her understanding of individual worth from the Declaration of Independence.[25] She goes so far as to call *Invisible Man* a "hymn to democracy" that "acknowledges its [democracy's] past failures as injustices rather than as the natural result of some people deserving a higher status than others." However, by imposing a "hermeneutics of suspicion" upon the novel, she undermines her recognition of "Ellison's humanism, his dedication to the absolute value of the individual" as "plausible and politically engaged."[26] In short, by suggesting that democracy masks an "ideology of domination," Eichelberger does not explain how to distinguish between the self-evident truths of the Declaration of Independence and the "false consciousness" that is the alleged product of American political and social institutions. If *Invisible Man* "constitutes a full-scale critique of American individualism," Eichelberger gives no principled basis for her own "bias in favor of democracy."[27] Eichelberger asserts that democracy is "the only acceptable means of organizing modern Western society" but offers no reason for this conclusion.

One interpretation of *Invisible Man* that examines its treatment of Marxist politics, while pointing out its drawbacks, is Gregory Stephens's *On Racial Frontiers: The New Culture of Frederick Douglass, Ralph Ellison, and Bob Marley* (1999).[28] Although Invisible Man ultimately failed as a leader in the Marxist Brotherhood (just as the Brotherhood failed Harlem), Stephens argues that Ellison's depiction of his Brotherhood experience suggests an alternative arena for political discourse: "These alternative or oppositional public spaces can play an important role in 'housing' new forms of identity and political alliances, and in critiquing the exclusionary practices of a larger public sphere."[29] Adding black nationalist and religious groups as other forms of "counter-publics," Stephens finds in *Invisible Man* a presentation of political alternatives that embody Ellison's notion of "antagonistic cooperation."[30] Stephens sees Ellison, along with Frederick Douglass and Bob Marley, as an "integrative ancestor" whose "mixed heritage" and "transracial consciousness" could "help us build a democracy in which commonality and difference could coexist." Unfortunately, by emphasizing the mixed racial and cultural heritage of Douglass, Ellison, and Marley, as well as "their interaction with a mixed public," Stephens comes close to offering a reductionist reading of their "common moral vision and cultural critique." In short, integrated messengers produce integrated messages. Nevertheless, *On Racial Frontiers* rightly points out their contribution to a "multiracial 'imagined community,' "[31] and, in particular, the options for political discourse latent in *Invisible Man*.

Donald B. Gibson includes a more direct commentary on the political lessons of *Invisible Man* in *The Politics of Literary Expression: A Study of Major Black Writers* (1981). Gibson sees Ellison's novel as "a social document," despite the narrative's focus on Invisible Man's progress in individual enlightenment as opposed to his political or social engagement.[32] However, he argues that *Invisible Man* emphasizes "the responsibility of the victim for his victimization," and concludes that Ellison, through his hibernating narrator, advocates a "politics of retreat." Because Ellison rejected "racial group solidarity" as a means of individual liberation, Gibson asserts that "the public policy implications of *Invisible Man* are murderous" for black Americans.[33] He acknowledges that the novel contains "myriad qualifications," especially in its epilogue chapter, where one finds that the "consciousness revealed there is in a healthier state." However, Gibson argues that this gives only "the appearance of ambiguity."[34] He rejects Invisible Man's closing epiphany as "tentative" at best, and not a ringing endorsement of America's political ideals.

Invisible Man certainly depicts someone who, in Ellison's words, refused "to run the risk of his own humanity"; this was Invisible Man's share of the responsibility for his predicament.[35] Nevertheless, Ellison did not excuse the various and sundry exploiters of Invisible Man's innocence. In his "Working Notes for *Invisible Man,*" he called the blind bigotry of the white American society within which his hero operates "a tragic national situation" that was inadequate "for the full development of personality."[36] Moreover, Ellison observed in his 1981 introduction to the novel that the hero was "a blues-toned laugher-at-wounds who included himself in his indictment of the human condition."[37] As the narrator discovers in the epilogue to his tale: "The fact is that you carry part of your sickness within you, at least I do as an invisible man. I carried my sickness and though for a long time I tried to place it in the outside world, the attempt to write it down shows me that at least half of it lay within me" (575). Both Invisible Man and American society share the blame for their mutual invisibility and blindness.

To his credit, Gibson recognizes that the formal chapters of the novel (excluding the prologue and epilogue) offer a "review of the past" that "has created order in the narrator's mind." But Gibson does not appreciate that the "order" in Invisible Man's mind was the product of his writing his tale down for the sake of an audience. This narrative device of Ellison's, the narrator making a novel of his experiences, should not be overlooked. Speaking of *Invisible Man* as the "memoirs" of his protagonist, Ellison observed: "It's a social act; it is not a resignation from society but the attempt to come back and to be useful."[38] It may have been "written underground," but it still had to surface (which means Invisible Man had to surface) in order for the story to reach the reader.[39] We conclude that both the novel's plot and its fictive manner of production demonstrate it is not a "retreat," or at least not a retreat that signifies an abandonment of social and civic responsibility.

Thomas Hill Schaub's *American Fiction in the Cold War* (1991) offers a more accurate assessment of Invisible Man's temporary departure from society: as a "strategic retreat," the narrator's literary hibernation helps him understand and communicate the pitfalls and possibilities of the spoken word. Schaub argues that Invisible Man "tells his story as a form of leadership, a prolonged dramatic discourse upon the ambivalence of the word." The narrator discovers this "only by first exhausting the options of leadership which he thought were available to him,"[40] and then turning to the written word as the remaining "socially responsible role to play."[41] By extricating Ellison's "stark social critique" of Jim Crow legislation and black leadership from the "mythic journey" more commonly noted by scholars of *Invisible Man,* Schaub recovers for post–Civil Rights Movement readers the unequal social and political climate for black Americans within which Ellison wrote his novel.[42] Yet, there remains much more of *Invisible Man's* social and political commentary to uncover.

Ellison consistently highlighted the novel's political engagement in the lectures, interviews, and essays he produced in the decades following the publication of *Invisible Man.* Two examples announce his social purpose directly in their titles: "The Novel as a Function of American Democracy" (a lecture) and "Society, Morality, and the Novel" (an essay).[43] Most importantly, what makes Ellison an apt subject for political inquiry is his clear appreciation of the land of his birth that also takes into account how Americans have fallen short of the nation's ideals. Like Alexis de Tocqueville, who wrote in *Democracy in America,* "It is because I was not an adversary of democracy that I wanted to be honest with it,"[44] Ellison saw himself as an appreciative critic of the United States. He said of the Declaration of Independence, "Though our history is one long list of struggles to make the values of that document manifest in the structure of our society, our history has also been marked by endless attempts to evade our moral commitment to the ideal of social equality."[45] Ellison wrote to recover this sense of responsibility, by both the artist and his audience, for the condition of American democracy.

Ellison's concern to measure what is wrong about America by what is right about America is almost completely missed by Ernest Kaiser, whose selective reading of Ellison says more about Kaiser's Marxism than it does about Ellison's alleged capitalist mindset. Kaiser's 1970 *Black World* essay, "A Critical Look at Ellison's Fiction and at Social and Literary Criticism by and about the Author," pulled no punches in its black militant assessment of Ellison's oeuvre to date: "Ellison has become an Establishment writer, an Uncle Tom, an attacker of the sociological formulations of the Black freedom movement," and "a denigrator of the great tradition of Black protest writing." As my prologue and the chapters that follow demonstrate, Kaiser fails to grapple sufficiently with the explicit and implicit criticisms of America that Ellison presented throughout his fiction and nonfiction. In addition, by placing Ellison firmly in the camp of the New Criticism of his day, Kaiser erroneously asserts that Ellison argued for a "separation of art and politics." Black literature, according to this line of reasoning, must be protest literature that "calls for a fight for freedom" in unambiguous terms. Kaiser concludes by questioning Ellison's "humanity" and claiming that Ellison exploits "Black people's folklore to show that Black human suffering has always existed and will always exist no matter what the Blacks do." In short, Kaiser interprets Ellison's writings as devoid of possibility, transcendence, and hope for black Americans.[46]

As a black writer in a predominantly white America, Ellison believed that a person's "individuality is still operative beyond the racial structuring of American society.[47] He emphatically denied that blacks were merely the sum total of their experiences under slavery or segregation. Ellison understood black Americans to possess the same will or moral agency that any other American possessed. To be sure, blacks confronted racism to one degree or another in the United States, which limited the scope of their personal initiative. But they were also participants in what Ellison called a "broader American cultural freedom" that reposed a responsibility to think and act in each citizen. As he once put it, "the obligation of making oneself seen and heard was an imperative of American democratic individualism."[48] This "obligation of freeing themselves"[49] had the makings of drama for Ellison, and so the story he told of black Americans wending their way through the contradictions of an ostensibly white America provides ample material for political inquiry. In so doing, he offered hope for continued progress in aligning the nation's practice with its principles.[50]

Invisible Man represents "political hope" in at least two ways: first, by what the narrator is able to learn and teach through his own journey *up* the river to freedom and enlightenment; second, by what the novel as a novel conveys about Ellison's demonstration of the freedom and possibilities available to black Americans, white Americans, and human beings, simply, when faced with barriers to their development as individuals.

It's no surprise that for someone whose claim to fame rests upon a novel entitled *Invisible Man,* Ellison believed the "moral perception" or vision of Americans white and black needed improvement.[51] His way of improving the moral vision of the nation was to make art of the ways black Americans dealt with their predicament as strangers in their own land. Robert Penn Warren neatly summarized *Invisible Man* as "the most powerful artistic representation we have of the Negro under . . . dehumanizing conditions; and, at the same time, it is a statement of the human triumph over those conditions."[52] That triumph, of course, is not only the narrator's but also Ralph Ellison's. As he acknowledged in his acceptance speech for the National Book Award, his achievement represented the culmination of a long "apprenticeship" in the art of the novel. But it also reflected a determination to express a profound understanding of the "diversity of American life" in "a prose which was flexible, and swift as American change is swift, confronting the inequalities and brutalities of our society forthrightly, yet thrusting forth its images of hope, human fraternity and individual self-realization."[53] In short, although Ellison gave credit to a few of his literary teachers (by name, Henry James, Mark Twain, and William Faulkner), the American novel had plenty of room to grow, and *Invisible Man* represented his initial foray into the thicket of artistic innovation and expression.[54]

Read as a "raft of political hope," *Invisible Man* pays homage to Mark Twain's *Adventures of Huckleberry Finn* for its critique of American mores. In an introduction written for the thirtieth anniversary edition of *Invisible Man,* Ellison shares that he learned from Twain that "a novel could be fashioned as a raft of hope, perception and entertainment that might help keep us afloat as we tried to negotiate the snags and whirlpools that mark our nation's vacillating course toward and away from the democratic ideal." Ellison added:

> So if the ideal of achieving a true political equality eludes us in reality—as
> it continues to do—there is still available that fictional vision of an
> ideal democracy in which the actual combines with the ideal and gives

us representations of a state of things in which the highly placed and the lowly . . . are combined to tell us of transcendent truths and possibilities such as those discovered when Mark Twain set Huck and Jim afloat on a raft.[55]

Huck Finn's depiction of the friendship between a free white boy and an escaped black slave offers an opportunity for Americans to step back from their day-to-day life and consider how their social and political practice at times contradicts their professed devotion to the ideals of equal humanity. Like Twain's *Huck Finn,* Ellison's *Invisible Man* presents the reader with a "tragic-comic" look at America's contradictions in hopes of pressing more of the nation's truths into political power.[56] Ellison believed it was this contradiction between America's "noble ideals and the actualities of our conduct" that drove "the American novel at its best."[57]

Addressing himself to readers, Ellison remarked that "in this so-called age of conformity we wish to discover some transcendent meaning in at least some of the turbulence which swirls through our lives. . . ."[58] As for the literary critic's responsibility, he must ensure that "the reader does not evade the crucial part of a fiction simply because of its difficulty." Ellison argued that critics must not "water down" a work and thereby "rob the reader of that transcendence which, despite his tendency to evade the tragic aspects of reality, he seeks in literature. The intent of criticism is frustrated, the fiction reduced to mere entertainment, and the reader is encouraged to evade self-scrutiny." Writing for democratic readers depended upon "the *individual's* ability to rise out of the mass and achieve the possibility implicit in the society," which reflected Ellison's literary hope that readers would "attain the finest perception of human value."[59]

Invisible Man begins with "I" and ends with "you," which suggests the connection the unnamed narrator, as well as Ralph Ellison, hopes to make with the reading public. Moving from the individual to society sounds easy enough, but as *Invisible Man* demonstrates, it's a precarious endeavor—a literary tour of duty made more difficult by the fact that our guide was to be an expelled student from a southern college for Negroes who, unbeknownst to himself, journeys to New York on a fool's errand. Ellison's hope is that by boarding his literary raft—guided by an invisible man, no less—the reader will learn to see more of America than he or she already knows. As Invisible Man confesses at the close of the novel: "And it is this which frightens me: Who knows but that, on the lower frequencies, I speak for you?" (581). Frightening, because the tale he has recounted is in many ways an unpleasant one. Yet, as Ellison pointed out, "it is in the unpleasant, in that which is charged with emotion, with fears, with irrationality, that we find great potential for transforming attitudes."[60] He expected his audience to include "articulate citizens," those open to self-scrutiny, as well as the "Bull" Connors of the world.[61] *"I would always write,"*

Ellison noted, "*as though the governor of Mississippi was looking over my shoulder.*"[62] As Ellison explained in his "Little Man at Chehaw Station" essay, living in America means never underestimating your audience.[63]

As the following essays demonstrate, *Invisible Man* offers hope for the citizen-reader by combining literary eloquence with capacious social observation and political commentary. In true Ellisonian fashion, the essays find unity in their exploration of freedom's possibilities and obstacles as reflected in *Invisible Man,* while approaching their respective interpretations from disciplines as diverse as literature, politics, law, and history.

James Seaton explores the enigmatic "principle" that *Invisible Man's* narrator claims must be affirmed in order to assume one's place in the hypocritical world of American society. Left undefined in the novel's epilogue, but what Ellison referred to elsewhere as "the omnipresent American ideal,"[64] the principle invites a definition by the reader that is general in application but rooted in the American experience. By examining the rejection of the principle by flawed—but instructive—characters in the novel, Seaton draws out some of the novel's political lessons. Most of these lessons are "negative," indicating doctrines, programs, or lifestyles to avoid. However, Seaton clarifies a few positive implications that derive from Invisible Man's tortuous discovery of the value of the principle of human equality, which has more to do with freedom and possibility than obeisance and uniformity. Danielle Allen interprets *Invisible Man* to depict democracy as a cruel political mistress, empowering her citizens only to disempower them. The novel illustrates what happens "when strangers try to act together," tied only by the bonds of citizenship and operating under pressure that bears on their interactions. Ellison shows how responsibility and reciprocity vie against exploitation and sacrifice for preeminence in the democratic order. Allen concludes that Ellison's most profound political wisdom will be found in the interaction and development of the characters, and not in some explicit display of protest or endorsement of a political program.

My own essay interprets *Invisible Man* as offering a complex portrait of the possibilities and pitfalls of American society, where individuals confront the challenge of what Ellison called "American democratic individualism." It examines key episodes and characters in *Invisible Man* that reveal Ellison's keen observations about the diverse livelihoods that black Americans made for themselves in the midst of racial discrimination. I also make extensive use of Ellison's post–*Invisible Man* essays, lectures, and interviews to show his abiding concern for the improved vision of American citizens and the progress of democratic freedom. Thomas Engeman argues that the ideals of equality and liberty were Ellison's initial political mainstays, finding their clearest expression in the epilogue to *Invisible Man.* These ideals, however, were not sufficient to create true community after slavery's demise. For the remedy, Engeman turns to Ellison's posthumously published novel *Juneteenth,* which suggests the need for a Christian conversion to redeem America from its white supremacist past—a conversion personified by A. Z. Hickman, the jazzman-turned-preacher and political visionary of *Juneteenth*.

Connecting *Invisible Man* to Ellison's nonfiction writings of the 1940s, William Nash shows how writing the novel transformed Ellison's early "politicized social criticism" into a more complex depiction of individual freedom in a prejudicial but democratic society. Specifically, Nash interprets Mary Rambo and the hospital and funeral scenes of *Invisible Man* as literary rebuttals to sociological accounts of black life as merely the product of white oppression. The universalism of *Invisible Man,* a book written as "a form of social power," invites the reader to reconsider his view of race and individuality in a way that political doctrines and propaganda sheets cannot match. Alfred Brophy interprets *Invisible Man* as signaling the sociopolitical changes afoot in post–World War II America that facilitated the modern Civil Rights Movement. He draws upon court precedents and newspaper editorials from the Oklahoma of Ellison's youth that highlight the primacy of individual freedom and the social costs of segregation. Brophy concludes that the *Brown v. Board of Education* decision of 1954 serves as *Invisible Man's* closest political analog.[65]

Kenneth Warren revisits the Little Rock desegregation crisis of 1957 and examines Ellison's debate with Hannah Arendt over the responsibility (or recklessness) of the parents of "the Little Rock Nine." Contrary to both Ellison and Arendt, Warren argues that the black children who integrated Central High became "cultural apprentices" of freedom and responsibility on their own initiative and did not merely follow their parents' lead into the Civil Rights Movement. Nevertheless, Warren affirms that their courage demonstrated Ellison's conviction that black Americans had never accepted their second-class status in American society passively. Warren sees in the Little Rock Nine, as well as the central figures of *Invisible Man,* a demonstration of how black American culture was both shaping and being shaped by the greater American culture. Taking the widest historical view, Charles Banner-Haley reads *Invisible Man* as an attempt to situate black Americans in the center of America's social and political development. By "removing the veil of invisibility" that has cloaked the contribution of black Americans, Ellison offered a portrait of American history more diverse than that presented by consensus historians. Moreover, in taking the reader on a literary journey from race to America and back to the individual, Ellison established himself not only as a major writer, but also as a public intellectual whose political views defy the claims of pundits on both the Right and the Left.

Moving from history to mystery, as Ellison might have put it,[66] Marc Conner draws out the sacred and historical significance of the "litany of things" that confront, puzzle, and ultimately help liberate Invisible Man as an individual and social being. From the central chapter's "yam" episode to *Invisible Man's* presentation of time, history, and memory, Conner shows how material objects compel the narrator to see America's contradictions more clearly. This frees Invisible Man to affirm *and* to reject as a way of contributing to an America more faithful to its professed ideals. Following this theme of affirmation and rejection, Herman Beavers offers a sophisticated account of how *Invisible Man* oscillates between stability (represented by documents) and chaos. Viewing Invisible Man as a "random element," epitomized by the famous Battle Royal scene, Beavers argues that the novel incorporates chaos theory and "turbulent flow" to illustrate the diverse and fluid character of American democratic society. Beavers suggests that Ellison's use of disorder takes on greater significance by representing not merely individual or social entropy, but also opportunities for growth by the narrator, the free society he intends to rejoin, and the reader of *Invisible Man.*

In a fitting tribute to the political focus of this collection of essays, John Callahan offers a lyrical and spirited ode to Ellison's understanding of the nexus between love and democracy. Connecting Invisible Man's funeral oration to his closing remarks in the Epilogue, Callahan interprets the narrator's social activism as "an expression of love" and not merely a personal ambition to lead. Reflecting on this theme's extended treatment in *Juneteenth,* and highlighting the political prescience of its provocative closing chapter, Callahan shows Ellison's concern to delineate the options available to those who would resolve America's contradictions.

At the end of *Invisible Man,* the protagonist declares that "there's a possibility that even an invisible man has a socially responsible role to play" (581).[67] Ellison's invisibility as a political commentator or activist has not hidden his considerable reflection on the sacred ideals that set the American republic into motion. He understood those ideals to form the ground of future progress and to mark the starting point for any writer ambitious enough to help readers bridge the gap between American promise and fulfillment. By showing how Ellison moved America's political ideals and shortcomings to the foreground of American literary consciousness, this volume offers *Invisible Man* as a raft of political hope to all who would join that community of "articulate citizens" envisioned by Ralph Ellison.

ENDNOTES

1. In his first debate with U.S. Senator Stephen A. Douglas, Lincoln observed, "In this and like communities, public sentiment is everything. With public sentiment, nothing can fail; without it nothing can succeed. Consequently he who moulds public sentiment goes deeper than he who enacts statutes or pronounces decisions. He makes statutes or decisions possible or impossible to be executed." "First Debate with Stephen A. Douglas at Ottawa, Illinois" (August 21, 1858), *The Collected Works of Abraham Lincoln,* ed. Roy P. Basler, 9 vols. (New Brunswick: Rutgers University Press, 1955), 3:27.

2. Ralph Ellison, "Brave Words for a Startling Occasion" (January 27, 1953), *The Collected Essays of Ralph Ellison,* ed. John F. Callahan (New York: The Modern Library, 1995), 152–53. Hereinafter cited as *Collected Essays;* emphases in original unless otherwise noted. He repeated this conviction almost forty years later: "In a sense the Constitution and Bill of Rights made up the acting script which future Americans would follow in the process of improvising the futuristic drama of American democracy. The Founders' dream was a dream of felicity, but those who inherited the task of making it manifest in reality were, alas, only human." "Address at the Whiting Foundation" (October 23, 1992), *Collected Essays,* 851.

3. Ralph Ellison, "Brave Words for a Startling Occasion," *Collected Essays,* 151. Over a decade later, Ellison commented, "The main stream of American literature is in me, even though I am a Negro, because I possess more of Mark Twain than many white writers do." Ralph Ellison, "Remarks at The American Academy of Arts and Sciences Conference on the Negro American, 1965" (May 14–15, 1965), in *New Black Voices: An Anthology of Contemporary Afro-American Literature,* ed. Abraham Chapman (New York: New American Library, 1972; orig. publ. in 95 *Daedalus* 1 [Winter 1966]), 406–7.

4. Ralph Ellison, "Society, Morality and the Novel" (1957), *Collected Essays,* 702.

5. Ralph Ellison, "Introduction to the Thirtieth-Anniversary Edition of *Invisible Man*" (November 10, 1981), *Collected Essays,* 483.

6. Ralph Ellison, "Going to the Territory" (September 20, 1979), *Collected Essays,* 591. Ellison found a parallel example of transcending race in comparative human performance on the athletic field:

> [W]hile baseball, basketball and football players cannot really tell us how to write our books, they do demonstrate where much of the significant action is taking place. Often they are themselves cultural heroes who are responsible for a powerful modification in American attitudes. They tell us in nonliterary terms much about the nature of possibility. They tell us about the cost of success, and much about the nonpolitical aspects of racial and national identity, about the changing nature of social hierarchy, and about the role which individual skill and excellence can play in creating social change.

"Remembering Richard Wright" (July 18, 1971), *Collected Essays,* 674. Contrary to Ellison's optimism, Maxine Lavon Montgomery's *The Apocalypse in African-American Fiction* (Gainesville: University Press of Florida, 1996) emphasizes "the blueslike absurdity of modern America and the apocalypse toward which the nation is moving" (51). Montgomery accurately sees in the novel's Harlem riot "a clash not just among people, but the various political ideologies posing as solutions to the race problem" (13). Moreover, she notes Invisible Man's rejection of "Ras's [black] nationalism and Brother Jack's scientific historicism" (51), two forces connected by the riot. However, Montgomery mentions but does not discuss the "chorus of affirmations" with which the narrator closes the tale that is the novel. Her only comment on "the democratic principles upon which America was founded" is that Invisible Man's "naïve belief" in them proves "deceptive" (50).

The focus on apocalyptic imagery in the novel leads her to conclude: "With *Invisible Man* there is no question that the end of the world is imminent" (41). Does this mean the end of America's democratic principles? Montgomery makes no attempt to square this with the narrator's "chorus of affirmations" or to explain what has enabled him, after all the reversals he has suffered, to "learn to love" (51).

7. Ralph Ellison, "Society, Morality and the Novel," *Collected Essays*, 722.

8. Ralph Ellison, "Introduction to the Thirtieth-Anniversary Edition of *Invisible Man*," *Collected Essays*, 482.

9. Ralph Ellison, "Going to the Territory," *Collected Essays*, 593.

10. See Ralph Ellison, " 'A Very Stern Discipline' " (March 1967), *Collected Essays*, 733–37, where he explains the destructiveness of stereotypes in literature and democratic thought and practice.

11. Ralph Ellison, "The Novel as a Function of Democracy" (June 1967), *Collected Essays*, 755–65.

12. Ralph Ellison, "Twentieth-Century Fiction and the Black Mask of Humanity" (1946), *Collected Essays*, 99. Ellison called *Invisible Man* not only an attempt to create a "work of art" but also "a social action in itself." "The World and the Jug," Part II (February 3, 1964), *Collected Essays*, 183.

13. Ralph Ellison, "On Initiation Rites and Power: A Lecture at West Point" (March 26, 1969), *Collected Essays*, 532.

14. Ralph Ellison, " 'A Very Stern Discipline,' " *Collected Essays*, 754.

15. Ralph Ellison, "Commencement Address at the College of William and Mary" (1972), *Collected Essays*, 409. Ellison referred repeatedly to the Declaration of Independence, Constitution, and Bill of Rights as "our sacred documents" (408–11).

16. Jerry Gafio Watts, *Heroism and the Black Intellectual: Ralph Ellison, Politics, and Afro-American Intellectual Life* (Chapel Hill: The University of North Carolina Press, 1994), 12.

17. Watts, 12 and 97. See also an account of the vilification of Ralph Ellison at an April 1965 Negro Writers' Conference in Harold Cruse, *The Crisis of the Negro Intellectual: From Its Origins to the Present* (New York: William Morrow & Company, Inc., 1971; orig. publ. 1967), "Negro Writers' Conferences—The Dialogue Distorted," 498–512. Cf. John McCormick, *Catastrophe and Imagination: An Interpretation of the Recent English and American Novel* (London: Longmans, Green and Co., 1957), an early recognition of political perception in *Invisible Man* that transcended the subject of race: "Although no other novelist has conveyed the bitterness of relations between whites and negroes so successfully, we do not read *Invisible Man* as a documentary study in race-relations; its allegory is broadly political, not narrowly racial. The novel is a work of high art, a full and brave statement of the need for men to be individuals and to be human" (293). McCormick listed *Invisible Man*, along with *The Great Gatsby, A Farewell to Arms, The Sound and the*

Fury, and *Light in August,* as a modern novel "which might still be read a century from now" (65). To which, Ellison commented: "Surely the man is on the weed." See Ralph Ellison, "Letter to Albert Murray" (April 4, 1957), in *Trading Twelves: The Selected Letters of Ralph Ellison and Albert Murray,* ed. Albert Murray and John F. Callahan (New York: The Modern Library, 2000), 157–58.

18. Watts, 57, 71, and 108. Watts concludes that "Ellison's blue ontology generates a less critical framework than [Richard] Wright's Marxism for confronting the political situation of blacks precisely because Ellison viewed the political-social order as a relatively insignificant shaper of black life" (85). Cf. Alan M. Wald, *Exiles from a Future Time: The Forging of the Mid-Twentieth-Century Literary Left* (Chapel Hill: The University of North Carolina Press, 2002), which focuses on Ellison's early association with the League of American Writers and his writing for Communist-supported journals (like the *New Challenge, Negro Quarterly,* and *New Masses*) as an attempt to integrate "Black literary Marxism" (285) and "Afro-cosmopolitanism" (xv). See also Wald, 206, 266, and 276–97. Grouping Ralph Ellison with Richard Wright, Wald asserts that "Marxism remained the touchstone for their political and creative thought for years" after the mid-1940s (294). However, he acknowledges that *Invisible Man,* written during the decade after Ellison and Wright broke with Communist regulars, represented a "deradicalization process" (289) for Ellison. See also William J. Maxwell, *New Negro, Old Left: African-American Writing and Communism Between the Wars* (New York: Columbia University Press, 1999) and Mark Naison, *Communists in Harlem during the Depression* (Urbana: University of Illinois Press, 1983).

19. H. William Rice, *Ralph Ellison and the Politics of the Novel* (Lanham, Md.: Lexington Books, 2003), 140.

20. See Rice, *Ralph Ellison and the Politics of the Novel,* chap. 3, "A Socially Responsible Role for an Invisible Man: Ellison the Essayist," 57–82.

21. T.V. Reed, "Invisible Movements, Black Powers: Double Vision and Trickster Politics in *Invisible Man,*" in his *Fifteen Jugglers, Five Believers: Literary Politics and the Poetics of American Social Movements* (Berkeley: University of California, 1992), chap. 3, 58–86; Reed, *Fifteen Jugglers, Five Believers,* 85.

22. Rice, *Ralph Ellison and the Politics of the Novel,* 109.

23. Reed, *Fifteen Jugglers, Five Believers,* 85.

24. Reed, *Fifteen Jugglers, Five Believers,* 85 and 86.

25. Julia Eichelberger, *Prophets of Recognition: Ideology and the Individual in Novels by Ralph Ellison, Toni Morrison, Saul Bellow, and Eudora Welty* (Baton Rouge: Louisiana State University, 1999), 2–3.

26. Eichelberger, *Prophets of Recognition,* 57 and 3.

27. Eichelberger, *Prophets of Recognition,* 57 and 5.

28. See Gregory Stephens, *On Racial Frontiers: The New Culture of Frederick Douglass, Ralph Ellison, and Bob Marley* (Cambridge, U.K.: Cambridge University Press, 1999),

chap. 3, "Invisible Community: Ralph Ellison's Vision of a Multiracial 'Ideal Democracy,'" 114–47.

29. Stephens, 147.

30. For Ellison on "antagonistic cooperation," see "The World and the Jug" and "The Little Man at Chehaw Station: The American Artist and His Audience" (1977/1978), *Collected Essays*, 188 and 492. Lawrence P. Jackson puts forth B. P. Rinehart as Ellison's depiction of "a political actor absolutely necessary to conceptualize emancipatory freedom." See "Ralph Ellison, Sharpies, Rinehart, and Politics in *Invisible Man*," 40 *The Massachusetts Review* 1 (Spring 1999), 71–85. See also Miele Steele, "Metatheory and the Subject of Democracy in the Work of Ralph Ellison," 27 *New Literary History* 3 (1996), 473–502.

31. Stephens, ix and 1–4. For something of a corrective, see Ross Posnock, *Color & Culture: Black Writers and the Making of the Modern Intellectual* (Cambridge, Mass.: Harvard University Press, 1998), which argues that Ellison's essays recover "implicitly the root sense of politics as civic participation in a public world, one emancipated from the private realm of the *ethnos* where social organization by natural descent reigns" (187).

32. Donald B. Gibson, *The Politics of Literary Expression: A Study of Major Black Writers* (Westport, Conn.: Greenwood Press, 1981), 93 and 63.

33. Gibson, 93–94. For Gibson, this retreat from a society that does not permit individual "integrity" seems like a rejection of politics, but actually results in "oppression by default, by refusal to oppose it" (94). He concludes that the Invisible Man must either join his oppressor or "remain the powerless, underground victim." Gibson affirms Marcus Klein's assessment that the Invisible Man has no positive role to play above ground: "[G]iven the social facts of America, both invisibility and what he now calls his 'hibernation' are his permanent condition." See Marcus Klein, "Ralph Ellison," in *After Alienation* (Cleveland: World Publishing, 1964), p. 74, cited by Gibson, 96 n. 15. S. P. Fullinwider agrees, concluding that Invisible Man "ended up living in an abandoned cellar in complete alienation. He had abandoned the idea of changing society." *The Mind and Mood of Black America* (Homewood, Ill.: The Dorsey Press, 1969), 199. Curiously, without any direct comment on the novel's epilogue, Fullinwider argues that *Invisible Man* teaches a more "Nietzschean ideal" of self-definition that rejects (scientific) reason in favor of "art" like jazz, which "defied convention" and "embraced chaos and from it created its forms." This interpretation does not account for the Epilogue's discussion of "the principle" Invisible Man comes to accept—a principle that derives in some way from the "Great Tradition" Fullinwider claims the novel's narrator rejected as masking "ruthless power and greed" (197).

34. Gibson, 61 and 94. Claiming that Ellison "bought the propaganda of the academic critics, accepted the image of the faceless, universal man, trapped in the narrow world of his own ego" along with "the modern idea of a raceless world," Addison Gayle, Jr. gives short shrift to the political implications of the novel's epilogue, which he calls an "assimilationist denouement." See Addison Gayle, Jr.,

The Way of the New World: The Black Novel in America (Garden City, N.Y.: Anchor Press/Doubleday, 1975), 212–13.

35. Ralph Ellison, "The Art of Fiction: *An Interview*" (Spring 1955), *Collected Essays,* 221.

36. Ralph Ellison, "Working Notes for *Invisible Man*" (undated), *Collected Essays,* 344.

37. Ralph Ellison, "Introduction to the Thirtieth-Anniversary Edition of *Invisible Man,*" *Collected Essays,* 481.

38. Ralph Ellison with Allen Geller, "An Interview with Ralph Ellison" (October 25, 1963), in *Conversations with Ralph Ellison,* ed. Maryemma Graham and Amritjit Singh (Jackson: University of Mississippi, 1995), 76; orig. publ. in *Tamarack Review* (Summer 1964), 221–27. As noticed by Thomas A. Vogler, "What is affirmative in both the structure and the existence of the book is that the invisible man does survive through turning his experience into art." See "*Invisible Man:* Somebody's Protest Novel," in *Ralph Ellison: A Collection of Critical Essays,* ed. John Hersey (Englewood Cliffs, N.J.: Prentice-Hall, Inc., 1974), 134.

39. Ralph Ellison, "The Art of Fiction: *An Interview*" (Spring 1955), *Collected Essays,* 220: "The hero comes up from underground because the act of writing and thinking necessitated it." See also Ralph Ellison with David L. Carson, "Ralph Ellison: Twenty Years After" (September 30, 1971), in Graham and Singh, 203, and Ralph Ellison with John O'Brien, "Interview with Ralph Ellison" (1973), in Graham and Singh, 230–31.

40. Thomas Hill Schaub, *American Fiction in the Cold War* (Madison: The University of Wisconsin Press, 1991), 104 and 105. To emphasize the rhetorical advantage gained by the narrator (and Ellison) by choosing the written over the spoken word, Schaub titles his chapter on *Invisible Man* "From Ranter to Writer." He borrowed the phrase from Ralph Ellison's 1958 *Partisan Review* essay: "The final act of *Invisible Man* is . . . that of a voice issuing its little wisdom out of the substance of its own inwardness—after having undergone a transformation from ranter to writer." See Ralph Ellison, "Change the Joke and Slip the Yoke," *Collected Essays,* 111.

Citing Invisible Man's speech at the white smoker, Homer Barbee's speech before the white trustees and black students, and Ras the Exhorter's transformation into Ras the Destroyer, Schaub reads *Invisible Man,* in part, as a critique of "speech-making itself as a form of leadership in which the ambiguities of the word may be collapsed into the monologue of ideology" and "especially suited to demagoguery" and "propaganda" (Schaub, 107–8, 111–13). Curiously absent from this interpretation is the narrator's eulogy to Tod Clifton, wherein he reflects to himself, "And could politics ever be an expression of love?" Given Invisible Man's perplexity over the reason for the gathered crowd at Clifton's memorial, "Did it signify love or politicized hate?" (452), Schaub's recovery of the novel's implicit but pervasive political commentary would have benefited from a stronger emphasis on the ambiguity of the spoken word's potential for good. For a more sympathetic and politically optimistic reading of the eulogy, see John F. Callahan, "Frequencies of Eloquence: The Performance and Composition of *Invisible Man,*"

In the African-American Grain: Call-and-Response in Twentieth-Century Black Fiction (Urbana: University of Illinois Press, 2001; orig. publ. 1988), 150–88, esp. 170–73.

41. Ralph Ellison, *Invisible Man* (New York: Random House, 1952; reprint, New York: Vintage Books, 1995), 581.

42. Schaub highlights the "disparity" between American principle and practice as the context for Ellison's writing: "In writing *Invisible Man,* Ellison made this long-standing hypocrisy a central theme of the novel, but his determination to make the experience of his central character resonate universally for all readers had the effect of mediating historical and political urgencies within the ahistoricism of mythic form and tragic vision so typical of post-war critical thought" (Schaub, 92). Similarly, John Whalen-Bridge calls *Invisible Man* "a kind of submerged call to political action" in *Political Fiction and the American Self* (Urbana: University of Illinois Press, 1998), 131; see also 137–42. See also Kenneth W. Warren, "Ralph Ellison and the Reconfiguration of Black Cultural Politics," 11 *Yearbook of Research in English and American Literature,* ed. Winfried Fluck (Tubigen: Gunter Narr Verlag, 1995), 139–57, for a discussion of the limited options for political and literary representation available to black Americans, which makes Ellison's *Invisible Man* all the more a cultural *tour de force.*

43. Ralph Ellison, "Society, Morality, and the Novel" and "The Novel as a Function of American Democracy," *Collected Essays,* 694–725 and 755–65, respectively. Cf. Ellison's famous reply to *Dissent* editor Irving Howe, where Ellison commented that the novel "is *always* a public gesture, though not necessarily a political one." Ralph Ellison "The World and the Jug," Part I (December 9, 1963), *Collected Essays,* 158. For Howe's critique, which (in Ellison's words) sees James Baldwin and Ralph Ellison as " 'black boys' masquerading as false, self-deceived 'native sons' " of America, see Irving Howe, "Black Boys and Native Sons," in Irving Howe, *A World More Attractive: A View of Modern Literature and Politics* (Freeport, N.Y.: Horizon Press, 1970; orig. publ. 1963), 98–122.

44. Alexis de Tocqueville, *Democracy in America,* intro. Sanford Kessler and trans. Stephen D. Grant (Indianapolis: Hackett Publishing Company, Inc., 2000), 169.

45. Ralph Ellison, "Notes for Class Day Talk at Columbia University" (1990), *Collected Essays,* 840.

46. Ernest Kaiser, "A Critical Look at Ellison's Fiction and at Social and Literary Criticism by and about the Author," 20 *Black World* 2 (December 1970), 95, 96, and 97. Of the New Critics that influenced Ellison, Kaiser writes: "This kind of writing, unemotional, uncommitted and uninvolved in the people's problems, is a cop-out and an escape in the heartbreak house of a dying, exploiting, murdering capitalistic society" (57). Moreover, he criticizes both Ellison and Richard Wright for ignoring the "great tradition of protest and fight-back" (59) in other black American writers. Commenting on Ellison's novel-in-progress, Kaiser surmises: "It is not much more than the Blacks' resignation to their oppression and fate. Where is man's great struggle to control his society and nature? It is not in

Ellison's fiction" (86). This issue of *Black World* monthly addressed "Ralph Ellison and His Literary Works and Status."

47. Ralph Ellison, "'A Completion of Personality': A Talk with Ralph Ellison," Part I (1974), *Collected Essays,* 799. Channeling the muse of Frederick Douglass, Ellison noted, "For Negroes the Supreme Court Decision of 1954 and the Civil Rights Act of 1964 induced no sudden transformation of character; it provided the stage upon which they could reveal themselves for what their experiences have made them, and for what they have made of their experiences." "If the Twain Shall Meet" (November 8, 1964), *Collected Essays,* 575.

48. Ralph Ellison, "A Special Message to Subscribers" (1979), *Collected Essays,* 351.

49. Ralph Ellison, "The World and the Jug," Part I (December 9, 1963), *Collected Essays,* 160 and 161. The publication of Ellison's second novel *Juneteenth* (edited by John F. Callahan from a work-in-progress at the time of Ellison's death in 1994) offers this restatement of the black American predicament: "This society is not likely to become free of racism, thus it is necessary for Negroes to free themselves by becoming their idea of what a free people should be" (356).

50. For a discussion of the political relevance of Ellison's writings to contemporary racial controversies, see the following articles by Lucas E. Morel: "Ellison's 'Invisible' Still Walk Among Us," *Los Angeles Times* (April 14, 2002), M1; "Ennobled by Jazz: Ralph Ellison and the Music of American Possibility," *Books & Culture: A Christian Review* (May/June 2002), 9–10; "America's Racial Divide: Of Debts Spoken and Unspoken," IX *On Principle* 3 (June 2001), 1, 3–4; and "On Becoming Visible: Race and the *Imago Dei,*" *Books & Culture: A Christian Review* (September/October 2000), 24–26. For an essay that that emphasizes the cultural, as opposed to political, freedom suggested by *Invisible Man,* see Morris Dickstein, "Ralph Ellison, Race, and American Culture," 18 *Raritan* 4 (Spring 1999), 30–50.

51. Ralph Ellison, "'A Completion of Personality': A Talk with Ralph Ellison," Part I (1974), *Collected Essays,* 805: "The point is one of moral perception, the perception of the wholeness of American life and the cost of its successes and its failures."

52. Cited in Robert Penn Warren, *Who Speaks for the Negro?* (New York: Random House, 1965), 354.

53. Ralph Ellison, "Brave Words for a Startling Occasion," *Collected Essays,* 151 and 153. Ellison asserted that the award must have been given to him for "my efforts rather than my not quite fully achieved attempt at a major novel" (151). However, a few months before the novel was published, he wrote to Albert Murray "that whether our books are miscarriages or what not, this kind of labor of love is never lost, not completely lost, because just the effort to do what has never been done before, to define in terms of the novel that which has never been defined before is never completely lost." Ralph Ellison, "Letter to Albert Murray" (January 8, 1952), in *Trading Twelves,* 25. He would state a few years later that he thought *Invisible Man* "failed of eloquence"; see Ralph Ellison, "The Art of Fiction: *An Interview*" (Spring 1955), *Collected Essays,* 217. Of course, this says more about the difficulty of doing literary justice to the mutable, American social and

political landscape than it does about Ellison's craft as a writer. This also goes a long way to explaining why he never finished the sprawling saga of race, religion, and politics from which John F. Callahan culled the posthumous novel *Juneteenth*.

54. As John F. Callahan noted, "Ellison chooses to write a patriotic novel, but on his terms." Callahan, "Frequencies of Eloquence," 184.

55. Ellison, "Introduction to the Thirtieth-Anniversary Edition of *Invisible Man*," *Collected Essays*, 482–3.

56. For Ellison's conviction that American culture could only be taken in as a whole through a "comic and tragic vision," see "Foreword to *The Beer Can by the Highway*" (1987), "Introduction to the Thirtieth-Anniversary Edition of *Invisible Man*," "Working Notes for *Invisible Man*," and "The World and the Jug," in *Collected Essays*, 847, 483, 344, and 177, respectively.

57. Ralph Ellison, "Hidden Name and Complex Fate: A Writer's Experience in the United States" (January 6, 1964), *Collected Essays*, 206–7: "I need only remind you that the contradiction between these noble ideals and the actualities of our conduct generated a guilt, an unease of spirit, from the very beginning, and that the American novel at its best has always been concerned with this basic moral predicament."

58. Ralph Ellison, "Society, Morality, and the Novel," *Collected Essays*, 706. For further discussion of transcendence and other Ellisonian themes, see Horace A. Porter, *Jazz Country: Ralph Ellison in America* (Iowa City: University of Iowa Press, 2001), 8–16.

59. Ralph Ellison, "Society, Morality, and the Novel," *Collected Essays*, 722.

60. Ralph Ellison, "On Initiation Rites and Power," *Collected Essays*, 540.

61. "Nevertheless, the hooded horrors parading, murdering and shouting defiance in the South today suggest that the psychic forces with which I tried to deal (in both dream and essay) are still there to be dispersed *or humanized*." Ralph Ellison, " 'Tell It Like It Is, Baby' " (June 1965), *Collected Essays*, 30; emphasis added.

62. Ralph Ellison, "Roscoe Dunjee and the American Language" (May 14, 1972), *Collected Essays*, 460.

63. Ralph Ellison, "The Little Man at Chehaw Station: The American Artist and His Audience" (1977/1978), *Collected Essays*, 489–519.

64. Ralph Ellison, "Society, Morality and the Novel," *Collected Essays*, 702.

65. For a recent law review issue that examines Ralph Ellison's connection to the development of American law, see Alfred L. Brophy, ed., "Ralph Ellison and the Law," 26 *Oklahoma City University Law Review* 3 (Fall 2001). The review is divided into the following sections: "Ellison's Cultural and Political Thought and Context," "*Invisible Man* and Other Ellison Texts," and "Ellison's Expanding Circle: Legal and Psychological Ramifications of Invisibility."

66. Recalling his early days of hunting, Ellison wrote that after a successful shot, the men would declare "in voices that throbbed with true American optimism, 'A

hit, my boy, is history!'" If they missed, Ellison observed that "they'd stare at the sky or cover and say, 'A miss, my boy, is a mystery!'" Ellison added that the writer's task was "to transform the misses of history into hits of imaginative symbolic action that aid their readers in reclaiming details of the past that find meaning in the experience of individuals." Ralph Ellison, "Address at the Whiting Foundation" (October 23, 1992), *Collected Essays,* 853.

67. Ellison noted many times that Invisible Man eventually forsook speaking for writing as his "socially responsible role," as shown by the novel presented fictionally as the narrator's memoirs. Similarly, in one of Ellison's last speeches, he described the civic duty of the American writer as follows: "Whether they be poets or novelists, essayists or dramatists, they are challenged to take individual responsibility for the health of American democracy." Ralph Ellison, "Address at the Whiting Foundation," *Collected Essays,* 852–53.

Chapter 1

Affirming the Principle

JAMES SEATON

A half century after the publication of *Invisible Man* there is very little controversy over its standing as one of the great literary works of the twentieth century, but the debate over the political implications of the novel and about Ralph Ellison's politics in general has continued, even though some issues have become moot. The question as to whether *Native Son* or *Invisible Man* provides the right model for African-American writers is happily irrelevant, given the number and variety of black novelists who have attained prominence in the last 50 years, and few are interested in reviving the often vehement attacks on the novel and on Ellison himself launched in the sixties. Ellison's opinions, however, still remain provocative. Indeed, the gulf between academic orthodoxy and the views expressed in the essays has only widened over the years, even as the reputation of *Invisible Man* has grown. A number of Ellison's most influential critics acknowledge the greatness of *Invisible Man* but go out of their way to distance themselves—and *Invisible Man*—from the views expressed in Ellison's essays. In addition, there are some new reasons why a study of the political implications of *Invisible Man* in the light of Ellison's essays would be controversial even if Ellison's own opinions had somehow lost their capacity to provoke. Assuming a continuity and coherence between the Ellison of the novel and the Ellison of the essays goes against the grain of prevailing theories about authorship, while the attempt to arrive at a reasonably accurate reading of the novel's political implications by any means at all is at odds with the dominant theories of interpretation.

The notion that a literary work is the product of a specific author or authors seems obvious to common sense but has been rejected by some of the most influential contemporary theorists. Roland Barthes's "The Death of the Author" and Michel Foucault's "What is an Author?" are the canonical statements on this theme. Neither attempts to refute the traditional conception of authorship by reasoned argument, but both speak with an oracular certainty that is surely one of the sources of their influence. Barthes writes about what "[w]e know now," in fortunate contrast to the ignorant ages before us:

> We know now that a text consists not of a line of words, releasing a
> single "theological" meaning (the "message" of the Author-God) but of
> a multidimensional space in which are married and contested several

writings, none of which is original: the text is a fabric of quotations, resulting from a thousand sources of culture.[1]

Echoing Barthes, Foucault announces that "criticism and philosophy took note of the disappearance—or death—of the author some time ago."[2] E. D. Hirsch argues carefully and at length in *Validity in Interpretation* that any attempt to distinguish between more accurate and less accurate readings of a text must rely on a conception of meaning based on the author's intention.[3] Barthes and Foucault do not disagree; the difference is that they want to rule out the ability to make any distinction between more or less accurate readings. Once one rejects the notion of authorship, Barthes observes with approval, "the claim to 'decipher' a text becomes entirely futile."[4] Foucault finds it authoritarian to find one analysis better than another, since the effect is to discount some readings as "wrong." The more readings, the better, no matter whether they are responsible or arbitrary, based on close reading or imposed from without. For him, then, to assert that the "author is the principle of thrift in the proliferation of meaning" is to justify the rejection of authorship as a concept. The notion of authorship warrants the strongest condemnation in Foucault's vocabulary: it is "ideological": "The author is therefore the ideological figure by which we fear the proliferation of meaning."[5] Today, however, partisans of "proliferation" are likely to find that it is precisely the hegemony of the postmodernist orthodoxy sponsored by figures like Barthes and Foucault that deters alternative views. My own study has the goal of discovering as accurately and fully as possible the political implications of *Invisible Man*. Contrary to the opinions of Barthes and Foucault, there is no need to worry that attempts like my own will discourage the "proliferation" of rival interpretations; it is rather the acceptance of theories that teach the impossibility of discovering the insights of authors like Ralph Ellison through reading their works that discourages reconsideration of texts like *Invisible Man*.

A number of critics express their admiration for Ellison's first novel but distance themselves from Ellison's stances in his essays.[6] Houston Baker analyzes the Trueblood episode in *Invisible Man* hoping to demonstrate that "the distinction between folklore and literary art evident in Ellison's critical practice collapses in his creative practice."[7] Alan Nadel, whose *Invisible Criticism* provides a perceptive and sympathetic study of *Invisible Man,* seems appalled by Ellison's politics, commenting that "Only someone naively seduced by the propaganda of the American Dream and an essentialist notion of individualism could articulate some of the positions that Ellison held."[8] Jerry Gafio Watts notes that Ellison has been "subjected to uncivil and ad hominem attacks by critics" but then goes on to attack in "ad hominem" fashion himself, going so far as to speculate that an "unsatisfiable 'great white master' may have taken up residence in Ellison's black superego"[9] and suggesting that Ellison's "phenomenal stature in American art and letters" is due not only to "the magnificent achievement of *Invisible Man*" but also to "Ellison's willingness to assume the air of a senior statesman of American letters and his fondness for being celebrated."[10] Not content to merely disagree with Ellison's allegiance to a "rather doctrinaire establishmentarian American ideology,"[11] Watts charges that Ellison adopted "an intensified elitist individuality as a social marginality facilitator."[12] It is not clear what this means, but it appears that Watts is charging that Ellison hypocritically expressed views not because he thought they were true but because he could rise in society by identifying himself with such positions—an "ad hominem" criticism if there ever was one. Meanwhile, Kerry McSweeney finds it possible to admire *Invisible Man* once it is viewed as an "early postmodernist text," but warns that Ellison's adamantly humanistic belief in what is "basic in man beyond all differences of class, race, wealth, or formal education" cannot help but "seem mystifying to some readers"; he himself finds Ellison's belief in a shared humanity "hardly either self-evident or universally accepted."[13] In contrast, this essay reconsiders the politics of Ellison's first novel on Ellison's terms, that is, by first looking closely at the novel itself and then turning to his *Collected Essays* for explication and confirmation. The hypotheses on which the study is based include the supposition that both *Invisible Man* and Ellison's essays convey valuable insights and the belief that the former and the latter are mutually illuminating.

Another premise is that the meaning of the assertion of the narrator in the Epilogue that "we were to affirm the principle on which the country was built"[14] is central to any study of the political implications of *Invisible Man.* By the end of the novel the narrator has come to believe both that his grandfather was a wise man whose advice should be followed and that this affirmation sums up the deeper meaning of his grandfather's cryptic deathbed utterance. Throughout *Invisible Man,* the narrator puzzles over the meaning of his grandfather's last words, which he had overheard as the old man spoke to his son, the narrator's father. The old man had told the narrator's father to "overcome 'em with yeses, undermine 'em with grins, agree 'em to death and destruction, let 'em swoller you till they vomit or bust open" (16). To the narrator, worrying that his youthful exemplary conduct will be taken as a sign of rebellion, "the old man's words were like a curse" (17). No matter how properly he behaves, he cannot help thinking that he may be in some sense a "traitor" like his grandfather:

> When I was praised for my conduct I felt a guilt that in some way I was doing something that was really against the wishes of the white folks, that if they had understood they would have desired me to act just the opposite, that I should have been sulky and mean, and that that really would have been what they wanted, even though they were fooled and thought they wanted me to act as I did. (17)

After brooding over his grandfather's words throughout the novel, the narrator finally reaches in the Epilogue some tentative certainty about what the

dying man meant: "Could he have meant—hell, he *must* have meant the principle, that we were to affirm the principle on which the country was built
and not the men, or at least not the men who did the violence" (574). This
conclusion, however, only leads to another set of questions:

> Did he mean say "yes" because he knew that the principle was greater
> than the men? . . . Did he mean to affirm the principle? . . . Or did he
> mean that we had to take the responsibility for all of it, for the men as
> well as the principle? . . . Was it that we of all, we, most of all, had to
> affirm the principle, the plan in whose name we had been brutalized and
> sacrificed? . . . Or was it, did he mean that we should affirm the principle
> because we, through no fault of our own, were linked to all the others in
> the loud, clamoring semi-visible world, that world seen only as a fertile
> field for exploitation by Jack and his kind, and with condescension by
> Norton and his, who were tired of being the mere pawns in the futile
> game of "making history"? Had he seen that for these too we had to
> say "yes" to the principle, lest they turn upon us to destroy both it and
> us? (574–75)

These questions are important, but the narrator leaves unasked the prior question, what principle? The narrator tells us only that it is "the principle on
which the country was built," adding that "the men"—presumably the
founders—"had dreamed [it] into being out of the chaos and darkness of the
feudal past." The narrator comments that the same men "had violated and
compromised [the principle] to the point of absurdity even in their own
corrupt minds" (574).

Perhaps the most likely candidate for the "the principle on which the
country was built" is the assertion in the Declaration of Independence that
"all men are created equal." It would make sense to say that it was the principle of human equality that the founders "had violated and compromised to
the point of absurdity even in their own corrupt minds" by their acceptance
of slavery. But answering this question leads to another question. If the equality of human beings is the key notion to be affirmed, why is it not identified
in some unmistakable way? Although there can be no certain answer to this
question, if one rewrites the Epilogue by replacing "the principle" with
"equality," one begins to suspect at least one reason. Naming "equality" as the
key value in all the contexts where the enigmatic phrase "the principle"
appears in the Epilogue has the effect of turning the "equality" referred to
repeatedly into a doctrine rather than a principle. Ellison's "principle" is not
only an idea but also the aspirations and possibilities with which the idea was
associated at the founding and since. Ellison's purposefully vague "principle" is
broader than any doctrine. Similarly, by characterizing "the principle" as one
"on which the country was built," and also the principle "in whose name we
had been brutalized and sacrificed," Ellison ties the ideal he invokes to

a specifically American context. The ideal he has in mind is not the *Égalité* of the French Revolution, nor the equality promised to the workers and peasants of Russia in 1917. It is the equality asserted by the Declaration of Independence, but it is also that equality as embodied in the Constitution and its amendments, not equality as a merely theoretical construction. Ellison's "principle" is tied, for better and for worse, to the history of the United States.

Ellison's essays rarely if ever invoke abstract concepts; repeatedly and emphatically he connects the ideals he affirms to the founding documents of the United States. Sometimes he gives first place to the Declaration's assertion of human equality. Ellison declares in 1990 that "[t]he Declaration is the moral imperative to which all of us, black and white alike, are committed"— though he hastens to add that "our history has also been marked by endless attempts to evade our moral commitment to the ideal of social equality."[15] Typically, however, Ellison does not single out the Declaration and its assertion of equality as the uniquely valuable element in the founding. Instead, he cites the Constitution and the Bill of Rights as well as the Declaration, a practice implying that they are all manifestations of "the principle" whose affirmation, the narrator of *Invisible Man* finally decides, was the message of his grandfather's last words. Thus Ellison's essay "Society, Morality, and the Novel" refers to the "moral imperatives of American life that are implicit in the Declaration of Independence, the Constitution, and the Bill of Rights."[16] In his 1972 "Commencement Address at the College of William and Mary," Ellison tells his audience that it is "the Declaration of Independence, the Constitution, and the Bill of Rights" that "I speak of as the 'sacred documents' of this nation."[17] Ellison's moving tribute to Roscoe Dunjee, the editor of the Oklahoma City newspaper, *The Black Dispatch,* credits the paper's editorials with instilling in him a faith that there was something in the Constitution and the other founding documents beyond their literal meaning, something that in this passage he calls "a mysterious binding force" and that in *Invisible Man* appears as "the principle":

> Roscoe Dunjee understood what it has taken me many years to understand. He understood that not only were the American people a revolutionary people, but that in the shedding of blood, sacrifice, agony, and anguish of establishing this nation, all Americans became bound in a covenant. Roscoe Dunjee understood, at a time when hardly anybody else did, that there was an irrational element in the American Constitution, a mysterious binding force which was the secret to moving people.[18]

Ellison stresses that the documents he treasures are valuable not simply because their ideas are valuable but because they are part of an action, the making of a "covenant": "As we fought this revolution in fire and blood and sacrifice, a covenant was made, and that covenant, to use biblical terminology, was the Constitution, the Declaration of Independence, and the Bill of Rights."

These are the grounds upon which we stand today."[19] Ellison writes that newspapers like Roscoe Dunjee's *Black Dispatch* responded to the need of African Americans "to inspirit the ideals of the Constitution, the Bill of Rights, and the Declaration of Independence into our own reality."[20]

Although the narrator of *Invisible Man* ponders the meaning of his grandfather's last words repeatedly over the course of the novel, the notion of "the principle on which the country was built" does not appear until the Epilogue. The narrator does not debate the meaning of American history or stop to ponder the significance of the founding documents at any point in the novel. No speech comparable to the oration of Boris Max in *Native Son* provides explicit guidance for the reader about what it might mean "to affirm the principle on which the country was built." The novel does, however, provide some implicit and broadly negative dramatic guidance. The narrator undergoes a series of adventures in which he is offered alternatives to affirming the principle. Neither Dr. Bledsoe nor Ras the Exhorter who becomes Ras the Destroyer has any interest in affirming the principle mentioned in the Epilogue. The Brotherhood poses a more difficult intellectual problem, since its members claim to be working for equality for all. On the other hand, neither Dr. Bledsoe nor Ras can be easily dismissed, whatever one thinks of their politics. The limitations of the alternatives they embody are made clear, but we are also allowed to sense the force of the real insights Bledsoe and Ras possess. If Ellison had been interested in writing a novel only to make a political point, he would surely have presented Bledsoe and Ras in a way that emphasized only their flaws. Instead, their portraits allow the reader to "become acquainted with ambivalence" (10), like the narrator in the dream sequence of the Prologue. This literary strategy does not, however, diminish the novel's political significance but instead enriches it. The narrator's willingness to allow readers to note the strengths as well as the failings of Bledsoe and Ras implies that he has incorporated the lessons he has learned in the course of the novel; his ultimate willingness to "affirm the principle" is not a sentimental expression of naive idealism but a result of hard-won experience.

Dr. Bledsoe, the narrator discovers, is without scruples. His motto might be the slogan now often associated with Malcolm X and emblazoned on tee shirts: "by any means necessary." He tells the narrator "I'll have every Negro in the country hanging on tree limbs by morning if it means staying where I am" (143). Power, not love or any principle, is the key to all human relationships. He explains that "Power is confident, self-assuring, self-starting and self-stopping, self-warming and self-justifying" (142). Dr. Bledsoe's concentration on the realities of power frees him from many of the illusions of the narrator. His recognition that white people have most of the power does not lead him to assume that whites are inherently superior. In contrast, the narrator had looked forward to delivering his speech before the leading white citizens of his town even while enduring the battle royal, since "I felt that only these men could judge truly my ability" (25). Discovering that the narrator had taken the white trustee Norton to Jim Trueblood's cabin simply because Norton had ordered him to do so, Bledsoe is angered that one of his students would be so foolish as to do something simply because a white man had ordered him to do it: "Dammit, white folks are always giving orders, it's a habit with them. . . . My God, boy! You're black and living in the South—did you forget how to lie?" (136). White people, he makes clear to the narrator, do not control him: "These are the facts, son. The only ones I even pretend to please are *big* white folk, and even those I control more than they control me. This a power set-up, son, and I'm at the controls" (142). His ability to see through talk of principles to the realities of power allows him to see through the propaganda of white supremacy: "These white folk have newspapers, magazines, radios, spokesmen to get their ideas across. . . . The white folk tell everybody what to think— except men like me. I tell *them;* that's my life, telling white folk how to think about the things I know about" (142). President Bledsoe's ability to tell the truth at least to himself and in private is evident when he declines to offer any justification for his actions. Instead, Bledsoe shocks the narrator with his unsparing honesty:

> "Shocks you, doesn't it? Well, that's the way it is. It's a nasty deal and I don't always like it myself. But you listen to me: I didn't make it, and I know that I can't change it." . . . I don't even insist that it was worth it, but now I'm here and I mean to stay—after you win the game, you take the prize and you keep it, protect it; there's nothing else to do." (143)

Ras the Exhorter, like Dr. Bledsoe, rejects white supremacy but, unlike Bledsoe, does so openly. Ras calls for black unity, while Bledsoe is ready to "have every Negro in the country hanging on tree limbs." President Bledsoe would, of course, disavow the latter sentiment in public and himself claims to work on behalf of the welfare of blacks. How does the reader know that Ras is any less cynical than Bledsoe in his private thoughts? Ras's speeches provide no certain answer, but his refusal to kill Tod Clifton when he has the chance shows that his actions match his words; the narrator sees Ras "draw back the knife and stop it in mid-air; draw back and stop, cursing; then draw back and stop again" (370). Ras's speech to Tod demonstrates the depth of his commitment to black solidarity:

> "You six foot tall, mahn. You young and intelligent. You black and beautiful—don't let 'em tell you different! You wasn't them t'ings you be dead, mahn. Ras the Exhorter raise dup his knife and tried to do it, but he could not do it. Why don't you do it? I ask myself. I will do it now, I say; but somet'ing tell me, 'No, no! You might be killing your black king!' " (373)

The novel makes it clear, however, that Ras's personal sincerity is no guarantee that his leadership will actually help black people. In fact, the Brotherhood has little difficulty in making use of Ras in their scheme to spark a race riot that will cause death and destruction in Harlem and thereby provide ammunition for propaganda that will assist the Brotherhood's international political strategy. Even before the riot begins, the narrator notices that something is wrong: "the violence was pointless and, helped along by Ras, was actually being directed against the community itself" (513). Stunned by the violence of the riot, the narrator vainly pleads with Ras's followers to recognize that they are being used:

> "They want the streets to flow with blood; your blood, black blood and white blood, so that they can turn your death and sorrow and defeat into propaganda. It's simple, you've known it a long time. It goes, 'Use a nigger to catch a nigger.' Well, they used me to catch you and now they're using Ras to do away with me and to prepare your sacrifice. Don't you see it? Isn't it clear? . . ." (558)

Ras's response—"Hang the lying traitor" (558)—suggests that his commitment to black solidarity, so movingly dramatized when he restrained himself from killing Tod Clifton, has its limits; a suggestion that gains added credibility from Ras's willingness to fire on "some joker with a big ole Georgia voice" (562) who yells down an insult from a window. The narrator's final thoughts about Ras are mixed: ". . . Ras was not funny, or not only funny, but dangerous as well, wrong but justified, crazy and yet coldly sane . . ." (564). This judgment parallels Tod Clifton's more succinct verdict: "That poor, misguided son of a bitch" (376).

President Bledsoe and Ras the Exhorter each have good reasons of their own for refusing to affirm "the principle on which the country was built." Having observed that, as Ellison himself put it in an essay written before be began writing *Invisible Man,* "the idealized ethic of the Constitution and the Declaration of Independence" seems to be "reserved for white men,"[21] both are convinced that an African American would have to be a fool to believe that those principles would ever be applied to all. Neither can believe in the promises of American democracy, and thus neither is willing to accept its obligations. Bledsoe and Ras differ in many ways, but both provide examples of a point of view that Ellison in his essays characterizes as "secessionism." The term is by no means simply derogatory. The narrator of the novel moves beyond both Bledsoe and Ras, but *Invisible Man* makes it clear that both have a good deal of evidence to support their refusal to accept an "idealized ethic" by which white Americans will not themselves be bound in their relations with black Americans. The author of the novel is, of course, well aware of the same evidence; he comments in a 1983 essay that "we are all at some point or another secessionists."[22] The impulse to secessionism is not always wrong, and it does not always directly involve race. In "Perspective of Literature" Ellison refers to "the attitudes of individual 'secessionism' displayed by the heroes of Ernest Hemingway."[23]

The notion of secessionism Ellison puts forward in his essays clarifies the political implications of the novel. Ellison's use of the term links the

Confederacy of the old South and their contemporary sympathizers with black separatists from Garvey to the present. Individuals, Ellison suggests, may choose to opt out of any social arrangement, and they may achieve a personal integrity in doing so, like Hemingway's heroes, but American political secessionism is doomed to failure. The Confederacy marked its high point, and the Confederacy itself ended in bloody defeat. Bledsoe and Ras both have personal qualities that deserve respect; Bledsoe possesses rare intelligence and intellectual honesty, while Ras has both personal courage and true feeling for other black people. As political leaders, however, both are terribly flawed. Paradoxically, it is the character who is personally less attractive, Dr. Bledsoe, whose leadership seems more benign. He himself may be interested in nothing but personal power, but to get more power he must do his best to increase the resources and the prestige of the black college he heads. Surely African Americans will indeed benefit from the expanded educational opportunities resulting from his efforts. Ras, however, whose overriding motive is a desire to help black people, encourages violence that has disastrous consequences for Harlem itself. The secessionism of both Bledsoe and Ras, however, is finally not a pragmatic attempt to work out a superior alternative to the status quo but a choice of death rather than the life possible in America. Bledsoe is ready to "have every Negro in the country hanging on tree limbs by morning if it means staying where I am," while Ras is willing to die himself and lead others to death rather than compromise.

The members of The Brotherhood are not secessionists; their official platform is presented only vaguely in *Invisible Man,* but on its face it seems compatible with American democracy. Brother Jack's answer to the narrator's half-formed question reveals about as much as we ever learn about its overall goals: "What are we doing? What is our mission? It's simple; we are working for a better world for all people. It's that simple. Too many have been dispossessed of their heritage, and we have banded together in brotherhood so as to do something about it" (304). The narrator and the reader do learn, however, that the members of the Brotherhood pride themselves on their grasp of history, which they consider a science. One of them, bothered that the narrator does not "speak more concretely," tells him "we call ourselves scientists here. Let us speak as scientists" (306). In the same conversation Brother Jack tells the narrator "We are all realists here, and materialists" (307). Ras reveals his insight into the Brotherhood's view of itself when he taunts Tod Clifton and the narrator: "Three black men fighting in the street because of the white enslaver? Is that sanity? Is that consciousness, scientific understahnding?" (372). Ras nevertheless fails to shake the narrator's confidence in the truth of the Brotherhood's claims:

> The world was strange if you stopped to think about it; still it was a world that could be controlled by science, and the Brotherhood had both science and history under control.

> . . . I was dominated by the all-embracing idea of Brotherhood. The organization had given the world a new shape, and me a vital role. We recognized no loose ends, everything could be controlled by our science. (381–2)

The narrator begins to lose his faith in the scientific control of human life and history only when he ponders Tod Clifton's decision to leave the Brotherhood and sell "Sambo" dolls: "It was as though he had chosen—how had he put it the night he fought with Ras?—to fall outside of *history*" (434). The death of Tod Clifton pushes the narrator to question the notion of an all-controlling science. Tod Clifton, the narrator muses, had made the decision to "deliberately plunge outside of history . . . to step off the platform and fall beneath the train." The narrator cannot understand why he chose "to plunge into nothingness, into the void of faceless faces, of soundless voices, lying outside history" (439). If Tod Clifton could make such a choice, however, perhaps there are others who are also outside of history. Perhaps human affairs do not lend themselves to scientific control as easily as the Brotherhood supposes. The Brotherhood has no interest in those left behind by history, and the narrator had at first acquiesced in this indifference. Now, however, he begins to ask himself if those for whom the Brotherhood has only contempt may be

> . . . the saviors, the true leaders, the bearers of something precious? The stewards of something uncomfortable, burdensome, which they hated because, living outside the realm of history, there was no one to applaud their value and they themselves failed to understand it. . . . What if history was a gambler, instead of a force in a laboratory experiment, and the boys his ace in the hole? What if history was not a reasonable citizen, but a madman full of paranoid guile and these boys his agents, his big surprise! His own revenge? (441)

Invisible Man does not challenge the specific theses that make up the Marxist theory of history—there are no debates about the nature of the proletariat, and nobody speculates on the historical implications of the labor theory of value. More radically, the novel questions the possibility of any attempt to achieve a scientific understanding of human life. The narrator begins to suspect that the human truth of history will not be found in any theory but might be captured in music or art or in a novel such as the one he finally decides to write. Walking through Harlem and hearing "a record shop loudspeaker blaring a languid blues," he wonders "Was this all that would be recorded? Was this the only true history of the times, a mood blared by trumpets, trombones, saxophones and drums, a song with turgid, inadequate words?" (443). He tells the members of the Brotherhood that they must do more than digest theories to understand Harlem. They must get "around to the gin mills and the barber shops and the juke joints and the churches,

Brother. Yes, and the beauty parlors on Saturday when they're frying hair. A whole unrecorded history is spoken then, Brother" (471).

The principle the narrator of *Invisible Man* finally decides to affirm is not the product of ratiocination but something "dreamed into being" (574). While the Brotherhood's favorite term of praise is "scientific," the term that Ellison uses repeatedly in his essays to convey the significance of the founding documents of the United States is "sacred." While the self-described "scientists" of the Brotherhood accept the basic principles of their doctrines as dogma that cannot be questioned, Ellison's regard for the "sacred" nature of the Declaration and the Constitution does not prevent him from recognizing that they are both "man-made" and in some sense "fictions":

> At some point people, and especially American people, are pushed to recognize that behind the Constitution which we say rests in principles that lie beyond the limits of death and dying, are really man-made, legal fictions. That doesn't stop them from being precious or sacred. . . .[24]

The principles are sacred not because they are dogma that must be accepted without questioning but because they have been "made sacred through acts of courage, sacrifice, and bloodshed."[25] The Constitution is not the logical product of a theory but a "covenant" and even a "script":

> I look upon the Constitution as the still-vital covenant by which Americans of diverse backgrounds, religions, races, and interests are bound. . . . The Constitution is a script by which we seek to act out the drama of democracy and the stage upon which we enact our roles.[26]

The most straightforward political lessons of *Invisible Man* are negative. Dr. Bledsoe's belief that power is the only reality may seem sophisticated (anticipating by more than a decade Michel Foucault's more elaborate articulations of a similar vision), but his nihilism, if accepted as a political credo, can lead, it seems clear, only to bloodshed. While Ras the Exhorter can effectively point to the exploitation of black people in the Brotherhood, his romantic appeals to racial identity lead ultimately, the novel suggests, to suicidal violence. Although Ras's rhetoric stresses the unity of all black people, his eagerness to hang the narrator as a traitor demonstrates that the purity he seeks can be purchased only by blood. The Brotherhood claims to represent the "dispossessed," but, as Brother Jack explains to the narrator, its scientific understanding allows it to treat those it regards as out of touch with history like "dead limbs that must be pruned away so that the tree may bear young fruit" (291).

Given the negative guidance supplied by the examples of Bledsoe, Ras, and the Brotherhood, one can at least hazard some speculations about the political significance of the grandfather's injunction. It is significant, surely, that the narrator's decision to "affirm the principle" results from his pondering of his grandfather's last words, not from reading any work of political theory. He finally realizes that he had been wrong when he had "thought my grandfather incapable of thoughts about humanity." His grandfather, the narrator now sees, had "accepted his humanity just as he accepted the principle. It was his, and the principle lives on in all its human and absurd diversity" (580). There is a close connection between the full realization of the humanity of the grandfather, a former slave, and the narrator's acceptance or affirmation of "the principle."

An acceptance of "the principle," Ellison seems to be saying, means a willingness to accept the "human and absurd diversity" it entails—the seemingly absurd possibility, for example, that a grandfather who had been a slave might possess a wisdom beyond that of university professors and scientific theoreticians. Ellison's essays provide many examples of this "human and absurd diversity," from the "light-skinned, blue-eyed, Afro-American-featured individual . . . clad in handsome riding boots and fawn-colored riding breeches of English tailoring" with a "dashy dashiki" and wearing "a black Homburg hat, tilted at a jaunty angle . . . on the crest of his huge Afro-coiffed head"[27] to the "tall young brown-skinned man" Ellison once encountered who, he reports, "strode toward me carrying himself with a proud military bearing subtly combined with a subdued version of Harlem strut" and "wearing a gray cap which bore the insignia of the Confederate Army."[28] The principle the narrator of *Invisible Man* decides to affirm is, it seems, very different from those seductive political ideals of the Brotherhood and Ras that in the name of equality for the workers or equality for black people, respectively, demand uniformity. The equality offered by "the principle" makes room for individuals to realize diverse possibilities. This individual diversity enriches everyday life but makes utopia impossible. Perhaps this negative correlation between the possibilities available to individuals and the possible triumph of utopian (or totalitarian) uniformity is among the most important political lessons of *Invisible Man*. As the narrator puts it, "Until some gang succeeds in putting the world in a strait jacket, its definition is possibility" (576).

Although "possibility" is a key concept for both the narrator of *Invisible Man* and for the book's author, it would be a mistake to assume that the narrator is nothing more than a mouthpiece for Ralph Ellison. Likewise, there are times when Ralph Ellison's comments on *Invisible Man* must be taken with a grain of salt, as when he declares in the 1955 *Paris Review* interview that "It's not an important novel" and expresses doubt that it will still be read in 20 years. On the other hand, his supposition that "If it does last, it will be simply because there are more things going on in its depth that are of permanent interest than on its surface" (217) seems right. After the publication of his first novel in 1952, Ellison—much to the frustration of all those expecting another novel—expended much of his talent and intellectual energy writing essays that work out the implications, or, to put it another way, bring to the surface, the "things going on in its depth." This is not to say that Ellison's essays deal in a superficial way with themes that the novel treats more deeply but rather to emphasize that they clarify, explicate, and often exemplify what is suggested in the novel. The study of the political implications of *Invisible Man* cannot ignore Ellison's brilliant essays, works of art in a different genre, merely because the concept of an author whose ideas and intentions are worthy of critical consideration seems to be outmoded, or for any other reason. To overlook Ellison's essays in reconsidering *Invisible Man* would be to neglect an invaluable resource and to underestimate Ellison's overall achievement through a failure to appreciate the unity-in-diversity of his *oeuvre*.

ENDNOTES

1. Roland Barthes, "The Death of the Author," *Image/Music/Text,* ed. and trans. by Stephen Heath (New York: Hill and Wang, 1977), 146.

2. Michel Foucault, "What is an Author?" *Textual Strategies: Perspectives in Post-Structuralist Criticism,* ed. Josué V. Harari (Ithaca, New York: Cornell University Press, 1979), 143.

3. E. D. Hirsch, Jr., *Validity in Interpretation* (New Haven: Yale University Press, 1967).

4. Barthes, 147.

5. Foucault, 159.

6. On the other hand, Robert O'Meally finds a consistent vision in all of Ellison's work. He depicts an Ellison "insisting in any company upon cultural pluralism and artistic integrity" and always emphasizing "the distinctive richness and beauty of Afro-American life and culture"; see *The Craft of Ralph Ellison* (Cambridge, Mass.: Harvard University Press, 1980), 179, 180. In an often reprinted essay, George E. Kent finds "almost a mathematical consistency between Ellison's critical pronouncements and his creative performance," though he admits to feeling "a certain unease" about Ellison's "relationship to the West" in both (56). See "Ralph Ellison and the Afro-American Folk and Cultural Tradition," 13 *CLA Journal* 3 (March 1969): 265–76; rpt. in Robert J. Butler, ed., *The Critical Response to Ralph Ellison* (Westport, Connecticut: Greenwood Press, 2000), 51–57. In his moving eulogy, John F. Callahan asserted the unity of Ellison's life and writings in a way directly relevant to the present essay: "Like his *Invisible Man,* Ralph affirmed 'the principle' on the page and in conversation, while he resisted the reduction of art, personality or, for that matter, politics, to categories or formulas" (200). See "Frequencies of Memory: A Eulogy for Ralph Waldo Ellison," 18 *Callaloo* 2 (1995), 298–309; rpt. in Robert J. Butler, ed., *The Critical Response to Ralph Ellison* (Westport, Connecticut: Greenwood Press, 2000), 199–209.

7. Houston A. Baker, Jr., "To Move Without Moving: An Analysis of Creativity and Commerce in Ralph Ellison's Trueblood Episode," 98 *PMLA* 5 (Octo-

ber 1983); rpt. in Robert J. Butler, ed., *The Critical Response to Ralph Ellison* (Westport, Connecticut: Greenwood Press, 2000), 74.

8. Alan Nadel, *Invisible Criticism: Ralph Ellison and the American Canon* (Iowa City: University of Iowa Press, 1988), 403.

9. Jerry Gafio Watts, *Heroism and the Black Intellectual: Ralph Ellison, Politics, and Afro-American Intellectual Life* (Chapel Hill: University of North Carolina Press, 1994), 120.

10. Watts, 31.

11. Watts, 117.

12. Watts, 119.

13. Kerry McSweeney, *Invisible Man: Race and Identity* (Boston: Twayne Publishers, 1988), 13. McSweeney's criticism of Ellison's assertion of human unity on the grounds that "it is hardly self-evident" suggests that he intends to also call into question the affirmation in the Declaration of Independence of certain "self-evident truths"; he is undoubtedly correct in making a connection between the two affirmations. Harry V. Jaffa provides a persuasive restatement of the validity of the Declaration's notion of "self-evident truths" that also supports Ellison's statement in *A New Birth of Freedom: Abraham Lincoln and the Coming of the Civil War* (Lanham, Md.: Rowman & Littlefield Publishers, Inc., 2000), 117–21.

14. Ralph Ellison, *Invisible Man,* (New York: Random House, 1952; reprint, New York: Vintage Books, 1995), 574. All subsequent citations will be noted parenthetically in the text by page number, and emphases in original unless otherwise noted.

15. Ralph Ellison, "Notes for Class Day Talk at Columbia University," *Collected Essays,* 840.

16. Ralph Ellison, "Society, Morality, and the Novel," *Collected Essays,* 702.

17. Ralph Ellison, "Commencement Address at the College of William and Mary," *Collected Essays,* 408.

18. Ralph Ellison, "Roscoe Dunjee and the American Language," *Collected Essays,* 452.

19. Ralph Ellison, "Roscoe Dunjee and the American Language," *Collected Essays,* 453–4.

20. Ralph Ellison, "Roscoe Dunjee and the American Language," *Collected Essays,* 457.

21. Ralph Ellison, "Twentieth-Century Fiction and the Black Mask of Humanity," *Collected Essays,* 90–91.

22. Ralph Ellison, "Presentation to Bernard Malamud of the Gold Medal for Fiction," *Collected Essays,* 465.

23. Ralph Ellison, "Perspective of Literature," *Collected Essays,* 779.

24. Ralph Ellison, "Perspective of Literature," *Collected Essays*, 771.

25. Ralph Ellison, "Commencement Address at the College of William and Mary," *Collected Essays*, 409.

26. Ralph Ellison, "Perspective of Literature," *Collected Essays*, 773.

27. Ralph Ellison, "The Little Man at Chehaw Station," *Collected Essays*, 505–6.

28. Ralph Ellison, "Notes for Class Day Talk at Columbia University," *Collected Essays*, 839.

Chapter 2

Ralph Ellison on the Tragi-Comedy of Citizenship

DANIELLE ALLEN

WHERE ARE THE POLITICS
IN *INVISIBLE MAN*?

Ellison's novel has been caught up in political questions ever since it appeared. Irving Howe criticized Ellison fiercely for not having written a protest novel; his interests seemed, in the 1950s and early 1960s, far too aesthetic.[1] But, recently and especially since Ellison's death in 1994, a spate of critics have turned toward analysis of the democratic theory that provides the backbone for Ellison's novels and extensive criticism.[2] And when I discussed the book with a retiree reading group, I discovered that Ellison had at last fallen from his empyrean heights and landed in the muck. These more recent readers found the book far too, and even painfully, political. There is, I think, a very specific reason for the divergence in these reactions and this has to do with where the novel's politics are to be found.[3]

For all that the novel is full of scenes likely to occasion urban protest (both in the novel and in life), no single policy issue can in any way be said to orient or shape the movement of the novel. But scholars and critics interested in the novel's politics have regularly gone after just such political events and details—hence the common conversation about whether the Brotherhood is to be construed as a parody of the American Communist party.[4] But our first clue about how to read the politics of the text comes from the very shadowiness of the Brotherhood party. Every time the reader, or a character, tries to focus on exactly what the Brotherhood is, the group seems to disappear; one can't fix it in one's mind. Indeed, none of the members, for instance, has a last name, and their very anonymity deflects attention from them. It seems that one isn't meant to focus on a particular event or institution and that these are not the phenomena that have captured Ellison's regard. In other words, the politics of the novel is not made apparent through positions taken by characters and backed up with institutions but in some other way. If in reading the novel, one is not meant to focus on events and institutions, toward what other focus is one's political attention directed?

A reader may not be able to conjure up a clear picture of what exactly the Brotherhood is, but she can easily recall and outline the structure of the protagonist's interactions with, say, Brother Jack and Brother Hambro. Throughout the novel conversations are rendered fully. The book is clearly about interactions between individuals, and perhaps this is the reason that *Invisible Man* at first seemed to be a book that had retreated from public, political questions. Moreover, the book is not simply about any and every type of interaction; we learn next to nothing about the precollegiate family life of our unnamed protagonist, whom I've taken to calling I. M. as a nickname.[5] Rather, most of the conversations have something to do with what happens when strangers try to act together.[6] The novel thus draws our attention to the basic democratic project: strangers, with nothing but common citizenship to tie them together, are supposed to decide together and then act. How are they to do so? How *do* they do so?

Indeed, Ellison brings analytical pressure to bear on the interactions between strangers, whose only relation to one another is that of common citizenship, until they tell us about the psychic lives of democratic citizens and therefore also about how the larger political body, made up of so many millions of strangers doing things with and to each other, works. In a 1945 letter to literary critic and philosopher Kenneth Burke, he described himself as "a Negro writer who writes out of his full awareness of the complexity of western personality and who presents the violence of American culture in psychological terms rather than physical ones."[7]

The politics in the novel lies, then, in the novel's account of what it is like, psychologically speaking, to be an individual in a democratic world of strangers, where large scale events are supposed to arise somehow out of one's own consent and yet never really do.[8] Democracy puts its citizens under a strange form of psychological pressure by building them up as sovereigns, and then regularly undermining any individual citizen's experience of sovereignty. Moreover, democracies claim to secure the good of all citizens, whereas in any particular democracy there are always some people who are benefiting less than others, or are positively harmed, by particular political decisions. The citizens who lose out in any given political battle need to find ways to reconcile their experience of loss and impotence with the notion that they are nonetheless sovereign.[9] *Invisible Man* addresses precisely this psychological tension, the psychic anxiety of being a powerless sovereign, and to the degree that the novel is existentialist, its existentialism is democratic.[10] If one reads not for protest but for character development in the novel—as the members of that retiree reading group were doing—one necessarily comes up against politics. Moreover, as we shall see, in *Invisible Man* the result of scrutinizing one individual's existential experience of democratic collaboration is a rich account of how democracy works at the level of interactions among citizens. Ellison aspired to an "imaginative integration of the total American experience."[11] In short, he aspired to move from depiction of one life to a totalizing account of democracy.

FROM INDIVIDUAL EXPERIENCE
TO DEMOCRATIC FACTS

How, then, did Ellison think it was possible for an author to get from descriptions of an individual life and its psychic struggles to the "total American [read: democratic] experience"? Here Ellison's idea of ritual is key. From T. S. Eliot's *The Wasteland* and Lord Raglan's *The Hero,* Ellison took a conviction that myth and ritual are fundamental to both human life and literature.[12] In fact, these are the phenomena that in his view connect particular events to broad social meanings. In his view, societies use rituals to create, justify, and maintain their social structures. These rituals may be as overt as the requirement that students say the Pledge of Allegiance in school every day or as little noticed as the adult habit of asking a child upon a first meeting, "What's your name and how old are you?"[13] Even the smallest interaction could serve Ellison's purpose and provide ritual elements. Indeed, the narrative structure of the novel itself reveals Ellison's habit of putting pressure on small interactions in order to identify the rituals beneath them and to make them yield large, general claims about politics. Three examples will show how Ellison moves from small interactions to truths about the larger political scene. I will begin with a scene that is obviously an initiation ritual in Ellison's own terms, the Battle Royal scene, and then turn to two less obviously ritualistic moments of social interaction.

Battle Royal

The Battle Royal scene has often been identified, by Ellison himself and also by critics, as an initiation rite. Young black men are taught their impotence through it. But the scene is and does much more than that, if one attends to I. M.'s experience of it. Let us begin our examination of the scene anew.

When I. M. begins his psychological and political odyssey, he has few words to explain his sufferance of physical and moral depredations of life in the South—the little he knows is that he endures for the sake of achieving a greater part in American democracy. He expects to be the next Booker T. Washington and believes that following the rules will get him there. As a young high school and college student, he describes his stance as one of humility, which he calls "the secret, indeed, the very essence of progress."[14] Notably, humility is a character trait, not an action.[15] When a high school graduation oration on humility wins him much praise and an invitation to deliver the same speech before a gathering of the town's foremost white citizens, one result will be a college scholarship for I. M.; the other, his inadvertent first step toward articulating the belief that what he is describing as humility is in fact not a character trait but a chosen *action,* one that is inspired by a belief in the centrality of reciprocity to democratic politics.

On the evening appointed for I. M. to deliver his speech for the second time, the town's eminencies are all drunk, nastily and lecherously so; they maul a stripteaser, who barely escapes the room unscathed, before turning to the entertainment they expect from "the shines." First there is a Battle Royal, a boxing match in which ten boys, blindfolded, are set upon each other.[16] I. M. too is made to participate and, along with the other boys, is first humiliated before the match by being forced to watch, while wearing scanty boxing shorts, the white woman's striptease and is then humiliated again after the match by being ordered to collect his pay in coin from a mat on the floor. (More even—the mat turns out to be electrified; the coins, merely buttons.) Bloodied and debased, I. M. is finally allowed to speak and begins, amid yells and laughter, in this context of *humiliation,* his paean to, of all things, *humility.* As the context for his speech has shifted, however, so too his memory has been jolted out of place, for instead of reciting, in accord with his written text, that he will devote himself to "social responsibility," I. M. instead resoundingly commits himself to "social equality." Ellison writes: "The laughter hung in the sudden stillness. I opened my eyes, puzzled. Sounds of displeasure filled the room. . . . 'Say that slowly son!' " Realizing his mistake, I. M. feels a flutter of fear before retracting his desire for "equality," affirming his commitment to "social responsibility," and finding himself rewarded. The men respond that they "mean to do right by [him], but [he's] got to know [his] place at all times" (31). We could call I. M.'s mistake a Freudian slip.[17] The psychological pressure on I. M. has led him to reveal, if only for a brief moment, the question raised by his focus on humility: How does social responsibility, obedience to laws and norms, relate to social equality or the ability to use common institutions to accrue benefit in the social and private sphere? In a democratic society, does the one not promise the other, despite his audience's refusal to acknowledge that promise?[18] The audience's insistence that I. M. accept social responsibility turns the narrative spotlight on the question of the sorts of political actions the invisible do in fact, despite being invisible, carry out. How can an account of citizenship be expanded to include their actions?

I. M. is being humble *in exchange* for future goods, and so he conceives of his humility as setting him in relation to the broader world of social and political interaction. The audience to his speech, however, disputes whether his humility does in fact give him grounds to consider himself a public actor. The novel therefore opens by staging a contest over how to interpret the relation between our institutionalized political obligations to one another and our everyday citizenly interactions: Do we not regularly enact democratic responsibility *outside* courtrooms and assemblies? In the eery moment when I. M. replaces the phrase "social responsibility" with the phrase "social equality," he brings to the surface a suppressed question about how ideas like "responsibility" and "obligation" work to support democratic agreement and democratic peace.[19] That they do is clear; I. M. averts possible violence to himself by publicly committing himself to "responsibility." And his audience vaguely senses that some "gift" is involved in the resulting release of tension. Wrongly, they think the gift is theirs: "We mean to do right by you, but you've got to know your place at all times," they say.

The novel will, time and again, make the point that remarks such as these mistake the exchange relations involved in the democratic gift; the assumption of responsibility is, in fact, the real benefaction. Here within invisibility itself, Ellison is revealing a political act (the acceptance of obligation in the face of loss) that founds peace; what makes I. M.'s acceptance of obligation not just sustaining of political order but more specifically democratic is that his assumption of obligation is based on an expectation, however attenuated, of reciprocity. Indeed, in democratic regimes those practices and habits by which citizens accept communal decisions with which they disagree must necessarily rest on highly developed structures and notions of reciprocity.[20] It should come as no surprise that in the literature of political theory, the topic of reciprocity always floats near the surface of discussions about democratic deliberation and agreement.[21] In Ellison's novel, the form of democratic action taken by the invisible is somehow exemplary of democratic reciprocity but highlights, too, how practices of reciprocity have gone badly awry. In the Battle Royal episode, Ellison is, as it were, turning an x-ray on ordinary human interaction in order to reveal the regularity of the skeletal structure supporting it; in this case, the structure links responsibility and equality, agreement and reciprocity. The regularity of structure beneath the seeming idiosyncrasy of our daily interactions thus has deeply political implications.[22]

Eventually I. M. becomes increasingly aware that his willingness to put aside his personal desire for respect, recognition, and social equality in order to gain access to the democracy's institutions of power—the schools and colleges that pave the way to positions of leadership, the public fora where the audience consists of those who make political decisions—has been abused precisely by not being recognized for what it is. It is, first of all, a gift that is more than a gift for it involves an assumption of loss. It is also, and more importantly, an act and not merely, like humility, an aspect of character. The action that he recognizes, but that no one else can see, is sacrifice. According to the Oxford English Dictionary definition, this is "the destruction or surrender of something valued or desired for the sake of something having, or regarded as having, a higher or more pressing claim" or "the loss entailed by devotion to some other interest." Sacrifice is, of course, one of Ellison's central terms in the novel and in his essays, and his focus on it excavates a central democratic fact. Although democracies claim to act for the good of all, every political decision inflicts some loss on some members of the polity, even in cases where the whole community generally benefits. Since democracy claims to secure the good of all citizens, it is people who benefit less than others from particular political decisions, but nonetheless accede to those decisions, who preserve the stability of political institutions. Their sacrifice makes collective democratic action possible. By presenting I. M.'s experience in terms of political categories like sacrifice, agreement, and responsibility, Ellison lays bare how politics structures ordinary life and ordinary psychic experience. "It is our fate as human beings always to give up some good things for other good things, to throw off certain bad circumstances only to create others."[23]

Or, if I were to use Ellison's terms to make that last point, it would go like this: By presenting I. M.'s experience in terms of political categories like sacrifice, agreement, and responsibility, Ellison names the rituals that give human life its meaning and that undergird our common actions. Indeed, my metaphor of his writing as an x-ray machine that reveals the skeleton of democratic life makes the same point that Ellison usually uses the word "ritual" to make.

Strangers Bumping into Each Other in the Dark

A second example of how Ellison moves from descriptions of small interactions to political analysis should help us refine our understanding of how broadly Ellison defines the rituals that reflect our common political life.

The novel begins with a rumination on responsibility as a democratic gift that presumes reciprocation. That rumination is inspired by nothing more than strangers bumping into each other in the dark. Ellison gives I. M. a prologue in which to explain why he is narrating his life history, and this prologue turns around I. M.'s account of how, being bumped in the dark by a stranger and called a name, he attacked the man and beat him within an inch of his life. Pondering whether this was an abdication of his social responsibilities, he reflects: "I can hear you say, 'What a horrible, irresponsible bastard!' And you're right. I leap to agree with you. . . . But to whom can I be responsible and why should I be when you refuse to see me . . . ? Responsibility rests upon recognition, and recognition is a form of agreement" (14). Ellison equips I. M. with the language of a political theorist—agreement, responsibility, recognition—as his protagonist epigrammatically relates his conclusions about democracy. He is willing to act responsibly by heeling to the limits of law and social custom, provided that his acts of responsibility are recognized as such: that is, as a gift other citizens have requested for their own good and for which they agree to give him a gift in exchange. His invisibility itself results from the failure of his proffer of reciprocity to be taken up—seen as citizenly action—by those around him. Again, Ellison puts pressure on small interactions until they yield conclusions about the political consequences of ordinary exchanges.

Regarding the man who bumped him in the dark, I. M. finally decides: "I was the irresponsible one; for I should have used my knife to protect the higher interests of society. . . . All dreamers and sleepwalkers must pay the price, and even the invisible victim is responsible for the fate of all. But I shirked that responsibility" (14).[24] As I. M. sees it, his real irresponsibility lies in his failure to put an end to the abdication of responsibility perpetrated by the sleepwalkers. In their refusal to see the presence of the gift at the heart of democratic responsibility, they reduce the possible sphere of democratic action. When the young I. M.'s drunk audience forces him to retract the phrase "social equality" and affirm "responsibility" without the promise of equality, they too erase the agreement beneath democratic institutions. Bumping into strangers in the dark is a metaphor for democratic citizenship. All our ordinary interactions with strangers are structured by rituals that define the life forms open to us within our democracies.

Importantly, Ellison's concern to reveal the rituals that constitute democratic citizenship is the source of the tight narrative tie among the book's many episodes.[25] The Battle Royal, the scene when I. M. bumps into a man in the dark and nearly kills him, and others, too, that are discussed in terms of agreement and responsibility all enact the same sort of ritual, whereby a citizen confronts, albeit in its most extreme version, the democratic fact of the powerlessness that dwells within any citizen's sovereignty. Moreover, the citizen confronts this democratic powerlessness amid a crush of strangers all also groping blindly in the dark. The problem with American life, in Ellison's view, is that insufficient creative energy has been directed to the problem of how to draw strangers into satisfactory relations of reciprocity with one another.[26] In an interview with Robert Penn Warren, he lamented life in the South in the following terms:

> [A]t certain moments a reality which is political and social and ideological asserts itself, and the human relationship breaks up and both groups of people fall into their abstract roles. Thus a great loss of human energy goes into maintaining our stylized identities. In fact, much of the energy of the imagination—much of the *psychic* energy of the South, among both whites and blacks, has gone, I think, into this particular negative art form.[27]

Ellison sought to discern precisely how democracy stylizes the identities of individuals and loads citizens up with psychic tasks. He seeks rituals in our interactions not only in order to explain how communities are made into integral wholes and to explain the ideas used to do that work, but also in order to show what the stakes of communal life are for the individual psyche. And as a literary artist able to rework rituals, Ellison saw himself as having the chance to intervene in the stylization of identities and therewith to reform politics.

Riots and the Central Democratic Fact of Sacrifice

My third example of how a small interaction is brought to be revealing of the larger political scene also reveals the degree to which Ellison's method of looking for the action patterns that link individual and political experience guided the growth of the story itself. The epiphanic climax of the novel comes at the end of the riot, after I. M. has fallen into the coal chute, when he has that wild, wild dream of castration. He says:

> . . . I lay beside a river of black water, near where an armored bridge arched sharply away to where I could not see. And I was protesting their holding me and they were demanding that I return to them and were annoyed with my refusal. . . .
>
> But now they came forward with a knife, holding me; and I felt the bright red pain and they took the two bloody blobs and cast them over the bridge, and out of my anguish I saw them curve up and catch beneath the apex of the curving arch of the bridge, to hang there, dripping down through the sunlight into the dark red water. And while the others laughed, before my pain-sharpened eyes the whole world was slowly turning red. (569)

This epiphany turns on a pun, and to catch it out will require a small digression back to the subject of sacrifice again.[28]

I. M.'s most rigorous analysis of the idea of sacrifice, and its role in politics, occurs in his conversation with Hambro after the Brotherhood has switched its policy and attention away from Harlem. I. M. is neither included in policy deliberations nor even forewarned of the change and confronts his Brotherhood tutor, Hambro, who admits: "It's unfortunate, Brother, but your members will have to be sacrificed" (501). Here Ellison at last brings I. M. face-to-face with what has, throughout the novel, kept him running and accepting loss in pursuit of some elusive gain: the repeated requirement that he sacrifice. "Sacrifice?" I. M. says, "You say that very easily."

Eventually, the conversation with Hambro about sacrifice results in I. M.'s discovery of three criteria for distinguishing legitimate from illegitimate sacrifices. Beginning a dialogue between them, Hambro answers:

> ". . . [T]he interests of one group of brothers must be sacrificed to that of the whole."
>
> "Why wasn't I told of this?" I said.
>
> "You will be in time, by the committee—Sacrifice is necessary now—"

"But shouldn't sacrifice be made willingly by those who know what they're doing? My people don't understand why they're being sacrificed. They don't even *know* they're being sacrificed—at least not by us. . . ." (502)

In I. M.'s resistance to Hambro, criteria for distinguishing illegitimate from legitimate sacrifice and for rejecting unreasonable sacrifices emerge. First and foremost, there are problems of agency. The grammatical distinction between Hambro's use of the passive voice—"your members will have to be sacrificed"—and I. M.'s reference to the *making* of sacrifices by choice and with foreknowledge accurately registers the conflict here. Scapegoats are sacrificed; a hero sacrifices and, for her sacrifice, gains the honor that accrues from having other citizens acknowledge that she, and not they, have borne the worst of it. The idea of "gift" does not have a semantic range wide enough to capture the "losses" involved in democratic politics, and so it is inadequate to the task of "honoring" those who give the gift of absorbing loss. Here already are two of the three criteria for distinguishing legitimate sacrifices. First, a legitimate sacrifice is made voluntarily and knowingly; second, democratic responsibility stems from the agreement to honor the voluntary sacrifice, which is more than a gift.

Hambro refuses to acknowledge the importance of these criteria and continues the argument thus:

". . . All of us must sacrifice for the good of the whole. Change is achieved through sacrifice. We follow the laws of reality, so we make sacrifices."

"But the community is demanding equality of sacrifice," I said. "We've never asked for special treatment."

". . . It's inevitable that some must make greater sacrifices than others. . . ."

"That 'some' being my people. . . ."

"In this instance, yes."

"So the weak must sacrifice for the strong. Is that it, Brother?"

"No, a part of the whole is sacrificed—and will continue to be until a new society is formed." (502–3)

Hambro hopes sacrifice will produce a new and internally consistent society. He, in other words, is engaged in the ritual driving out of a scapegoat, or a ritual of purification.[29] In response, I. M. asks whether it is possible to keep those who sacrifice within the community so that society becomes different but not new. A discourse of sacrifice can function only within the context of a fallibilistic approach to politics, where it is not the perfect resolution of the problem of coercion that is sought, but only a just resolution. Losses do not disappear but must be acknowledged to be part of the fabric of society.

I. M. articulates one last criterion for determining the legitimacy of particular sacrifices: sacrifice becomes illegitimate when one person or group regularly sacrifices for the rest. Instead, sacrifices must be reciprocated. The weak
have been incorporated into the democratic polity only when they are in an
equal position to request sacrifice from others; "equality of sacrifice" is the
third criterion of legitimacy. I. M. learns that Hambro is merely cynical when
the latter remarks: "I thought that you had learned . . . [that] it's impossible *not*
to take advantage of the people. . . . The trick is to take advantage of them in
their own best interest" (504). I. M. realizes that Hambro "didn't have to deal
with being both sacrificer and victim; . . . he didn't have to put the knife
blade to his own throat" (506). In Hambro's world, those who sacrifice are victims, or scapegoats, because someone else controls the sacrifice. The Brotherhood's policies undo the democratic promise that one can choose one's own
sacrifices, and thus their policies also undermine the limits on sacrifice and
the distinction between sacrifice and scapegoating established by the need for
consent. The Brotherhood's policies separate the agency of sacrifice from the
experience of it. Democracy, however, opens a distinction between those who
give up their interests consensually and those who do not, between sacrificers
and victims, aiming to reduce as much as possible the category of victim.
Moreover, a democratic sacrifice opens a covenant—it is not mere sufferance
of someone else's abuses—so that those who benefit from the sacrifice must
see themselves as recipients of gifts in respect to which they must act responsibly. It is in constantly reopening democratic covenants, and in requiring the
cultivation of trust to do so, that the practice of mutual sacrifice does most of
its political work. If democracies are to distribute political losses as justly as
possible, their citizens must work to see that sacrifices are voluntary, honored,
and reciprocated.

I. M.'s account of his invisibility is intimately bound up with the failure of
the political world in the novel to take proper stock of different citizens' sacrifices. At the end of the conversation with Hambro, I. M. shouts:

> Look at me! Look at me! Everywhere I've turned somebody has wanted
> to sacrifice me for my good—only *they* were the ones who benefited. And
> now we start on the old sacrificial merry-go-round. At what point do we
> stop? Is this the true definition, is Brotherhood a matter of sacrificing the
> weak? If so, at what point do we stop? (501)

No account of democratic sacrifice that fails to acknowledge that communal decisions inevitably provide private benefit to some members of the
community at the expense of others can provide a realistic or legitimate basis
for collective action. I. M.'s attempt to get Hambro to see him—"Look at me!
Look at me!"—reveals the point of his critique of Hambro's failure to consider who benefits from democratic agreements. I. M. is underscoring the fact
that when the recipients of the gift of sacrifice fail to acknowledge the gifts

they receive, they render invisible, or cease to see, those who sacrifice. Hambro, looking *through* I. M., sees only the transparent agreement achieved by the party's "committee." I. M.'s original, meta-narrative plan to show his readers what they are "looking through" (581) when they do not see him now becomes his central project within the narrative, too. Agreements never look transparent if we see that they require some citizens to accept lesser fulfillment of their interests than do others.

If democratic citizens are going to address the problem of sacrifice adequately, they must, then, ask three questions: Who is sacrificing for whom? Is the sacrifice voluntary and honored? Will the sacrifice be reciprocated? I. M. does not deny that political practice entails sacrifice and disappointment, but he discerns that "sacrifice" cannot be said easily: It is a political action that should be accompanied by the democratic concern fostered by these three questions. Indeed, the politics of democratic agreement, in order to advance legitimacy, must be able to develop such a democratic concern for loss.

But we began this discussion about sacrifice in order to find the pun that motivates the castration dream. Where, o where, has that little pun gone? With all this analysis, I've now buried it, so let me repeat it. When I. M. complains about the Brotherhood policy change, Hambro says, "It's unfortunate, Brother, but your *members* will have to be sacrificed" [emphasis added].[30] There it is, the source of the castration dream, a "linked verbal echo," to use Ellison's words, that appears approximately sixty pages before the surreal grand finale of the dream. "Ellison's transitions, puns, images, and allusions create a ghost network of language and craft that integrate the sundry aspects of the American [Dream/]Nightmare."[31]

By positioning the dream as the last word on the riot scene, and also the last word in I. M.'s conversation with Hambro, Ellison explicitly links what he has discovered about sacrifice through I. M.'s personal interactions, including his conversation with Hambro, to large-scale political events. The reader gets to see the same ritual of sacrifice enacted on both personal and political levels. It's as if the riot tells us how existentially and politically bracing are ordinary citizens' everyday experiences of loss and sacrifice; the riot, oddly enough, becomes a metaphor for an ordinary part of democratic life. Indeed, if we assimilate it to the dream, and consider the dreamy riot and dream sequence to originate in I. M.'s earlier personal experiences of sacrifice, the end of the novel makes a powerful statement about the psychic pressures of democratic life, where citizens are by definition empowered only to be disempowered.[32] The dream scene also confirms that the democratic ritual in which Ellison has been most interested, sacrifice, turns out, in the novel and in I. M.'s experience, to be, inevitably, castration. The world inhabited by I. M. has failed to find a sufficiently democratic response to the necessary fact of loss and sacrifice in democratic politics and, instead, simply unmans citizens. First asking for their consent, it then does what it will with them.

THE ACCURACY OF ELLISON'S
X-RAY VISION

Ellison's intuition that sacrifice is central to the meaning of democratic citizenship was absolutely accurate.[33] In fact, he zeroed in on a central but generally ignored term in the social contract tradition. The enlightenment philosophers Thomas Hobbes, John Locke, and Jean-Jacques Rousseau all draw on the same Old Testament story about Jepthah (*Judges* 11) in order to ground their accounts of consent and political obligation. Jepthah, who had been cast out of the Israelite tribe as a bastard, gains his place both in the tribe and as the leader of the Israelites by fighting for them and winning. He wins when he vows to God that, if given the victory, he will sacrifice the first thing he sees when he gets home. His daughter, of course, comes out to greet him, and when he is torn about what to do—whether he should carry out the sacrifice he has promised to Yahweh—she tells him that since he promised the Lord to sacrifice, he must do so. She will go with her friends to the hills for two months to lament her virgin death, and then she will let her father sacrifice her. Jepthah gains his citizenship through military sacrifice; he cements a system of promise and consent on the basis of his daughter's self-sacrifice. Jepthah's promise to God is for Hobbes paradigmatic of the promises that underlie consent-based politics, but the daughter's self-sacrifice is the basic model for the relationship between citizen and sovereign (*Leviathan* 21.7). Beneath the promise and consent that found the social contract is the most extreme loss. Ellison's novel thus unearths, through astute observation of practice, the principle buried beneath the operations of a consent-based politics.[34]

In sum, Ellison's pursuit of the rituals inherent in ordinary life led him to the following "tragi-comic" discovery about democratic politics. A legitimate account of collective democratic action must begin by acknowledging this "paradox of politics": that communal decisions inevitably benefit some members of a community at the expense of others, even in cases where the whole community generally benefits.[35] Since democracy claims to secure the good of all citizens, it is the people who benefit less than others from particular political decisions, but nonetheless accede, who preserve political stability. Their sacrifice makes collective democratic action possible. Toward the end of the castration dream, I. M. dreams of saying to Jack and Bledsoe and old Emerson and Norton and Ras: "But if you'll look, you'll see. . . . It's not invisible . . . there hang not only my generations wasting upon the water. . . . But your sun. . . . And your moon. . . . Your world. . . . There's your universe, and that drip-drop upon the water you hear is all the history you've made, all you're going to make. Now laugh, you scientists. Let's hear you laugh!" (570). The blood that drains from him constitutes the world of his tormentors and their only legacy. So too the sacrifices of some citizens are the bedrock of other citizens' lives. Ellison challenges us to look at our comforts and see the sacrifices of others that have made them possible.

Once the sacrifices of our political life become visible, democracy must be seen not as a static end state that achieves the common good by assuring the same benefits or the same level of benefits to everyone, but rather as a political practice by which the diverse negative effects of collective political action, and even of just decisions, can be distributed equally, and constantly redistributed over time, on the basis of consensual interactions.[36] The viability of democratic citizenship depends on how well a democratic polity deals with the necessary presence of loss in politics. Indeed, the problem of loss highlights the fundamental paradox of democratic citizenship: Democratic citizens are encouraged to think of themselves as all-powerful even in the very moments that power is being taken from them. Democratic citizens, therefore, regularly need to recover the agency that is supposed to be their birthright in the face of its degradation. Citizenship consists partly of rituals used to manage the psychological tension that arises from the experience of being a powerless sovereign, and some future democracy may—Ellison is hopeful—one day find healthy rituals with which to do this. The democracy in which I. M. lives, however, has adopted castration as its solution. Through that ritual, some citizens are made to bear the marks of the impotence with which all the rest are also afflicted. They become apotropaic off-scourings in an extreme ritual of purification.

THE TRAGI-COMEDY OF CITIZENSHIP

American representative democracy, Ellison suggests in *Invisible Man,* has long been running along a road of failure, along the inseparable tracks of tragedy and comedy, leaving citizens to feel, like I. M., "as though [they'd] been watching a bad comedy." I. M. continues: "Only it was real and I was living it and it was the only historically meaningful life that I could live. If I left it, I'd be nowhere. As dead and as meaningless as Clifton" (478). I have used the term "tragi-comic" to describe Ellison's discovery of the place of sacrifice in democratic politics because it is his own term for describing a suitably democratic political vision. He talks about the relationship between tragedy and comedy frequently,[37] but let me quote just one remark from a foreword Ellison wrote for someone else's novel. John Kouwenhoven's *The Beer Can by the Highway,* Ellison wrote, "has been quietly teaching Americans to discern in things both great and small, dignified and pedestrian, that which is essentially 'American' about American civilization. It . . . was written by a critic who has looked long and hard at American culture with that native mixture of comic and tragic vision which is so necessary if we are to make sense of our diverse, pluralistic society."[38] In *Invisible Man* the juxtaposition of tragedy and comedy comes out perhaps most clearly in the riot scene. Face to face with burning Harlem, I. M. reflects: "I wanted to laugh, for suddenly I realized that I didn't know whether I had been part of a sellout or not" (480). But unlike I. M., the rioters "were in no mood for laughter." Tragedy and comedy arise from the same situation, but they differ depending on whether the situation is experienced with or without understanding of it by those who participate in it. Moreover, to view any particular event as tragic or comic is to learn to accept it by one of two different strategies.[39]

Reflecting on invisibility, Ellison says: "Men in our situation simply cannot afford to ignore the nuances of human relationships. And although action is necessary, forthright action, it must be guided—tempered by insight and compassion. Nevertheless, isn't this what civilization is all about? And isn't this what tragedy has always sought to teach us?"[40] Tragedy teaches one not to take advantage of the necessary suffering of others, but to see and acknowledge it.

We are perhaps less familiar, however, with what comedy has to offer politics. Ellison describes his coming to know his protagonist's voice thus:

> But then as I listened to its *taunting laughter* and speculated as to what kind of individual would speak in such accents, I decided that it would be one who had been forged in the underground of American experience *and yet managed to emerge less angry than ironic. That he would be a blues-toned laugher-at-wounds who included himself in his indictment of the human condition.* I liked the idea, and as I tried to visualize the speaker I came to relate him to those ongoing conflicts, tragic and comic, that had claimed my group's energies since the abandonment of the Reconstruction. (*Invisible Man,* Introduction, xviii; emphasis added)

In the face of one's own necessary suffering, comedy teaches a citizen to laugh. As far as Ellison is concerned, laughter and irony, and not merely forgiveness, enable citizens satisfactorily to assimilate the political imposition of losses and sacrifices.[41] Forgiveness fails to involve those who have *not* suffered from a communal decision in that suffering—they remain objects of others' attention but do not themselves participate in any way in the event of the suffering. But laughter does draw even those who have not suffered into awareness and experience of the loss.[42] Those who *have* suffered do not pursue revenge but make sure those who *have not* suffered are aware of their beneficence. "A comic ethics provides a mandate for rhetoric: namely, for confronting our differences and communicating across them. This ethics encourages 'charitability' toward the motives of others; indeed, the alternative is an assumption of universal cunning and hypocrisy that would make social cooperation impossible."[43] Here one suspects that Ellison follows Kenneth Burke, who interpreted the physiology of laughter as indicating an evolution from the gesture of the threat—open mouth, bared teeth, guttural sounds—to the gesture asking for cooperation and, even, love.[44] In coming to hear I. M.'s voice, Ellison hears "taunting laughter," which suggests a similar sort of evolution.

Pure anger may be a motivation to speak, but it cannot determine the form that rhetoric takes if speech is to undo invisibility and facilitate democratic representation. In *Invisible Man* Harlem has its one fury, Ras, a Caribbean-born political activist who preaches revenge on his street corner: He shouts, "Blood calls for blood! You remember that" (376). I. M. rejects Ras's "shrill," anger-driven rhetoric almost immediately upon arriving in Harlem. Seconds after he notices him, he is surprised to observe two policemen standing mere feet away, chatting and laughing with each other, and ignoring Ras (159–60). He realizes that anger can rarely make people visible to one another, for it derives from specificity of experience and particularized views of how the world should be.[45] In search of visibility, public language, the language we use for talking to strangers, must generate a transition away from the anger (or other particular interest) that drives someone to speak and to a language that can integrate standpoints. Laughter, in contrast to anger, arises from a shared recognition that aligns different standpoints, even if only temporarily.[46] "The elements of identity shared between sacrificer, victim, and audience can emerge into consciousness when the clown or the fool of comedy can laugh along with everyone else—all laugh at, and thereby sacrifice, requisite bits of their self."[47] Laughter must somehow issue from anger and transform it; comedy teaches the forms of imagination that allow a metamorphosis in one's assessment of one's interests.

To see the paradox of democratic citizenship—that it empowers only to disempower—and to weep teaches sympathy for one's fellow citizens; to see this paradox and to laugh is to make another democratic sacrifice, enabling further political action. Here, then, are two possible strategies for dealing with the fact of loss in politics. Tragi-comic citizenship blends them. Finally, a tragic-comic citizen has this to say about democratic politics: "Oh, what a joke on us it is, that our democratic ideals are so noble, and raise our desires to such a pitch, and are also so far beyond our grasp. Let's hope the joke is good enough to keep us at it."

ENDNOTES

1. I. Howe (1963), "Black Boys and Native Sons," *Dissent.* Cf. R. Ellison, 1995 [1963–64] "The World and the Jug," in *Collected Essays* (New York: The Modern Library). For another example of this critical perspective, see D. Gibson (1981), *The Politics of Literary Expression: A Study of Major Black Writers* (Westport, Conn.). On the political critiques of Ellison, see L. Neal (1974), "Ellison's Zoot Suit," in J. Hersey, ed., *Ralph Ellison: A Collection of Critical Essays* (NJ: Prentice Hall), 58–79 [Reprinted from *Black World,* Vol. 20, no. 2, Dec. 1970, 31–50]; and M. Dickstein (1999), "Ralph Ellison, Race, and American Culture," *Raritan* 18: 30–50.

2. Two scholars in particular have been building a body of work in this area: Meili Steele (1996), "Metatheory and the Subject of Democracy," *New Literary History* 27: 473–502; (1996), "Democratic Interpretation and the Politics of Difference," in *Comparative Literature* 48: 326–342; (2002), "Arendt versus Ellison on Little Rock: the Role of Language in Political Judgment," in *Constellations* 9: 184–206 and Kenneth Warren (1995), "Ralph Ellison and the Reconfiguration of Black Cultural Politics," in *Yearbook of Research in English and American Literature* 11: 139–57; (2000), "As white as anybody": Race and the Politics of Counting as Black," in *New Literary History* 31: 709–26. There has also been a proliferation of free-standing pieces on the subject: J. M. Albrecht (1999), "Saying Yes and Saying No: Individualist Ethics in Ellison, Burke, and Emerson," in *PMLA* 114: 46–63; T. Parrish (1995), "Ralph Ellison, Kenneth Burke, and the Form of Democracy," in *Arizona Quarterly* 52: 117–148; D. S. Allen (2001), "Law's Necessary Forcefulness: Ellison vs. Arendt on the Battle of Little Rock," in 26 *Oklahoma City University Law Review* 3 (Fall 2001), 857–900; D. S. Allen (2004), *Talking to Strangers* (Chicago: University of Chicago Press).

The best place to start with criticism of Ellison is A. Nadel (1988), *Invisible Criticism: Ralph Ellison and the American Canon* (Iowa City: University of Iowa Press); K. Bentson., ed. (1987), *Speaking for You: The Vision of Ralph Ellison* (Washington, D.C.: Howard University Press); H. Baker (1984), *Blues, Ideology, and Afro-American Literature: A Vernacular Theory* (Chicago: University of Chicago Press); H. L. Gates, Jr. (1988), *The Signifying Monkey: A Theory of African-American Literary Criticism* (Oxford: Oxford University Press). The most helpful text on Ellison that I have found is B. Eddy, 1998, *The Rites of Identity: The Religious Naturalism and Cultural Criticism of Kenneth Burke and Ralph Ellison.* Unpublished Dissertation. Dept. of Religion. Princeton University. She addresses sacrifice, tragedy, and comedy in Ellison, as well as many of the other concepts that come up in his work. On Ellison's politics and the political ideas in his writings generally (as opposed to his "democratic theory"), see J. G. Watts (1994), *Heroism and the Black Intellectual: Ralph Ellison, Politics, and Afro-American Intellectual Life* (Chapel Hill: University of North Carolina Press); J. Callahan (1988), "Frequencies of Eloquence: the Performance and Composition of *Invisible Man*," in R. O'Meally, ed. 1988. *New Essays on Invisible Man* (Cambridge: Cambridge University Press), 55–94; B. Ostendorf, (1988), "Ralph Waldo Ellison: Anthropology, Modernism, and Jazz," in R. O'Meally, ed. 1988., *New Essays on Invisible Man* (Cambridge: Cambridge University Press), 95–122, S. E. Hyman (1974), "Ralph Ellison in Our Time," in J. Hersey. *Ralph Ellison: A Collection of Critical Essays* (NJ: Prentice-Hall), 39–42 (Reprinted from *The New Leader,* Vol. 47, no. 22, Oct. 26, 1964, 21–22); B. Foley, 1999, "Reading Redness: Politics and Audience in Ralph Ellison's Early Short Fiction," in *Journal of Narrative Theory* 29.3: 323–39. But for Eddy, I have not yet come across a text that investigates Ellison's idea of sacrifice, the subject of this essay.

3. Ellison sought characters "possessing broad insight into their situations [and] the emotional, psychological, and intellectual complexity which would allow them to

possess and articulate a truly democratic world view" ("Twentieth-Century Fiction and the Mask of Humanity," *Collected Essays,* p. 93).

4. See, for instance, the early interviews, "The Art of Fiction: *An Interview,*" from 1955 and "On Initiation Rites and Power: A Lecture at West Point," from 1969. Both are available in *Collected Essays,* ibid.

5. I am certainly not the first. Ellison suggests it with his riff on "I am what I am," and "I yam what I yam" (266, 269). Albert Murray confesses in a letter to Ellison, dated Feb. 9, 1952, that he does, too. "(By the way, *Invisible Man* equals IM equals I'M equals I AM . . .)," (A. Murray and J. Callahan, eds., 2000, *Trading Twelves: The Selected Letters of Ralph Ellison and Albert Murray,* New York: Vintage Books).

6. As many commentators have pointed out, I. M.'s relationship with Mary is the only one to which Ellison provides any strong emotional warmth. And she drops almost entirely out of the plot after a brief centrality. Repeatedly, the conversations Ellison develops involve strangers: the Reverend Barbee's encomium to the founder of the College reports on past efforts at collaboration; there is the union meeting at the paint factory; and I. M.'s effort to work with his quasi-mentor at that factory. All of his meetings with Brotherhood members and his experiences at the eviction, at his first public speech, and at Tod Clifton's funeral focus attention precisely on the relationships among strangers who are trying to act together. I. M.'s encounter with the young Mr. Emerson perhaps brings this theme out the best, when the young Emerson asks, "Do you believe that two people, two strangers who have never seen one another before can speak with utter frankness and sincerity? . . . [D]o you believe it is possible for us, the two of us, to throw off the mask of custom and manners that insulate man from man, and converse in naked honesty and frankness?" (*Invisible Man,* p. 186).

7. Cited in T. Parrish (1995), "Ralph Ellison, Kenneth Burke, and the Form of Democracy," *Arizona Quarterly* 52: 117.

8. Ellison regularly makes the argument that, whereas white Americans have been able to live with illusions about how democracy works, blacks in contrast "are an American people who are geared to what *is,* and who yet are driven by a sense of what it is possible for human life to be in this society" ("What America Would Be Like Without Blacks," *Collected Essays,* p. 584). African Americans, in his argument, understand the ways the collective decisions of a democracy impose on some citizens. White Americans have been able to avoid that knowledge because one minority group was assigned to bear the bulk of these burdens. "When we look objectively at how the dry bones of the nation were hung together, it seems obvious that some one of the many groups that compose the United States had to suffer the fate of being allowed no easy escape from experiencing the harsh realities of the human condition as they were to exist under even so fortunate a democracy as ours" ("What America Would Be Like Without Blacks," *Collected Essays,* p. 583); "these Americans were designated as perfect victims for sacrifice" ("Perspective of Literature," *Collected Essays,* pp. 777–78). The thrust of this argument is to take the black experience of living under Jim Crow as a metaphor

for a basic democratic experience of having the majority make decisions to which one does not concur, and may even actively resent. The Jim Crow period, in this analysis, is therefore not an aberration but fundamentally revealing of some of the most difficult problems to be faced by democratic peoples.

9. Cf. D. S. Allen, "Law's Necessary Forcefulness: Ralph Ellison vs. Hannah Arendt on the Battle of Little Rock," 26 *Oklahoma City University Law Review* 3 (Fall 2001), 857–900.

10. Nadel (2001, 396) writes: "We can view Ellison's art, in other words, as exploring the tension between conscious America and the American unconscious."

11. "On Initiation Rites and Power," *Collected Essays,* p. 525.

12. Ellison invokes the idea of ritual throughout his essays. For instance, in "The Myth of the Flawed White Southerner," (*Collected Essays,* p. 553) he refers to himself as "a novelist interested in that area of national life where political power is institutionalized and translated into democratic ritual and national style." To piece together Ellison's account of ritual, see particularly "Twentieth-Century Fiction and the Black Mask of Humanity," "The Art of Fiction: *An Interview,*" "Hidden Name and Complex Fate," and "On Initiation Rites and Power," in *Collected Essays,* pp. 81–99, 210–24, 189–209, and 520–41, respectively.

13. "Hidden Name and Complex Fate," *Collected Essays,* p. 195.

14. Ralph Ellison, *Invisible Man,* (New York: Random House, 1952; reprint, New York: Vintage Books, 1995), 17. All subsequent citations will be noted parenthetically in the text by page number, and emphases in original unless otherwise noted.

15. Notably, Kenneth Burke too was concerned to distinguish humility and humiliation (B. Eddy, 1998, *The Rites of Identity: The Religious Naturalism and Cultural Criticism of Kenneth Burke and Ralph Ellison.* Unpublished Dissertation. Dept. of Religion. Princeton University, pp. 156–8).

16. This scene has been much analyzed, partly because it was published as an excerpt of the novel before the novel appeared. See Eddy, ibid; M. Nussbaum, 1999, "Invisibility and Recognition: Sophocles' *Philoctetes* and Ellison's *Invisible Man,*" in *Philosophy and Literature* 23: 257–83.

17. Ellison certainly drew heavily on Freud. Young Emerson is reading *Totem and Taboo* when the protagonist goes to visit him (p. 180), and Ellison's preoccupation with taboos generally and with incest in particular also indicate the connection.

18. S. E. Hyman (1974. "Ralph Ellison in Our Time," in J. Hersey. *Ralph Ellison: A Collection of Critical Essays.* NJ: Prentice Hall. 39–42. [Reprinted from *The New Leader,* vol. 47, no. 22, Oct. 26, 1964, 21–22]) is one of the few critics to recognize the importance of "responsibility" to Ellison. Now see Morel, chap. 3 in this volume.

19. J. Callahan (1988. "Frequencies of Eloquence: The Performance and Composition of *Invisible Man,*" in R. O'Meally, ed. 1988. *New Essays on Invisible Man.* Cambridge: Cambridge University Press. 55–94, p. 64) offers a similar reading. Similarly,

Callahan in this volume makes the positive argument for fraternity and civic friend-ship that is necessitated by the discovery of the problem of loss discussed in this essay.

20. Ellison insists that even the politically oppressed position of African Americans in the U.S. during the period of segregation nonetheless required that African Americans engage in systems of reciprocity. Thus, he remarks on "the complexity of circumstances which go to make up the Negro experience, and which alone go to make the obvious injustice bearable" ("Hidden Name and Complex Fate," *Collected Essays,* p. 208).

21. Reciprocity is central to all the deliberative democracy literature. Here I cite only the central texts and two critical pieces: J. Habermas, 1990. *Moral Consciousness and Communicative Action.* Trans. by Christian Lenhardt and Shierry Weber Nicholsen. Cambridge, MA: MIT University Press; J. Rawls, 1993. *Political Liber-alism;* S. Benhabib, 1986. *Critique, Norm, and Utopia: A Study of the Foundations of Critical Theory.* New York: Columbia University Press (esp. chap. 8); S. Cham-bers, 1995. "Discourse and democratic practices," in S. White, ed. *The Cambridge Companion to Habermas.* 233–62; A. Honneth, 1995. "The other of justice: Habermas and the ethical challenge of postmodernism," in S. White, ed. *The Cambridge Companion to Habermas.* 289–324; M. Williams, 1988, *Voice, Trust, and Memory: Marginalized Groups and the Failings of Liberal Representation.* Princeton: Princeton University Press.

22. The everyday requires sacrifice. Thus, Ellison writes, "It is our fate as human beings always to give up some good things for other good things, to throw off certain bad circumstances only to create others" ("Hidden Name and Complex Fate," *Collected Essays,* p. 208).

23. "Hidden Name and Complex Fate," *Collected Essays,* p. 208. Almost everyone with whom I have discussed these materials has objected that the term "sacrifice" does not properly belong to politics and is too dangerous to introduce to political discussion. And yet, despite general disavowals of the topic, the word comes up frequently in political theory and political discussions. In fact, from a quick and casual survey, it's a fair bet that the majority of works published in political theory use the term at some point.

24. One should note in this passage how Ellison begins with clichéd notions of responsibility (two opposed clichés) and then moves from these to a completely counterintuitive version of the term ("I was the irresponsible one for I should have used my knife"). This strategy of beginning with what is familiar in order to take the reader to something else is central to Ellison's writing. Thus, in "On Ini-tiation Rites and Power," (*Collected Essays,* p. 532) he writes, "I could not violate the reader's sense of reality, his sense of the way things were done, at least on the surface. My task would be to give him the surface and then try to take him into the internalities, take him below the level of racial structuring and down into those areas where we are simply men and women, human beings living on this blue orb, and not always living so well." Cf. "The Little Man at Chehaw Sta-tion," *Collected Essays,* p. 496.

25. The work with rituals is also the source of the book's formal unity.

26. We might take I.M.'s reflections on his funeral oration for Tod Clifton as focusing on this problem. The strangers there share something like Brotherhood, "something for which the theory of Brotherhood had given me no name," (p. 453).

27. R.P. Warren, *Who Speaks for the Negro?,* 344; emphasis in original.

28. Alan Nadel (2001, "Ralph Ellison and the American Canon," *American Literary History,* p. 394; cf. pp. 395, 397ff.) discusses Ellison's interest in puns and acknowledges their psychological force: "they reveal connections that have to be repressed so as to expedite the 'normal' flow of information."

29. These analytical terms are not far off those Ellison himself uses to describe the political behaviors of whites who want to "get shut" of blacks and Garveyites. "Both would use the black man as a scapegoat to achieve a national catharsis, and both would by way of curing the patient, destroy him," in "What America Would Be Like Without Blacks," *Collected Essays,* p. 579.

30. Id. Ellison follows the same analytical moves of this passage of the novel in his essay, "What America Would Be Like Without Blacks." Thus, just before the passage cited above, he remarks that the early eighteenth-century attempt to export all blacks back to Africa "would have amounted to the severing of a healthy and indispensable member" (p. 579). He was aware of the pun.

31. Nadel 2001, 400.

32. This line of analysis is consistent with Nadel (2001, 397), who writes:

> In this context, it becomes imperative to regard the term *American Dream* as a pun that pervasively informs Ellison's fiction. The term signifies both America's conscious ideals and the deluded unconsciousness with which it evades and undermines them. These two forms of the American Dream intersect in that demimonde of the collective and individual psyche, the marginal space where the visionary is sightless and dream verges on nightmare, the surreal meeting place of the symbolic and the grotesque.

33. We can tell that Ellison meant his term "sacrifice" to be used for political and not only psychological analysis because he makes it the centerpiece of a criticism of Hannah Arendt's arguments about school desegregation and Little Rock (Warren 1965, pp. 343–44).

34. Ellison discussed the founding of the U.S. in precisely such terms (see n. 8). He also regularly invoked the idea that the Constitution was founded on the blood sacrifice of the Revolutionary War. See, for instance, "On Initiation Rites and Power."

35. William Connolly ([1991], *Identity/Difference: Democratic Negotiations of Political Paradox,* Ithaca: Cornell University Press, p. 94) has recently called this the "paradox of politics": "[e]very form of social completion and enablement also contains subjugations and cruelties within it. Politics, then, is the medium through which these ambiguities can be engaged and confronted, shifted and stretched."

36. Here is a section of the interview with Robert Penn Warren in which Ellison criticizes Arendt for not understanding the place of sacrifice in politics:

> Warren: Here in the midst of what has been an expanding economy you have a contracting economy for the unprepared, for the Negro.
> Ellison: That's the paradox. And this particularly explains something new which has come into the picture; that is, a determination by the Negro no longer to be the scapegoat, no longer to pay, to be sacrificed to—the inadequacies of other Americans. We want to socialize the cost. A cost has been exacted in terms of character, in terms of courage, in determination, and in terms of self-knowledge and self-discovery. Worse, it has led to social, economic, political, and intellectual disadvantages and to a contempt even for our lives. And one motive for our rejection of the old traditional role of national scapegoat is an intensified awareness that not only are we being destroyed by the sacrifice, but that the nation has been rotting at its moral core. (Warren 1965, 339)

37. For example, "Address to the Harvard College Alumni, Class of 1949," "That Same Pain, That Same Pleasure," and "Working Notes for *Invisible Man,*" in *Collected Essays,* pp. 415–26, 63–80, and 341–45, respectively.

38. "Foreword to *The Beer Can on the Highway,*" *Collected Essays,* 847.

39. On the tragic and comic in Ellison, and as "two aspects of the individualist ethics that connect Emerson to Ellison and Burke," see Albrecht, ibid., esp. pp. 50ff. See also Houston Baker (1983), "To Move without Moving: An Analysis of Creativity and Commerce in Ralph Ellison's Trueblood Episode," *PMLA* 98 (1983): 828–45.

40. Warren 1965, 343.

41. Cf. the essay, "On Being the Target of Discrimination," where he writes: "segregation is far more than a negative social condition; it is also a perspective that fosters an endless exercise of irony, and often inspires a redeeming laughter" (*Collected Essays,* p. 821).

42. On Arendt on the subject of irreversibility and forgiveness, see B. Honig (1993), *Political Theory and the Displacement of Politics* (Ithaca: Cornell University Press), 76–79, 84–87. On irreversibility in Ellison, see Eddy 1998, 207.

43. Albrecht 2001, p. 53.

44. Eddy (ibid.), 149.

45. D. S. Allen, 2000, *World of Prometheus,* Princeton: Princeton University Press, chap. 7. See also J. Braithwaite, 2000, "Survey Article: Repentance Rituals and Restorative Justice," *Journal of Political Philosophy* 8: 115–31.

46. Cf. H. Bergson, 1911. *Laughter: An Essay on the meaning of the Comic* (authorized translation, by Cloudesley Brereton and Fred Rothwell). New York: Macmillan.

47. Eddy 1998, 143.

Chapter 3

Ralph Ellison's American Democratic Individualism

LUCAS E. MOREL

*I'll stand on that as I stand on what I see and feel and on what I've heard,
and what I know.*

—*INVISIBLE MAN*

Ralph Ellison chose to write as a means of expressing and affirming his individuality, his excellence, and his free humanity in America. This exercise of his personal responsibility, despite American segregation, was his basic message to the Negro American: As he put it in a note to his *Juneteenth* manuscript, "This society is not likely to become free of racism, thus it is necessary for Negroes to free themselves by becoming their idea of what a free people should be."[1] There was no need to get all of his instruction in liberty from a racist society. It was incumbent upon the Negro to draw upon his own wit, resources, and the free institutions of American society to free himself and show what he thought freedom was all about. To do otherwise—to protest one's oppression but not exercise even the limited freedom he already possessed—was a dead-end.[2] This school of hard knocks was a way station to the eventual regime of freedom that American democracy promised and hence a necessary preparation for an arena of activity yet to come.[3] Laws and court decisions would only be the beginning of black freedom, not an end game itself. Case in point, Ralph Ellison's *Invisible Man* did not write itself! Even the Negro folklore that informs *Invisible Man* was put there by his imagination and craft, and not the necessary outcome of a mere change in laws.[4]

The formal chapters of *Invisible Man* begin with a speech (Chapter 1) and end with a riot (Chapter 25), which on the surface poses two possibilities for guiding the American republic. Invisible Man's speech at the Battle Royal, which he first delivered at his high school graduation to wide acclaim, is not truly his but merely the ritual utterance of an aspiring black youth seeking to garner favor with the white movers and shakers of his hometown. Because it's really the audience's speech and not Invisible Man's, he remains voiceless. This predicament leads to the voice of chaos and destruction—a riot for those who have the freedom to *act* if their *words* fail to gain credence with the society at large.[5] When some connected *Invisible Man's* riot episode to the tenement burnings that occurred in the decade following its publication, Ellison reminded one interviewer that he had reported on the Harlem Riot of 1943 for the *New York Post*. "I certainly wasn't recommending that people burn buildings," Ellison added, "but was suggesting that this was a negative alternative to more democratic political action. When it is impossible to be heard within the democratic forum, people inevitably go to other extremes."[6] This political antithesis anticipates Malcolm X's speech, "The Ballot or the Bullet,"[7] which is really a gloss on Abraham Lincoln's statement that "ballots are the rightful, and peaceful, successors of bullets."[8] What could be more American than the struggle to solve social and political conflict by talking instead of fighting?

Ellison used the phrase "American democratic individualism" in a brief preface written in 1979 for the Franklin Library edition of *Invisible Man*. There he describes the context of black American achievement:

> And, since black folks did not look at themselves out of the same eyes with which they were viewed by whites, their condition and fate rested within the eye of the beholder. If this were true, the obligation of making oneself seen and heard was an imperative of American democratic individualism.[9]

In this context, a condition where blacks could not wait for whites to "see" or acknowledge them, due to racism's hold on their moral perception, visibility was each individual's duty. As Invisible Man puts it in his first speech for the Brotherhood, "You see, all I needed was a chance. You've granted it, now it's up to me!" (341). Here is American democratic individualism in a nutshell.

Ralph Ellison saw his calling as a writer as having a direct impact on American culture and hence political practice. Criticizing W. E. B. Du Bois's signature statement about the American Negro's "double consciousness," Ellison replied: "My problem is not whether I will accept or reject American values. It is, rather, how can I get into a position where I can have the maximum influence upon those values."[10] He added that he wanted to see a more thorough and consistent application of the "American ideals" set forth in the nation's founding documents. In short, he believed his writings would help America, as Martin Luther King, Jr. put it, "Be true to what you said on paper."[11]

Ellison once likened the creation of fictional characters to a chief aim of democratic society: "the development of conscious, articulate citizens."[12] Both the writer and a free society are responsible to give voice, to give "eloquence," to their respective dramatis personae.[13] And as Ellison liked to remind us, the American cast of characters has always included the Negro. Ellison saw in

Negro American culture, displayed in the verve and elegance of "jazzmen and prize fighters, ballplayers and tap dancers," an "affirmation of life beyond all question of our difficulties as Negroes."[14] For Ellison, "individuality" was "still operative beyond the racial structuring of American society."[15]

So, when critics chastised Ellison for preaching individualism to blacks instead of racial solidarity,[16] he referred them to the jazz giants of old, whom he called the "stewards of our vaunted American optimism."[17] Ellison argued that blacks took pride in Duke Ellington and Johnny Hodges "not because they were anonymous bumps within the crowd, but because they were themselves." He reminded them, "If the white society has tried to do anything to us, it has tried to keep us from being individuals," and noted the irony in black leaders decrying black individualism while they themselves were "doing all they can to suppress all individuality but their own."[18] Proud to be a Negro American, Ellison still did not believe true freedom or human excellence would be found down the road of color consciousness: "I recognize that we are bound less by blood than by our cultural and political circumstances."[19] For him the politics of the American regime, despite the segregation he experienced, left sufficient room for aspiring Negro individuals to make their mark.

For Ellison, racism posed a barrier to individual thought and expression not only for the bigoted white, but for blacks who sought to affirm something about themselves *as blacks* in the face of color prejudice. Those unable to free themselves from the "straitjacket of racist ideology," Ellison warned, would elevate an individual's race "to a position of total (really totalitarian) importance."[20] Of the prospects for black appreciation and preservation of their distinctively American past, Ellison said, "I would think that so much of what happens is up to people of our background; but very often they're so full of ideology—what they call *blackness*—that they don't quite know what to do about it, except sometimes to boast about it."[21] In other words, Ellison saw little hope in black consciousness to produce true progress for blacks in American society.

Curiously, just as American democracy allowed room for jazz to develop, Ellison saw a democratic ethos at work within jazz music: "true jazz is an art of individual assertion within and against the group."[22] Jazz served as a fitting analogy for the society of free individuals that the American republic was intended to secure. For Ellison, the American founders represented a jazzy assemblage of political connoisseurs: "Out of the democratic principles set down on paper in the Constitution and the Bill of Rights they were improvising themselves into a nation. . . ."[23] Moreover, Ellison saw jazz as both a means and an end of Negro American freedom: It not only existed as a body of musical expression, with its own techniques and traditions, but also testified to the capacity of black Americans to thrive as artists within segregated America. By creating music that gave opportunity to excel across the color line, black Americans offered a beacon of hope to others who would dare to succeed in what little or great scope of freedom the majority-white society permitted.

As black musical excellence made itself known to wider audiences, but especially to black audiences, interests beyond musical ones were piqued. The young Ralph Ellison would, at first, strive to become a world-class trumpeter and classical composer, only to be emboldened further to try his hand at writing. Ellison once shared that he became a writer "because I had gotten the spirit of literature and had become aware of the possibilities offered by literature—not to make money, but to feel at home in the world."[24] He described himself as "a writer who is American, a Negro, and most eager to discover a more artful, more broadly significant approach to those centers of stress within our national life where he finds his task and being."[25] Ellison saw this as the goal of aspiring, democratic writers:

> Indeed, the integration of American society on the level of the
> imagination is one of this young writer's basic tasks. It is one way in
> which he is able to possess his world, and in his writings help shape the
> values of large segments of a society which otherwise would not admit his
> existence, much less his right to participate or to judge.[26]

One cannot help but hear Ralph Ellison's autobiography in this statement, and a sentiment that informs *Invisible Man*.

Of course, *Invisible Man* is not autobiographical, per se. In interviews, Ellison distinguished the narrator's experiences from his own, disavowing any strict correlation between events in the novel and his own life's journey.[27] An important reason for this distinction should almost go without saying: Ellison was an artist, a writer, who knew from personal experience that novels do not write themselves—even novels by Negro authors about the Negro experience in America. He once wrote that "even homeboys must do their homework."[28]

Although Ellison did not like to have his novel interpreted in autobiographical terms, there is a parallel between Invisible Man's quest for leadership—his desire to persuade men and to make a difference—and Ellison's own desire to make his mark in an America in need of social progress and political reformation. Concluding he could not match the grace, elegance, and mastery of the art of music like Duke Ellington or Louis Armstrong, the former trumpeter and aspiring composer turned to literature.[29] He became a writer in hopes of offering a corrective to the written record of American history and a spur to greater progress in securing freedom to all Americans.

It was this lonely, individual process that Ellison was protecting from the injection of racial determinism by those he considered ignorant practitioners of literary and social criticism. Of the Negro writer's experience, Ellison observed that like other writers, "he will have to go it alone! He must suffer alone even as he shares the suffering of his group, and he must write alone and pit his talents against the standards set by the best practitioners of the craft."[30]

Recall how the narrator of *Invisible Man* recollects his English professor pronouncing that "blood and skin do not think!" (354).[31] This is left for the individual. Here the novel subverts what Ellison called "the divisive mystification of race."[32] Ellison believed "the critical intelligence must perform the difficult task which only it can perform," even when it came to writing on subjects where conventional wisdom attributed "special insight" to black people.[33]

Ellison wanted to take the Negro American experience and make it a part of the American literary tradition before it was forgotten. Just as Invisible Man eventually recognizes that Harlem's residents "were outside the groove of history, and it was my job to get them in, all of them" (443), Ellison's writing of *Invisible Man* constituted his fight to get the Negro into the written record of American history. As he told Albert Murray, "The trick is to get mose lore [i.e., Negro folklore] into the novel so that it becomes a part of the tradition."[34] He does not declare blackness as a virtue in itself, for as he noted a few years after the novel was published, "I know of no valid demonstration that culture is transmitted through the genes."[35] For Ellison, the Negro American experience was a distinct, cultural heritage; nevertheless, given America's selective memory, the Negro's vital contribution to the pluralistic American culture required the talents and ingenuity of ambitious individuals.

The preservation of that heritage, the collective product of individual achievements in the arts of humanity, would require the same individual effort that helped to produce it. Invisible Man recalls his English professor, "half-drunk on words and full of contempt and exaltation," saying, "Our task is that of making ourselves individuals. The conscience of a race is the gift of its individuals who see, evaluate, record. . . . We create the race by creating ourselves and then to our great astonishment we will have created something far more important: We will have created a culture" (354). Ellison wrote as one individual striving to contribute to a community of diverse individuals, an endeavor that did not mean simply assimilating himself into a supposedly monolithic American culture.

For example, in the Liberty Paints factory, Invisible Man acts out an allegory of crude American assimilation by measuring ten black drops of "dope" into buckets of glossy white paint—headed for a national monument, no less—and stirring until they disappeared (199–200). The contribution of the black drops is essential, but the blackness is quickly submerged in an ocean of white—the ostensible color of freedom. For Ellison, the test of the American melting pot, and with it "the extension of the democratic process in the direction of perfecting itself," was "the inclusion, *not* assimilation, of the black man."[36] As he put it elsewhere, "we keep talking about 'black awareness' when we really should be talking about black American awareness, an awareness of where we fit into the total American scheme, where our influence is."[37] In other words, for Ellison, "This is a pluralistic society and culturally the melting pot really melts."[38]

A pivotal example of the cultural melting pot in *Invisible Man* takes shape at Brother Tod Clifton's funeral. One unifying element of the melting pot of humanity that assembles for the funeral is the song "There's Many a Thousand Gone." Initiated by an older Negro man, it is soon taken up by a euphonium horn that then leads the steadily massing crowd as they march and bear along the coffin bearing Brother Tod. The singing crowd included "white brothers and sisters," as well as those who "had been born in other lands" (453). It is no surprise that Ellison highlights music as a unifying element of the cultural melting pot he saw operating in the United States. An old Negro spiritual about slavery, an abiding reminder of what Ellison called America's "original sin,"[39] provides an ironic means of reunifying Americans: "And yet all were touched; the song had touched us all." Riffing on the "racial mountain" referred to by Langston Hughes in his famous 1926 *Nation* essay,[40] Ellison places Clifton's funeral at Mount Morris Park, which is then climbed by an integrated community of mourners. He thereby illustrates how Negro Americans can lead Americans of all races into a unity of purpose. There, despite Invisible Man's lack of religious faith, he issues a eulogy that serves as a "sermon on the mount" for the somber, sweltering crowd.

Frustrated over his lack of words, Invisible Man tells the crowd, "What are you waiting for, when all I can tell you is his name?" (455). The name "Tod Clifton" means the world to Invisible Man (and Ellison), for each individual is like Tod Clifton, a person "jam-full of contradictions," as Invisible Man later declares to the Brotherhood (467). Therein lies a clue to America's greatness— the "diversity" of individualism. In the Epilogue, Invisible Man draws out an important, political implication of individual diversity: "Let man keep his many parts, and you'll have no tyrant states" (577). If, as Invisible Man declares, "America is woven of many strands; I would recognize them and let it so remain," then a society that intends to remain free must begin by protecting each individual's freedom, regardless of race. In *Invisible Man,* Ellison does so threefold with his *own* decision to write a novel featuring an *individual* who highlights the life and death and especially the name of yet *another individual,* Tod Clifton. As one of the many strands that constitute America, Tod Clifton deserved to be remembered.[41] Like the dead commemorated by Abraham Lincoln in his Gettysburg Address,[42] Tod Clifton's death will not have been in vain if the diverse multitude assembled for his funeral unites in their recognition of each name, each individual, each strand of the American tapestry. In short, they must answer in the affirmative Invisible Man's plaintive cry, "And could politics ever be an expression of love?" (452). Ironically and fittingly, Ellison brings to life the nation's motto, *E pluribus unum* ("Out of many, one"), at an integrated funeral—where "crowds approached the park from all directions" to "stand touching and sweating and breathing and looking in a common direction."

Ellison embeds Tod Clifton in the reader's memory through a scene that closes with strong allusions to a cooking or, dare I say, melting pot. The concluding paragraphs of the funeral chapter contain references to boiling and vegetables: "the crowds that seemed to boil along" and the "crowd boiled, sweated, heaved"; "market carts . . . shading the withering fruits and vegetables"; "the stench of decaying cabbage" along with a "watermelon huckster . . . holding up a long slice of orange-meated melon"; "Oranges, cocoanuts and alligator pears" (460). Even a reference to "the dazzling reds, yellows and greens of cheap sport shirts and summer dresses" adds the proper mix of color for a stew pot. Last, for those who might miss Ellison's sympathetic image of "the great unwashed," Invisible Man describes the crowd as "boiling figures seen through steaming glass from inside a washing machine." Ellison suggested as much by making the grave diggers Irish and, hence, emblematic of the immigrants that would seek assimilation or "inclusion"[43] (Ellison's preferred term) into the New World that was America. The chapter concludes with a reference to the tension of the crowd as palpable and in need of organization "before it simmered away in the heat" (461).[44]

At the close of the funeral, Invisible Man passed through the crowd and saw "not a crowd but the set faces of individual men and women" (459). In other words, as an orator and aspiring leader, he finally got to the place where his speech to a crowd produced in him a clear vision of his audience— "individual men and women." Unlike at the start of the novel, where he recalls his college library's display of "photographs of men and women in wagons drawn by mule teams and oxen, dressed in black, dust clothing, people who seemed almost without individuality, a black mob that seemed to be waiting, looking with blank faces" (39), he was now beginning to recognize all of the "strands" of the fabric of American society. He would eventually learn to "let it so remain." Julia Eichelberger draws the same conclusion in her examination of Invisible Man's "hibernation": "Through his withdrawal, Ellison's protagonist learns that he can and must recognize others, that he must 'speak for' (581) the individual and against the belief that 'individuals . . . don't count' (291)."[45]

Ellison understood the novel as "a product of the *integrative* and *analytical* play of the imagination." He went on to observe that "imagination itself is *integrative*," and therein lies the hope for a more humane, more free, and hence more "articulate" citizenry that offered the best prospects for an American practice more consistent with its ideals. For if the "human imagination is integrative,"[46] this gave hope for the integration of society. As Alan Nadel points out while discussing Ellison's understanding of integration, "In an unequal society, however, art that integrates the sensibilities reveals the integrated history of American culture."[47]

If "conscious, articulate citizens" were the goal of a successful democracy, then Ellison stood a chance of shaping those same citizens by crafting a work of art out of the American story. He commented that "it's futile to *argue* our humanity with those who willfully refuse to recognize it, when art can *reveal* on its own terms more truth while providing pleasure, insight and, for Negro readers at least, affirmation and a sense of direction."[48] Ellison did not even rule out the Bull Connors of the world from learning from his book. As he put it in 1972, *"I would always write as though the governor of Mississippi was looking over my shoulder."*[49]

Ellison's optimism, his hope for writing as an artist and not a propagandist, derived from his appreciation of the great writers who had preceded him. Upon receiving the National Book Award in 1953 for *Invisible Man,* he commented that his own attempt to write a major novel derived from a feeling that "except for the work of William Faulkner something vital had gone out of American prose after Mark Twain." He continued,

> I came to believe that the writers of that period took a much greater responsibility for the condition of democracy and, indeed, their works were imaginative projections of the conflicts within the human heart which arose when the sacred principles of the Constitution and the Bill of Rights clashed with the practical exigencies of human greed and fear, hate and love.[50]

He understood the craft of great writers, to which he aspired, to be reducing certain aspects of the world "everyone knows" to "a symbolic form which will simultaneously involve the reader's sense of life while giving expression to his, the writer's, own most deeply held values."[51]

However, Ellison believed that art did not have to make explicit, political statements in order to promote social or political progress. He particularly resisted the label of "protest novel" for *Invisible Man.* Even Random House, in their press release announcing the novel's imminent publication on April 14, 1952, emphasized that the novel "goes far beyond the confines of the 'race novel' to become a valid and powerful interpretation of the human condition, Negro and white."[52] Nevertheless, Ellison went on to explain that his novel, like all good novels, does protest in a more grandiloquent way:

> [T]he protest lies in my trying to make a story out of these elements without falling into the clichés which have marked and marred most fiction about American Negroes—that is, to write literature instead of political protest. Beyond this, I would say simply that in the very act of trying to create something, there is implicit a protest against the way things are, a protest against man's vulnerability before the larger forces of society and the universe.[53]

In short, Ellison believed the task of the novelist was "to present the human, to make it eloquent, and to provide some sense of transcendence over the given."[54] Thus, *Invisible Man,* read as Invisible Man's memoirs, presents itself as the protest not of a race but of an individual mind for the consideration of other individual minds.[55]

In many ways, Ellison's novel defends the truth of the Declaration of Independence—that all men are created equal. By having his narrator wrestle with staying below ground, far from the madding crowd that is America in all its contradictions, professing this but practicing that, Ellison seeks to show a human being who cannot help but live out his humanity even after he has sought and found an escape underground, away from human society: "In going underground, I whipped it all except the mind, the *mind*" (580). He cannot help but awake from his self-imposed hibernation because his mind, his human mind, will not let him sleep.[56] Ellison begins the central chapter of the novel with Invisible Man trying to read, "but my mind kept wandering back to my old problems" (261). His natural compulsion to think about his condition, and that of American society, marks him as a member of that worldwide community of reasoning beings to which the Declaration of Independence appeals. This restlessness of the mind would eventually give birth to his memoirs we now know as *Invisible Man*.

His thinking about life, both the good and the bad, leaves him unsatisfied with a solitary life of eating sloe gin poured over vanilla ice cream and listening to the bluesy jazz of Louis Armstrong. The five phonographs Invisible Man intends to acquire, so that he can "hear five recordings of Louis Armstrong playing and singing 'What Did I Do to Be so Black and Blue'—all at the same time" (8), may have been a crude way of hitting all of his senses, but a life of mere sensory existence would not suffice. No decent human being would be satisfied with this. The mind, signifying reason (*logos*) as well as the story-telling part of the human soul, would not rest in solitude—at least not for long. As Invisible Man notes in the final paragraph before the Epilogue: "So I would stay here until I was chased out. Here, at least, I could try to think things out in peace, or *if not in peace*, in quiet. I would take up residence underground" (571; emphasis added). His body may be at rest, but his mind leads him to activity, especially one that will lead him above ground to rejoin in some way the rest of society.

Furthermore, if his mind is not at rest, perhaps he can gamble on that of his listener, Ellison's reader. Invisible Man concludes as much near the end of the novel's epilogue: "Being invisible and without substance, a disembodied voice, as it were, what else could I do? What else but try to tell you what was really happening when your eyes were looking through" (581)? Ellison wrote that one of his difficulties was in getting readers to give members of a despised class a respectful hearing: "How does one . . . make the illiterate and inarticulate eloquent enough so that the educated and more favorably situated will recognize wisdom and honor and charity, heroism and capacity for love when found in humble speech and dress?"[57] It is no accident that as Invisible Man narrates his memoirs, he does not announce at the outset that he is black. The references to race come indirectly, dawning upon the reader as the narrator tells how others have reacted to his presence. By first engaging the minds of his readers, and not their physical eyes, Invisible Man (and, one infers, Ralph Ellison) attempts to make this connection to readers who might not otherwise listen to, or be persuaded by, an unemployed but library-bred and college-educated black youth.

American democracy affirms the public role of reason or the mind by making justice its end and not mere majoritarian interest or will. In short, republics respect and secure the rights of the individual but only do so precisely because said protection not only is the raison d'etre of government but also because it is good for all concerned. As Ellison observed, "democracy is, or should be, the most disinterested form of love."[58] If self-government did not promote justice and the common good, then it would simply be another form of rule by might. What Aristotle called "reason unaffected by desire or appetite"[59] or as the *Federalist Papers* puts it, "the cool and deliberate sense of the community,"[60] must therefore guide the political community.

Ellison placed great importance upon the mind of each individual. He even likened the narrator of *Invisible Man* to Dostoyevsky's in *Notes from Underground* by virtue of their respective intellects: "My narrator, like Dostoievsky's, is a thinker, and this is true despite the fact that my character doesn't think too clearly or too well. Nevertheless, my protagonist does possess a conscious philosophical dimension and is, since he lives by ideas, an intellectual."[61] If man is a political or rational animal,[62] the novel shows that this nature of humanity and therewith political society begs a different interpretation by the characters of the novel. For Jack and the Brotherhood Committee, the reason of the individual as expressed in political debate and compromise is replaced by the alleged scientific historicism of the Brotherhood leadership, which requires little input from the rank and file. This never sits well with Invisible Man, who is uncomfortable with the Brotherhood's lack of sociability when they are working. Whenever he gets picked up for a Brotherhood event, no one is talking in the car: "No one spoke. . . . It was as though we were mere chance passengers in a subway car" (299).[63] Real conversations, which are few and far between at the Brotherhood, involve personalities, individuality, differences of opinion, diversity, and sentimentality—in short, a respect for intellectual diversity that could lead to the agreement or unity in thinking that creates political communities. This camaraderie of the mind marks the classical understanding of the city, and makes a misnomer of "the Brotherhood." Not surprisingly, Jack asks only that Invisible Man "work hard and follow instructions" (308), a job description not far removed from that of a slave.

Instead of walking a picket line with a clapboard declaring, "I Am A Man," and waving an American flag, Ellison chose to write man-to-man, and wove an American flag in lyrical prose that gave all the colors—red, white, and especially blue—their due. As Invisible Man puts it at the close of his memoirs, "America is woven of many strands; I would recognize them and let it so remain. It's 'winner take nothing' that is the great truth of our country or of any country" (577). *Invisible Man* was a sign that never needed to be put down.[64] It was intended to be read and considered as long as minds were open to its message, which means as long as minds were open to reflecting on the meaning of America as played out in the lives of a diverse people united in principle but at times divided in practice.

Of course, Ellison wrote not only to expand the moral horizon of whites, but also to show blacks their freedom and opportunities even in the face of a discriminatory society. In a 1953 letter of thanks to the *Chicago Defender,* which chose Ellison for its annual honor roll, he wrote, "I addressed my book to Negroes and now, at last, through you my own people have answered."[65] Two years before *Invisible Man* was published, he thanked his good friend Albert Murray "for seeing to it that a few Negroes read my reviews; I get the feeling that most times the stuff is seen only by whites and that, I'm afraid, doesn't mean much in the long run."[66] Both whites and blacks needed liberation.

This is why Ellison insisted he was a charter member of the Civil Rights Movement despite not joining the struggle in the streets during the 1950s and 1960s: "I *have* served a certain apprenticeship in the streets and even touch events in the Freedom Movement in a modest way. . . . For, you see, my Negro friends recognize a certain division of labor among the members of the tribe. Their demands, like that of many whites, are that I publish more novels."[67] In keeping with the title of his landmark novel, Ellison believed his main, civic duty as an American writer was to help readers see each other better. Part of this responsibility, as expressed in the Epilogue to *Invisible Man,* meant affirming "the principle on which the country was built" (574): namely, that all men are created equal. Black Americans were duty-bound to preserve this principle "because we were the heirs who must use the principle because no other fitted our needs." Invisible Man adds, "Not for the power or for vindication, but because we, with the given circumstance of our origin, could only thus find transcendence."

Some critics have argued that *Invisible Man*'s narrator comes to this appreciation of America as a land of freedom and opportunity too easily, with nary a mention by the protagonist of the source of his devotion to the American regime.[68] If the story offers little explanation for Invisible Man's patriotism, then his American optimism or faith in democratic principles may only express Ralph Ellison's belief in the American dream; his story, critics charge, assumes it on the part of Invisible Man without showing its narrative source. In short, if the tale and not the teller is to be trusted, the novel—as Invisible Man's memoirs—remains unconvincing in its portrayal of Negro American transcendence over racial bigotry and the general exploitation of individual against individual.

One answer to this criticism has to do with Ellison's narrative strategy. One objective of his writing was to point out how black Americans, both individually and communally, found ways to exercise their liberty as people free by nature but constricted by racial discrimination. In the novel, Ellison shows a variety of ways his black characters, across the moral spectrum of virtue and vice, negotiate the "briar patch" of American life.[69] Among the most admirable characters in the novel is Mary Rambo. Although Mary appears in just a few scenes, she demonstrates her freedom and fortitude not only by supporting herself as a single woman in New York, but also by helping others navigate the vast freedom of that quintessential northern city.[70] After being released from the Liberty Paints factory hospital, Invisible Man stumbles out of the subway and collapses into Mary's arms, when she says: "You take it easy, I'll take care of you like I done a heap of others . . ." (252). As a Good Samaritan of Harlem, Mary Rambo provides for his physical well-being by feeding and housing him, even when his money runs out. To his consternation, she also encourages him with "her constant talk about leadership and responsibility" (258) and exhorts him with words Ralph Ellison attributed to his own mother: "It's you young folks what's going to make the changes . . . You got to lead and you got to fight and move us on all up a little higher" (255).[71]

Most especially, Mary demonstrates her freedom by maintaining her own individuality amidst the hullabaloo of the big city. As she warned Invisible Man: "Don't let this Harlem git you. I'm in New York, but New York ain't in me, understand what I mean? Don't git corrupted."[72] She is in New York, but not of it, and her memory of the past is a key to her maintaining her identity in the midst of urban anonymity.[73] "Up here," she intones, "too many forgits. They finds a place for theyselves and forgits the ones on the bottom" (255). She later tells him that even his "hard times" will prove to have "helped you a heap" (258).

Mary Rambo teaches Invisible Man how the freedom of New York (or America, generally) is really the freedom and initiative of the individuals who make of New York what they will.[74] As he eventually learns, moving to New York freed him in some ways but exposed him to the mischief—not just the mercy—of others. In short, the freedom of New York is merely the testing ground for whatever an individual brings with him or her. One might call it Ellison's fictionalized version of "a fair field of testing,"[75] wherein Negroes, along with the rest of the mass of humanity pouring into that city, could be expected to test their mettle. Apparently, the "land of the free" must become the "home of the brave" for individuals to make good on that freedom.

"New York!" as the vet from the Golden Day declares, "That's not a place, it's a dream" (152). He counseled Invisible Man to learn how to play its game: "Learn how it operates, learn how *you* operate" (153–54). The city symbolized the greater opportunities that would come not long after Ellison's novel was published. As Ellison later put it, "For Negroes the Supreme Court Decision of 1954 and the Civil Rights Act of 1964 induced no sudden transformation of character; it provided the stage upon which they could reveal themselves for what their experiences have made them, and for what they have made of their experiences."[76] Invisible Man certainly experienced no sudden transformation of character upon arriving in New York from the

South, but meeting folks like Mary Rambo ultimately helped him see how his past could inform his present and therewith help shape his future.

So much for the sunny side of the street. Turning to the president of the southern college for Negroes, one finds the cynical virtuosity of Dr. A. Hebert Bledsoe. Invisible Man observes that he wears the mask of a servile porter when dealing with the white trustees of the college,[77] but underneath is a political operator who has carved out his own fiefdom in the lion's mouth of a segregationist South:

> The white folk tell everybody what to think—except men like me. I tell *them;* that's my life, telling white folk how to think about the things I know about. . . . . It's a nasty deal and I don't always like it myself. But you listen to me: I didn't make it, and I know that I can't change it. But I've made my place in it and I'll have every Negro in the country hanging on tree limbs by morning if it means staying where I am. (143)[78]

His northern counterpart, a co–practitioner of self-centered freedom within a racist context, is Lucius Brockway, the wily, old paint formulator of the Liberty Paints factory. He has made himself the indispensable man of the company: "Without what I do they couldn't do nothing, they be making bricks without straw. . . . [C]aint a single doggone drop of paint move out of the factory lessen it comes through Lucius Brockway's hands. . . . Liberty Paints wouldn't be worth a plugged nickel if they didn't have me here to see that it got a good strong base" (214–15). Brockway continues:

> And that's another reason why the Old Man ain't goin' to let nobody come down here messing with me. *He* knows what a lot of them new fellers don't; *he* knows that the reason our paint is so good is because of the way Lucius Brockway puts the pressure on them oils and resins before they even leaves the tanks. . . . They thinks 'cause everything down here is done by machinery, that's all there is to it. They crazy! Ain't a continental thing that happens down here that ain't as iffen I done put my black hands into it! Them machines just do the cooking, these here hands right here do the sweeting. (218)

Like Bledsoe, Brockway has worked himself into a position of authority at an ostensibly white-controlled institution. As Brockway puts it, "[T]his here's the uproar department, and I'm in charge" (212).

As for the Invisible Man's freedom, the novel begins with his confession that he has been draining away electricity from the putative Monopolated Light & Power without paying for it. The fact that he has wired his ceiling to power 1,369 light bulbs as "an act of sabotage" demonstrates his ingenuity in the face of an institution that only appears to possess a monopoly on light and power. Not only does he "use their service and pay them nothing at all," he plies his invisibility to "live rent-free in a building rented strictly to whites, in a section of the basement that was shut off and forgotten during the nineteenth century." Invisible Man, treated as such by society, confesses to his audience that he gave up his "old way of life" because it was "based upon the fallacious assumption that I, like other men, was visible" (5, 6). Why act responsibly within an irresponsible society? American society wanted to have *his* cake and eat it, too, and this he could not abide. It represented a double standard in practice that gave the lie to the equality in principle upon which the nation declared its independence.

Admittedly, some of these examples of freedom betray an illicit compromise. Perhaps this was Ellison's way of getting white readers involved in the story: to wit, taking his characters seriously, and hence taking their situation seriously enough, to insist that justice be served—"He shouldn't steal electricity!"—while also rectifying (in the abstract if not immediately in practice) the unjust conditions (i.e., unequal protection of the laws and a moral perception that treats black Americans as aliens in their own land) that lead some blacks to take matters into their own "criminal" hands.

Of course, the chief expression of Invisible Man's freedom is the novel itself, an autobiographical tale that Ellison referred to as "a memoir written underground."[79] Whereas he initially allowed his voice to be exploited, most especially by Jack and the Brotherhood,[80] he eventually turned it to his own benefit—and society's[81]—by applying his invisibility as a writer.[82] Thwarted in his hopes to become an orator, a master of the spoken word, he literally finds his voice and his freedom in the written word. This medium first "disarmed" him in his attempt to "throw my anger in the world's face," and then prompted him to share his experience with whomever would listen to "a disembodied voice." He explains, "[B]ut now that I've tried to put it all down the old fascination with playing a role returns, and I'm drawn upward again" (579–81). Ellison explained, "The hero comes up from underground because the act of writing and thinking necessitated it. He could not stay down there."[83] Ellison described this "final act" of Invisible Man as "a voice issuing its little wisdom out of the substance of its own inwardness—after having undergone a transformation from ranter to writer."[84]

This was no easy journey. As the novel testifies, Invisible Man matures even as he tells his story. He learns by his own candid recounting of the events that forced him to face his own invisibility—events he believed, right up to the Epilogue, proved his incompatibility with an American society hamstrung by self-centeredness compounded by racial prejudice. After "first being 'for' society and then 'against' it," Invisible Man now assigns himself "no rank or any limit"; his world became "one of infinite possibilities" (576). But this is only a preliminary conclusion. Like the Prologue to the memoir that constitutes the novel, this statement in the first part of the Epilogue is only a first stab at resolving his conflicts with the free society above ground. As he says at the outset of the Epilogue, "So there you have all of it that's important. Or at least you *almost* have it" (572).[85]

The shift comes near the close of the Epilogue, when he declares, "Till now, however, this is as far as I've ever gotten, for all life seen from the hole of invisibility is absurd" (579). He goes on to explain why he decided to write, "torturing myself to put it down": "Because in spite of myself I've learned some things." By this account, Invisible Man (and Ellison) trusted that some individuals might decide to take a chance on their own self-recollection, their own honest accounting of what their experiences have made of them and hence what they might yet make of their experiences.

Put simply, the novel is about freedom, which Ellison depicts in a counter-intuitive way. Instead of showing freedom as the untrammeled exercise of human will, he offers episode upon episode where the narrator encounters Negro Americans who deal with racial discrimination on their own terms. Ellison seems to overwhelm the reader with the lack of control, choice, or responsibility of black characters in the ostensibly white world that is America, only to show the careful reader how in the midst of overwhelming environmental pressures—sociologists, take note!—the Negro American can still exercise freedom.[86]

The famous Battle Royal episode serves as a case in point. Ellison takes care to describe the narrator's responses to external commands in a way that indicates his choice or freedom in the matter. The narrator recalls how he and the other nine black boys were herded into the ring for the boxing free-for-all: "All ten of us climbed under the ropes and *allowed ourselves* to be blindfolded with broad bands of white cloth" (21; emphasis added). He adds that as he "felt the cloth pressed into place," he "frowned so that it would be loosened" when he relaxed. His quick thinking shows an attempt to see despite the blindfold. Moreover, the narrator, who was invited to the smoker to give a speech but told to get in the ring with the neighborhood toughs, remembers "going over my speech" while the blindfolds were put on: "In my mind each word was as bright as flame." Constrained but not entirely restricted by the boxing ring and influential white audience, in the midst of his anxious preparation for physical battle, Invisible Man's mind was at work, free and active. Alas, it would not be the last time others would blindfold him as he sought to exercise his freedom.

The Battle Royal scene also offers a civic example of black freedom and perspicacity. Invisible Man's ode to accommodation, delivered to the raucous assembly seemingly "deaf with cotton in dirty ears," unwittingly reflects an experience with freedom that Invisible Man found in the segregated South. When he mistakenly says "social equality" instead of "social responsibility," a marker of accommodation, the narrator recalls it as a phrase he "had often seen denounced in newspaper editorials," but "heard debated in private" (30, 31). Here the reader learns that Negro Americans did not accept a definition of their humanity that contradicted their own perception of reality—even if it were printed in the newspaper. "We have been disciplined," Ellison remarked elsewhere, "to accept our *own* sense of life regardless of what those antagonistic to us thought about us."[87] Freedom of speech may have been restricted for black southerners, but this did not stop them from articulating a rebuttal among themselves—away from the overtly public sphere, to be sure, but at least in affirmation of what was true to their own experience.[88]

The vet from the Golden Day, whom Invisible Man meets again as they take a bus North, also affirms the freedom of Negro Americans in the face of racial discrimination. Speaking of the "game" of life, the vet exclaims that "that game has been analyzed, put down in books. But down here they've forgotten to take care of the books and that's your opportunity." The vet highlights a significant blind spot of white Southerners regarding the Negro intellect: "They wouldn't see you because they don't expect you to know anything, since they believe they've taken care of that. . . ."[89] He believes that by reading books—most of which, presumably, were written by whites—Invisible Man could learn how the world operates and "learn how *you* operate" (153–54). Invisible Man takes this lesson to heart. After settling into New York, but unable to find work after distributing what he thought were letters of recommendation from Dr. Bledsoe to New York supporters of his college for Negroes, Invisible Man spends his time, "when not looking for work, in my room, where I read countless books from the library" (258). At the dedication of an Oklahoma City branch library named in his honor, Ellison closed his remarks by calling the library "the nexus of dreams" and "the place where we are able to free ourselves from the limitations of today, by becoming acquainted with what went on in the past and thus we project ourselves into the future."[90]

As a budding writer who frequented the New York Public Library, Ellison wrote "out of other books" and, thus, drew from many sources irrespective of the color line: "Books which seldom, if ever, mentioned Negroes were to release me from whatever 'segregated' idea I might have had of my human possibilities."[91] Of course, one of the glories of *Invisible Man* is its demonstration "that Negro American folk tradition constitutes a valuable source for literature." Nevertheless, Ellison adds:

> My point is that the Negro American writer is also an heir of the human experience which is literature, and this might well be more important to him than his living folk tradition. For me, at least, in the discontinuous, swiftly changing and diverse American culture, the stability of the Negro American folk tradition became precious as a result of an act of literary discovery. . . . [B]ut for the novelist of any cultural or racial identity, his form is his greatest freedom, and his insights are where he finds them.[92]

In like manner, after being falsely accused of self-promotion by jealous members of the Brotherhood and offered the alternative of lecturing on "the

Woman Question," the Invisible Man reflects on his own decision to keep an open mind about sources of enlightenment:

> No, despite my anger and disgust, my ambitions were too great to surrender so easily. And why should I restrict myself, segregate myself? I was a *spokesman*—why shouldn't I speak about women, or any other subject? Nothing lay outside the scheme of our ideology, there was a policy on everything, and my main concern was to work my way ahead in the movement. (407)

When "all the secrets of power and authority still shrouded from me in mystery appeared on the way toward revelation," Invisible Man confesses he did not want to foreclose any avenue to fulfill his ambition. Along these lines, Ellison observed of Richard Wright that he was "as much a product of his reading as of his painful experiences." Ellison repeatedly cited Wright's example as a writer who saw no idea or thinker off limits to him: "And during the days when I knew him well he certainly didn't allow racial considerations to limit the free play of his intellect."[93] Ellison even identified with James Baldwin as "not the product of a Negro storefront church but of the library, and the same is true of me."[94] Ellison said that his own reading beyond the racial canon of his day was "a very liberating discovery," for even as a child, "nobody got in the way of me being the hero!"[95]

To be sure, Ellison never claimed that freeing oneself would be easy. This is why he made so much of the Negro's exhibition of "grace under pressure" throughout American history.[96] This grace turned out to be an historical, providential pun as southern Negroes discovered that the key to greater freedom was with them all along in the form of the black Protestant church. Martin Luther King, Jr., noted Ellison, tapped into this quintessential Negro institution for support and empowerment:

> Negro religion has been a counterbalance to much of the inequality and imposed chaos which has been the Negro American experience. When Martin Luther King, Jr., emerged as an important American figure, it was an instance of the church making itself visible in the political and social life and fulfilling its role in the realm of morality.[97]

The strategy of nonviolent protest and passive resistance was a new groove through which Southern Negroes channeled their history-long struggle for social, civil, and political freedom. Here, Ellison found it strange that white Americans, the vast majority of whom were churchgoers, could mistake the humility of the Negro for weakness or servility. How could they miss the humble strength and authoritative meekness of their professed Lord and Savior Jesus Christ as embodied in the Negroes who served them so consistently and intimately?[98]

One of the last essays Ellison wrote was entitled "On Being the Target of Discrimination."[99] He was careful not to use the word "victim," for it implied a lack of freedom—a lack of options from which the aggrieved might choose to deal with an incivility or injustice. One may not be able to avoid being the "target" of discrimination, but in the world Ellison grew up in—the world of segregated Oklahoma and Alabama, not to mention the discrimination he experienced in New York—one could choose how to respond as well as how to contribute to the greater society. As he put it:

> If we can resist for a moment the temptation to view everything having to do with Negro Americans in terms of their racially imposed status, we become aware of the fact that for all the harsh reality of the social and economic injustices visited upon them, these injustices have failed to keep Negroes clear of the cultural mainstream; Negro Americans are, in fact, one of its major tributaries.[100]

Ellison understood the cultural pluralism of America to be "an important source of Negro American optimism—just as that optimism was a support of the general faith in the workability of the American system."[101] Similar to the aim of the Montgomery Improvement Association,[102] he sought the improvement not only of the Negro condition but also that of White America: as he put it, "we are aware that each of our victories increases the area of freedom for all Americans, regardless of color."[103]

Ellison also believed that while black Americans were certainly the targets of racism, they possessed a "freedom to broaden our personal culture by absorbing the cultures of others."[104] He spoke from his own experience as a boy growing up in segregated Oklahoma, but guided by the supervisor of music for Oklahoma City's Negro schools. Reflecting on Zelia N. Breaux's "gift," what Ellison called an "important bit of equipment for living," he concluded, "Even more important was the fact that we were being taught to discover and exercise those elements of freedom which existed unobserved (at least by outsiders), within our state of social and political unfreedom."

For example, Ellison noted that when segregation replaced slavery in the South, the races may have looked like they were separated, but their public distance belied the private intimacy that was required if the inferiority of blacks vis-à-vis whites was to be maintained. He loved to point out the impossibility of whites keeping blacks out of their affairs by the simple fact that if a segregated society wanted clean clothes, their Negro employees had to look at their dirty laundry! He observed, "[E]verywhere you look, even in the deepest, most rabid part of the South, the Negroes are not separate but right in the bedrooms, in the kitchens."[105] Moreover, what Negro Americans have observed and experienced constitutes what Invisible Man calls "a whole unrecorded history" that is spoken in "the gin mills and the barber shops and the juke joints and the churches" (471).

Reflecting on the relevance of *Invisible Man* in a changing, increasingly free America, Ellison observed: "[S]o much which we've gleaned through the harsh discipline of Negro American life is simply too precious to be lost. I speak of the faith, the patience, the humor, the sense of timing, the rugged sense of life and the manner of expressing it which all go to define the American Negro." Ellison worried that a lack of awareness of what Negroes have to offer—even those raised under segregation—and what they have experienced and hence learned by that experience, would hinder them from capitalizing on the freedoms newly protected by the 1964 Civil Rights Act and 1965 Voting Rights Act. "I see a period," Ellison confessed, "when Negroes are going to be wandering around because, you see, we have had this thing thrown at us for so long that we haven't had a chance to discover what in our background is really worth preserving."[106]

The discrimination that targeted them as victims certainly limited the scope of their freedom as human beings and as citizens; however, it did not drive their freedom, initiative, creativity, ingenuity, and improvisation to extinction. Ellison's 1989 essay, "On Being the Target of Discrimination," illustrates his belief that being the "target" of discrimination was just the beginning of the Negro American's response to his environment.[107] For Ellison, the modern-day use of the word "victim" to describe the Negro American gave away the game. As he put it, "[S]ometimes you can get so *uptight* about your *dis*advantages that you ignore your advantages."[108] The history of jazz, just to mention one American cultural institution, belies any notion of black victimization that suggests their incapacity to create and excel even in the face of social and political discrimination.

Ellison observed early on in his public career that *Invisible Man* is not simply a series of reverses imposed upon the protagonist from without. Invisible Man had a responsibility in every episode, a choice to make when faced with an individual that did not have his best interest in mind. After all, Ellison stated that the problem with Richard Wright's *Native Son* was that it was all environment and no individual responsibility. Despite "having the confidence of his talent," Wright produced fiction that does not account for his *own* liberation from a quite dismal environment.[109] Bigger Thomas and black Americans, in general, were simply rats in the racist maze of America. Or, as Ellison put it famously, "Wright could imagine Bigger, but Bigger could not possibly imagine Richard Wright."[110] *Invisible Man,* on the other hand, accounts for the individual *and* the environment. Thus, for Ellison, the briar patch of American segregation had all the makings of drama.[111] As noted earlier in the discussion of the Battle Royal scene, even the novel's most famous episode is written to preserve Invisible Man's partial responsibility for his fate at the white smoker.

Thus, the legacy of slavery accounts for only part of the social conditions within which black Americans try to be all they can be in a post–Civil Rights

Movement era. The clear "costs" of being black in America must be considered in light of what Ellison viewed as the underappreciated "benefits" of a hard-fought and expensively bought legacy of Negro-American discipline, improvisation, and transcendence.[112] He explained:

> I started with the primary assumption that men with black skins, having retained their humanity before all of the conscious efforts made to dehumanize them, especially following the Reconstruction, are unquestionably human. Thus they have the obligation of freeing themselves . . . by depending upon the validity of their own experience for an accurate picture of the reality which they seek to change, and for a gauge of the values they would see made manifest.[113]

What Ellison calls "the obligation of freeing themselves" bears a striking resemblance to the struggle the American founders underwent as they declared and fought for independence from England,[114] giving additional evidence for the patriotism informing Ellison's critique of his country.

At bottom, *Invisible Man* is a book for citizens, especially American citizens, those who live in "the land of the free and the home of the brave." Would the free see Ellison's fictional raft as a sure vessel to brave the turbulent waters of American racial tension? "The real questions," as Ellison posed them so famously to Irving Howe, "seemed to be: How does the Negro writer participate *as a writer* in the struggle for human freedom? To whom does he address his work? What values emerging from Negro experience does he try to affirm?"[115] The good news is, *Invisible Man* is still in print a half century later, still being read, and therefore still suggesting ways to improve the "moral perception" of the nation and the world, one reader at a time.[116]

ENDNOTES

1. Ralph Ellison, *Juneteenth: A Novel,* ed. John F. Callahan (New York: Random House, 1999), 356.

2. "And if we stop living to give ourselves over to complaint the best we can expect is more frustration." "Letter to Charles Davidson" (July 10, 1971), *Living with Music: Ralph Ellison's Jazz Writings,* ed. Robert G. O'Meally (New York: The Modern Library, 2001), 252.

3. Ellison argued that "you prepare yourself for desegregation and the opportunities to be released thereby *before* this freedom actually exists." "If the Twain Shall Meet" (November 8, 1964), *The Collected Essays of Ralph Ellison,* ed. John F. Callahan (New York: Modern Library, 1995), 575. Hereinafter cited as *Collected Essays;* emphases in original unless otherwise noted. Also, "For Negroes the Supreme Court Decision of 1954 and the Civil Rights Act of

1964 induced no sudden transformation of character; it provided the stage upon which they could reveal themselves for what their experiences have made them, and for what they have made of their experiences" (575). Last, "Civil rights are only the beginning." "Letter to Albert Murray" (September 28, 1958), *Trading Twelves: The Selected Letters of Ralph Ellison and Albert Murray,* ed. Albert Murray and John F. Callahan (New York: The Modern Library, 1999), 196.

4. "The protest is there not because I was helpless before my racial condition, but because I *put* it there." Ralph Ellison, "The World and the Jug," Part II (February 3, 1964), *Collected Essays,* 183. See also Ralph Ellison, "My Life and Yours" (n.d.), corrected, typed transcript ("excerpts") of University of Chicago lecture, Box 174, Ralph Ellison Papers, Library of Congress, 21: "I believe in the blackness of my skin just as I believed in the whiteness of some of my people's skin, but it didn't help when I was alone trying to write."

5. Invisible Man marvels at Dupre and Scofield as they, paradoxically enough, "organize" the riot: "They've done it, I thought. They organized it and carried it through alone; the decision their own and their own action. Capable of their own action." Ralph Ellison, *Invisible Man* (New York: Random House, 1952; reprint, New York: Vintage Books, 1995), 548. All subsequent citations will be noted parenthetically in the text by page number, and emphases in original unless otherwise noted.

   Dupre's leadership exemplifies an alternative community of thought and action to that of the socialistic Brotherhood: "First we gets a flashlight for everybody. . . . And let's have some organization, y'all. Don't everybody be running over everybody else. Come on" (542)! Dupre uses the flashlights later to clear his tenement building of its occupants before he sets it ablaze. This admittedly riotous course of action includes acts of responsibility, as when Dupre announces, "I wants all the women and chillun and the old and the sick folks brought out" (546). This orderly liberation of his tenement building also contrasts with the eviction of the elderly couple, which first introduced Invisible Man to Jack and the (faux) Brotherhood.

6. Ralph Ellison, " 'A Completion of Personality' " (1982), *Collected Essays,* 816–17.

7. Malcolm X, "The Ballot or the Bullet" (April 3, 1964), in *Malcolm X Speaks: Selected Speeches and Statements,* ed. George Breitman (New York: Grove Weidenfeld, 1965), 23–44. For example, after criticizing the American political system for parties that fail to live up to their campaign promises and southern states that do not allow blacks to vote, Malcolm X concludes: "That's why, in 1964, it's time now for you and me to become more politically mature and realize what the ballot is for; what we're supposed to get when we cast a ballot; and that if we don't cast a ballot, it's going to end up in a situation where we're going to have to cast a bullet. It's either a ballot or a bullet" (30).

8. Abraham Lincoln, "Message to Congress in Special Session" (July 4, 1861), *Collected Works of Abraham Lincoln,* ed. Roy P. Basler, 9 vols. (New Brunswick: Rutgers University Press, 1955), 4:439.

9. Ralph Ellison, "A Special Message to Subscribers" (1979), *Collected Essays,* 351.

10. Cited in Robert Penn Warren, *Who Speaks for the Negro?* (New York: Random House, 1965), 327.

11. Martin Luther King, Jr., "I See the Promised Land" (1968), *I Have A Dream: Writings and Speeches that Changed the World,* ed. James M. Washington (San Francisco: HarperSanFrancisco, 1992), 197. Ellison said as much: "Thus we are determined to bring America's conduct into line with its professed ideals." Warren, *Who Speaks for the Negro?* 339.

12. Ralph Ellison, "Introduction to the Thirtieth-Anniversary Edition of *Invisible Man*" (November 10, 1981), *Collected Essays,* 482. Similarly, in "The Little Man at Chehaw Station: The American Artist and His Audience" (1977/1978), Ellison wrote: "To the extent that American literature is both an art of discovery and an artistic agency for creating a consciousness of cultural identity, it is of such crucial importance as to demand of the artist not only an eclectic resourcefulness of skill, but an act of democratic faith." *Collected Essays,* 494.

13. "The Constitution is a script by which we seek to act out the drama of democracy, and the stage upon which we enact our roles." Ralph Ellison, "Perspective of Literature" (1976), *Collected Essays,* 773.

14. Ralph Ellison, "Introduction to *Shadow and Act*" (May 1964), *Collected Essays,* 54. Recalling his early friendship with Richard Wright, Ellison remarked that Wright's literary expertise "gave me something of that sense of self-discovery and exaltation which is implicit in the Negro church and in good jazz." Ralph Ellison, "Remembering Richard Wright," *Collected Essays,* 672.

15. Ralph Ellison, " 'A Completion of Personality' " (1974), *Collected Essays,* 799.

16. For example, see Ernest Kaiser, "A Critical Look at Ellison's Fiction and at Social and Literary Criticism by and about the Author," 20 *Black World* 2 (December 1970), 53–59, 81–97; Lloyd L. Brown, "The Deep Pit," in *Twentieth Century Interpretations of* Invisible Man*: A Collection of Critical Essays,* ed. John M. Reilly (Englewood Cliffs, N.J.: Prentice-Hall, Inc., 1970), 97–99, orig. publ. in *Masses and Mainstream,* V (June 1952), 62–64; and Addison Gayle, Jr., "Cultural Strangulation: Black Literature and the White Aesthetic," in *Within the Circle: An Anthology of African American Literary Criticism from the Harlem Renaissance to the Present,* ed. Angelyn Mitchell (Durham: Duke University Press, 1994), 207–12, orig. publ. in Addison Gayle, ed., *The Black Aesthetic* (New York: Doubleday, 1971).

17. Ralph Ellison, "Homage to Duke Ellington on His Birthday" (April 27, 1969), *Collected Essays,* 678. For a good introduction to Ellison's understanding of the cultural heroism of black musicians in the early twentieth century, see Horace A. Porter, *Jazz Country: Ralph Ellison in America* (Iowa City: University of Iowa

Press, 2001), "Jazz States" (Introduction) and chaps. 1–2. See also Berndt Ostendorf, "Anthropology, Modernism, and Jazz," in *Ralph Ellison: Modern Critical Views*, ed. and intro. Harold Bloom (New York: Chelsea House Publishers, 1986), 145–72.

18. Ralph Ellison, "Indivisible Man" (December 1970), *Collected Essays*, 394.

19. Ralph Ellison, "'A Very Stern Discipline'" (March 1967), *Collected Essays*, 750.

20. "Study and Experience: An Interview with Ralph Ellison," *Conversations with Ralph Ellison*, ed. Maryemma Graham and Amritjit Singh (Jackson: University Press of Mississippi, 1995), 327 and 328.

21. Ralph Ellison, "'My Strength Comes from Louis Armstrong': Interview with Robert G. O'Meally, 1976" (May 1976), *Living With Music*, 275.

22. Ralph Ellison, "The Charlie Christian Story" (May 17, 1958), *Collected Essays*, 267. Earlier in the essay he noted, "Jazz, like the country which gave it birth, is fecund in its inventiveness, swift and traumatic in its developments and terribly wasteful of its resources" (266).

23. Ralph Ellison, "Study and Experience: An Interview with Ralph Ellison," ed. Graham and Singh, 336.

24. Ralph Ellison, "What These Children Are Like" (September 1963), *Collected Essays*, 550.

25. Ralph Ellison, "'Tell It Like It Is, Baby'" (June 1965), *Collected Essays*, 30.

26. Ralph Ellison, "'A Very Stern Discipline'" (March 1967), *Collected Essays*, 754.

27. "Let me say right now that my book is not an autobiographical work." Ralph Ellison, "The Art of Fiction: *An Interview*" (Spring 1955), *Collected Essays*, 210.

28. Ralph Ellison, "Letter to Robert O'Meally" (April 17, 1989), "'American Culture is of a Whole': From the Letters of Ralph Ellison," *New Republic*, intro. John F. Callahan (March 1, 1999), 47.

29. In the formative period of Ellison's writing career, his friendship with Richard Wright served him well as he made the transition from musician to writer. In fact, Ellison found in Wright much that reminded him of his musical heroes: "He had the kind of confidence jazzmen have. . . . He was well aware of the forces ranked against him, but in his quiet way he was as arrogant in facing up to them as was Louis Armstrong in a fine blaring way." "Remembering Richard Wright" (July 18, 1971), *Collected Essays*, 667 and 668.

30. Ralph Ellison, "The World and the Jug," Part II (February 3, 1964), *Collected Essays*, 184.

31. Elsewhere Ellison noted, "I know of no valid demonstration that culture is transmitted through the genes." "Some Questions and Some Answers" (May 1958), *Collected Essays*, 291. See also "The Little Man at Chehaw Station" (1977/1978), *Collected Essays:* "Well, if you ask me, artistic talent might have

something to do with race, but you do *not* inherit culture and artistic skill through your genes" (514).

32. Ralph Ellison, "Study and Experience: An Interview with Ralph Ellison," ed. Graham and Singh, 339.

33. Ralph Ellison, "Blues People" (February 6, 1964), *Collected Essays,* 287.

34. Ralph Ellison, "Letter to Albert Murray" (June 2, 1957), *Trading Twelves,* 166.

35. Ralph Ellison, "Some Questions and Some Answers" (May 1958), *Collected Essays,* 291.

36. Ralph Ellison, "What America Would Be Like Without Blacks" (April 6, 1970), *Collected Essays,* 582. He added that "whatever else the true American is, he is also somehow black" (583).

37. Ralph Ellison, "Indivisible Man" (December 1970), *Collected Essays,* 373.

38. "Ralph Ellison's Territorial Advantage" (1976), *Living With Music,* 25. See also Ralph Ellison's "Haverford Statement" (May 30–31, 1969), *Collected Essays,* 430, and "The Little Man at Chehaw Station" (Winter 1977/1978), *Collected Essays,* 507–12.

39. Ralph Ellison, "Perspective of Literature" (April 27–30, 1976), *Collected Essays,* 778.

40. Langston Hughes, "The Negro and the Racial Mountain," *Nation* (June 23, 1926), in *Crossing the Danger Water: Three Hundred Years of African-American Writing,* ed. Deirdre Mullane (New York: Anchor Books, 1993), 504–507.

41. My thanks to Monea Tamara Hendricks, a student in my Black American Politics course (Winter 2002), for pointing out that "Tod" in German means "dead" or "death." So, when Invisible Man muses to himself, "Tod Clifton's *Tod*" (460), Ellison pays tribute to the sophistication of his narrator—and Ellison's own mischievous sense of humor.

42. "It is for us the living, rather, to be dedicated here to the unfinished work which they who fought here have thus far so nobly advanced. It is rather for us to be here dedicated to the great task remaining before us—that from these honored dead we take increased devotion to that cause for which they gave the last full measure of devotion—that we here highly resolve that these dead shall not have died in vain—that this nation, under God, shall have a new birth of freedom—and that government of the people, by the people, for the people, shall not perish from the earth." Abraham Lincoln, "Address Delivered at the Dedication of the Cemetery at Gettysburg—Final Text" (November 19, 1863), *Collected Works of Abraham Lincoln,* ed. Roy P. Basler, 7:23.

43. Ralph Ellison, "What America Would Be Like Without Blacks" (April 6, 1970), *Collected Essays,* 582: "[T]he true subject of democracy is not simply material well-being, but the extension of the democratic process in the direction of perfecting itself. The most obvious test and clue to that perfection is the inclusion, *not* assimilation, of the black man."

44. "Out of the fire and into the melting pot" (152) is how the vet from the Golden Day describes the Negro's initial experience of freedom in New York.

45. Julia Eichelberger draws the same conclusion in her examination of Invisible Man's "hibernation": "Through his withdrawal, Ellison's protagonist learns that he can and must recognize others, that he must 'speak for' (581) the individual and against the belief that 'individuals . . . don't count' (291)." *Prophets of Recognition: Ideology and the Individual in Novels by Ralph Ellison, Toni Morrison, Saul Bellow, and Eudora Welty* (Baton Range: Louisiana State University, 1999), 57.

46. Ralph Ellison, "Introduction to the Thirtieth-Anniversary Edition of *Invisible Man*" (November 10, 1981), *Collected Essays*, 482. Ellison wrote that "the very process of the imagination as it goes about bringing together a multiplicity of scenes, images, characters, and emotions and reducing them to significance is nothing if not integrative." "Haverford Statement" (May 30–31, 1969), *Collected Essays*, 430.

47. Alan Nadel, "Ralph Ellison and the American Canon," 13 *American Literary History* 2 (2001), 394.

48. Ralph Ellison, "'A Very Stern Discipline'" (March 1967), *Collected Essays*, 736 (emphasis added). The preceding sentence reads: "Here revelation is called for, not argument."

49. Ralph Ellison, "Roscoe Dunjee and the American Language" (14 May 1972), *Collected Essays*, 460.

50. Ralph Ellison, "Brave Words for a Startling Occasion" (January 27, 1953), *Collected Essays*, 152–53.

51. Ralph Ellison, "On Initiation Rites and Power: A Lecture at West Point" (March 26, 1969), *Collected Essays*, 532.

52. Random House press release (March 25, 1952), Box 154, Ralph Ellison Papers, Library of Congress.

53. Ralph Ellison, "On Initiation Rites and Power" (March 26, 1969), *Collected Essays*, 540. See also "The World and the Jug," Part II (February 3, 1964), *Collected Essays:* "The protest is there not because I was helpless before my racial condition, but because I *put* it there" (183).

54. Ralph Ellison, "On Initiation Rites and Power" (March 26, 1969), *Collected Essays*, 541.

55. In a note he jotted to himself as he wrote *Juneteenth*, Ellison recorded that his second novel should place the mind even more at the heart of the narrative: "The mind becomes the real scene of the action" (352).

56. "I couldn't be still even in hibernation. Because, damn it, there's the mind, the *mind*. It wouldn't let me rest. Gin, jazz, and dream were not enough. Books were not enough." (573).

57. Ralph Ellison, "Society, Morality and the Novel" (1957), *Collected Essays*, 724. For an interpretation of the novel that sees Invisible Man's tale, especially as

framed by the Prologue and Epilogue, as the product of his above-ground expe-
riences and subsequent restless hibernation, see Robert B. Stepto, "Literacy and
Hibernation: Ralph Ellison's *Invisible Man,*" in *From Behind the Veil: A Study of
Afro-American Narrative* (Urbana: University of Illinois Press, 1979), 163–94.

58. Ralph Ellison, "Letter to Albert Murray" (August 17, 1957), *Trading Twelves,* 175.

59. Aristotle, *Politics,* trans. Carnes Lord (Chicago: University of Chicago Press,
1984), Bk. 3, chap. 16, p. 114 (my translation).

60. James Madison, *The Federalist,* Jacob E. Cooke, ed. (Middletown, Conn.: Wesleyan University Press, 1961), no. 63, 425.

61. Ralph Ellison, "Letter to Stanley Edgar Hyman" (May 29, 1970), " 'American
Culture is of a Whole': From the Letters of Ralph Ellison," *New Republic,* intro.
John F. Callahan (March 1, 1999), 41–42.

62. See Aristotle, *Politics,* trans. Carnes Lord, Bk. 1, chap. 2, p. 37: "[M]an is by
nature a political animal."

63. See also *Invisible Man,* 333 ("As before, no one spoke a word") and 356 ("Then,
as he got the car under way, he became silent, and I decided not to ask any
questions. That was one thing I had learned thoroughly"). When he is grilled by
the Brotherhood for accepting a high-profile magazine interview, Invisible Man
exclaims, "What's happened to everybody? You act as though none of you has
any contact with me at all" (405).

64. For Ellison as a writer who "created his own picket line of the mind," see
Porter, *Jazz Country,* 136.

65. "Somehow, despite all of the fine reviews and other acts of recognition, it was
seeing my name among those honored by the *Chicago Defender* that gave me a
real sense of accomplishment." "Letter to John H. Sengstacke" (January 15,
1953), Box 213, Ralph Ellison Papers, Library of Congress. A leading black
newspaper during the modern Civil Rights era, the *Chicago Defender* described
its honor roll as paying "tribute to the individuals and organizations, who in its
opinion have extended the area of democracy in the United States and throughout the world," as well as "those who have served beyond the call of duty and
who have contributed materially to the advancement of better race relations
everywhere." See award program entitled "49th Year of Progress: 1953 Seventh
Annual Robert S. Abbott Memorial Award Presentation" (May 16, 1953), Box
213, Ralph Ellison Papers, Library of Congress.

66. Ralph Ellison, "Letter to Albert Murray" (January 24, 1950), *Trading Twelves,* 7.

67. Ralph Ellison, "The World and the Jug," Part II (February 3, 1964), *Collected
Essays,* 187–88. He confessed, "I assure you that no Negroes are beating down
my door, putting pressure on me to join the Negro Freedom Movement, for
the simple reason that they realize that I am enlisted for the duration." He also
remarked, "I am known as a bastard by certain of my militant friends because
I am not what they call a part of the Movement. That is, they figure I don't cuss
out white folks enough. All right, I cuss them out in my own ways." Ralph

Ellison, William Styron, Robert Penn Warren, and C. Vann Woodward, "The Uses of History in Fiction," 1 *The Southern Literary Journal* 2 (Spring 1969), 74. Robert Bone conveyed this well when he observed: "The Negro writer, who is surely not free of social responsibility, must yet discharge it *in his own fashion,* which is not the way of politics but art; . . . Without repudiating his sense of obligation to the group, Ellison has tried to express it through services which only the imagination can perform" (emphasis in original). See "Ralph Ellison and the Uses of Imagination," in *Ralph Ellison: A Collection of Critical Essays,* ed. John Hersey (Englewood Cliffs, N.J.: Prentice-Hall, Inc., 1974), 110.

For a discussion of *Invisible Man* as "a novel of the civil rights years" but which summed up "every ideology roiling the turbulent waters of black life," see Morris Dickstein, "Ralph Ellison, Race, and American Culture," 18 *Raritan* 4 (Spring 1999), 30–50. See also Cushing Strout, " 'An American Negro Idiom': *Invisible Man* and the Politics of Culture," in *Approaches to Teaching* Invisible Man, ed. Susan Resneck Parr and Pancho Savery (New York: The Modern Language Association of America, 1989), 79–85. For a summary Ellison provided of his early political activism, see "Introduction to the Thirtieth-Anniversary Edition of *Invisible Man*" (November 10, 1981), *Collected Essays,* 479–80.

68. For example, see Irving Howe, "Black Boys and Native Sons," in *A World More Attractive: A View of Modern Literature and Politics* (New York: Horizon Press, 1970; orig. publ. 1963), 98–122, esp. 114–15; Edward Margolies, *Native Sons: A Critical Study of Twentieth-Century Black American Authors* (Philadelphia: J.B. Lippincott Company, 1968), 148; Addison Gayle, *The Way of the New World: The Black Novel in America* (New York: Doubleday, 1976); Donald B. Gibson, *The Politics of Literary Expression: A Study of Major Black Writers* (Westport, Conn.: Greenwood Press, 1981); Timothy Brennan, "Ellison and Ellison: The Solipsism of *Invisible Man*," *CLA Journal* 25 (December 1981), 162–81; Barbara Foley, "The Rhetoric of Anticommunism in *Invisible Man*," 59 *College English* 5 (September 1997), 530–47; Houston A. Baker, Jr., "Failed Prophet and Falling Stock: Why Ralph Ellison was Never Avant-Garde," 7 *Stanford Humanities Review* 1 (1999), 4–11. See also Larry Neal, "Ellison's Zoot Suit," in *Ralph Ellison,* ed. John Hersey, 58–79, esp. 61–64, which recounts several of Ellison's more strident critics "both in the white left and the Black left" (61); Kerry McSweeney, *Invisible Man: Race and Identity* (Boston: Twayne Publishers, 1988), 116–25; and Thomas Hill Schaub, *American Fiction in the Cold War* (Madison: The University of Wisconsin Press, 1991), chap. 5, "From Ranter to Writer: Ellison's *Invisible Man* and the New Liberalism," 91–115.

69. Ellison explains literature's "social function" within the nexus between American political principle and practice in "Perspective of Literature" (April 27–30, 1976), *Collected Essays,* 766–81.

70. Ellison omitted a chapter, entitled "Out of the Hospital and Under the Bar," that further developed the character of Mary Rambo. In a note to the published version of the chapter, which appeared in 1963, Ellison writes that "it was Mary, a woman of the folk who helped release the hero from the machine" at the Liberty

Paints factory hospital. He invited readers to "imagine what this country would be without its Marys." See Ralph Ellison, "Out of the Hospital and Under the Bar," in *Soon, One Morning: New Writing by American Negroes, 1940–1962,* ed. Herbert Hill (New York: Alfred A. Knopf, 1963), 243 and 244.

71. Ralph Ellison, "That Same Pain, That Same Pleasure: An Interview" (Winter 1961), *Collected Essays,* 75. Speaking of his "sense of mission" and responsibility, Ellison recalls "my mother's insistence, from the time I was a small boy, that the hope of our group depended not upon the older Negroes but upon the young—upon me, as it were. . . ." Ellison dedicated *Invisible Man* to his mother, Ida, who died in 1937. Cf. Lawrence Jackson, *Ralph Ellison: Emergence of Genius* (New York: John Wiley & Sons, 2002), 413, who argues that Ellison dedicated the novel to Ida Guggenheimer, a long-time benefactor. The uncertainty owes to the dedication's brief, ambiguous wording, "To Ida," which may simply be Ellison's way of honoring both of them.

72. One can trace Mary's warning against biting too much of the Big Apple to a 1939 interview Ellison conducted while working for the Writer's Project of the federal Works Progress Administration: "Ahm in New York, but New York ain't in me. You understand?" See "Eddie's Bar," in *A Renaissance in Harlem: Lost Voices of an American Community,* ed. Lionel C. Bascom (New York: Avon Books, Inc., 1999), 36.

73. Compare Brother Jack, who tells Invisible Man to "put aside your past" (309) and even gives him a new name, with the blueprints jive-talker Peter Wheatstraw, who reminds Invisible Man not to deny his past (172–77).

74. Cf. Claudia Tate, "Notes on the Invisible Women in Ralph Ellison's *Invisible Man,*" in *Speaking for You: The Vision of Ralph Ellison,* ed. Kimberly W. Benston (Washington, D.C.: Howard University Press, 1987), 163–72, where Mary Rambo gets credit for helping Invisible Man with no strings attached, but so much so that Tate believes he is incapable of leaving the "the inanimate womb of the underground" (171). Tate reads the novel as ending where it began, with Invisible Man stuck in his basement cell with "no mother to give him birth." Read as Invisible Man's memoirs, the novel (especially its culmination in the final three pages of the Epilogue) is testimony of the protagonist's successful rebirth into the society above-ground. See infra notes 56, 57, and 81–83.

75. Ralph Ellison, "On Being the Target of Discrimination" (April 16, 1989), *Collected Essays,* 826.

76. Ralph Ellison, "If the Twain Shall Meet" (November 8, 1964), *Collected Essays,* 575. The "Supreme Court Decision of 1954" Ellison referred to was the landmark *Brown v. Board of Education* ruling, which announced the desegregation of public schools. For a recent reappraisal of *Brown*'s significance, see James T. Patterson, *Brown v. Board of Education: A Civil Rights Milestone and Its Troubled Legacy* (New York: Oxford University Press, 2001).

77. "The honored guests moved silently upon the platform, herded toward their high, carved chairs by Dr. Bledsoe with the decorum of a portly headwaiter."

Invisible Man recollects that although Bledsoe "was physically larger" than the white trustees, he adopted a "posture of humility and meekness which made him seem smaller." After Dr. Bledsoe scolds Invisible Man for taking a trustee to the slave-quarter section of the college town, the narrator recollects, "As we approached a mirror Dr. Bledsoe stopped and composed his angry face like a sculptor, making it a bland mask, leaving only the sparkle of his eyes to betray the emotion that I had seen only a moment before." *Invisible Man,* 114, 115, and 102.

78. Dr. Bledsoe adds: "I's big and black and say 'Yes, suh' as loudly as any burrhead when it's convenient, but I'm still the king down here. I don't care how much it appears otherwise. Power doesn't have to show off. . . . The only ones I even pretend to please are big white folk, and even those I control more than they control me. This is a power set-up son, and I'm at the controls" (142).

79. Ralph Ellison, "The Art of Fiction: *An Interview*" (Spring 1955), *Collected Essays,* 220.

80. After Emma wonders aloud if Invisible Man could not have been "a little blacker," Jack rebukes Emma: "We're not interested in his looks but in his voice" (303).

81. Ellison emphasizes the social aspect of the narrator's chronicle in a 1963 interview: "*Invisible Man* is a memoir of a man who has gone through that experience and now comes back and brings his message to the world. It's a social act; it is not a resignation from society but an attempt to come back and to be useful." Allen Geller, "An Interview with Ralph Ellison" (October 25, 1963), *Conversations with Ralph Ellison,* ed. Maryemma Graham and Amritjit Singh (Jackson: University Press of Mississippi, 1995), 76.

82. Thomas Hill Schaub rightly discerns how "Invisible Man and *Invisible Man* coincide, as the book's words and its hero's 'disembodied voice' stand as the only reality presented to the reader." See Schaub, *American Fiction in the Cold War,* 104. Ross Posnock also recognizes Invisible Man's "socially responsible role" (581) as "an intellectual, which he has discovered in the act of putting his life down on paper" in *Color and Culture: Black Writers and the Making of the Modern Intellectual* (Cambridge, Mass.: Harvard University Press, 1998), 76. While Posnock recognizes Invisible Man's affirmation of "invisibility *as* responsibility," he believes "invisible man remains in a hole and only says he is coming out" (Posnock, 77, emphasis in original). Unlike Schaub, Posnock does not notice that the novel as a memoir proves that the narrator left his hole to bring his message to the world.

83. Ralph Ellison, "The Art of Fiction: *An Interview*" (Spring 1955), *Collected Essays,* 220. Ellison explained, "The fact that you can read the narrator's memoirs means that he has come out of that hole." He went on to describe the novel's self-presentation as a man's memoirs as "a form beyond the form." See also "On Initiation Rites and Power: A Lecture at West Point" (March 26, 1969), *Collected Essays,* where Ellison says that Invisible Man "comes out of the ground, and this can be seen when you realize that although *Invisible Man* is *my* novel, it is really *his* memoir" (537). Cf. H. William Rice, *Ralph Ellison and the Politics of*

the Novel (Lanham, Md.: Lexington Books, 2003), which acknowledges the novel as "the fruit of the underground" (11) but concludes that Ellison left the narrator in a more ambiguous state. See especially the Introduction and chaps. 1 and 2, which elaborate upon Yonka Kristeva, "Chaos and Pattern in Ellison's *Invisible Man,*" 30 *Southern Literary Journal* 4 (Fall 1997), 68: "Ellison focuses on a liminal state, a process of transition and becoming which is unresolved at the end of the novel" (Rice, 11–12).

84. Ralph Ellison, "Change the Joke and Slip the Yoke" (Spring 1958), *Collected Essays,* 111.

85. To an incredulous interviewer, Ellison justified the inclusion of the Epilogue by saying it "was necessary to complete the action begun when he [Invisible Man] set out to write his memoirs." "The Art of Fiction: *An Interview*" (Spring 1955), *Collected Essays,* 220.

86. In a review of Gunnar Myrdal's *An American Dilemma,* which he wrote for the *Antioch Review* but never saw published, Ellison observed: "Are American Negroes simply the creation of white men, or have they at least helped to create themselves out of what they found around them? Men have made a way of life in caves and upon cliffs; why cannot Negroes have made a life upon the horns of the white man's dilemma?" Ralph Ellison, "*An American Dilemma:* A Review" (1944), *Collected Essays,* 339. For the circumstances that led to Ellison's assignment of the review and its eventual nonpublication, see Jackson, *Ralph Ellison,* 302–303.

87. Ralph Ellison, "Harlem's America," *The New Leader* (September 26, 1966), 24.

88. In "Ralph Ellison's Territorial Advantage" (1976), *Living With Music,* Ellison notes how black Americans kept civically aware in segregated Oklahoma: "Oklahoma had and still has one of our most famous papers, the *Black Dispatch.* It was published and edited by Roscoe Dungee [sic] and was widely read for its editorials" (14). In his tribute to the *Dispatch* founder, "Roscoe Dunjee and the American Language" (May 14, 1972), *Collected Essays,* Ellison praises Dunjee for understanding "what newspapers were supposed to do": namely, "to instill democratic ideals" (452 and 456). Recalling his days as a newspaper boy, Ellison wrote, "I grew up selling Dunjee's paper, reading it, and talking with my peers and friends about what appeared in it" (454). For further discussion of Roscoe Dunjee's influence on Ralph Ellison, see Alfred L. Brophy, "*Invisible Man* as Literary Analog to *Brown v. Board of Education,*" chap. 6, in this volume.

89. In a letter to Albert Murray (April 9, 1953), Ellison recounts a lecture he gave where he cited the Tuskegee library as an example of "the kind of freedom that lies available in the south but which is too often ignored" (*Trading Twelves,* 46). Richard Wright managed to check out books from a Memphis public library open only to whites by pretending to check them out for a white card-holder. See his quasi-autobiographical account in *Black Boy (American Hunger): A Record of Childhood and Youth,* intro. Jerry Ward, Jr. (New York: Perennial Classics/HarperCollins Publishers, 1998; orig. publ. by Harper & Brothers, 1945), chap. 13.

90. "Ellison's Library Speech" (June 21, 1975), handwritten transcript in folder entitled "June 21, 1975—Dedication Ellison Branch Library," Box 171, Ralph Ellison Papers, Library of Congress, 12. See also "Interview with WKY-TV, Oklahoma, 1976" (August 22, 1976), *Living With Music*, 262: "The library is the university, it's the grade school of the novelist. He writes out of other books. That's how he learns his craft." For a brief account of the library dedication, see Bob Burke and Denyvetta Davis, *Ralph Ellison: A Biography* (Oklahoma City: Oklahoma Heritage Association, 2003), 280–84.

91. Ralph Ellison, "The World and the Jug," Part I (December 9, 1963), *Collected Essays*, 164. Ellison added: "It requires real poverty of the imagination to think that this can come to a Negro *only* through the example of other Negroes. . . . Need my skin blind me to all other values?" (164–65).

92. Ralph Ellison, "Change the Joke and Slip the Yoke" (Spring 1958), *Collected Essays*, 112.

93. "Study and Experience: An Interview with Ralph Ellison," ed. Graham and Singh, 327. Cf. W. E. B. Du Bois's famous statement: "I sit with Shakespeare and he winces not. Across the color line I move arm in arm with Balzac and Dumas. . . . I summon Aristotle and Aurelius and what soul I will, and they come all graciously with no scorn nor condescension. So, wed with Truth, I dwell above the Veil." *The Souls of Black Folk: Authoritative Text, Contexts, Criticism*, ed. Henry Louis Gates, Jr. and Terri Hume Oliver (New York: W. W. Norton & Company, 1999), 74. In "Remembering Richard Wright," Ellison recalls that "when I knew him he was not shrinking from the challenges of his existence. Nor complaining that he'd been 'buked and scorned.' Nor did he feel that he had handicaps that could not be overcome because of his identity as a Negro writer. Instead he was striving to live consciously—at least artistically and intellectually—at the top of his times" (667).

94. Ralph Ellison, "The World and the Jug," Part I (December 9, 1963), *Collected Essays*, 163. "One reason why I tell black kids to read novels is that we've been choked off from knowing how society operates. And often American novels . . . do tell us something about the dilemmas of people and institutions, of areas of American life from which we are restricted because of our race." "Indivisible Man" (December 1970), *Collected Essays*, 385. See also "The Little Man at Chehaw Station" (1977/1978), *Collected Essays*, where Ellison explains: "As a citizen, the little man endures with a certain grace the social restrictions that limit his own social mobility, but *as a reader,* he demands that the relationship between his own condition and that of those more highly placed be recognized" (498–99).

95. "Interview with WKY-TV, Oklahoma, 1976" (August 22, 1976), *Living With Music*, 263.

96. "Negro Americans had to learn to live under pressure. . . . We were forced into segregation, but within that situation we were able to live close to the larger society and to abstract from it enough combinations of values, including

religion and hope and art, which allowed us to endure and impose our own idea of what the world should be, of what man should be, and of what American society should be. I'm not speaking of power here, but of vision, of values and dreams. Yes, and of will." Ralph Ellison, "'A Very Stern Discipline'" (March 1967), *Collected Essays,* 747. See also "An Extravagance of Laughter" (1985), *Collected Essays,* where Ellison wrote: "I had read Hemingway's definition, but for Negroes, 'grace under pressure' was far less a gauge of courage than of good common sense" (631–32).

97. Ralph Ellison, "'A Completion of Personality'" (1982), *Collected Essays,* 813.

98. Ralph Ellison, "Indivisible Man" (December 1970), *Collected Essays,* 376: "But we keep getting this mixed up with obsequiousness or with fear, which is the way the *white* man interprets it."

99. Ralph Ellison, "On Being the Target of Discrimination" (April 16, 1989), *Collected Essays,* 819–28.

100. Ralph Ellison, "What America Would Be Like Without Blacks" (April 6, 1970), *Collected Essays,* 580.

101. Ralph Ellison, "Haverford Statement" (May 30–31, 1969), *Collected Essays,* 430. In a statement made before the Senate Subcommittee on Executive Reorganization, Ellison observed, "But of one thing I am certain: We were hopeful . . . and we lived as we could live and had to live, because we had great hopes and great confidence in the promises of American democracy." *The New Leader* (September 26, 1966), 24.

102. The Montgomery Improvement Association, led by Martin Luther King, Jr., organized the bus boycott in Montgomery, Alabama, that helped desegregate public transportation and catapulted the Civil Rights Movement to national prominence. The name of the organization reflected the group's belief that desegregation was good for every citizen of Montgomery, not just the persecuted Negroes. See Martin Luther King, Jr., *Stride Toward Freedom: The Montgomery Story* (New York: Harper & Row, Publishers, 1958).

103. Ralph Ellison, "Some Questions and Some Answers" (May 1958), *Collected Essays,* 300.

104. Ralph Ellison, "Going to the Territory" (September 20, 1979), *Collected Essays,* 605. See also "The Little Man at Chehaw Station" (1977/1978), where Ellison speaks of "America's social mobility, its universal education, and its relative freedom of cultural information" that amounts to "an incalculable scale of possibilities for self-creation" (493 and 494).

105. Cited in Richard Kostelanetz, "Ralph Ellison: Brown Skinned Aristocrat," *Shenandoah* (Summer 1969), 57. See also Ralph Ellison, "Indivisible Man" (December 1970), *Collected Essays:* "By being in it and outside you can evaluate. Housekeepers, bellhops, domestics, have done this for years . . . But in terms of their position in the social hierarchy, they were outside but right in the *bedroom*" (384). See also "'A Completion of Personality'" (1974), *Collected Essays,* 803–804.

106. Ralph Ellison, "That Same Pain, That Same Pleasure: An Interview" (1961), *Collected Essays,* 79. Ellison's appreciation of Negro American heritage can be found throughout his essays and interviews: for example, see "Some Questions and Some Answers" (May 1958), *Collected Essays,* 300; "The World and the Jug," Part I (December 9, 1963), *Collected Essays,* 160–61; and "What These Children Are Like" (September 1963), *Collected Essays,* 549–50.

107. Ralph Ellison, "On Being the Target of Discrimination" (April 16, 1989), *Collected Essays,* 819–28.

108. Ralph Ellison, "Indivisible Man" (December 1970), *Collected Essays,* 393.

109. Ralph Ellison, "Remembering Richard Wright" (July 18, 1971), *Collected Essays,* 667.

110. Ralph Ellison, "The World and the Jug," Part I (December 9, 1963), *Collected Essays,* 162.

111. Ralph Ellison, "'A Completion of Personality'" (1974), *Collected Essays,* 802.

112. For a discussion of these and other Ellisonian themes, see Porter, *Jazz Country,* 8–16.

113. Ralph Ellison, "The World and the Jug," Part I (December 9, 1963), *Collected Essays,* 161.

114. For a brief interpretation of the Declaration of Independence as the first American "emancipation proclamation," see Lucas E. Morel, *"Juneteenth:* American Democracy in Theory and Practice," *Christian Science Monitor* (June 19, 2000), 9.

115. Ralph Ellison, "The World and the Jug," Part I (December 9, 1963), *Collected Essays,* 161.

116. See Ralph Ellison, "'A Completion of Personality'" (1974), *Collected Essays,* 804–805, where Ellison states: "To repeat myself, this society has structured itself to be unaware of what it owes in both the positive and negative sense to the condition of inhumanity that it has imposed upon a great mass of its citizens. The fact that many whites refuse to recognize this is responsible for much of the anger erupting among young blacks today. . . . The point is one of moral perception, the perception of the wholeness of American life and the cost of its successes and its failures."

Chapter 4

Invisible Man and Juneteenth: Ralph Ellison's Literary Pursuit of Racial Justice

THOMAS S. ENGEMAN

More than most major writers, in numerous essays and speeches, Ralph Ellison steadily commented on the importance of literature for life, and the principles of American democracy for racial justice. Because *Invisible Man* and *Juneteenth* are at bottom "novels of ideas," a brief introduction to Ellison's reflections on literature and democracy will prepare us for a study of racial justice in the novels.

While often deploying the pyrotechnics of surrealism, including extended dream sequences and wild comic conceits, Ralph Ellison argued the goal of his writing is literary realism:

> [W]hat one listens for in a novel: the degree to which it contains what Henry James termed "felt life," . . . that quality conveyed by the speaker's knowledge and feeling for the regional, racial, religious, and class unities and differences within the land, and his awareness of the hopes and values of a diverse people struggling to achieve the American promise in their own time, in their own place, and with the means at hand.[1]

Unlike his "enemy" the social scientist, the writer invents images to capture the world's complex reality. Literature best reveals the possibilities of human knowledge and action; art must be a guide for "ordinary" experience:

> But hope and aspiration are indeed important aspects of the reality of Negro American history, no less than that of others. Besides, it's one of our roles as writers to remind ourselves of such matters, just as it is to make assertions tempered by the things of the spirit. It might sound arrogant to

say so, but writers and poets help create or reveal hidden realities by asserting their existence. . . .

I do not find it a strain to point to the heroic component of our experience, for these seem truths which we have long lived by, but which we must now recognize consciously.[2]

Knowledge of the literary classics elevates social science's negative realism: "We (Negroes) depend upon outsiders—mainly sociologists—to interpret our lives for us. It doesn't seem to occur to us that our interpreters might well be not so much prejudiced as ignorant, insensitive, and arrogant. It doesn't occur to us that they might be of shallow personal culture, or innocent of the complexities of actual living."[3] In artistically reconstructing the world, writers must inspire it with their greater understanding of human possibility: "You must pay the Negro community the respect of trying to see it through the enrichening perspectives provided by great literature, using your own intelligence to make up for the differences. . . . Human beings are basically the same and differ mainly in lifestyle. Here revelation is called for, not argument."[4]

Ellison also maintains the importance of the Declaration's principles of equality and liberty for racial justice. These principles were mainly embodied in the Constitution and later refined by Abraham Lincoln. He referred to this nearly sacred trinity as "the framers of Declaration, the Constitution, and Lincoln."[5]

[T]he Declaration of Independence marked the verbalization of our colonial forefathers' intentions of disposing of the king's authority. . . . The Constitution marked the gloriously optimistic assertion and legitimization of a new form of authority and the proclaiming of a new set of purposes and promises. . . . Through the dramatic conflict of democratic society, it would seek to fulfill its revolutionary assertions.[6]

We made a formulation here of what we were and who we were, and what we expected to be, and we wrote it down in the documents of the Bill of Rights, the Constitution, the Declaration of Independence. I mean that we put ourselves on the books as to what we were and would become, and we were stuck with it. And we were stuck with it partially through a process of deification which came through the spilling of blood and through the sacrifices which were endured. . . .[7]

Ellison also admired the "agonistic . . . conflict of democratic society." Competition results in a creative society in all fields; Americans, thus, recreate themselves through the revolutionary principles of the Declaration. But, as we will see, *Juneteenth* radically qualifies Ellison's view of "self-creative" individualism.

A life-long defender of the Declaration's color-blind teaching of equality and individual liberty, Ellison was highly critical of Black liberation movements, illustrated in *Invisible Man* by the Black Nationalist Ras's politics of race and violence:

> "Brothers are the same color; how the hell you call these white men *brother?* . . . We sons of Mama Africa, you done forgot? You black, Black! . . . They hate you, mahn. You African. AFRICAN! . . . They sell you out. . . . They enslave us—you forget that? How can they mean a black mahn any good?"[8]

For Ellison, Ras's racial nationalism revives the recently buried specter of Nazism, and, ultimately, of white racial superiority as the justification for slavery:

> The Germany which produced Beethoven and Hegel and Mann turned its science and technology to the monstrous task of genocide; one hopes that when what are known as "Negro" societies are in full possession of the world's knowledge and in control of their destinies, they will bring to an end all those savageries which for centuries have been committed in the name of race. From what we are witnessing in certain parts of the world today, however, there is no guarantee that simply being non-white offers any guarantee of this. The demands of state policy are apt to be more influential than morality.[9]

Therefore, liberal principles—guaranteeing opportunity, but demanding excellence—offer the only safe basis for liberation:

> Democracy is a collectivity of individuals.
>
> The great writers of the nineteenth century and the best of the twentieth have always reminded us that the business of being an American is an arduous task, as Henry James said, and it requires constant attention to our consciousness and conscientiousness. The law ensures the conditions, the stage upon which we act; the rest of it is up to the individual.[10]

But the individual liberation explored in *Invisible Man* is hostile to the kind of fellow feeling and social knowledge required to help liberate others. Indeed, the existential search for self-knowledge through a flight to solitude appears altogether hostile to society. The invisible man's existential "visibility" first appears in isolation from society: his family, college, political party, and work. If *Invisible Man* offers a radical, existential approach to the Declaration's natural rights outlined in Ellison's essays and speeches, *Juneteenth* appears at the opposite, communitarian edge. The second novel explores the obscure connection between the Declaration and American religion.

INVISIBLE MAN

Invisible Man seeks individual liberation through freedom from social oppression. "Invisible man," or IM, like Nietzsche's Zarathustra, finds freedom from "the flies of the market-place" only in solitude.[11] After leaving his family, IM eventually escapes the racism of Southern and Northern life altogether. Invisible in racist America, he gains the "visible" he craves by living alone, under the crowded streets of New York.

Invisible Man's exploration of race relations is similar to W. E. B. Du Bois's *The Souls of Black Folk*. (The other common theme of these works is pessimism about piercing the Veil, breaching the color line, of racial segregation). The differences between the two works are also instructive. Du Bois mainly wrote vignettes in his own name, while Ellison's nameless IM is a purely literary creation. Moreover, the subtleties and humor of IM's quixotic quest go far beyond Du Bois's sociological essays.

Nevertheless, *Invisible Man* and *The Souls of Black Folk* share many themes: (1) the insufficiency of Booker T. Washington's accommodationism; (2) the pervasiveness of racism in both the North and South; (3) the centrality of music in Negro culture; and, most significantly, (4) the "double sightedness" of Black existence, causing Black invisibility. Du Bois observes:

> The Negro is a sort of seventh son, born with a veil, and gifted with second-sight in this American world—a world which yields him no true self-consciousness, but only lets him see himself through the revelation of the other world. It is a peculiar sensation, this double-consciousness, this sense of always looking at one's self through the eyes of others, of measuring one's soul by the tape of a world that looks on in amused contempt and pity.[12]

Invisible Man explores the effects of Du Bois's double consciousness on Blacks. But all Americans are enslaved by race prejudice. Regarding his writing, Ellison said: "I will not ignore the racial dimensions at all, but I will try to put them into a human perspective." He added, "For it is our fate as Americans [white and Negro] to achieve that sense of self-consciousness through our own efforts."[13] Therefore, he insists on the origin of *Invisible Man* in Fyodor Dostoevsky's philosophical *Notes from Underground,* not the political/racial writings of Richard Wright's *Native Son* and Du Bois's *Souls of Black Folk.*

While racism *is* the reality IM overcomes to obtain self-conscious freedom, every human is similarly fated to illusion and oppression. IM learns that Reverend Homer Barbee, the blind seer of his beloved College, is both physically *and* intellectually blind to the difference between illusion and reality. Jack, the glass-eyed leader of the "Brotherhood," has become blind to the meaning of justice. If IM eventually triumphs over his social blindness, attaining a rare liberation, he remains uncertain how his new knowledge can be used to destroy racism and segregation.

IM grows up in the rural, segregated South. With one exception, his family comprises "good Negroes," followers of Booker T. Washington. They believe personal honesty, hard work, and ability are rewarded in America. "[T]hey were told they were free, united with others of our country in everything pertaining to the common good, and, in everything social, separate like the fingers of the hand. And they believed it. They exulted in it. They stayed in their place [and] worked hard" (15–16). The exception to the family's foolish docility is IM's grandfather, who believes "our life is a war." He teaches them to "live with your head in the lion's mouth. I want you to overcome them with yeses, undermine 'em with grins, agree 'em to death and destruction, let 'em swoller you till they vomit or bust wide open." This unfathomable call to arms remains the central and "constant puzzle" for IM; it is so opposed to every view of race taught him by whites and Negroes alike. He soon learns that in searching for the liberating truth, he finds himself "carrying out his advice in spite of myself" (16).

If comically told, the racial landscape Ellison paints is uniformly bleak. The only aid crossing the color line comes from a gay man who helps the hero as an act of revenge against his father (190–192). Moreover, in racist America influential Negroes become agents of oppression. IM's greatest enemy is President Bledsoe, the hypocritical successor of his College's benevolent Founder (a Booker T. Washington-like figure).[14]

The novel opens with a display of overt racism in IM's small southern town. The white leaders' monthly "smoker" features various adult entertainments. Prominent among them is a free-for-all with local black "boys." The top graduate of the colored high school, IM discovers he must first brawl in the "battle royal" before presenting his honorific address, and receiving their award for his achievement. Speaking through his bloodied mouth, IM repeats the accepted views of voluntary segregation presented by Booker T. Washington at the Atlanta Exposition. Receiving the whites' praise as a "boy" who will "some day lead his people in the proper paths," IM gladly accepts their scholarship to Bledsoe's college, which will "encourage him in the right direction" (32).

The sterile Tuskegee-like college *appears* a model of Booker T. Washington's benevolent ideal of progress through education, although it proves only an empire of illusion and tyranny. The college corrupts students by demanding they accept segregation, and their own inferiority, enabling their oppressor, President Bledsoe, to become wealthy and honored. A realist, Bledsoe tells IM the stark truth: "Well, that's the way it is. It's a nasty deal and I don't always like it myself. But you listen to me: I didn't make it, and I know that I can't change it. But I've made my place in it, and I'll have every Negro in the country hanging on tree limbs by morning if it means staying where I am" (143).

The College presents a sanitized view of Negro life to attract the support of its idealistic white benefactors. Donors pay the college to atone for the exploitation of Negroes in their northern factories. Unwilling to seek racial justice in the North, the trustees willingly accept Bledsoe's comfortable vision of racial decorum and progress. The students dutifully play the game, appearing to conform to the strict ideals of a New England education.

The collegians are forbidden contact with the inmates of a local insane asylum. IM learns why when forced to take a Trustee to a black brothel when the inmates are there. Educated black war veterans, who treat whites as their equals, they have been committed for their insane lack of social awareness. For exposing the College's ridiculous racial tableaus, IM is permanently exiled.

Still believing in Bledsoe's goodness, IM accepts his letters of introduction to the College's wealthy New York friends. After inexplicable failures, he learns the letters are not those of grace. Recipients are encouraged to deceive IM about the College's willingness to help him, or permit his return:

> Thus, while the bearer is no longer a member of our scholastic family, it is highly important that his severance with the college be executed as painlessly as possible. I beg of you, sir, to help him continue in the direction of that promise which, like the horizon, recedes ever brightly and distantly beyond the hopeful traveler. (191)

IM reformulates the letter's message: "The Robin bearing this letter is a former student. Please hope him to death, and keep him running" (194).

Having escaped the total racism and hypocrisy of Southern society, in the North IM tries his luck at Liberty Paint, manufacturer of the purest paint made in America. "Optic White" is used by the (still segregated) United States Government; "Keep America Pure with Liberty Paints" is the company's (and the Government's) motto. Lucius Brockway, the old defender of the company's paternal racial order, wrote the company's tag line: "If It's Optic White, It's the Right White." He has made the Negro slogan *pay:* "If you're white, you're right." IM is made Brockway's assistant, working the basement boilers brewing the "base" for the greatest white "covering" in the world. Lucius cynically brags: "Our white is so white you can paint a chunka coal and you'd have to crack it open with a sledge hammer to prove it wasn't white clear through" (217–218).

IM becomes the catalyst for the plant's racial conflicts. The white boss considers Negroes incompetent, but is unable to instruct IM in mixing the hard white paint. Since young Negro college students, like IM, are hired to replace more highly paid whites, the union members believe he is management fink, and "undeveloped" as a worker. The third camp are Negroes like Brockway, who, like President Bledsoe, have made the system work for them and will now "hang from a tree" any agents of change. When the hero tells Brockway he accidentally attended a union meeting, the latter explodes: "I knowed you belonged to that bunch of troublemaking foreigners! I knowed it! Git out! . . . Git out of my basement!" (224). When IM refuses to give him his personal allegiance, Brockway blows up a boiler in revenge. In the plant's infirmary, the white medical staff employ a new electric lobotomy machine to cure the hero's antisocial rebelliousness. Once again, IM remains oppressed and invisible to the warring racial forces, but ever optimistic, he still believes there is an accepted way to pass through the Veil to liberation and "visibility."

IM's turn to political leadership is prepared through his friendship with his landlady, Mary Rambo. Mary thinks Negroes no longer require the economic enlightenment and moral uplift of Booker T. Washington, but the leadership of W. E. B. Du Bois's "Talented Tenth," and the NAACP. Breaking down legal barriers, a new Negro elite will liberate the black masses. IM finds living with Mary pleasant, "except for her constant talk about leadership and responsibility. . . . Mary reminded me constantly that something was expected of me, some act of leadership, some newsworthy achievement" (258). But it is only a small step from Du Bois's elitist democracy to the violence of the Brotherhood's warlike Party.

A brilliant speaker, IM is drafted into the (Communistic) Brotherhood to be its Harlem spokesman. He soon begins to question the Brotherhood's authoritarianism. Suppressing his doubts, IM stays with the Brotherhood until convinced belatedly of its indifference to Negroes. In the face of the Black Nationalist Ras's opposition, IM builds the Party in Harlem, only to be suddenly removed. Ras rapidly increases his agitation, causing Harlem to erupt in violence. IM understands the Brotherhood deliberately caused the riot; it was ordered by "Moscow." By showing American racism to the world, the riot was intended to checkmate American foreign policy. "I could see it now, see it clearly and in growing magnitude. It [the riot] was not suicide, but murder. The committee had planned it" (553).

But the great riot reveals aspects of humanity obscure in peace. Once liberated, the Negro "masses" demonstrate genuine virtues. Remarkably courageous, they have a genuine sense of community and organizational ability (545–548), virtues normally hidden in their segregated, shadow world.

Wearing a disguise to avoid Ras's revenge, the hero accidentally takes on the persona of the "renaissance man" of Harlem, Rinehart. The incredible Rinehart is a numbers runner, pimp, gang leader, police pay master, minister of the gospel, and, all round celebrity; his success illustrates the disordered individualism resulting from urban segregation. Rinehart, rind heart or heartless, offers a radical alternative to the leadership tradition of both Booker T. Washington and W. E. B. Du Bois. He represents the tyrannical self-enrichment possible through the ruthless exploitation of the Negro community by its "Talented Tenth." IM rejects Rinehartism, as he had earlier rejected the enforced political "liberation" of the Brotherhood, W. E. B. Du Bois's elitism, and Booker T. Washington's hopeful passivity. But the possibility of his "leadership" teaches IM about the trauma of the oppressed urban Blacks, as the riot provided him an insight into their virtues.

Freed from his last illusions about racial justice and liberation, IM now lives underground, totally free and "visible," but without social purpose. He resists oppression by fueling his subterranean vaults with pirated electricity from Monopolated Light and Power. His 1,369 (and growing) lights enable him to see himself. He is no longer invisible, as he had been when forced to see himself through the eyes of those, black and white, who denied him individuality.

Having told his story in the novel, IM is a different man. He lives, as had his grandfather, in the light of the great principles of the Declaration of Independence—while acutely aware of the distance between principle and practice.

> Did he [his grandfather] mean "yes" because he knew that the principle was greater than the men, greater than the numbers and the vicious power and the methods used to corrupt its name? Did he mean to affirm the principle, which they themselves had brought into being out of the chaos and darkness of the feudal past, and which they had violated and compromised to the point of absurdity even in their own corrupt minds? Or did he mean that we had to take the responsibility for all of it, for the men as well as the principle, because we were the heirs who must use the principle because no other fitted our needs? (574)

Living the Declaration's principles, he loves and hates his oppressors, who were also victims of racial stereotypes.

> And I defend (them) because in spite of all I find that I love. *In order to get some of it down I have to love.* I sell you no phony forgiveness, I'm a desperate man—but too much of your life will be lost, its meaning lost, unless you approach it as much through love as through hate. So I approach it through division. So I denounce and I defend and I hate and I love. (580; emphasis added)

Like *The Souls of Black Folk*, *Invisible Man* ends pessimistically. Is the underground teacher of the evils of invisibility still a person? "I remind myself that the true darkness lies within my own mind, and the idea loses itself in gloom." Unlike Dostoevsky's underground man, IM still thinks "there's a possibility that even an invisible man has a socially responsible role to play" (579, 581). Yet, his isolation from the struggles, illusions, and passions of political life suggests that understanding, forgiveness, and even love, are insufficient bases for humanity.

Ellison continued to seek a better ground for justice and liberation than the higher individualism found in artistic existentialism or liberal individualism of *Invisible Man*. In *Juneteenth,* Ellison rejects the brilliant, self-created individualism of Senator Adam Sunraider, to celebrate the Negro, Christian community that raised him.

RECONCILIATION AND
SOCIAL SALVATION

As we have seen, Ellison's understanding of liberation in *Invisible Man* is totally secular. When religion does briefly appear, it is a powerful source of oppression. The blind Reverend Homer Barbee passionately exhorts the collegians to accept President Bledsoe as a divinely inspired follower of the great

Founder, while the omniscient Rinehart ordains himself to further his Harlem scam. Similarly, Ras appeals to "divine Mother Africa" to justify his violence against all those who do not hate Whites. In short, religion in the early novel is an ideological support of oppression and alienation.

At some point, Ellison discovered a new path to liberation, and racial reconciliation, in American religion. In the capacious, unpublished novel he wrote and rewrote in the decades following the publication of *Invisible Man*, Ellison made a fundamental reformulation of the American racial "mystery." That part of his project posthumously published as *Juneteenth* offers a revaluation of religion and Christianity in American society. In his second sailing, Ellison suggests only Christianity possesses the emotional and spiritual sinews capable of uniting the fractured American communities still warring at the conclusion of *Invisible Man*.

In *Juneteenth*, Ellison enlists Christian morality and the rhetorical power of Negro dramaturgy to argue for a religious view of race relations. The novel is told from the perspective of the ancient patriarch, Reverend Alonzo Hickman. Unlike the invisible, existential intellectual IM, seeking liberation through "fleeing the flies of the marketplace," the Reverend Hickman has a different goal. Once a freedom-living, pleasure-loving jazzman, Hickman now loves his Christian community. While his duty is contained in the commandment to love one's neighbor as oneself—not IM's search for individual liberation— Hickman is a towering figure. Hickman's vision of Christian leadership is revealed at the Lincoln Memorial:

> "Sometimes, yes . . . sometimes the good Lord . . . I say sometimes the good Lord accepts His own perfection and closes His eyes and goes ahead and takes His own good time and He makes Himself a *man*. Yes, and sometimes that man gets hold of the idea of what he's supposed to do in this world and he gets an idea of what it is possible for him to do, and then that man lets that idea guide him as he grows and struggles and stumbles and sorrows until finally he comes into his own God-given shape. . . ."[15]

Hickman admires and emulates the great president. Lincoln was the political messiah, the president who first realized for Blacks the equality promised in the Declaration of Independence, while going beyond the principles of the Declaration. In his "Second Inaugural Address," Lincoln argued for a Christian magnanimity toward the suffering of those "who had borne the battle, their widows, and orphans" in the North *and* South. Hickman believes the end of racial war, like the end of the Civil War, could be accomplished through the spirit of Christian reconciliation.

Reverend Hickman gave up the free life of an itinerant jazzman when presented with an extraordinary child to raise. To protect her lover, an aristocratic woman had accused Hickman's brother, Bob, of raping her. Her charge resulted in Bob's brutal murder and the death of their mother. Nevertheless, on the night of her delivery, Bob's accuser comes to Alonzo for his help with the birth, and to make him a gift of the child. Hickman, who wishes only revenge—"Those eyes for Bob's eyes; that skin for Bob's flayed skin; those teeth for Bob's knocked-out teeth; those fingers for his dismembered hands" (296)—only reluctantly listens to her confession. "I'm a Christian! . . . Yes, a *Christian*. I lied. Yes. I bore false witness and caused death. Yes, and I'm a murderess. Can't you see that I understand?" (295). Confronting her great need and his absolute despair, Hickman delivers the child and begins his own conversion. "But to who else could she go, Hickman? Who but to the one who had suffered deep down to the bottom of the hole, down where there's nothing to do but come floating up lifting you in his own arms into the air, or die?" (298). Redemption, reconciliation, and love become the principles of Hickman's new ministry.

While Reverend Hickman raises the remarkable child, Bliss, to become a Negro Abraham Lincoln, white racial pride ever remains the enemy of racial equality. Bliss is told that he is white, and therefore superior to Daddy Hickman and the Negroes who are lovingly rearing him. Bliss's new sense of superiority fires his ambition.

Leaving his "Daddy" and "extended family," Bliss recreates himself as Adam Sunraider, the only race-baiting Senator from a Northern state. In a key scene, Senator Sunraider impiously extols the virtues of his own self-creating individualism on the Senate floor:

> "Ours is the freedom and obligation to be ever the fearless creators of ourselves, the reconstructers of the world. We were created to be Adamic definers, namers and shapers of yet undiscovered secrets of the universe!
>
> Therefore let the doubters doubt, let the faint of heart turn pale. We move toward the fulfillment of our nation's demand for citizen-individualists possessing the courage to forge a multiplicity of creative selves and styles. We shall supply its need for individuals. . . ." (23)

Hickman and his flock come to Washington to prevent Bliss/Sunraider's assassination. But Sunraider is shot on the Senate floor by his rejected Black son. Near death, and wishing reconciliation, the Senator sends for Daddy Hickman. As he had done on many death vigils, Hickman consoles and inspires the white Senator. In this strange case, the Reverend speaks not of the promise of eternal life but to Sunraider's own despair at his hollow life. Hickman seeks to renew the Senator's memory of his Christian community so he may be reconciled with his true self (Bliss) and his true people. Hour after hour, Hickman speaks of Bliss's happy childhood, and the faithfulness and love of the Negroes for him. Many of the Reverend's happiest memories are remembered darkly by Sunraider, but they lead him to remember other happy times. After deserting Hickman, Bliss had a single affair of the heart with a mixed-race woman in the Oklahoma Territory:

> . . . And I could tell you how I drew her close then and how her surrender was no surrender but something more, a materialization of the

heart, the deeper heart that lives in dreams—or once it did—that roams out in the hills among the trees, that sails calm seas in the sunlight; that sings in the stillness of star-cast night . . . I tried to read the mystery of myself within her eyes. (93, 94)

This relationship offered his last chance for the love Daddy Hickman had prepared him for. But racial pride fueled a great ambition: "I was working my way to where I could work my way to" (97).

Hickman's love slowly effects a reconciliation of the fallen son with his father. But as old memories replace those of his self-created self, Bliss confronts a recurrent image. Sunraider had fractiously warned his Senate colleagues of the "take over" of General Motors by the Cadillac Fleetwood's conversion into a "coon" car:

> "Indeed, I am led to suggest, and quite seriously, that legislation be drawn up to rename it the "Coon Cage Eight." And not at all because of its eight superefficient cylinders, nor because of the lean, springing strength and beauty of its general outlines. Not at all, but because it has now become such a common sight to see eight or more of our darker brethren crowded together enjoying its power, its beauty, its neo-pagan comfort, while weaving recklessly through the streets of our great cities and along our superhighways." (23)

Now standing between life and death, Sunraider is ominously assailed by another car driven by "our darker brethren." This "more than mortal machine" he realizes is "no Cadillac, no Lincoln, Oldsmobile, or Buick nor any known make of machine." The car is able to fly, and be in two places at the same time—"dividing itself and becoming simultaneously both there in the distance and here before him." It is better than any Roadmaster ever made by General Motors.

The three devils riding in the car are the embodiment of black hatred for whites, paralleling Bliss's own denial of human love and community. One has the same Jamaican accent as the Black Nationalist, Ras the Destroyer. Enforcers of Satan's supreme "No" to God's love, they make the Senator join them on a journey to Hades. Such is the result of Sunraider's love of his "devilish" Senatorial identity (343), and rejection of a reconciliation to Negro life which would have permitted him to enter the heaven created by Reverend Hickman's uncompromising love for all humankind. Even entering the modern chariot of the damned, Bliss "*seemed to hear* the sound of Hickman's consoling voice, calling from somewhere above" (348).

Reverend Alonzo Hickman acquires a Mosaic stature. Possessing the classical virtues of courage, prudence, and magnanimity, his ultimate power is as a law giver. His classical virtues are perfected by Christian ones: faith, hope, and charity. Negroes become fully human as they are led to live a Christian life. Hickman transforms isolated individuals into believers and citizens. If *Invisible*

Man shows the variety of injustices oppressing Negroes (and whites), in *June-teenth,* Hickman engages in the continual creation of Christian community. Hickman's failure to convert Sunraider illustrates man's complex liberty and loves, not the untruth of his word. Even God cannot save Satan's legions of the damned. As "God's Trombone," the Reverend combines powers spiritual and temporal. In a note, Ellison suggests Hickman is a forerunner of the Negro ministers who became political leaders beginning in the 1950s.[16]

Whether Hickman is clearly superior to IM is unclear. Never a college student, Hickman has little formal education and none in theology. "Hickman is intelligent but untrained in theology. . . . Devout and serious, he is unable to forget his old, profane way of speaking and of thinking of experience. Vernacular terms and phrases bloom in his mind even as he corrects them with more pious formulations."[17] But the Reverend offers the clearest answer to the problem of action and rational individualism found in *Invisible Man;* IM has no practical solution to racism and human alienation. Unable to pierce the color line, the wisest voice IM heard was his grandfather's counsel of total resistance: "yes" them to death. The racial wars remain. If *Invisible Man* sounds an optimistic note about the hero's ultimate utility, his grandfather's "no" remains authoritative pending an as yet unrevealed solution to the "color line." The solution IM sought is offered in *Juneteenth.*

Juneteenth realizes Ellison's emergence as a Christian communitarian, reversing the central themes of *Invisible Man.* Where the earlier novel described Negro life in the South as a continual nightmare, *Juneteenth* cele-brates the religious, rural communities of the South and West. The change between the two novels results from Ellison's greater acknowledgment of Christianity's influence within the Negro communities he knew. In *Juneteenth,* these rural communities, existing behind the times like the celebration of Juneteenth itself, are the perfection of Black social life.

CONCLUSION

A classical/Christian realist, Ellison sought to make Americans admire Negro life by placing it within the sweep of the Western literary tradition and the reality of American culture. This great task finally required two contrasting accounts of Black life. *Invisible Man* is a philosophic/literary treatment of the American "color line" or the "Veil," earlier explored by W. E. B. Du Bois in *The Souls of Black Folk.* Ellison thoroughly realized Du Bois's passionate soci-ology as literature, ennobling the Negroes' struggle within the Veil. Ellison's Negroes are a hardy and resilient people, if one still bedeviled by racism and beguiled by false prophets (like Reverend Homer Barbee, President Bledsoe, and Ras the Destroyer) and outright charlatans (like Rinehart).

Juneteenth, in contrast, reconnects existential liberation and the Declaration of Independence with the saving grace of Christian community. While Reverend Hickman's faith in Christ's commandments appears antithetical to IM's desire for liberation, both aspects of American life were united in Abraham Lincoln. Lincoln personified, for Ellison, the Founders' belief that a religious society supported the principles of the Declaration and Constitution. This connection was also described by Alexis de Tocqueville in *Democracy in America.* Tocqueville famously observed: "Religion sees in civil freedom a noble exercise of the faculties of man; . . . Freedom sees in religion the companion of its struggles and its triumphs, the cradle of its infancy, the divine source of its rights."[18] Tocqueville (and the Founders) argued that since American religions teach that God made men free and equal, only democratic government is compatible with man's Divine creation. Tocqueville observed:

> The greatest part of English America has been peopled by men who, after having escaped the authority of the pope, did not submit to any religious supremacy; they therefore brought to the New World a Christianity [Reformed Protestantism] that I cannot depict better than to call it democratic and republican: this singularly favors the establishment of a republic and of democracy in affairs. From the beginning, politics and religion were in accord, and they have not ceased to be so since.[19]

Juneteenth reconnects IM's pursuit of liberation to Christian faith and practice. Ellison's reflection on the intersection of reason and faith, freedom and community, are manifest in Hickman's attempt to raise Bliss to become a new Lincoln. Finally, Daddy Hickman forgives his "son's" spectacular fall, and through the power of his word, almost resurrects Bliss by restoring his love for the heaven created by Christian Negro life.

Escaping the Veil, Ralph Ellison traveled far on his pilgrimage to America's mysterious heart. The depth of his new intellectual and spiritual understanding is manifest in *Juneteenth*'s complex political, religious, and literary allusion and symbolism. His eventual insight into America's unique union of reason *and* faith places Ellison among a small band of novelists who freed themselves from the twentieth century's scientific modernism. If at times lacking the artistic polish of *Invisible Man*'s brilliant social satire, *Juneteenth*'s often ribald invocation of the mysterious American union of freedom and faith is a remarkable advance over the first novel's sterile individualism.

ENDNOTES

1. Ralph Ellison, "The Myth of the Flawed White Southerner" (1968), *The Collected Essays of Ralph Ellison,* ed. John F. Callahan (New York: Modern Library, 1995), 556. Hereinafter cited as *Collected Essays.*

2. Ralph Ellison, " 'A Very Stern Discipline' " (1965), *Collected Essays*, 737.

3. Ibid., 747.

4. Ibid., 736.

5. Ibid., 728.

6. Ralph Ellison, "Perspective of Literature" (1976), *Collected Essays*, 774.

7. Ralph Ellison, "On Initiation Rites and Power: A Lecture at West Point" (March 26, 1969), *Collected Essays*, 526.

8. Ralph Ellison, *Invisible Man* (New York: Random House, 1952; reprint, New York: Vintage Books, 1995), 370–71. All subsequent citations will be noted parenthetically in the text by page number, and emphases in original unless otherwise noted.

9. Ralph Ellison, "Some Questions and Some Answers" (May 1958), *Collected Essays*, 300.

10. Ralph Ellison, "Perspective of Literature" (1976), *Collected Essays*, 781.

11. Friedrich Nietzsche, *Zarathustra. Collected Works of Friedrich Nietzsche*, ed. Walter Kaufmann (New York: Viking/Penguin, 1982), 163.

12. W. E. B. Du Bois, "Of Our Spiritual Strivings," *The Souls of Black Folk*, ed. Henry Louis Gates, Jr. and Terri Hume Oliver (New York: W.W. Norton & Company, 1999), 10–11.

13. Ralph Ellison, "On Initiation Rites and Power" (March 26, 1969), *Collected Essays*, 528.

14. See *Invisible Man*, 305, where IM says of Booker T. Washington, "Well, I guess I don't think he was as great as the Founder."

15. Ralph Ellison, *Juneteenth: A Novel*, ed. John F. Callahan (New York: Random House, 1999), 282; emphasis in original. All subsequent citations will be noted parenthetically in the text by page number, and emphases in original unless otherwise noted.

16. Ibid., "Notes," 360.

17. Ibid., "Notes," 353.

18. Alexis de Tocqueville, *Democracy in America*, ed. and trans. Harvey C. Mansfield and Delba Winthrop (Chicago: The University of Chicago Press, 2000), 43–44.

19. Ibid., 275.

Chapter 5

Invisible Man as "a form of social power": The Evolution of Ralph Ellison's Politics

WILLIAM R. NASH

One might reasonably approach discussing Ellison's *Invisible Man* as a political novel with some trepidation. This is not because one cannot find political content in it. Rather, it is because Ellison was himself so clear about just what sort of political moves he sought to *avoid* in his writing. As Jerry Gafio Watts notes, Ellison once claimed that "when writers write about politics, usually they are wrong. The novel at its best demands a sort of complexity of vision which politics doesn't like. Politics has as its goal the exercise of power—political power—and it isn't particularly interested in truth in the way that the novel form demands that the novelist must be."[1]

Despite the author's stated resistance to the political, we must not embrace the generalization that plagued Ellison in the late 1960s, when some Black Aestheticians like Larry Neal and Addison Gayle deemed him a slave to the dictum that art must be "pure" and therefore cannot be political. Critics who fell deeply into that trap would do well to review Ellison's 1954 comments to Alfred Chester and Vilma Howard about the social function of art: "I recognize no dichotomy between art and protest. . . . If social protest is antithetical to art, what then shall we make of Goya, Dickens, Twain?"[2] On first glance, for me at least, this presents a dilemma: how one can simultaneously eschew politics and affirm the validity of social protest? One finds Ellison's answer, or at least one of his answers, by considering his understanding of how the novelist is "interested in truth."

In 1965, the year that a group of American scholars and authors named *Invisible Man* as the "best single novel of the post-war period,"[3] Ellison told an interviewer for the BBC that

> the good novelist tries to provide . . . vivid depictions of certain crucial and abiding patterns . . . by reducing the chaos of human existence to artistic form. And when successful he provides the reader with a fresh vision of reality. For then through the symbolic action of his characters and plot he enables the reader to share forms of experience not immediately his own. And thus the reader is able to recognize the meaning and value of the presented experience and the essential unity of human experience as a whole. This may, or may not, lead to social change. . . . But it is, nevertheless, a form of social action, and an important task. Yes, and in its own right, a form of social power.[4]

Certainly we can all agree that Ellison fits his own criteria for what it means to be a "good artist." Without reservation, *Invisible Man* also exercises precisely this sort of social power in its articulation of an integrative impulse that pushes us all to acknowledge our common humanity. This essay explores the particulars of how the articulation of that message fits into the process of Ellison's artistic empowerment.

In 1964, Ellison published *Shadow and Act,* a collection of essays that reinforced his reputation as a major voice in American letters; it also provided attentive readers with numerous insights into the richness and depth of *Invisible Man.* As Robert O'Meally notes briefly in *The Craft of Ralph Ellison,* one can find specific analogues in the novel for elements of particular essays.[5] Equally significantly, one also gets a sense of the cultural-political milieu Ellison sought to introduce his readers to in 1952. Many of the pieces in the collection first appeared after Ellison won the National Book Award for *Invisible Man;* it is perhaps not at all surprising that these essays would treat the Big Book, as it were, in some way or another.

More striking in this context, though, are the pieces in *Shadow and Act* that Ellison wrote before the publication of his first novel: essays like "The Way it Is" (1942), "Harlem is Nowhere" (1948), and "*An American Dilemma*: A Review" (1944). Through their various presentations of African-American life, they convey a sense of the common humanity that Americans share across racial borders and reject the notion that race is an indelible stain. One finds in them individuals or ideas that correlate closely with characters and concepts appearing in *Invisible Man.* Although the essays are all, to varying degrees, political in the sense that Ellison objects to, it is in the transformation of these figures from the essays, where he freely engages in politicized social criticism, that he achieves his synthetic vision. Looking at the hospital, Mary Rambo, and funeral episodes in the novel in the context of these particular source materials, one sees how Ellison took his early, more explicitly political writings and transformed their particular details into the universal, unifying, democratic message that he conveys in *Invisible Man*.

Ellison wrote "Harlem is Nowhere," in 1948, after work on *Invisible Man* was well underway. The essay, which broadly describes the psychological impact of racism on blacks that "are in desperate search for an identity," takes as its specific subject the LaFargue Mental Hygiene Clinic.[6] This institution, which served the Harlem community from 1946 until 1959, provided low-cost mental care for "old and young, black and white."[7] Its integrationist practice is one with its political mission. According to Lawrence Jackson, "the clinic treated mental health disorders in order to promote social justice," a term defined in this context as "not only destroying the forces of oppression, but healing psychic wounds, especially those suffered by the black poor."[8] Along with Richard Wright, Ellison devoted himself to the establishment of the clinic in an effort to assist the African-American community, to transform his call for political protest into specific action.

As Jackson notes, "even though [Ellison] was involved in the important work of the clinic, the business of writing continued" to be pressing for him.[9] With "Harlem is Nowhere," the author fuses those aims. In addition to promoting the work of the clinic, which Ellison refers to as "an underground extension of democracy," the essay also explores the broader questions of how white racism has affected the black psyche, how African Americans can forge identity in the face of what the author calls "a capricious reality in which even the most commonly held assumptions are questionable."[10] In this instance, both the patients and the physicians realize that the problems they must battle are larger than the individuals involved, more a symptom of the social order's sickness than the disparate pathologies of random individuals. The great gift to the patients in this is the doctors' willingness to really see them, to attempt "to give each bewildered patient an insight into the relation between his problems and his environment, and . . . to reforge the will to endure in a hostile world."[11] With this level of sensitivity and compassion, they are a far cry from their fictional counterparts in the factory hospital.

In describing the operations of the LaFargue clinic, Ellison mentions several fundamental premises about African-American identity that shape treatment of every patient:

He is viewed as a member of a racial and cultural minority, as an American citizen caught in certain political and economic relationships, and as a modern man living in a revolutionary world. Accordingly, each patient, whether white or black, is approached dynamically as a being possessing a cultural and biological past who seeks to make his way toward the future in a world wherein each discovery about himself must be made in the here and now at the expense of hope, pain, and fear—a being who in responding to the complex forces of America has become confused.[12]

Would that such humane treatment was afforded to Invisible Man after the accident at Liberty Paints. Unfortunately, the doctors who (mis)treat him in the factory hospital see his past only as a potential impediment to Invisible Man's treatment. One could argue that they do approach it dynamically, but to the altogether different end of making the narrator a sort of *tabula rasa* that they can shape to their own ends. In effect, we might read their attempts to "cure" the narrator as the obverse of the work done at the LaFargue clinic. By taking the reader to this other extreme, Ellison moves away somewhat from an emphasis on what causes the psychic wound, and focuses more fully on how the victim might most effectively heal himself.

In the factory hospital, the doctors, intent primarily on getting him "started again," use electroshock in an attempt to cauterize his psychic wounds (232). Readers should expect nothing less (more?) from them given that they appear primarily as an indistinguishable mass, with occasional faces and disembodied voices floating in and out of Invisible Man's restricted range of vision. The voices are most telling; almost always, at least until they think they have "cured" him, they address the narrator directly only as "boy." It is as if they want to ensure that he will keep to his place while they are in the act of erasing his independent sense of self. When they talk around, or over him, one can see clearly where he fits into their worlds. Apart from some banter like "they really do have rhythm, don't they? Get hot, boy! Get hot!" to describe Invisible Man's writhing, shocked body, the clinical discussion is a loose acknowledgment of the history of racial oppression melded with speculation about how best to handle this particular case.

Small wonder, then, that the narrator conceives of this environment as a "vast whiteness in which [he him]self was lost" (238). The room itself, all of its fixtures, and all of its inhabitants save the narrator, are white. As such, it represents the logical extension, in a sense, of the "bath of whiteness" that Invisible Man gets in the explosion at Liberty Paints (230). He floats, unaware of the separation point between his body and the "crystal and white world," experiencing a profound crisis of identity, losing himself in a "scale of receding grays" (238). Meanwhile, the doctors work to make sure that he has forgotten his heritage. Their apparent familiarity with this process makes the notion that this is a "factory hospital" all the more disturbing. Perhaps it is merely a facility connected with Liberty Paints; however, it also seems to be dedicated to turning out unraced African Americans, individuals who "experience no major conflict of motives" and make no trouble for society. This is coded language for unreserved accommodationism, which is their ultimate goal (236).

One of the wonderful ironies of this passage manifests itself in Invisible Man's tricksterism, as he retreats into what he calls "the blackness of my mind" to try to find an effective response to the white doctors' questions (239). The very process designed to strip him of his black identity gets him "started again" in another sense, setting him on the road to real self-awareness.

As O'Meally notes, he "thwarts" the official plan by calling the African-American folk tradition to mind. The narrator recalls one of his grand-mother's songs, a scatological childhood rhyme, the identity of Buckeye the Rabbit and Brer Rabbit, and the mechanisms of the dozens; in the process, says O'Meally, "Invisible Man does not lose his identity; he falls back upon it in wonderment."[13]

On a cultural level, O'Meally is correct. And yet, Invisible Man does not "fall back" on this heritage uncritically. As the onslaught begins, Invisible Man thinks, "maybe I was just this blackness and bewilderment and pain, but that seemed less like a suitable answer than something I'd read somewhere" (240). As essential as the African-American folk tradition is to him in this instance, he will not rest with a narrow view of himself as "just" one set of anything. Instead, he will make a concerted effort to know himself, realizing as he does that, "When I discover who I am, I'll be free" (243). This reminds the reader that true self-knowledge demands a balance of cultural identification with a healthy awareness of what distinguishes the individual from the group. As such, it represents the successful application of the fundamental principles of the LaFargue clinic. Invisible Man has been reminded of his past, albeit unin-tentionally, and he recognizes his need to rebuild his sense of self on that foundation. Armed with that awareness, he is potentially every bit as danger-ous to "the system" as the other trickster figures he recalls.

Clearly, however, simple tricksterism is not the defining attribute of the narrator's existence. He learns, tragically, in the course of the Harlem riots, that this approach leaves the practitioner vulnerable to external manipulation: "The committee had planned it. And I had helped, had been a tool. A tool just at the very moment I had thought myself free" (553). This makes sense, as tricksterism is, by definition, an adversarial activity. What the narrator must learn is the mechanism for creating unity out of conflict, the way to get to the point where he can ask the novel's famous final question with conviction.[14] In taking the narrator the final steps along that path, Ellison must push his political views from the positions of the earlier essays towards the universalism that he finally achieves in *Invisible Man*. Part of that comes from his encoun-tering Mary Rambo and from his giving Tod Clifton's funeral speech. In both instances, he learns to move beyond the masses to the point of discerning individuals; in that process, he learns to see himself as well.

But a crucial starting point for that process occurs in the hospital scene, or more correctly, in the director's office as Invisible Man awaits release. When the administrator informs him that he will be released from the hospital but not allowed to return to work, Invisible Man asks, "how shall I live?" (246). This seemingly innocuous question in fact contains the seeds of the meta-physical survival program that the narrator must undertake—and, as such, it relates directly to the political implications of the text. Quite a lot of impact from four words; and yet, if one turns to the work of the "other Ralph Waldo" in American literature, one can perhaps understand what Ellison has accomplished with this off-hand remark.

In 1851, after the deaths of his son Waldo and his friend Margaret Fuller, and at least partially in response to the passage of the Fugitive Slave Act of 1850, Emerson composed an essay titled "Fate," which he eventually published in *The Conduct of Life* (1860). In it, Emerson shifts from the bold claim in *Nature* that "Undoubtedly we have no questions to ask which are unanswerable," to a recognition of uncontrollable social and environmental forces marshaled against humanity.[15] Rather than simply denying or submitting to them, however, he advocates confrontation, keeping always in mind this question: "How shall I live?"[16] Only by resisting these forces, he argues, can one gain true freedom.

This is precisely the sort of process that Invisible Man needs to undergo, the sort of freedom that he needs to obtain for himself. In the early stages of his quest, he has the sense that all will become clear for him, that there are indeed no unanswerable questions. Furthermore, up until his encounter with Emerson, Jr., he has believed that the State College ideology held all of those answers for him. Now, in the aftermath of the explosion, emerging from his baptism in whiteness and from the renaissance of his blackness, the narrator must determine what precisely he is to do for himself. Having been born again in the hospital, in effect, he must go out and face the hostilities and pressures of American life. In this brief moment, he suggests the value of trying to make that journey deliberately, with as much awareness as possible—and, in that process, of forging individual connections that transcend labels and transform one's consciousness.

Fortunately for Invisible Man, despite his disorientation upon hitting the streets, he knows enough to head for Harlem, the territory where he can nurture and revitalize the community consciousness that the hospital has tried to burn out of him. Equally fortunately, once he arrives there, he literally stumbles into Mary Rambo, the one who will help him move forward towards the achievement of his goals. In his characterization of Mary Rambo, Ellison draws on material that preceded his starting the novel, specifically an essay called "The Way It Is." "The Way It Is" appeared in the October 20, 1942 issue of *New Masses,* which was largely devoted to African Americans' contributions to the war effort. As Lawrence Jackson notes, the piece "provided a real human component to the more academic pieces of sociology and political science (and outright propaganda) in the magazine."[17] Ellison's account of a conversation he had with a widowed domestic worker named Mrs. Jackson (her first name is never given) describes the particulars of one family's suffering in the face of racial and economic injustice. Although wary of Ellison as a potential relief investigator in disguise, she eventually relaxes enough to tell him the details of her life.

Her initial hesitation to open up to him, although humorous and a bit ironic in the telling, demonstrates something troublesome about her situation, and the situation of other African Americans caught in the grip of the war's pressures. At the point in the essay when she challenges Ellison's identity, the reader already knows that her oldest son, Wilbur, is away in the Army; he has not yet learned, but soon will, that Mrs. Jackson's nephew, William, has died aboard a torpedoed Merchant Marine ship. What Ellison presents, then, is a woman who has fully and freely sacrificed her family to a government that repays her with manipulation and deception, a bureaucracy that, in her experience, seeks to deprive her of what little financial support she qualifies for. With the patience of Mary Rambo, she withstands these hardships, as well as a long string of insults and offenses that includes her having been "dispossessed" in 1937. Furthermore, although Ellison finds her "gloomy" and vocal about things like the inadequacy of housing in Harlem ("these ole holes we have to live in can get mighty cold. Now can't they though?"), she endures even the worst outrages of her life with generally good humor.[18] Not so Ellison, whose apparent frustration moves him to "make more" of her story than she has herself.

When he has given Mrs. Jackson her chance to speak on her own terms, he appends a political analysis of her circumstances. As Lawrence Jackson puts it, he uses her story to "invoke the necessity of extending the powers of government" to combat the abuses that the African-American community faces.[19] This is, undeniably, an effective means of making his case. In the process, however, he tempers the celebration of her fortitude with a pragmatic (almost sociological) emphasis on her environment. He also transforms the individual "she" into a nameless "they"; furthermore, and perhaps most strikingly, he intrudes on the boundaries of her personal identity, referring in the course of his analysis to the "Mrs. Jacksons of Harlem" as a group that "offers one of the best arguments for the stabilization of prices and the freezing of rents."[20]

This is not an inappropriate method for making the case that Ellison wants to make in 1942; indeed, the essay is quite compelling in its balance of personal anecdote and political platform. But in this instance, the political program seems somewhat externally imposed. When, for instance, Ellison claims at the end of the essay "Mrs. Jackson's reality must be democratized so that she may clarify her thinking and her emotions," one has the sense that someone else's definition of "clarify" is in play here.[21] The real Mrs. Jackson, as Ellison ably demonstrates, is perfectly clear about how she feels and what there is to be done about it. Perhaps the young writer himself needs to clarify his position on her views, his sense of what it truly means to "democratize [her] reality." The reader finds the fruit of that process in the novel.

One might read Mary Rambo as a reimagined Mrs. Jackson. The two women have much in common, from their head-of-household status to their nurturance of an unnamed young black man who needs their assistance. Ellison even evokes the parallel by naming Mary's assistant in lifting Invisible Man Ralston Jackson; when he says, "*I'm Jenny Jackson's boy, you know I know you Miss Mary,*" she responds enthusiastically by enumerating his entire family and reminiscing about things she and his mother did together years ago. For all the value of these similarities, however, the two are most significantly alike (to borrow a phrase from the "other" Ralph Waldo) as representative women. Like Mrs. Jackson, Mary Rambo exists in the narrative as a type, although one that shows markedly different characteristics in the final analysis. She is, the novel tells us, a "stable, familiar force" that helps Invisible Man regain his sense of balance, both literally and figuratively.

Notably, Mary's help proves "painful" to the narrator at some points; her expectation that his education suits him to be a leader of the black community clashes with his own recent disillusionment about Bledsoe and the whole system associated with the State College for Negroes, after all (258). Still, she is a positive presence, a foundation that enables Invisible Man to begin reconciling the fragmentation of his identity that torments him throughout most of his quest. And, in making her initial case to him about his responsibilities to the community, she sounds a hopeful note that contrasts Mrs. Jackson's voice in "The Way It Is." While Invisible Man eats the soup she provides, Mary points out to him that young people like him "got to lead and you got to fight and move us all on up a little higher." She also notes "it's the ones from the South that's got to do it, them what knows the fire and ain't forgot how it burns." Having charged him with this, she then offers the following caution: "don't let this Harlem git you. I'm in New York, but New York ain't in me, understand what I mean?" (255).[22]

Mary's refusal to submit to her environment enables her to maintain a strong sense of self and thereby to become something of a community icon. As such, she provides Invisible Man the foundation on which to build his own sense of self. Strikingly, though, Mary's positive resistance to Harlem counters the statements of the "real" Mrs. Jackson in "The Way It Is." As Ellison prepares to leave her, Mrs. Jackson remarks "A friend of mine that moved up on Amsterdam Avenue . . . wanted to know why I don't move out of Harlem. So I told her it wouldn't do no good to move 'cause anywhere they let us go gets to be Harlem right on."[23] For all of her resilience in the face of suffering, Mrs. Jackson sounds a note of resignation here that shifts the reader's perception of her situation. It also prepares the reader, in a sense, for the political conclusion of the essay, the abstraction of this individual woman into a crowd of "Mrs. Jacksons."

In contrast, Mary's statement helps set Invisible Man on the road to reconciling his present and past, the quest that will finally lead him to some understanding of his identity. This is, of course, not a smooth path; but one of the pitfalls that he encounters along the way and its relationship to his time with Mary is particularly important in relation to this question, too. Mary makes Invisible Man aware enough of his world to move him to speak out for the evicted couple. That, in turn, spins him into the vortex of the Brotherhood, arguably one of the most nefarious forces he encounters in his journey.

In "The Way It Is," one striking element is the resonance between the Brother-hood's program and the final paragraphs of the *New Masses* essay. Both become, at least temporarily, a framework for making sense of experience. But, as Invisible Man eventually learns, the Brotherhood is not the answer that he seeks.

By moving his fictional narrator from an encounter with the individual, through the reliance on the political left, and beyond it to some new vision of selfhood, Ellison completes the arc of unified human experience that he describes so forcefully in the BBC interview. He thereby takes the initial accomplishment of his *New Masses* essay a significant step farther towards that larger "truth" that he says the novelist should be concerned with. And, ulti-mately, it is not just the radical left that Ellison objects to with this revision. In *The Craft of Ralph Ellison,* O'Meally makes a compelling case that the Brotherhood stands in the novel not just for the Communist Party but for the multiple groups of "white American activists" who "betray their black coun-trymen" and "use blacks and their art for narrow political ends."[24] This sug-gests even greater significance for the encounter with Mary Rambo, as it effectively makes her the touchstone for the narrator's (and thereby the author's) resistance to all corrupting political agendas.

Cast a bit more broadly, that rejection of confining political opinions also includes Ellison's suspicions of politicized social science, especially sociology. Lawrence Jackson dates Ellison's disaffection from sociology to his Tuskegee years, when he read Robert Park's work[25] for Professor Ralph Davis.[26] Out-raged by Park's sweeping generalizations about "innate black passivity," the author steeled himself against racial essentialism, a stance that he would maintain throughout his life.[27] In 1944, he brought his distrust of sociology and his repu-diation of essentialism to bear in *"An American Dilemma:* A Review," an essay written for the *Antioch Review* that remained unpublished until its inclusion in *Shadow and Act.* The review begins with an accounting of Ellison's early strug-gles with sociology, and then assesses the weaknesses of Myrdal's two-volume work. In taking the Swedish sociologist to task for his minute description of black suffering and his complete inability to see African-American culture, Ellison sounds a call for a new way of seeing the community.

Myrdal's study, which comprises 11 sections, 45 chapters, 10 appendices, and some 1,400 pages, takes as its central theme the notion "that the race prob-lem was a conflict between verbally honored American ideals and the pervasive practice of white racism."[28] As Walter Jackson notes, "Myrdal's book . . . pro-vided a detailed analysis of racial discrimination and an argument that interven-tion at a number of points by governments and private groups could break the vicious circle."[29] In these terms, the book has much to offer an American pub-lic not intimately acquainted with, or at least not necessarily willing to address, the horribly oppressive conditions under which most African Americans lived in the moments of the book's composition and publication. Indeed, these attributes have much to do with the book's success. Although it was hardly uniformly praised, "for two decades" it was a touchstone text for "people of various persuasions" concerning "black-white relations."[30] Indeed, it was particularly important for African Americans; David Southern notes that blacks tended to review the book favorably, although, he notes, "Ralph Ellison and Carter Woodson . . . unleashed hostile attacks . . . that anticipated the black nationalists of the 1960s."[31]

When Ellison takes up the task of critiquing the book, he does not overlook its accomplishment. Indeed, in cataloguing Myrdal's "microscopic" analysis of African-American life, he goes so far as to note "some of the insights are brilliant, especially those through which he demonstrates how many Negro personality traits, said to be 'innate,' are socially conditioned."[32] Admitting that, he nevertheless objects to the narrowness of Myrdal's conclusions, complaining that the Swedish sociologist relegates black life to a pattern of reactions to white pressures. With barely contained outrage, he asks "can a people . . . live and develop for over three hundred years simply by *reacting*? Are American Negroes simply the creation of white men, or have they at least helped to create themselves out of what they found around them?" The answers to Ellison's questions are, in his view, obvious; he has little patience with this reductive view of African-American culture, and suggests an alternative response for blacks. In Lawrence Jackson's terms, he sees that Myrdal should have concerned himself with "an analysis of the cultural forms and rituals which Negroes have actively chosen in the face of the 'higher values' of white America."[33] He subsequently answers that charge in his novel, which is of course replete with considerations of black cultural forms.[34] One finds an especially evocative response in the description of Invisible Man's eulogy for Tod Clifton and his assessment of the crowd's reaction to his speech.

The very act of staging the funeral marks an important realignment of the narrator's priorities. As he looks down at the crumpled Sambo doll he took from Clifton in the moments before his murder, Invisible Man thinks, "the incident [the sale of the dolls] was political. . . . The political equivalent of such entertainment is death" (447). And yet, all of his Brotherhood training to the contrary, Invisible Man cannot rest comfortably with that notion. Were he merely able to follow the party line, he would disassociate himself with Clifton immediately. Because he is more human than that, though, he thinks the situation through and sees how he can both honor Clifton's life and use his death to serve the community. Or at least he thinks it will serve the community, because he has not yet fully realized the depths of betrayal that the Brotherhood is capable of. Unlike the other members, he can still see Clifton the individual beyond the obscenity of his actions. This awareness, which will ultimately set him at odds with, then apart from, Brother Jack and the rest of the committee, sustains him as he moves forward to the funeral and prepares him for one of the most important realizations he has on the path to enlightenment.

As the crowd moves Clifton's coffin forward to the temporary platform in Mount Morris Park, they sing a song, "There's Many A Thousand Gone," which is started by an elderly black man walking in the procession. Invisible Man watches intently, recognizing the heritage and the emotional impact of the song.[35] Fleetingly jealous of the singer for his ability and willingness to raise the song, he realizes in the moment before he is to speak that he has just confronted "something for which the theory of Brotherhood had given [him] no name" (453). Disarmed by this insight, he nevertheless must find something to say to this crowd that has assembled at his behest. And so, with "no idea of a ritual" to keep the event a "Brotherhood funeral," he speaks simply and from the heart (454). The short, declarative sentences and the clinical descriptions almost threaten to depersonalize the account of Clifton's life and death; but, throughout the speech, Invisible Man keeps repeating the phrase that saves this speech from detachment: "His name was Clifton" (455).

In making this point, Invisible Man keeps the eulogy from being "political" in the conventional sense. He knows this as he does it, and he reacts with despair, recognizing that "Brother Jack probably wouldn't approve of it at all" but also aware that this is the speech that he has to give under these circumstances (457). What the reader and author know, despite the narrator's convictions to the contrary, is that the great strength of the speech is its transcendence of conventional rhetoric to achieve the remarkably personal insights that come from the recurrent emphasis on the slain individual. By telling the particulars of Clifton's story as he does, Invisible Man finds a way to touch on the universal experiences of injustice and exploitation that the crowd knows. When he figuratively puts the community in the coffin with Clifton, for instance, he has a powerful metaphor for substandard housing.[36] When he talks about the cop with "an itching finger and an eager ear for a word that rhymed with 'trigger,'" Invisible Man effectively evokes the systemic racism that affects the majority of interactions between police and community members. Still, throughout this process, he maintains a crucial balance. Even as he traces the inevitability of Clifton's murder to its logical conclusion, he does not let his congregation forget the individual who has been lost.

He also keeps another important kind of equilibrium in play here. As he gets to the universals of pain, he also finds the universals of joy that the crowd can share. Counseling them against reaction (a point that evokes Ellison's problem with Myrdal's thesis), he recounts the pleasures awaiting the members of the congregation in their community: cold beer, good music, conversation, and entertainment. He does this neither to cheapen the suffering nor to mock the crowd; rather, he uses these simple examples to demonstrate the richness, the complexity, of African-American life. This is not a monolithic community which has been uniformly violated; it is, in fact, a group of people, each of whom will react in his or her own way to this tragedy. Through his telling of Clifton's story, Invisible Man comes to know this. Ellison conveys that in the narrator's remark as the service ends: "as I took one last look I saw not a crowd but the set faces of individual men and women" (459). This statement is a far cry from Ellison's earlier assertion about "the Mrs. Jacksons" of Harlem; as such, it refutes the social scientific assumptions about dealing with "the race," assumptions that Myrdal also falls victim to.

Perhaps even more importantly, though, the view of the crowd as individuals repudiates one of Myrdal's fundamental premises about "the Negro problem." If, as he claimed, it is "really a white problem," then one need not be aware of the black community as folks—only as the folk, and with little, if any, concern for the state of their souls.[37] What Ellison provides in the account of Clifton's funeral is a look at the narrator coming awake, once again able to see the community as folks. In doing so, he achieves a version of the "deeper science" that Ellison calls for in 1944, the medium that will allow for effective analysis of "what is happening among the masses of Negroes."[38] In this instance, what is happening is a community-derived ritual that takes the place of any politicized, formal agenda. As the spontaneous eruption of the spiritual indicates, it is a ritual saturated with cultural significance, the product of a history that is part of how "Negroes have made a life upon the horns of the white man's dilemma."[39] By creating the fictional context that conveys the truth of these experiences to readers who have no lived frame of reference for either the murder or the ritual, the author taps into the universal undercurrents that convey the novel's social power.

The heart of that social power lies in the novel's ability to change the reader's perception of the boundaries and connections that define individual and racial identity. Again, with its famous final question, the novel calls on each of us to rethink all of our beliefs about the self. And this transformative power of Ellison's word obviously, and undeniably, lives on, in the continuing significance of this landmark novel.

Perhaps Ellison's greatest contribution to the elevation of the *body politic* beyond the limitations of conventional, racialist constructions of identity is his conveyance of this challenge to the readers. By figuring out how we shall live, we can know who we are. And, as Ellison tells us, when we know who we are, we will be free.

ENDNOTES

1. Jerry Gafio Watts, *Heroism and the Black Intellectual* (Chapel Hill: University of North Carolina Press, 1994), 49.

2. Alfred Chester and Vilma Howard, "The Art of Fiction: An Interview" (1954), in *Conversations with Ralph Ellison*, eds. Maryemma Graham and Amritjit Singh (Jackson: University of Mississippi Press, 1995), 8.

3. Richard Kostelanetz, "An Interview with Ralph Ellison" (1965), in *Conversations with Ralph Ellison,* eds. Maryemma Graham and Amritjit Singh (Jackson: University of Mississippi Press, 1995), 87.

4. Kostelanetz, 97.

5. O'Meally, 53.

6. Ralph Ellison, "Harlem is Nowhere" (1948), in *The Collected Essays of Ralph Ellison,* ed. John Callahan (New York: Modern Library, 1995), 322.

7. Lawrence Jackson, *Ralph Ellison: Emergence of Genius* (New York: John Wiley & Sons, 2002), 497.

8. Jackson, 497.

9. Jackson, 498.

10. Ellison, "Harlem is Nowhere," 320, 325.

11. Ellison, "Harlem is Nowhere," 327.

12. Ellison, "Harlem is Nowhere," 321.

13. O'Meally, 99, 100.

14. "And it is this which frightens me: Who knows but that, on the lower frequencies, I speak for you?" Ralph Ellison, *Invisible Man* (New York: Random House, 1952; reprint, New York: Vintage Books, 1980), 581.

15. Ralph Waldo Emerson, "Nature," in *Selections from Ralph Waldo Emerson,* ed. Stephen E. Whicher (Boston: Houghton Mifflin, 1957), 22.

16. Emerson, "Fate," in *Selections from Ralph Waldo Emerson,* ed. Stephen E. Whicher, 330.

17. Jackson, 414.

18. Ralph Ellison, "The Way It Is" (1942), in *The Collected Essays of Ralph Ellison,* ed. John Callahan (New York: Modern Library, 1995), 317.

19. Jackson, 414.

20. Ellison, "The Way It Is," 318.

21. Ellison, "The Way It Is," 319.

22. Cf. "Eddie's Bar," a transcript of a 1939 interview Ralph Ellison conducted as part of the Writer's Project of the federal Works Progress Administration: "Ahm in New York, but New York ain't in me. You understand?" *A Renaissance in Harlem: Lost Voices of an American Community,* ed. Lionel C. Bascom (New York: Avon Books, Inc., 1999), 36.

23. Ellison, "The Way It Is," 317.

24. O'Meally, 54.

25. Robert E. Park and Ernest W. Burgess, *Introduction to the Science of Sociology* (Chicago: University of Chicago Press, 1921).

26. Jackson, 226.

27. Jackson, 227.

28. David W. Southern, *Gunnar Myrdal and Black-White Relations: The Use and Abuse of* An American Dilemma, *1944–1969* (Baton Rouge: Louisiana State University Press, 1987), 54.

29. Walter A. Jackson, *Gunnar Myrdal and America's Conscience: Social Engineering and Liberalism, 1938–1987* (Chapel Hill: University of North Carolina Press, 1990), 240.

30. Southern, 71.

31. Southern, 72.

32. Ralph Ellison, "*An American Dilemma:* A Review" (1964), in *The Collected Essays of Ralph Ellison,* ed. John Callahan (New York: Modern Library, 1995), 339.

33. Jackson, 450.

34. Michel Fabre argues that with *Invisible Man,* Ellison was "aiming to rebut Gunnar Myrdal's sociology and to show that in Negro culture there was much of value for America as a whole." "From *Native Son* to *Invisible Man:* Some Notes on Ralph Ellison's Evolution in the 1950s," in *Speaking for You: The Vision of Ralph Ellison,* ed. Kimberly Benston (Washington: Howard University Press, 1987), 214.

35. For a discussion of Invisible Man's epiphany about the spiritual, see Robert G. O'Meally, *The Craft of Ralph Ellison* (Cambridge: Harvard University Press, 1980), 96–97.

36. "Such was the short bitter life of Brother Tod Clifton. Now he's in this box with the bolts tightened down. He's in the box and we're in there with him, and when I've told you this you can go. It's dark in this box and it's crowded. It has a cracked ceiling and a clogged-up toilet in the hall. It has rats and roaches, and it's far, far too expensive a dwelling." *Invisible Man,* 458.

37. Southern, 56.

38. Ellison, "*An American Dilemma:* A Review," 340.

39. Ellison, "*An American Dilemma:* A Review," 339.

Chapter 6

Invisible Man as Literary Analog to Brown v. Board of Education

ALFRED L. BROPHY

The year 2002 marked the fiftieth anniversary of the publication of *Invisible Man* as well as the one-hundred-fiftieth anniversary of another novel that remade Americans' understanding of race and law. For in 1852, one hundred years before Ralph Ellison's novel, *Uncle Tom's Cabin* appeared. Harriet Beecher Stowe responded—and helped shape the response of Americans—to the Fugitive Slave Act of 1850 and ultimately the institution of slavery itself. *Uncle Tom's Cabin* taught Americans to view blacks as humans and with humanity. Once we saw the Christ-like Uncle Tom, we could no longer abide slavery. With *Invisible Man* we again had a great, popular novel that signaled—and perhaps propelled—the changes that were coming in American law and culture. We could see the Invisible Man's humanity—and would no longer abide courts' duplicitous treatment of blacks so common in pre–World War II America.

Invisible Man captured Americans' emerging ideas about racial equality. It and *Brown v. Board of Education* (1954) drew upon a common reservoir of thinking—given strength by America's participation in World War II—about the imperative for equal treatment of individuals and for the need to eliminate the racial categorization so prevalent in Germany (as well as the United States). Both crystallized for Americans the costs of discrimination, while humanizing those discriminated against. As the novel and the court case uncovered the connections between black and white societies, they taught us how much black society had contributed to American society. As we learned that dropping black dye into white paint makes the white paint even whiter, we learned that discrimination had many costs. Some of those costs were born by the people who ostensibly were doing the discriminating, for they lost valuable assets.

This essay describes those growing sentiments in American legal culture and then suggests some ways that they parallel *Invisible Man*. It begins with an exploration of the baseline, the Supreme Court's 1896 decision in *Plessy v. Ferguson*, then explores the way that its "separate but equal" doctrine was modified over the next 58 years, until we reached *Brown*. After describing that legal doctrine, the essay contemplates the connections between *Invisible Man* and *Brown*, and suggests ways the Invisible Man authored *Brown*.

THE BASELINE: *PLESSY v. FERGUSON* AND THE ORIGINS OF SEPARATE BUT EQUAL

The central story is the doctrine announced in *Brown v. Board of Education* that black children must be treated indistinguishably from white children, and, ultimately, that race should be a factor in the government's decision making only in the most compelling of circumstances. But a baseline is needed to evaluate the development in legal doctrine and cultural understanding that makes that result possible. That baseline is the United States Supreme Court's 1896 decision in *Plessy v. Ferguson*. The Court addressed the constitutionality of a Louisiana statute that required railroads to provide separate accommodations for whites and blacks. Homer Plessy, a light-skinned black man, challenged the statute, arguing that it deprived him of the equal treatment of the law, because it segregated him from whites. The Court took Plessy's argument as resting on the belief that segregation stamped him as inferior. Yet, it rejected the possibility that segregation was unconstitutional because it stamped blacks as inferior. It concluded that how particular people felt is irrelevant in determining the constitutionality of an act:

> We consider the underlying fallacy of the plaintiff's argument to consist in the assumption that the enforced separation of the two races stamps the colored race with a badge of inferiority. If this be so, it is not by reason of anything found in the act, but solely because the colored race chooses to put that construction upon it.[1]

The Fourteenth Amendment protected political equality, so states could not draw distinctions based on race regarding political rights.[2] However, social relations received no such constitutional protection; they were subject to a low level of scrutiny.[3] *Plessy* said that the state could legislate social relations, such as where people could ride in railroad cars, as long as it established that there was a reasonable basis for drawing distinctions based on race.[4] With such a low burden to meet, it was easy for Louisiana to advance a rationale to support discriminatory legislation.

The opinion rests, as many have noted, upon nineteenth-century notions of the desirability of racial segregation, which taught the inferiority of blacks to whites and the need for accommodation between the races. "If the two races are to meet upon terms of social equality, it must be the result of natural affinities, a mutual appreciation of each other's merits and a voluntary consent of individuals. . . . If one race be inferior to the other socially, the Constitution of the United States cannot put them upon the same plane." The Court's fear of social equality, and contempt for anything that might tend to put blacks and whites together, resonated well with American culture at the time. It is not surprising that *Plessy* was decided a few months after Booker T. Washington's 1895 Atlanta Exposition Address, where he received applause for stating, "The wisest among my race understand that the agitation of questions of social equality is the extremest folly, and that progress in the enjoyment of all the privileges that will come to us must be the result of severe and constant struggle rather than of artificial forcing."[5] The Court's conclusion was based upon a view of the social inferiority of blacks and the belief that the law should take that difference in status into account.[6]

Justice Harlan's dissent reminds us that there existed at the time a strong opposition to *Plessy*'s wide discretion to the state to segregate based on race. He provided one of the most memorable phrases in all of American constitutional history by declaring that "our Constitution is color-blind."[7] He told what was obvious to any fair-minded observer at the time: that segregation was itself an incident of slavery. As Southern whites struggled to regain political and social control in the days following Reconstruction, black codes established segregation, extinguished voting rights for blacks, and limited opportunities for economic advancement. Harlan struggled for a legal interpretation that might show that everyone was equal before the law.[8] In language reminiscent of Mr. Norton (the white trustee whom Invisible Man chauffeurs around town), Harlan wrote about the common destiny of blacks and whites: that destiny "require[s] that the common government of all shall not permit the seeds of race hate to be planted under the sanction of law."[9] Yet, *Plessy* nurtured those seeds; it was the legal analog to the violence and racial legislation sweeping the South.[10]

Yet, there were others who carried on that struggle outside of the courts. Their advocacy of an alternative vision of equal protection held out the possibility of a different world. Some of those people lived in Oklahoma during Ellison's youth.

THE OKLAHOMA ORIGINS OF *BROWN:* OF ROSCOE DUNJEE, *McLAURIN v. OKLAHOMA STATE REGENTS*, AND . . . *INVISIBLE MAN*?

The Oklahoma of Ellison's youth was a place of struggle between competing visions of American race. Freed slaves and their descendants had come to the Oklahoma territory seeking a life less constrained by the norms of racial caste of more traditional Southern states. Yet white Southerners had also come to the territory and sought to replicate the society and the hierarchy they had known. The segregationists seemed to be winning the struggle. We see that in the persistent attempts by the Oklahoma legislature to prevent blacks from voting, to maintain unequal, segregated schools,[11] in the Oklahoma courts' failure to abide by even rudimentary standards of due process (embodied in the Jess Hollins case), and in the lynching that took place while law enforcement officials looked the other way—when they were not supervising it.[12]

But some blacks living in Oklahoma, like Roscoe Dunjee, had confidence that the rule of law (not the rule of police officers known as "laws") would someday prevail. As Ralph Ellison reminds us in "Perspective of Literature" and in "Roscoe Dunjee and the American Language,"[13] the Constitution—particularly through its equal protection clause—contains the seeds of justice. The idea is that the Constitution's covenant binds Americans to the dream that people should be treated equally. Dunjee expressed his confidence in the pages of his weekly paper, the Oklahoma City *Black Dispatch*. His editorials articulated an alternative worldview and an alternative view of the Fourteenth Amendment's "equal protection" clause. He argues that there should be uniform rules applied to all regardless of race.[14] Thus, there should be equal voting rights (and registration requirements); equal funding for schools, even if the schools were separate; equal (even if separate) treatment on railroads; and no laws requiring segregation in housing.[15]

The Growing Meanings of Equality:
The Protection of Personal Rights

Roscoe Dunjee's faith in the federal courts was sometimes fulfilled. Several important cases leading to *Brown* arose in Oklahoma. In the 1910s, the United States Supreme Court decided two cases from Oklahoma. The first, *McCabe v. Atchison, Topeka, and Santa Fe Railway* (1914), struck down Oklahoma's railroad passenger segregation statute, which permitted railroads to provide luxury accommodations only to those groups who rode with sufficient frequency to make such accommodations economically feasible. In essence, the statute permitted railroads to provide luxury accommodations to whites only. The statute was challenged unsuccessfully in both the lower federal courts and the Oklahoma Supreme Court. But in the United States Supreme Court, Justice White rejected the proposition that economic considerations might dictate result. White looked to the effect of the statute on each person to whom it was applied, not to blacks as a group.

> Whether or not particular facilities shall be provided may doubtless be conditioned upon there being a reasonable demand therefore, but, if facilities are provided, substantial equality of treatment of persons traveling under like conditions cannot be refused. It is the individual who is entitled

to the equal protection of the laws, and if he is denied by a common carrier, acting in the matter under the authority of a state law, a facility or convenience in the course of his journey which under substantially the same circumstances is furnished to another traveler, he may properly complain that his constitutional privilege has been invaded.[16]

McCabe was part of the Supreme Court's slow movement towards an understanding that the equal protection clause protected individual, not collective rights.[17] It became an important precedent, and was built upon in the education cases, which came to the court at the end of the 1930s. Those cases evaluated the equal protection clause as guaranteeing personal rights.

The second case to arise from Oklahoma in the 1910s was *Guinn v. United States.* It struck down Oklahoma's voter registration statute in 1915, which subjected registrants to a strict reading test. But those whose ancestors had been eligible to vote in January 1866—just before the Fifteenth Amendment (which guaranteed voting rights regardless of race) was ratified in 1870—were automatically eligible to vote. In essence, whites were eligible to vote because their grandfathers had been eligible; blacks were excluded. Chief Justice White again wrote the unanimous opinion for the court. Although the statute was neutral on its face—it did not establish a different standard for blacks and for whites—the court looked to the effect of the statute and concluded that the statute operated "in direct and positive disregard of the Fifteenth Amendment."[18] Where an NAACP official concluded that "[L]aw and order methods absolutely insure 'white superiority' in every way in which that superiority is real," the Supreme Court was beginning to understand that equal protection of the law required that the court look to the effect of legislation.[19] The Supreme Court began taking a realistic, rather than a formalist, view of racial legislation. In the wake of *Guinn,* the Oklahoma legislature passed another stringent registration law, which gave blacks only a few weeks to register. Otherwise, they were perpetually barred from registering. That law, too, was struck down—in 1939![20]

Oklahoma continued to provide cases for the Supreme Court to explore the meaning of the equal protection clause. In 1935, the Supreme Court overturned a death sentence against Jess Hollins for rape on the grounds that blacks had been systematically excluded from the jury rolls.[21] Each of those cases was part of the emergence of principles that aspired to (1) treat race realistically and (2) move in the direction of an understanding of the equal protection clause that guaranteed equal treatment to each individual. The question was, what constituted equal treatment?

Those Oklahoma cases inspired and were expanded by other cases, arising from other jurisdictions. In 1917, shortly after *McCabe,* the Supreme Court struck down racial zoning in *Buchanan v. Warley.* It addressed Louisville's zoning ordinance, which prohibited blacks from buying property on majority-white blocks and vice versa. Though the case arose from Louisville, it could just as easily have arisen from Oklahoma, for both Tulsa and Oklahoma City had similar ordinances and blacks in both places were making efforts to challenge the ordinances. *Buchanan,* relying upon *McCabe,* focused on the personal rights of homebuyers. *Buchanan* recognized the racial conflict underlying the zoning ordinance, but refused to allow those considerations to outweigh the constitutional rights of individual blacks. Despite the "feelings of race hostility which the law is powerless to control," the Court concluded that "its solution cannot be promoted by depriving citizens of their constitutional rights and privileges."[22]

Missouri ex rel. Gaines v. Canada, decided in 1938, shows the importance of *McCabe's* focus on personal rights. It is an important transition between *Plessy* and *Brown. Gaines* struck down a Missouri statute that segregated the University of Missouri Law School. Because there was no separate law school in Missouri, the state paid for blacks who wanted to attend law school to go to a neighboring state's school. *Gaines* struck down the statute on the grounds that the education provided was unequal:

> The white resident is afforded legal education within the State; the Negro resident having the same qualifications is refused it there and must go outside the State to obtain it. That is a denial of the equality of legal right to the enjoyment of the privilege which the State has set up, and the provision for the payment of tuition fees in another State does not remove the discrimination.[23]

Gaines's reasoning contained the destruction of the separate-but-equal principle, for once the Court found that geography could determine equality—that a law school located beyond the state's border was unequal—then there was little reason why separate facilities within a state should be equal, either. There was a strange formalism about the majority's opinion, for it drew a distinction based on the location of the alternate law school outside the state's borders. Thus, though it was attacking segregation, the *Gaines* majority clung to a formalist reasoning style, reminiscent more of the majority opinion in *Plessy* than Harlan's realistic dissent. And it was Justice McReynold's dissent, joined by Justice Butler, who emphasized a more practical look at what was actually happening: "The state should not be unduly hampered through theorization inadequately restrained by experience."[24] McReynolds saw two possibilities, each bad: Missouri may "abandon her law school and thereby disadvantage her white citizens without improving petitioner's opportunities for legal instruction; or she may break down the settled practice concerning separate schools and thereby, as indicated by experience, damnify both races."[25]

Meanwhile, back in Oklahoma, Roscoe Dunjee, by then on the national board of the NAACP, was still talking about filing lawsuits to demand equal treatment in the schools. After World War II, as in the 1910s, Oklahoma generated two important Supreme Court decisions. One of the most important cases leading into *Brown* arose from the University of Oklahoma's refusal to admit 68-year-old George McLaurin, a black teacher, to their Ph.D. program in education. Following a lower federal court's decision that the statute was unconstitutional, the Oklahoma legislature altered its statute regarding segregated education, allowing McLaurin to register, but requiring him to maintain strict separation from whites. Mr. McLaurin "was required to sit apart at a designated desk in an anteroom adjoining the classroom; to sit at a designated desk on the mezzanine floor of the library, but not to use the desks in the regular reading room; and to sit at a designated table and to eat at a different time from the other students in the school cafeteria."[26]

The Supreme Court recognized in *McLaurin,* as it had in cases since *McCabe,* that the University of Oklahoma's discrimination implicated Mr. McLaurin's personal rights. The restrictions "impair and inhibit his ability to study, to engage in discussions and exchange views with other students, and in general, to learn his profession."[27] But even worse was the effect that the restrictions would have on McLaurin's students:

> Our society grows increasingly complex, and our need for trained leaders increases correspondingly. [McLaurin's] case represents, perhaps, the epitome of that need, for he is attempting to obtain an advanced degree in education, to become, by definition, a leader and trainer of others. Those who will come under his guidance and influence must be directly affected by the education he receives. Their own education and development will necessarily suffer to the extent that his training is unequal to that of his classmates. State-imposed restrictions which produce such inequalities cannot be sustained.[28]

McLaurin recognized both the harms to individuals of discrimination based on race and the harm to people other than those most directly discriminated against.[29] *McLaurin* stood for the proposition that discrimination harmed the entire society—not just those who received the brunt of the discrimination. It recognized that discrimination has many costs. Most are borne by the people who are denied an adequate education, but society pays the cost for that discrimination, as well.

This convergence of legal doctrine, hence, began as a series of cases in the 1910s, gathering real force leading into the 1940s, and culminated in the understanding that treatment of blacks by the state in ways that made them unequal are prohibited unless done with compelling rationale. And though Roscoe Dunjee's faith in the courts was laughable to much of his community in the 1910s,[30] within his lifetime that faith in law was vindicated. To achieve such vindication, judges would look to the practical effect of legislation, and not just to the ambiguous statute, written in dissembling language. It would be only a small step, then, to the conclusion that segregation stamped one as inferior.

Running parallel to the evolution of legal doctrine was a host of cultural factors that pointed towards the breakdown of legally mandated segregation.

There was Americans' willingness to follow the equal protection principles and treat people equally, which owed much to the black press's demonstration of the hypocrisy of fighting wars for Democracy abroad and keeping segregation at home. There was also rising black political power and an increasingly integrated, mobile economy and society. World War II altered black aspirations and increased political and economic opportunity. The Cold War further changed the politics of race, as it exposed the hypocrisy of the United States' treatment of blacks.[31]

THE MEANINGS OF *BROWN*

So, the issues were aligned in May 1954 for a decision regarding the constitutionality of *Brown* that addressed several issues. On the lowest frequency, Chief Justice Warren's opinion explores what equal protection means: May the state separate people on the basis of race and then send the black children to different (and in most cases inferior) schools? Or, as Warren phrased the question, "Does segregation of children in public schools solely on the basis of race, even though the physical facilities and other 'tangible' factors may be equal, deprive the children of the minority group of equal educational opportunities?"[32] It is about treating American citizens as individuals, each deserving equal opportunity for education (and ultimately the right to participate in democracy) and the treatment of individuals fairly, without distinctions based on race.

Brown represents an important culmination of trends. First, and from a legal perspective, most important, are two trends in pre–World War II jurisprudence: a realist approach to racial legislation, looking to the actual effect of legislation on blacks, and a growth in the equal protection principle. Those changes have analogs in popular culture.[33] Warren exposes the lies of white southern existence and points to their actual effects. To get beyond the doctrine of "separate but equal," Warren asks how things appear in the "*light*" of public education's "full development and its present place in American life throughout the Nation."[34] He will look beyond mere questions of whether funding is equal (though in many instances it obviously was not). "Our decision . . . cannot turn on merely a comparison of these tangible factors in the Negro and white schools involved in each of these cases." We must look instead to "the effect of segregation itself on public education."[35] He acknowledges the centrality of education to life—much as the voting rights cases acknowledged the centrality of voting rights to achievement of other rights, really to democracy itself.[36] With such a realist approach to the effects of segregation, it is then an easy step to the conclusion that segregated education is "inherently unequal."[37]

Warren looks to the two cases in 1950 that involved segregation in higher education: *Sweat v. Painter* and *McLaurin*. Both struck down segregation statutes because the education facilities were unequal. *McLaurin* may be particularly helpful here, since Warren points out the detrimental effects of separate education (though he does not mention the harm to the community identified in *McLaurin*). He surmises that separating children from others "of similar age and qualifications solely because of their race generates a feeling of inferiority as to their status in the community that may affect their hearts and minds in a way unlikely ever to be undone."[38]

The second trend that *Brown* represents in pre–World War II jurisprudence is the development of the equal protection principle (and the corollary that the equal protection clause protects personal rights). Those cases were discussed in the previous section, mostly as outgrowths of the 1914 *McCabe* case arising from Oklahoma. The precedents multiplied in the years leading into *Brown*.[39]

Warren's elegant opinion avoided the moral evasions of previous judges; as the justices' conference notes illuminate, he understood the realities of segregation. It was part of the stamp of inferiority. As Warren said (quoting the Delaware trial court that had found segregation unconstitutional), "The policy of separating the races is usually interpreted as denoting the inferiority of the negro group."[40]

Brown represents, then, both a culmination of trends developing for decades before—many of whose doctrines were first articulated in Oklahoma cases—as well as reasoning based on *Plessy*. *Brown* held that separate facilities are unequal because they stamp blacks as inferior *and* whites as superior. Thus, *Brown* is in line with the separate-but-equal standard established by *Plessy*.[41] *Brown* is also forward-looking. It establishes what will, from then on, be the standard for judging invidious racial classification: that distinctions based on race are subject to close scrutiny and there must be compelling (not just reasonable) justifications for doing so. *Brown* represents the evolution of legal doctrine. Those doctrines emerged in conjunction with cultural changes that made segregation, at least at the national level, impractical and politically and socially unacceptable. Now let's turn to one of the cultural analogs to *Brown* and hear what the Invisible Man has to say about *Brown*. There are six ways that *Brown* and *Invisible Man* function as analogs.

HEARING THE INVISIBLE MAN'S MESSAGE: ANOTHER OKLAHOMA ROOT OF *BROWN*?

The excitement at the decision was such that as soon as he heard about it, Ellison wrote to his friend, M. D. Sprague, the librarian at the Tuskegee Institute:

> Well so now the Court has found in our favor and recognized our human psychological complexity and citizenship and another battle of the Civil War has been won. The rest is up to us and I'm very glad. The decision came while I was reading *A Stillness at Appomattox,* and a study of the

Negro Freedman and it made a heightening of emotion and a telescoping of perspective, yes and a sense of the problems that lie ahead that left me wet-eyed. I could see the whole road stretched out and it got all mixed up with this book I'm trying to write and it left me twisted with joy and a sense of inadequacy. . . . Well, so now the judges have found and Negroes must be individuals and that is hopeful and good. What a wonderful world of possibilities are unfolded for the children![42]

Those elegant sentences, which thanks to John Callahan's scholarship can be found seemingly everywhere, capture key elements of Ellison's optimism and vision.[43] There is the optimism that Ellison tells us about the triumph of the rule of law—not the rule of "laws" (or law enforcement officers).

That paragraph can serve as a starting point for linking Ellison, *Invisible Man*, and *Brown*. The specific elements of the Supreme Court's decision that capture Ellison's attention are the court's recognition of citizenship and recognition of blacks as individuals. Those points are central to both *Invisible Man* and *Brown*.

The analogy between *Invisible Man* and *Brown* begins at the point of *recognition of individualism and humanity of individuals*. Some of the scenes in *Invisible Man* are transparent in their depiction of group identity and the failure of whites to care about or even recognize the humanity of individuals: the Battle Royal scene, the statement to Invisible Man afterwards that "we mean to do right by you, but you've got to know your place at all times,"[44] and the accompanying realization that whites maintain a caste system that "keeps this Nigger boy running, but in the same old place." Other scenes explore in more complex ways the denial of humanity. The law, through the eviction of the elderly couple (who had themselves once been slaves), denied their humanity. While we could see the substance of their lives on the street, we could also see that the "laws"—the law enforcement officers as well as the New York landlord-tenant code—cared not at all about their life, or that they had freedom papers, expired life insurance policies, or pictures of Abraham Lincoln and Frederick Douglass. We learn that Tod Clifton, who met his death by "resisting reality in the form of a .38 caliber revolver in the hands of the arresting officer" (458), meant little to the police officer who shot him. Tod was there for the amusement of white people, and when he tried to act outside of "history" or to deny his place—when he acted outside of the expected modes of action—he was killed (457–58). "Our task," as Invisible Man discovers, "is that of making ourselves individuals" (354).[45] Through the novel, he accomplishes that task. The scenes correlate with *Brown*'s rejection of the American caste system. At the most base level, both are about the centrality of treating people as individuals, rather than groups. They both request that we look to individual characteristics and allow people to advance based on those characteristics.

For Ellison, the recognition of humanity, and the legal recognition that blacks shall no longer be subject to state-imposed discriminatory treatment, means that the rest of his message can be heard. As he wrote in his essay "Perspective of Literature," in language reminiscent of his first reaction to *Brown,* "The law ensures the conditions, the stage upon which we act; the rest of it is up to the individual."[46] Now we can telescope outward, looking at ways that *Invisible Man* relates in more distant ways to *Brown.*

At a close level, though not necessarily one that Ellison recognized in his letter to Sprague, *both the novel and the decision stem from a similar moral vision and both reject moral evasions.* Both are about looking at race through clear lenses and seeing what is actually happening, especially the actual effects of discrimination. Or, as the veteran at the Golden Day said, "for God's sake, learn to look beneath the surface. . . . Come out of the fog young man" (153). Part of the success of *Invisible Man* is that it makes us all look out from our veil of ignorance and see life as Invisible Man sees it. We are able to recognize moral evasions.[47] What else, after all, was the Invisible Man doing, but trying to teach us "what was really happening as [we] looked through?" (581).

During the eviction of the elderly couple from their Harlem apartment, we learn that there was a "Great Constitutional Dream Book" (280). But law had obscured it, making it difficult to read.[48] We see the difference between grand constitutional ideas and "law": namely, the law that enforced the landlord's rights and the law enforcement officers who carried out the eviction. Law represented a particular corruption of moral thought for Ellison. Though the elderly couple (and blacks more generally) was a "law abiding people," by which he meant they played on the unfair terms established by white society, they still were left without protection. Law had pushed out even religiously inspired ideas of fair treatment.[49]

That conflict between religion and law appears again in *Juneteenth,* when the jazz musician Alonzo Hickman, whose brother has been lynched following the false accusation that he raped a white woman, takes in the accuser. Hickman wanted to kill her, but he cannot. Instead, he delivers her child (whom he names Bliss), and then raises him with black ideals and morality in hopes that Bliss might eventually speak the truth to white America. The burden thus placed upon both Hickman, who becomes a minister, and Bliss is enormous. Too great, it seems, for Bliss is enticed away by visions of a white movie actress. Later in life he emerges as a Northern politician, the race-baiting Senator Adam Sunraider. During part of his last speech on the floor of Congress, Sunraider seems to speak from behind his mask of racism. Yet, Sunraider cannot quite break free; his speech returns to its typical racist imagery, and then he is shot by a black spectator.

The murder of Hickman's brother is yet another example of the breakdown of justice at the hands of "laws." As Hickman tried to make something more meaningful out of the surface violence, he turned from a career as a jazz musician (an occupation Ellison found admirable) to the ministry. *Juneteenth* depicted the conflict between law and religion: between Oklahoma "the city, with police power and big buildings and factories and the courts and the National Guard; and newspapers and telephones and telegraphs and all those folks who act like they've never heard of your Word" (137) and Hickman's religious teachings. Yet, Ellison sought to infuse moral values into the legal arena, for Hickman asks, "How the hell do you get love into politics or compassion into history?" (264)

Similarly, *Brown* recognizes that the mere equal facilities (if there were such a thing) cannot be equal.[50] That is part of remaking the equal protection clause; it is also part of the postwar realism of American courts. They cast aside their formal, analogical reasoning and asked what was really happening.[51] That rejection of dissembling cost the Supreme Court, just as it cost Invisible Man, for as he recalled at the end of the novel, "I was never more hated than when I was honest" (572). The same was true for the Supreme Court.[52]

Invisible Man and *Brown* look to the costs to the entire society: *The costs of discrimination fall upon both whites and blacks.*[53] Among the many examples in *Invisible Man,* one might look at the Liberty Paint scene, where workers were pitted against one another and where race played a part in both formation of union identity and in breaking unions. There is black on black discrimination, too. For example, Dr. Bledsoe threatens to lynch all blacks who challenge his power.[54] During the riot, Invisible Man recognizes the ways that Brotherhood fostered violence for their own means. The riot served many purposes, for whites and certain blacks, though not for the people of Harlem.[55]

McLaurin, which is one of the two key pillars of *Brown,* focuses explicitly on the cost of discrimination to the entire society. *Brown* focuses most of its attention on the costs of discrimination to blacks, addressing more obliquely the costs to society generally. *Brown* recognizes the centrality of education to American society and highlights the democratic costs to us all of the failure of proper education.

Brown looks primarily to the costs of discrimination to blacks, and part of its evidence (though a much smaller part than people believed at the time) comes from social science research. On those points, Ellison departs from *Brown.* Gunnar Myrdal's *American Dilemma: The Negro Problem and Modern Democracy* (1944), which was cited in a footnote in *Brown,* comes under particularly harsh attack by Ellison in a 1944 review written for *The Antioch Review,* but not published until 1964.[56] Ellison saw modern social science as a way of rationalizing and justifying the methods of economic and social control of the South.[57] Myrdal's social science left little room for blacks to be seen as anything other than objects, never more than the sum of their oppression. He found that both troubling and offensive. He observed, "Men have made a way of life in caves and upon cliffs; why cannot Negroes have made a life upon the horns of the white man's dilemma?"[58] Ellison thought that the "solution of the problem of the American Negro and democracy" rested only in part on white action. The solution required also "the creation of a democracy in which the Negro will be free to define himself for what he is and, within the larger framework of that democracy, for what he desires to be."[59] So, there may be some tension between *Brown's* citation of Myrdal and Ellison's rejection of parts of his work. Nevertheless, *Brown* derives from an understanding that blacks demand participation in the political and educational system.[60]

All of which brings one to a rationale that *Brown* uses to justify itself: *the cost to democracy of the failure to provide an education.*[61] Here *Brown* taps an important theme of Cold War America: the preservation of democracy. There was much work to be done after *Brown* to ensure voting rights for blacks, including the Voting Rights Act of 1965, which eliminated discriminatory voter registration requirements. In *Juneteenth,* Ellison offers a replacement for the invisibility trope, which more accurately captures the legal system's treatment of blacks: they are people "among the counted but not among the heard" (4). Thus, blacks are not completely invisible, but for the most important purposes are still ignored.

Invisible Man also makes us wonder about the possibilities of democracy. Invisible Man is skeptical of the motives of many who appear as leaders and even of those who follow them. Why did thousands appear to mourn Tod Clifton's death? To seek a thrill? (454). Were they his friends or were they using his death as a focal point? If so, was it "to stand touching and sweating and breathing and looking in a common direction?" (452). That leads to the question, "And could politics ever be an expression of love?" Later, Invisible Man is saddened that there were no politicians who saw blacks as anything more than "convenient tools for shaping their own desires!" (511). There were great potentialities, but the barriers to achievement were great. Blacks seeking to use the political process had little money, friends in government, unions, or business, and limited ability to communicate "except through unsympathetic newspapers" or Pullman porters. Yet, Ellison still has an optimism about the potential of democracy to reform, and of people to ultimately remake their world. Both the novel and the decision draw on an ideology of reform rather than maintenance of a racial caste system.

Moving toward further generality, *Invisible Man* and *Brown* both address *the malleability of history and its contribution to dissembling.* Invisible Man recognizes the power of history and Ellison presents two versions of its operation in the novel—the real versus the mythic, or the true way of seeing versus the self-delusional way. The legal framework contends against how people behave within it. These two versions of history, like the two versions of law (justice and dictates of the "laws"), clash in the novel just as they do in American society.

Invisible Man presents a montage of scenes from black history. Invisible Man's grandfather lived through much of that history—from Reconstruction, when blacks had some freedom (enough, at least, to purchase guns and to vote), through the dark ages afterwards, when the grandfather gave up his weapon, lived with his head in the lion, and agreed the white man to death. Similarly, the eviction scene presents vignettes from the complex history of black Americans from the pre–Civil War period through the 1930s in objects like the manumission papers and the newspaper clipping about Marcus Garvey. That history, of people laboring under terribly harsh conditions and still abiding by the law, exists alongside another history: the formalized, artificial version of history told by whites. Both of those histories, the myth and the reality, coexist and each exerts influence over the present.

This disjunction between myth and fact also appears in Tod Clifton's execution. When he tried to live outside of history, outside of the role that he was expected to play by the police officer and white society more generally, Clifton was killed. The way that Clifton's death was remembered in Harlem also conditioned how people there reacted. So the riot began because of what they understood about Clifton's execution.[62] And the way Clifton's death would be remembered by whites was defined by the white police officer.

While we might think that history is neutral, that it records "the patterns of men's lives" and that "all things of importance are recorded," the reality was quite different. As Invisible Man observed, "For actually it is only the known, the seen, the heard and only those events that the recorder regards as important that are put down, those lies his keepers keep their power by" (439). For Clifton, the police officer was judge, witness, *and* historian. To provide an alternative explanation, there was only the Invisible Man. He was left wondering, as happened so often in events involving race in American history, "Where were the historians today? And how would they put it down?" He also wondered, what would become of people who had no historians and who wrote no novels?

Those myths of history—of how blacks are expected to behave—condition the behavior "laws" (law enforcement officers, prosecutors, and judges) expect. When Brother Tarp tried to resist a white man who was taking advantage of him, Tarp paid with a life prison sentence. Tarp would likely never have gotten out, except that he took advantage of the fact that his jailors lost track of his identity and just lumped him together with others who had drowned during a flood. On this occasion, group identity had some benefits!

That is what *Brown* is about at the level of jurisprudence: a true history that looks through to events as they actually are. *Brown* also understands that segregation sprang up well after the Civil War ended—the history of which C. Vann Woodward called *The Strange Career of Jim Crow* (1955). Moreover, *Brown* recognizes that history works a magic of changing the conditions, the assumptions, and the understandings of the Constitution.[63] When *Plessy* offered fictitious histories of precedent and of the necessity of segregation, the Supreme Court could not break down the barriers of segregation. But when a new understanding of history and social reality came forth, bequeathed to us in works like W. E. B. Du Bois's *Black Reconstruction* (1935), then a more comprehensive history helped us understand that segregation was neither natural nor desirable.

Brown also represented a conception that the Constitution might change. We know from the Justices' conference notes that they believed that the Constitution's meaning might evolve. Here, there is a strange divergence between Ellison and the *Brown* Court, for Ellison drew a distinction between law as it was—or as it appeared—and what it ought to be.[64] Justice Black had the ability to see through the obfuscation. "I am compelled to say for myself that I can't escape the view that the reason for segregation is the belief that Negroes are inferior. I do not need a book to say that."[65] Or, as Chief Justice Warren said in conference, "The more I read and hear and think, the more I come to conclude that the basis of the principle of segregation and separate but equal rests upon the basic premise that the Negro race is inferior."[66]

Both the novel and the decision understand the fluid nature of history and what it means for us. Ellison sees *Brown* as another battle of the Civil War—and so do the justices. Ellison also sees the guarantee of equality as an original idea of the Constitution. His conception is not that the Constitution changes, but that we can return to that original covenant. Here, of course, he may be engaging in his own creation myth!

At the highest level of generality, there is yet another way that *Brown* connects to *Invisible Man*. It is the issue of *Dream vs. Reality: the dream of integration and of equal protection versus the reality of segregation.* This reality produced laws that compelled people to labor with little hope of advancement. The elderly couple evicted from their apartment were a law-abiding people, a theme that is repeated in *Juneteenth.* Yet, they are not given the benefit of justice. They had worked their whole lives and were left with virtually nothing. In fact, they had so little that the Invisible Man asked, How could they be evicted? From what would they be dispossessed? Their story was of the Constitutional Dream Book, which in 1952 held out so much hope—but had fulfilled it in such small ways. There are two stories in *Brown,* as well: the dream of the justices and the hard reality of entrenched segregation.

Ellison's mentor, Roscoe Dunjee, saw the possibility of the Constitution. Ellison did not at first see that possibility; he and his friends viewed Dunjee's confidence as a joke. They looked up to jazz musicians rather than hypocritical politicians and judges. But within a generation, Dunjee's ideas triumphed in the Supreme Court. That optimism, that world of possibility, appears in *Invisible Man* and makes it effective as a social novel. Much like *Uncle Tom's Cabin,* there is a prescription at the end. Where Stowe invites her readers to feel right and pray,[67] Ellison also had a personal prescription: to see others' humanity. Like Stowe, within a short time after it is published, *Invisible Man's* agenda is realized in law, at least, if not in reality.

ENDNOTES

1. *Plessy v. Ferguson,* 163 U.S. 537, 551 (1896).

2. *Plessy,* 544: "The object of the [Fourteenth] amendment was undoubtedly to enforce the absolute equality of the two races before the law, but, in the nature of things, it could not have been intended to abolish distinctions based upon color, or to enforce social, as distinguished from political, equality, or a commingling of the two races upon terms unsatisfactory to either."

3. *Plessy,* 544: "Laws permitting, and even requiring, their separation in places where they are liable to be brought into contact do not necessarily imply the inferiority of either race to the other, and have been generally, if not universally, recognized as within the competency of the state legislatures in the exercise of their police power."

4. *Plessy,* 550.

5. Booker T. Washington, *Up From Slavery: An Autobiography,* intro. Langston Hughes (1965), 142.

6. *Plessy,* 551: "Legislation is powerless to eradicate racial instincts or to abolish distinctions based upon physical differences, and the attempt to do so can only result in accentuating the difficulties of the present situation."

7. *Plessy,* 559: "The white race deems itself to be the dominant race in this country. And so it is, in prestige, in achievements, in education, in wealth, and in power. So, I doubt not, it will continue to be for all time, if it remains true to its great heritage, and holds fast to the principles of constitutional liberty. But in view of the Constitution, in the eye of the law, there is in this country no superior, dominant, ruling class of citizens. There is no caste here. Our Constitution is color-blind, and neither knows nor tolerates classes among citizens."

8. Harlan identified the discriminatory intent behind such legislation:

   It seems that we have yet, in some of the States, a dominant race—a superior class of citizens, which assumes to regulate the enjoyment of civil rights, common to all citizens, upon the basis of race. The present decision, it will be apprehended, will not only stimulate aggressions, more or less brutal and irritating, upon the admitted rights of colored citizens, but will encourage the belief that it is possible, by means of state enactments, to defeat the beneficent purposes which the people of the United States had in view when they adopted the recent amendments to the Constitution. . . . (*Plessy,* 560).

9. *Plessy,* 560.

10. See Ralph Ellison, *Going to the Territory,* in *The Collected Essays of Ralph Ellison,* ed. John F. Callahan (New York: Random House, 1995); J. Morgan Kousser, *Dead End: The Development of Nineteenth-Century Litigation on Racial Discrimination in Schools* (New York: Oxford University Press, 1986).

11. For example, see *Black v. Geissler,* 159 P. 1124 (Okla. 1916), which upheld discriminatory voting legislation passed in 1916 in the wake of the Supreme Court's invali-

dation of Oklahoma's grandfather clause and *Lane v. Wilson,* 307 U.S. 268 (1939), which struck down that same legislation. For commentary on the voting registration statutes, see "An Inflammatory Appeal," *Black Dispatch* 4 (October 15, 1920): "This law operated, as it was intended by its sponsors, to place the Negroes at a disadvantage although it did not bar them from the right of registration. It was the nearest approach to a grandfather clause that could be enacted at that time in face of the stringent attitude of the federal government against franchise discrimination because of race"; "Senseless Negroes," *Black Dispatch* 4 (July 9, 1920): "The ballot is the only medium with which in a democracy, one may protect his life, his property, and his happiness. It is a thing about which men of other races have fought and died. It is a thing which, when fully and completely in our hands, WILL STOP LYNCHING AND EVERY SORT OF DISCRIMINATION THAT HAMPERS US." See also Jimmie Lewis Franklin, *Journey Toward Hope: A History of Blacks in Oklahoma* (1982), which discusses violence and segregation legislation.

12. See *Hollins v. Oklahoma,* 295 U.S. 394 (1935). The Oklahoma Attorney General investigation of two lynchings that took place the last weekend in August 1920— of a black man in Oklahoma City and a white man in Tulsa—revealed evidence of law enforcement complicity in both cases. See "Investigation of Lynching of Roy Belton," Attorney General File 1018, Oklahoma State Archives, Oklahoma City; "Investigation of Lynching of Claude Chandler," Attorney General File 1017, Oklahoma State Archives, Oklahoma City.

13. Ralph Ellison, "Perspective of Literature" and "Roscoe Dunjee and the American Language," *Collected Essays,* 766–81 and 449–60, respectively.

14. "Upright Men Shall be Astonished," *Black Dispatch* 4 (August 15, 1919), which argued that rights were "equality with the white man to have his person, property and family protected from every form of lawlessness"; "Oklahoma's Rotten Educational Law," *Black Dispatch* 4 (January 21, 1921), which explained differential funding between black and white schools; "White Justice Likened Unto White Sepulchers," *Black Dispatch* 4 (June 4, 1920), which criticized the quality of justice in courts. See also "The Negro Before the Law," *Black Dispatch* 4 (January 28, 1921), a reprint of an editorial from the *Savannah Tribune,* which began, "There can be little inducement nowadays for Negro people to have confidence in the laws by which we are governed, in view of the brand of justice which is being meted out to Negroes in our courts."

15. I explore the content of these ideas, as well as the context where they arose, in Alfred L. Brophy, *Reconstructing the Dreamland: The Tulsa Riot of 1921— Race, Reparations, and Reconciliation* (New York: Oxford University Press, 2002) chaps. 1, 4.

16. *McCabe v. Atchison, Topeka, and Santa Fe Railway,* 235 U.S. 151, 161–62 (1914).

17. It rejected cases like *Cumming v. Richmond County Board of Education,* 175 U.S. 528 (1899), which had allowed the school board to close a high school for black students. In its place, the school board paid students' tuition at private schools, up to the amount of money the school board had spent on the students at the school that it closed (544).

18. *Guinn v. U.S.* 238 U.S. 347, 365 (1915).

19. See "Terrible Lessons," *Black Dispatch* 4 (August 22, 1919).

20. See *Lane v. Wilson,* 307 U.S. 268 (1939).

21. *Hollins v. Oklahoma,* 295 U.S. 394 (1935).

22. *Buchanan v. Warley,* 245 U.S. 60, 80–81 (1917). *Buchanan* thus distinguished between what was right and what was expedient, a calculation that *Plessy* had ignored.

23. *Missouri ex rel. Gaines v. Canada,* 305 U.S. 337, 349–50 (1938).

24. *Gaines,* 354.

25. *Gaines,* 353. He continued: "Whether by some other course it may be possible for her to avoid condemnation is matter for conjecture."

26. *McLaurin v. Oklahoma State Regents,* 339 U.S. 637, 639 (1950). Before the case came to the United States Supreme Court, the University ameliorated some of the more egregious discrimination.

27. *McLaurin,* 641.

28. *McLaurin,* 641.

29. In conference, Justice Jackson said, "Whites as well as blacks are victims of this system." Del Dickson, *The Supreme Court in Conference, 1940–1985* (2001), 640.

30. For example, see "The Facts Remain the Same," *Tulsa Star* 8 (September 18, 1920), which questioned the manhood of Dunjee's community, which trusted in the law enforcement rather than itself in protecting against lynching.

31. Michael Klarman provides a comprehensive catalog of the factors leading to *Brown.* See Michael Klarman, *Rethinking the Civil Rights and Civil Liberties Revolutions,* 82 *Virginia Law Review* 1 (1996). See also Carl Landauer, *Deliberating Speed: Totalitarian Anxieties and Postwar Legal Thought,* 12 *Yale Journal of Law & Humanities* 171 (2000). Klarman under-emphasizes both the legal and cultural significance of *Brown:* namely, the way it consolidated previous advances in civil rights law and legislation, as well as provided a catalyst and rallying-point, a staging base, for the legislative and court-based triumphs of the 1960s. The fact that the revolution has not been sustained is not the fault of *Brown,* nor of the justices, for revolutions are difficult to sustain. Once the fighting has pushed down the oppressive old system, it takes even more energy to create society anew. Moreover, old forces are not washed away in a brief fight, as historians of the American Revolution and Civil War know well. The power of conservatism is strong. Even those seeking a break with the past, as Ralph Waldo Emerson reminds us, are bound by it: "[S]o deep is the foundation of the existing social system, that it leaves no one out of it. . . . The past has baked your loaf, and in the strength of its bread you would break up the oven." Ralph Waldo Emerson, *The Conservative,* in *Ralph Waldo Emerson: Essays and Lectures,* ed. Joel Porte (New York: Library of America, 1983), 173, 178. The civil rights revolution needed perhaps even more energy to sustain it than to overcome segregation.

32. *Brown v. Board of Education of Topeka,* 347 U.S. 483, 493 (1954).

33. I avoid claiming any magic bullet status for *Brown.* While many recent interpretations of *Brown* fail to pay it sufficient reverence for its importance in the Civil Rights Revolution, it is also incorrect to credit it with the power to make changes by itself. See James T. Patterson, *Brown v. Board of Education: A Civil Rights Milestone and Its Troubled Legacy* (New York: Oxford University Press, 2001).

34. *Brown,* 492–93 (emphasis added).

35. *Brown,* 492.

36. Here, the cases were prescient, for it was growing black political strength in the North that made *Brown* conceivable.

37. *Brown,* 495.

38. *Brown,* 494. Here there is a significant divergence between *Invisible Man* and *Brown,* for Warren focuses on the oppression of children rather than the harm to the larger community. But in the intersection of law and literature, one would not expect an exact congruence between rationals.

39. For example, see *Shelley v. Kraemer,* 334 U.S. 1 (1948).

40. *Brown,* 494.

41. The words "separate but equal" do not appear in the majority opinion of *Plessy,* though they do in Harlan's dissent; see *Plessy,* 552. Indeed, it is not until *McCabe* (which struck down the Oklahoma railroad segregation statute) that a majority opinion in the Supreme Court uses that formulation and credits it to *Plessy.* See *McCabe,* 235 U.S. 151, 160.

42. Ralph Ellison, "'American Culture is of a Whole': From the Letters of Ralph Ellison," *New Republic,* intro. John F. Callahan (March 1, 1999), 38–39. The letter continues:

> For me there is still the problem of making meaning out of the past and I guess I'm lucky I described Bledsoe before he was checked out. Now I'm writing about the evasion of identity which is another characteristically American problem which must be about to change. I hope so, it's giving me enough trouble. Anyway, here's to integration, the only integration that counts: that of the personality. (39)

It has become fashionable to criticize *Brown* because it failed to sufficiently undo white supremacy or because it relied on rhetoric of damage done to the black psyche. See, e.g., Daryl Michael Scott, *Contempt and Pity: Social Policy and the Image of the Damaged Black Psyche,* 1880–1996, 119–36 (Chapel Hill: University of North Carolina, 1997); *cf. What Brown v. Board of Education Should Have Said* (Jack M. Balkin, ed.) (New York: New York University Press, 2001). It remains important to remember at the time, however, the optimism—even ecstasy with which the opinion was greeted. For just as *Invisible Man* drew criticism as perspectives changed, so has *Brown.* It is not so clear to me, however, that the first impression—in either case—was wrong.

43. For example, see Patterson, *Brown v. Board of Education,* xiv (quoting Ellison).

44. Ralph Ellison, *Invisible Man* (New York: Random House, 1952), 31. All subsequent citations will be noted parenthetically in the text by page number, and emphases in original unless otherwise noted.

45. It is a problem of the individual against the group. Ellison carefully pointed out the dangers of subordinating the individual to community values. For example, see *Invisible Man,* 502, and Julia Eichelberger, *Prophets of Recognition: Ideology and the Individual in Novels by Ralph Ellison, Toni Morrison, Saul Bellow, and Eudora Welty* (Baton Rouge: Louisiana State University Press, 1999).

46. Ralph Ellison, "Perspective of Literature," *Collected Essays,* 781.

47. For example, see Ellison's 1981 introduction to *Invisible Man,* where he recalls a poster for a revival of an *Uncle Tom* show that reminded him of "the tenacity which a nation's moral evasions can take on when given the trappings of racial stereotypes, and the ease with which its deepest experience of tragedy could be converted into blackface farce" (xvi).

   The rejection of moral evasions, the human search for a direct relationship with the Universe, links Ellison to his namesake Ralph Waldo Emerson. Emerson urged American scholars (and by implication judges) to reject out-moded ideas. In his 1837 essay *Nature,* Emerson reminded Americans, "There are new lands, new men, new thoughts." It was natural, then, for them to "demand our own works and laws and worship." Ralph Waldo Emerson, *Nature* in *Emerson's Essays,* 7. Ellison gives us a twentieth century novelist's presentation of those same ideas.

   In other places, like Senator Sunraider's speech in Ralph Ellison's *Juneteenth* (New York: Random House, 1999), Ellison presents a parallel with Emerson's American Scholar Address. The Senator, speaking through his mask of racism, recalls the transcendent (perhaps Transcendental?) ideas behind the Nation's founding (14). Americans headed for the Territory in an attempt to break with the past. Americans had an optimism about the future because they are not bound by the past. Echoing what Emerson said in "The Conservative," Senator Sunraider tells us about the power the past exercises, for it has taught us lessons. Yet, we can move beyond the past. (15)

48. Perhaps it was the "eye of the law," which Justice Harlan referred to in *Plessy,* that had been clouded? See *Plessy,* 559.

49. "*Laws,* that's what we call them down South! Laws! And we're wise, and law-abiding. And look at this old woman with her dog-eared Bible. What's she trying to bring off here? She's let her religion go to her head, but we all know that religion is for the heart, not for the head." *Invisible Man,* 278.

   As the Invisible Man was appealing to the police officers and the crowd to let the elderly couple stay, he contrasted law's dispossession with religion: "They're facing a gun and we're facing it with them. They don't want the world, but only Jesus. They only want Jesus, just fifteen minutes of Jesus on the rug-bare floor. . . . How about it, Mr. Law? Do we get our fifteen minutes worth of Jesus? You got the world, can we have our Jesus?" (279) Later, he concluded, that law had excluded the possibility of religion: "All we have is the Bible and this Law here rules that out" (280). See also *Invisible Man*, 500: "Hambro's lawyer's mind was too narrowly logical." Ellison follows in the tradition of Harriet Beecher Stowe, who also contrasted warm sentiments of the heart with the cold, logical legal mind in her trilogy on slave law: *Uncle Tom's Cabin, A Key to Uncle Tom's Cabin*, and *Dred: A Tale of the Great Dismal Swamp*. See Alfred L. Brophy, *Humanity, Utility, and Logic in Southern Legal Thought: Harriet Beecher Stowe's View in* Dred: A Tale of the Great Dismal Swamp, 78 *Boston University Law Review* 1113–61 (1998).

50. Ellison's later work also emphasized the inability to measure equality in purely economic terms. He deals in similar terms with the theme of debasing that takes place when something is associated with blacks. In "Cadillac Flambé," Senator Sunraider proposed using law to rename a Cadillac and thus cheapen the Cadillac because of its association with blacks. In turn, Sunraider's renaming would debase blacks. "It's that he would low-rate a thing so truly fine as a *Cadillac* just in order to degrade *me* and my *people*. He was accusing *me* of lowering the value of the auto, when all I ever wanted was the very best!" Ralph Ellison, *Cadillac Flambé*, 16 *American Review* (1973), 261. The renaming took away the equality that LeeWillie Minifees' success had purchased: "*Money?* LeeWillie, can't you see that it ain't no longer a matter of money? Can't you see it's done gone way past the question of money? Now it's a question of whether you can afford it in terms *other than money*."

51. For democracy as a central value, see Morton J. Horwitz, *The Warren Court and the Pursuit of Justice: A Critical Issue* (New York: Hill and Wang, 1998).

52. See Morton J. Horwitz, *The Transformation of American Law, 1870–1960: Crisis of Legal Orthodoxy* (Cambridge: Harvard University Press, 1992), which discusses academics' vitriolic reaction to *Brown*, and James T. Patterson, *Brown v. Board of Education*, 86–117 (New York: Oxford University Press, 2001).

53. Richard Case's review of *Invisible Man* phrased the central vision of *Invisible Man* as how whites cannot *see* blacks as individuals, and how that fate befalls everyone, now. Richard Case, *A Novel is a Novel*, 14 *Kenyon Review* (1952), 678–84; reprinted in *The Critical Response to Ralph Ellison*, ed. Robert J. Butler (Westport, Conn.: Greenwood Press, 2000), 35, 37.

54. See *Invisible Man*, 143: "The white folk tell everybody what to think—except men like me. I tell *them;* that's my life, telling white folk how to think about the things I know about. . . . I'll have every Negro in the country hanging on tree limbs by morning if it means staying where I am." See also *Invisible Man*, 372, for the argument between Clifton and Ras the Exhorter.

55. See *Invisible Man*, 558: "They want the mobs to come uptown with machine guns and rifles. They want the streets to flow the blood, black blood and white blood, so that they can turn your death and sorrow and defeat into propaganda. It's simple, you've known it a long time. It goes, 'Use a nigger to get a nigger.' "

56. Ralph Ellison, *"An American Dilemma:* A Review" (1944), *Collected Essays,* 328.

57. *"An American Dilemma:* A Review," *Collected Essays,* 329–30.

58. *"An American Dilemma:* A Review," *Collected Essays,* 329.

59. *"An American Dilemma:* A Review," *Collected Essays,* 329. There is that conflict between religion and law in *Invisible Man,* which is expanded in *Juneteenth;* for example, see *Juneteenth,* 137 and 266.

60. One wonders what the opinion written by the Invisible Man might have looked like! How might the "great constitutional dreambook" (280) differ from *Brown* if the Invisible Man—or his mentor, Roscoe Dunjee—had written it?

61. *Brown,* 493: "Compulsory school attendance laws and the great expenditures for education both demonstrate our recognition of the importance of education to our democratic society. . . . It is the very foundation of good citizenship."

62. For example, see *Invisible Man,* 448: "[I]t was necessary that we make it known that the meaning of [Clifton's] death was greater than the incident or the object that caused it. Both as a means of avenging him and of preventing other such deaths"; *Invisible Man,* 447: "The shooting was all that was left of him now, Clifton had chosen to plunge out of history and, except for the picture it made in my mind's eye, only the plunge was recorded, and that was the only important thing."

63. See Lawrence M. Friedman, *"Brown* in Context," *Race, Law, and Culture: Reflections on* Brown v. Board of Education, ed. Austin Sarat (New York: Oxford University Press, 1997), 49, 60.

64. Ellison was concerned with the disjuncture between the way law defined people and the reality of facts. His notes to *Juneteenth* express the conflict between how law defined blacks and the facts of their lives:

> The law deals with facts, and down here the facts are that we are weak and inferior. But while it looks like we are what the law says we are, don't ever forget that we've been put in this position by force, by power of numbers, and the readiness of those numbers to use brutality to keep us within the law. Ah, but the truth is something else. We are not what the law, yes and custom, says we are and to protect our truth we have to protect ourselves from the definitions of the law. Because the law's facts have made us outlaws. Yes, that's the truth, but only part of it; for Bliss, boy, we're outlaws in Christ and Christ is the higher truth. (354)

> Ellison set that disjuncture between law and reality in "Cadillac Flambé," when LeeWillie Minifees protested the proposed law renaming the Cadillac the "Coon Cage Eight." By renaming the Cadillac, Senator Sunraider's proposed law would have labeled and degraded blacks.

65. Dickson, *The Supreme Court in Conference,* 648 (conference notes for December 13, 1952). One might compare Black's progressive view with Justice Stanley Reed's support for segregation. Reed projected gradual accommodation, much like, one imagines, Bledsoe or the trustee:

The race came out of slavery a short time ago. . . . Negroes have not thoroughly assimilated. There has been some amalgamation of the races. . . . We must try our best to give Negroes benefits. We must start with the idea that there is a large and reasonable body of opinion in various states that separation of the races is for the benefit of both. Then there is the determination of when the changes are to be made. There has been great, steady progress in the South in the advancement of the interests of the Negroes. . . . Segregation is gradually disappearing.

66. Dickson, *The Supreme Court in Conference,* 654. *See also id.* at 660 (Justice Minton) ("The only justification for segregation is the inferiority of the Negro. So many things have broken down these barriers. Slavery went out with the Civil War. Then came the Fourteenth Amendment, which was intended to wipe out the badges of slavery and inferiority. . . . The Fourteenth Amendment says *equal rights,* not *separate but equal. Separate* is a lawyer's addition to the language that came in by this Court.").

67. Harriet Beecher Stowe, *Uncle Tom's Cabin* (New York: Penguin, 1983), 472–73.

Chapter 7

Ralph Ellison and the Problem of Cultural Authority: The Lessons of Little Rock

KENNETH W. WARREN

In her controversial essay "Reflections on Little Rock," originally written for *Commentary* magazine but published in the 1959 volume of *Dissent,* Hannah Arendt questioned the wisdom of the NAACP for deciding to place children on the front lines during the 1957 school integration crisis in Little Rock, Arkansas. Insisting on her *"sympathy for the cause of the Negroes as for all oppressed or underprivileged peoples,"* Arendt nonetheless faulted the desegregation effort for having contributed to recent social trends "abolishing the authority of adults" by denying "their responsibility for the world into which they have borne their children" and their "duty of guiding them into it."[1] Arendt's critique of the NAACP's tactics and strategy derived from her general fear, reiterated throughout her writings during the 1950s, that a failure to distinguish properly among political and social realms of human behavior gravely threatened political freedom.[2] The chief error of what she termed "forced integration" was that it confused the political realm with the social realm and thus failed to recognize that what "equality is to the body politic— its innermost principle—discrimination is to society."[3] The point she drew from her reflections was that forcing "parents to send their children to an integrated school against their will means to deprive them of the rights which clearly belong to them in all free societies—the private right over their children and the social right to free association."[4]

Predictably, Arendt's comments did not strike a positive note among liberal readers. Not only had *Commentary* found the article problematic when Arendt originally submitted it (and consequently attached conditions for publication that led Arendt to withdraw it),[5] but *Dissent,* in agreeing to publish it, had insisted on preceding "Reflections" with a disclaimer ("We publish it not because we agree with it—quite the contrary!") and on following it with two essays, by David Spitz and Melvin Tumin, respectively, attacking Arendt's arguments.[6] In deference to Arendt, *Dissent* also agreed to give her space in a subsequent issue to reply to her critics, and in making her response, Arendt elaborated her argument in the following way:

> The point of departure of my reflections was a picture in the newspapers, showing a Negro girl on her way home from a newly integrated school; she was persecuted by a mob of white children, protected by a white friend of her father, and her face bore eloquent witness to the obvious fact that she was not precisely happy. The picture showed the situation in a nutshell because those who appeared in it were directly affected by the Federal Court order, the children themselves. My first question was: What would I do if I were a Negro mother? The answer: Under no circumstances would I expose my child to conditions which made it appear as though it wanted to push its way into a group where it was not wanted.[7]

Arendt's "Reply," which focused on the news photograph of a young black girl being taunted by white teenagers and adults, was an attempt to make vivid the charge she had leveled in her original essay: The desegregation crisis in Little Rock represented the triumph of mob rule—the "sorry fact" that "the town's law-abiding citizens left the streets to the mob, that neither white nor black citizens felt it their duty to see the Negro children safely to school."[8] Her elaboration amounted to a reiteration of her main charge that school desegregation as pursued in Little Rock had devolved into the evacuation of all legitimate authority, particularly parental authority, from the scene of the crisis.

Arendt's critics were not confined to the pages of *Dissent* and of these critics perhaps the most significant was Ralph Ellison, who took advantage of several occasions to mention what he felt was Arendt's severe misreading of the Little Rock events. In "The World and the Jug," Ellison—no doubt relishing the irony of his gambit—disparaged Irving Howe's "Black Boys and Native Sons" by observing that Howe, who as editor of *Dissent* had distanced himself from Arendt's position on Little Rock, had now "written with something of the Olympian authority that characterized Hannah Arendt's 'Reflections on Little Rock.' "[9] This Olympian distance, which derived from Arendt's (and Howe's) lack of cultural knowledge of the Negro's situation in the South, had been fatal to the accuracy of their analyses. Both writers, Ellison contended, had missed the full human dimension of the situations they were observing.

Ellison subsequently built his case against Arendt in Robert Penn Warren's *Who Speaks for the Negro?* when he remarked that Arendt's criticisms of black mothers had overlooked the way in which the black parents in Little Rock were instilling in their children an "ideal of sacrifice" necessary to move the nation forward on its quest for true democracy. In alleging that Negro parents were "exploiting their children during the struggle to integrate the school," Arendt had demonstrated her "failure to grasp the importance of this ideal among Southern Negroes caus[ing] her to fly way off into left field." Arendt clearly had "absolutely no conception of what goes on in the minds of Negro parents when they send their kids through those lines of hostile people." What she had missed was that the parents had placed their children in harm's way at Central High because they were

> aware of the overtones of a rite of initiation which such events actually constitute for the child, a confrontation of the terrors of social life with all the mysteries stripped away. And in the outlook of many of these parents (who wish that the problem didn't exist), the child is expected to face the terror and contain his fear and anger precisely because he is a Negro American.[10]

Reiterating a favorite theme, that being a Negro in America required a stern discipline, Ellison found in Little Rock further evidence of the Negro's capacity to forge and express a sense of humanity not circumscribed by the narrow limits of the Jim Crow south. His point was not lost on Arendt, who, shortly after *Who Speaks for the Negro?* was published, wrote to Ellison saying, "It is precisely this ideal of sacrifice which I didn't understand."[11]

Arendt's concession, however, was only partial. As Elisabeth Young-Bruehl points out, although Ellison was the only one of her critics to whom Arendt "gave ground," she "remained convinced that education should not be the sole or even the most important source of social or political change."[12] By contrast Ellison was more the social interventionist in matters of education, arguing that among the failures of American education was that "many American children have not been trained to reject enough of the negative values which our society presses upon them."[13] Nonetheless, Arendt and Ellison were in accord on some crucial points in their readings of the Little Rock crisis and in their thoughts on society in general. In regard to the former, both presumed that the only legitimate agency to be reckoned with on the scene at Central High School was parental agency. Reading the child's unhappiness through her facial expression, Arendt believed that the Little Rock Nine were on the frontlines solely at the behest of, or through abdication of, the authority of their parents. Arendt's reading took for granted that parents had the final say in determining whether or not their children participated in the battle to integrate the nation's schools. Likewise Ellison's rebuttal of Arendt's "Reflections" focused on "the minds of Negro parents." Thus, although they drew diametrically opposed conclusions as to whether or not it had been exercised, both agreed that parental authority was the focal point of the event.

Yet, the children who participated in Civil Rights struggles in Little Rock and elsewhere often did so either without the approval of, or over the objection of, their parents. For an example, the 1951 student strike at Farmville, Virginia's

R. R. Moton High School was spearheaded by 16-year-old Barbara Johns, niece of Vernon Johns (who preceded Martin Luther King, Jr. as pastor of Montgomery, Alabama's Dexter Avenue Baptist Church). Barbara Johns had become outraged by the failure of local authorities to "fulfill commitments to improve the conditions of the high school set aside for black students," where students were forced "to sit in the shacks with coats on through the winter."[14] Fed up with the situation and acting without the approval of her parents, Johns organized a student strike, and in conjunction with other students, "sent out appeals to NAACP lawyers, who, completely misreading the source of the initiative, agreed to come to Farmville for a meeting provided it was not with 'the children.'" Although the resulting suit was one of those that contributed to the NAACP's attack on school desegregation in the 1954 *Brown v. Board of Education of Topeka* case, the organization's tactics were clearly not centered on making heroes and martyrs of children, who had thrust themselves into the middle of a social and political movement.

More directly related to the Little Rock crisis are the reminiscences of Melba Patillo Boyd, one of the Little Rock Nine. In recounting how she came to be one of the students who defied segregation, Boyd recalls somewhat painfully having made the decision on her own. She was among those who raised her hand "[w]hen my teacher asked if anyone who lived within the Central High School District wanted to attend school with white people." Having raised her hand in response to the teacher's question, Boyd had set in motion a process in which her parents were placed in the position of reacting to, rather than directing, their daughter's actions. To be sure, Boyd did not always feel comfortable having made such a momentous decision without consulting her parents. In the long period before divulging her decision to them, she agonizes, "When had I planned on telling them? Why did I sign my name to the paper saying I lived near Central and wanted to go, without asking their permission?"[15] Yet, however keen Boyd's discomfort, her hardships were willingly undertaken and not thrust upon her by her parents.

That these young women acted without (and in Johns's case, in defiance of) immediate parental authority does not mean that black adults played no role in shaping the scene that unfolded in Little Rock. The family histories of Boyd and Johns testify that the home life of both girls was far from a political vacuum and the girls' political sensibilities were partially shaped by the family circle. Yet, these young women were also taking responsibility for shaping the world they were preparing to inherit. As important as black parents were, the stories of Johns and Boyd also show that parents were far from being the only initiators of actions leading to school desegregation. Young people were themselves following national court rulings and faulting the behavior of local officials. It was in part their awareness of these larger events that prompted these students to go forward even when their parents and grandparents counseled caution. In fact, these young women were able to go forward because they were readers of the news in addition to being creatures of their culture.

Nonetheless, in interpreting the Little Rock event, Arendt and Ellison accord student agency a minor or nonexistent role. Instead they describe the young people as, respectively, victims of misplaced adult activism or cultural apprentices being trained into the discipline of the Negro's life world. Ellison echoed his opinion about the Little Rock Nine in an interview with Richard Stern that appeared in print in *Shadow and Act* under the title, "That Same Pain, That Same Pleasure." Here, Ellison asked, rhetorically, "How do you account for Little Rock and the sit-ins? How do you account for the strength of those kids?" By way of an answer he pointed to their heritage as both Negroes and Americans. The "thin-legged little girls who faced the mob in Little Rock" were avatars of "those human qualities which the American Negro has developed despite, and in rejection of, the obstacles and mean-nesses imposed upon us." Even more so, "the spirit which directed their feet is the old universal urge toward freedom."[16] However powerful and compelling Ellison's sentiments may be, his interpretation, in effect, looks past the children as individuals compelled by their own motives in order to see them as some-thing possibly more passive—the fulfillment of something ancient. Facing what may have been an unprecedented moment in American life, Ellison described it as something "old." The Little Rock Nine had not broken with the past; they embodied it.

This is not to say that Ellison always valued the past over the present. On the contrary, the Ellisonian project often called for criticizing tradition and convention. As much as he revered the past, he also believed "that to embrace uncritically values which are extended to us by others is to reject the validity, even the sacredness, of our own experience."[17] Respecting one's own experi-ence often meant challenging the truths imposed by authority and question-ing the values handed down from one generation to the next. The children in Little Rock might have been avatars of an "old universal urge," but they were also acting out of motivations deriving from having come of age in a world that was in many ways unlike that of their parents. The culture and traditions that authorized these youthful challenges to segregation were themselves part of the Jim Crow world that was under assault; consequently, "these children" could fulfill the dreams of the previous generation only by challenging that generation's authority and wisdom.

Ellison's remarks on the Little Rock crisis were not merely responses to the events of the late 1950s. They also reflected some of the concerns that had shaped the writing of *Invisible Man* (1952) and remained the focus of his essays and interviews from the years following the publication of his novel. Ellison continuously probed the nature of American and Negro identities and their interrelation to one another, as well as the ways that both Negro culture and American democracy, though fashioned within the constraints of slavery and segregation, did not merely reflect those conditions but pointed towards their transcendence. The sometimes positive, sometimes negative, effects of having lived as a Negro and as an American meant that the counsels of one's elders were often laced with ambiguities that could make them more of a burden than a comfort to the social initiate. Although the protagonist of *Invisible Man* represents a rather extreme case of a young person prematurely burdened with the responsibility of addressing the nation's social problems, his difficulties give us some insight into Ellison's understanding of what the children at Little Rock's Central High meant.

Obsessed with doing what he ought to do, the protagonist of *Invisible Man,* not surprisingly, is confounded at those moments when, as with his grandfather's deathbed instructions, his policy of following to the letter the commands of white authority—saying "yes" when *they* expect you to do so—is described as a means of corroding the very logic on which authority depends. Through the words the old man confides to his grandson ("over-come 'em with yeses," he tells the boy, and "undermine 'em with grins, agree 'em to death and destruction"), obedience becomes defiance.[18] Adding to the young man's confusion is the fact that there is no obverse—defiance does not automatically translate into obedience. The protagonist does indeed speculate momentarily that if whites truly knew something about the mind of blacks in the south, they would "have desired me to act just the opposite, that I should have been sulky and mean" rather than cheerfully compliant. Yet, he also declares that he was "afraid to act any other way because they [whites] didn't like that at all" (17). As far as Ellison's naïf can tell, black obedience is the only prescribed course for getting along in the segregationist South, and yet, according to his grandfather, being black and obedient also undermined the very people whom one was attempting to appease.

The social order of Jim Crow America, which Ellison knew both inside and out, was one that asserted black/white racial difference as both the ground and the goal of social and political life. Racial difference had to be taken for granted as the natural order of things, and yet, somewhat contradictorily, this difference also had to be enforced continually as if it could exist only by fiat. It was this tension between the idea of race as something natural and the idea of race as something merely imposed that signaled an instability in the nation's racial order that Ellison's novel—through plot and metaphor—was only too eager to exploit. The impossibility of guaranteeing white purity (the spoiled white paint at the Liberty Paint factory is one of the novel's most obvious metaphors for this) opened up an avenue for social critique that Ellison was to take repeatedly in his writings over the course of his career. The nation's white supremacist regime could always be embarrassed by its own inability to cordon off whiteness from blackness and to segregate black from white throughout all of the many tiers of human experience. Thus, if authority in the South (and in the nation for that matter) depended on always being able to distinguish black from white, authority would always find itself in crisis. To invoke another of *Invisible Man*'s organizing metaphors, authority could be maintained only through a willed blindness.

It was also true, however, that authority could not be challenged on the white side of the color line without facing the same threat on the black side. If the white college trustee, Mr. Norton, tumbles into psychosexual chaos as a result of the excessive willingness of a young black man, whom the trustee describes as "my fate" (42), to do his bidding, then so is the regime of the black college president, Mr. Bledsoe, rattled by the same will to obedience. With his power resting largely on his ability to stage-manage a presentation of black reality (in Bledsoe's words, "haven't we bowed and scraped and begged and lied enough decent homes and drives for you to show him?" [138]), Bledsoe's throne cannot avoid being shaken by the young man's alacrity to follow "the white line." White should not be black, but as the Invisible Man acts as chauffer to the college trustee he admits, "I identified myself with the rich man reminiscing on the rear seat" (39).

To understand *Invisible Man*'s inveterate irreverence towards authority, black as well as white, one can and should start with what Ellison saw mid-century as the bankruptcy of black politics—what he called the "ambiguity of Negro leadership." He writes:

> This was the late forties, and I kept trying to account for the fact that when the chips were down, Negro leaders did not represent the Negro community.
>
> Beyond their own special interests they represented white philanthropy, white politicians, business interests, and so on. This was an unfair way of looking at it, perhaps, but there was something missing, something which is only now being corrected. It seemed to me that they acknowledged no final responsibility to the Negro community for their acts, and implicit in their roles were constant acts of betrayal.[19]

This is also to say that because Negro authority, on an everyday basis, demonstrated, its illegitimacy, surrendering judgment to those in charge was either foolish or suicidal. Bledsoe, who tells the horrified narrator, "I've made my place . . . and I'll have every Negro in the country hanging on tree limbs by morning if it means staying where I am" (143), is a case in point. No crime is too heinous if its commission contributes to securing the position of black leadership, a term that turns out to be merely a different way of saying tyranny.

The corruption represented by Bledsoe is, of course, a matter of history. The reign of Jim Crow required whites to seek to undermine, suppress, or co-opt any political power they saw emerging among black Americans. It should go without saying that these efforts were not always, and could not have been, uniformly successful—force and fraud were often countered with resistance. Yet, the extent to which the compromising of black political power had been successful became a leitmotiv in criticisms and representations of black political praxis. The lament of an Alabama minister of the black Methodist Episcopal

Church writing to the *Chicago Defender* during the first great migration was far from unusual: "As leaders we are powerless for we dare not resent such or to show even the slightest disapproval."[20] During the decades between the Harlem Renaissance and the publication of *Invisible Man,* the ineffectualness, cowardice, and duplicity of black leadership was a common theme among African American authors, whether in Langston Hughes's poem "To Certain Negro Leaders," which sneered at those "Voices crying in the wilderness/At so much per word/From the white folks,"[21] or in Richard Wright's depiction of Reverend Taylor at the beginning of his short story "Fire and Cloud," which finds the black preacher bemoaning in Depression-Era America, "Here Ah is a man called by Gawd t preach n whut kin Ah do?"[22]

The peculiar features of the white-dominated regime of the South would have justified Ellison's treating the problem of black leadership as more of a practical than a philosophical or theoretical problem. The relative weakness and the constrained circumstances of blacks in positions of power during Jim Crow would seem to make their behaviors and habits a somewhat sterile ground for exploring broader or more abstract questions about the nature of legitimate power and authority. A racially segregated America represented a simple abuse of power and the replacement of authority with tyranny. Yet, from another angle, these very same circumstances serve quite nicely to frame an inquiry into the idea of authority in the modern world, as well as to highlight the way that Arendt and Ellison function as interlocutors.

In her discussion of the nature of authority, Arendt observes that the "most conspicuous characteristic of those in authority is that they do not have power."[23] Given that authority is often taken to be synonymous with power, Arendt's remark, on its face, may seem counterintuitive (the reasoning behind Arendt's claim will be addressed in greater detail). But her words open up the possibility that the relative powerlessness of black Americans during Jim Crow could prove to be less an obstacle than an aid to an investigation of the notion of authority. To be clear on this point, Arendt was not partial to the idea that victims of oppression enjoyed any clarity of insight regarding the nature of political freedom. Quite the contrary; in her prefatory remarks to "Reflections," she wrote, "*oppressed minorities were never the best judges on the order of priorities in such matters and there are many instances when they preferred to fight for social opportunity rather than for basic human or political rights.*"[24] Several years later, in a letter to Mary McCarthy in which she commented vituperatively on recent trends in the Civil Rights movement, Arendt reiterated her rather dim view of the capacity of the oppressed to set proper political and intellectual priorities. In words that would more than pass muster in contemporary far-right political circles, Arendt complained:

> Negroes demand their own curriculum without the exacting standards of white society and, at the same time, they demand admission in accordance to their percentage in the population at large, regardless of standards.

In other words they actually want to take over and adjust standards to their own level. This is a much greater threat to our institutions of higher learning than the student riots.[25]

Once again the combination of obtuseness and insight by Arendt derived from her commitment to the importance of maintaining the integrity of the public, social, and private spheres. In her view, blacks, as they had done in the Little Rock crisis, were carrying the principle of equality necessary to the public realm into the realm of the social, the very existence of which depended on granting groups the right to make discriminations and enforce their own standards. Arendt's use of the term "white society" was, of course, more damaging to her argument than she realized in that it conceded the very argument that many black activists were making: namely, that the educational standards in institutions of higher learning, which should have been based on intellectual ability and achievement, had, throughout the nation's history, been determined by the goal of preserving white dominance.

What makes Arendt's ruminations on authority illuminating in a discussion of Ralph Ellison and *Invisible Man,* however, is not her clarity on the various political aims of black Americans. Rather, the distinction she draws between authority and power is suggestive in working through a problem that Ellison's pursues relentlessly. The challenge embedded in Arendt's attempt to pin down the nature of authority is to find some account of authority's "binding force" that does not rely on coercion on the one hand or persuasion on the other. Authority, Arendt writes, must be

> "more than advice and less than a command, an advice which one may not safely ignore," whereby it is assumed that "the will and the actions of the people like those of children are exposed to error and mistakes and therefore need 'augmentation' and confirmation through the council of elders." The authoritative character of the "augmentation" of the elders lies in its being mere advice, needing neither the form of command nor external coercion to make itself heard.[26]

Operating in a manner akin to the way that "the binding force of the *auspices*" revealed "divine approval or disapproval of decisions made by men," authority, as it had existed in previous civilizations, had been "sanctified" by a tradition that "preserved the past by handing down from one generation to the next the testimony of the ancestors."[27]

The figure of the grandfather in *Invisible Man,* whose words of advice may not be safely ignored by the protagonist, reveals the curious nature of the "testimony of the ancestors" in Ellison's world. The old man's words are not underwritten by force or violence; his is a wisdom that began when "I gave up my gun back in the Reconstruction." Neither are they simply an indication of the way that the adult world imparts knowledge to children, for the narrator's parents warn their son "emphatically to forget what he had said" (16). But forget he cannot, and the binding force of his grandfather's words is such that the narrator feels, "I was carrying out his advice in spite of myself" (16). He obeys even when he tries to do otherwise and disobeys when he intends to comply. What *Invisible Man* urges us to contemplate is the idea that if the existence of proper authority implies obedience, there may be no legitimate authority if, at every turn, obedience results in subverting or misconstruing the very commands it intends to follow. This problem, which does emerge from the specific racial landscape of the South, nonetheless opens onto the larger problem of how in the modern era one can ground authority. In his notes on the protagonist of *Invisible Man*, Ellison wrote, "The boy would appease the gods; it costs him much pain to discover that he can satisfy the gods only by rebelling against them."[28] If that boy is also, as Ellison calls him, "the Negro individualist" whose god is himself, he must in turn embark on the seemingly impossible task of rebelling against his own rebellion. Thus, the gods must speak only to be defied, and the children must defy only to be rebuked.

Invisible Man's narrator introduces himself to us by admitting, "All my life I had been looking for something, and everywhere I turned someone tried to tell me what it was. I accepted their answers too, though they were often in contradiction and even self-contradictory" (15). Because he seeks authority around every corner, one could say that the narrator simply makes the mistake of believing that anyone able to offer a response to the questions he asks counts as an authority. This is, of course, an egregious error (and one might add, a stupid one: Why should anybody want to believe everything he's told?). Yet, if Ellison's novel is interested in establishing the possibility for legitimate authority, then one might say that the Invisible Man's stupidity turns out to be fortunate: Authority in the novel may not necessarily be in crisis. The problem may simply be that the narrator lacks the discernment to determine when a voice ought to count as an authority. For Ellison's naïf, the simple fact of someone's being able to give a response to his questions is sufficient to compel his trust that the answers offered by his respondent are based on considered judgment. Proper authority, however, would be able to emerge only when the narrator reaches a place where he learns to judge, and because the novel is a bildungsroman, the entire engine of the narrative is chugging along to get the narrator to the place where he can learn to discern.

The questions for which the Invisible Man is seeking authoritative answers, however, are by no means small ones: Who am I? How should I, as a young black man, live? When should I submit? When should I defy? Given the dangers that come with living in Jim Crow America, his very survival would seem to depend on his answering at least these questions successfully. Complicating the narrator's plight is that the nature of these questions might also lead us to wonder who, aside from the young man himself, is in a position to answer them? Indeed the narrator's tautological declaration, "I am nobody but myself"—a certainty he claims as the hard-won discovery of his "painful boomeranging"—points toward an almost anarchistic answer to the problem of authority in which each individual acts as his own authority (15). Keeping one's own counsel opens up the possibility for self-authorization.

Ellison's story, however, gives us ample reason to doubt the efficacy of this solution. Late in the novel when the protagonist seeks to avoid being physically attacked by the followers of Ras the Exhorter, he dons a disguise of a hat and dark glasses, precipitating a sequence in which he is repeatedly mistaken for Bliss Proteus Rinehart. Equally comfortable as a preacher, numbers runner, gambler, and ladies man, Rinehart represents a figure whose identity, ever shifting, cannot determine behavior from moment to moment. Described by Ellison as "the personification of chaos," Rinehart stands for "a country with no solid past or stable class lines; therefore he is able to move about easily from one to the other."[29] In such a country, the "natural" course of action would be to do as one likes, consulting no authority higher than one's whims or desires. However, as shown by the protagonist's near fatal experience while masquerading as Rinehart, *Invisible Man* is a novel that does not endorse surrendering to the chaos that would result from unchecked self-authorization. Rather, Ellison's fiction strives to balance a necessary flouting of authority with a corresponding deference to some idea of order.

It is, of course, no news to readers of Ellison that order cannot be established in a once-and-for-all-time manner. Instead the novel suggests that what order exists is best seen as an ongoing process that begins with the discovery that the patterns imposed on chaos are merely imposed and do not derive their authority from accurately representing things as they are. The reality of human existence as defined by Ellison is that we are surrounded by chaos, which means that all orderly and authoritative representations of reality are falsifications whose inadequacies will get exposed, given enough time. Positively speaking, this knowledge does arm the protagonist (and presumably the reader) with reasons for not acceding to the authority of Bledsoe, Jack, or Ras, and their demands for complete submission. But as useful as this knowledge is in providing reasons not to conform to certain patterns, it offers no clear guidelines for selecting one pattern over another. When should one heed the counsel of authority? From the standpoint of representational adequacy, all coherent patterns fall short of the truth. As bad as, say, Brother Jack's vision might be, it is no blinder than any of the other visions the novel makes available.

There is one potential remedy that *Invisible Man* offers as the narrator winds his story towards its conclusion. He insists that "a plan of living must never lose sight of the chaos against which that pattern was conceived" (580). That is, patterns of conduct should always at some point call attention to the fact they are fictive and not given. Presumably this would prevent any individual from believing he or she has the right to impose a plan of living on someone else. This injunction is fair enough, and very much in accordance with liberal theories of individual restraint in which one person's rights end at the point where the other fellow's nose begins. Ellison's narrator, however, extends the scope of this adage beyond the realm of individual conduct in asserting the importance of never "losing sight of the chaos" by saying that this adage "goes for societies as well as for individuals" (580). But extending this truth from individuals to societies is far from straightforward, because societies necessarily impose obligations on others. Societies always infringe on the individual's absolute freedom. How can an effort not to lose sight of chaos help create a plan to which the individual might willingly accede?

The novel's advocacy of a pattern of order that anticipates, makes room for, or otherwise acknowledges chaos, seeks to find its authorization not in logical argument but rather in aesthetic practice. Louis Armstrong's singing and playing, "Open the window and let the foul air out," introduces the narrator's peroration. The narrator quickly clarifies Armstrong's words by saying, "Of course Louie was kidding, *he* wouldn't have thrown old bad Air out, because it would have broken up the music and the dance, when it was the good music that came from the bell of old Bad Air's horn that counted" (581). The vision here is the idea of music made perfect by its imperfection, the plan made complete by virtue of the hole it leaves for disorder. In equating the necessity of bad air with the idea of diversity, the narrator seems to be claiming that the formula for making good art is the same as that for making a just society: "Diversity is the word. Let man keep his many parts and you'll have no tyrant states" (577). A good society would be like a good jazz song.

The protagonist puts forward this idea quite seriously and the novel wants us to see this formulation as being the right one. The narrator's sentiments, after all, resemble those that Ellison expressed three years after the publication of *Invisible Man* in an essay entitled "Living With Music": "The delicate balance struck between strong individual personality and the group during those early jam sessions was a marvel of social organization." Recounting his own youthful attempts to become a musician, Ellison insists that he "had learned too that the end of all this discipline and technical mastery was the desire to express an affirmative way of life through its musical tradition, and that this tradition insisted that each artist achieve his creativity within its frame. He must learn the best of the past, and add to it his personal vision."[30] Learning to be a good artist appears to be a lot like learning how to live well and democratically. Yet, as much as one might want to accede to Ellison's lesson, there are reasons to resist this conclusion. In touting Louis Armstrong's singing, the narrator is not just arguing that keeping the bad air is ethically and politically sound. It is equally important that putting the two together *sounds* good. That is, the narrator accepts the bad air with the good because he likes the sound of the music he hears blaring from the horn of Bad Air. The narrator can get away with this justification because we all like (or he presumes that we should like) Armstrong. But it leaves one to wonder what would happen if we didn't? Given the diversity of human tastes, the linking of taste with authority would appear to raise almost as many problems as it solves. If there is no disputing tastes, there is no adjudicating of them either. An arbiter of taste could only be arbitrary.

If neither representational adequacy nor aesthetic compatibility determines whether or not we should respect a particular authority, then where are we to turn? Perhaps back to what Ellison has termed "the validity, even the sacredness, of our own experience." As a defense against the theories of those who claimed to know something about their lives, Negroes (as Ellison was to admonish Irving Howe in his "World and the Jug" essays) had to depend "upon the validity of their own experience for an accurate picture of the reality which they seek to change, and for a gauge of the values they would see made manifest."[31]

At first glance, this move seems to take us back to the idea of each individual navigating according to her own internal compass. In this case, however, the plural pronoun is hardly accidental. Ellison always sought to place individual experience within a larger group context, whether "Negro," "American," or some combination of the two. In fact Ellison's larger point was that, had we the courage to admit it, the inescapable combination of the two was not only the truth of our individual experiences but also the inescapable implication of America's founding documents. It comes as no surprise to anyone familiar with Ellison's writings that the ideas expressed in the founding texts of the American republic underwrote the seriousness with which he approached the artistic enterprise. The title he gave to a 1967 lecture, "The Novel as a Function of American Democracy," exemplifies his many musings on the relationship between art and society. He "emphasize[d] that the American nation is based upon revolution, dedicated to change through basic concepts stated in the Bill of Rights and the Constitution. It is dedicated to an *open* society. . . . With such a society, it seems only natural that the novel existed to be exploited by certain personality types who found their existence within the United States."[32] There was then a necessary correlation between America's founding documents, the art of the novel, the aesthetics of the jazz musician, and the actual experiences of Americans.

Acknowledging these truths meant acknowledging the Negro's humanity: a truth, Ellison felt, that white America was still unwilling to face, but Negro Americans of necessity had known all along. Knowing something about their own humanity—the Invisible Man's grandfather, for example, "never had any doubts about his" (580)—placed black Americans somewhere ahead of whites in the struggle to make sense of the world. In his final effort to make sense of his grandfather's words, the invisible man speculates:

> Was it that we of all, we, most of all, had to affirm the principle, the plan in whose name we had been brutalized and sacrificed—not because we

would always be weak nor because we were afraid or opportunistic, *but because we were older than they, in the sense of what it took to live in the world with others?* (574; emphasis added)

The Negro as Ellison knew him had never been young—naïve, perhaps, as is the hero of Ellison's only completed novel—but not someone who came into the world unknowing. That is, while there is much that Ellison's protagonist does not know, it is more so the case that he seems to have forgotten things rather than having not yet learned them—remembering himself is to remember his past. This position, which Ellison had reached even before the publication of *Invisible Man* in 1952, became doubly important in the early 1960s when he found it necessary to counter Stanley Elkins's assertion in his controversial study *Slavery* that the Negro, as a result of the closed society of plantation slavery, had been a perpetual child.[33] Ellison's response before the fact was that the Negro could not have afforded himself such a luxury. Childhood had never been an option, as one could see in the courage of the children in Little Rock, who in some curious way were not really children. Ellison concludes that were the Negro merely to accept his second-class status, had the children of Little Rock merely acceded to the desires of segregationists, the vision of American democracy would fail in its attempt to compel assent to its credos, and its innermost principle of equality would become a dead letter. Perhaps more importantly, Ellison believed that even this possibility not quite fulfilled in his lifetime (and not even yet) would have been foreclosed had the Negro not possessed the cultural resources sufficient, in the teeth of outright denial, to authorize that defiance.

ENDNOTES

1. Hannah Arendt, "Reflections on Little Rock," 6 *Dissent* 1 (Winter 1959), 46.

2. Elisabeth Young-Bruehl's *Hannah Arendt: For Love of the World* (New Haven: Yale University Press, 1982) is especially good in tying Arendt's interventions into social crises of the 1950s to Arendt's *The Human Condition,* published in 1957; see 318–22.

3. Arendt, "Reflections on Little Rock," 51.

4. Ibid., 55.

5. See Young-Bruehl, 313–15.

6. Editors, Untitled Note, 6 *Dissent* 1 (Winter 1959), 45.

7. Arendt, "A Reply to Critics," 6 *Dissent* 2 (Spring 1959), 179.

8. Arendt, "Reflections on Little Rock," 49.

9. Ralph Ellison, "The World and the Jug," in *The Collected Essays of Ralph Ellison,* ed. John F. Callahan (New York: Modern Library, 1995), 156. Hereinafter cited as *Collected Essays.*

10. Interview with Ralph Ellison in Robert Penn Warren, *Who Speaks for the Negro?* (New York: Random House, 1965), 343–44.

11. Arendt to Ellison (July 29, 1965), Library of Congress, quoted in Young-Bruehl, 316.

12. Young-Bruehl, 317.

13. Ralph Ellison, "What These Children Are Like," in *Collected Essays,* 549.

14. Taylor Branch, *Parting the Waters: America in the King Years, 1954–63* (New York: Simon and Schuster, 1988), 20.

15. Mary Patillo Boyd, *Warriors Don't Cry: A Searing Memoir of the Battle to Integrate Little Rock's Central High* (New York: Pocket Books, 1994), 32.

16. Ralph Ellison, "That Same Pain, That Same Pleasure," *Collected Essays,* 79, 80.

17. Ralph Ellison, "Hidden Name and Complex Fate," in *Collected Essays,* 208.

18. Ralph Ellison, *Invisible Man* (New York: Random House, 1952; reprint, New York: Vintage Books, 1995), 16. All subsequent citations will be noted parenthetically in the text by page number, and emphases in original unless otherwise noted.

19. Ralph Ellison, "That Same Pain, That Same Pleasure," in *Collected Essays,* 76–77.

20. Unsigned letter to the *Chicago Defender,* Newbern, Ala., *Journal of Negro History* (April 7, 1917), 420.

21. Langston Hughes, "To Certain Negro Leaders," in *The Collected Poems of Langston Hughes,* ed. Arnold Rampersad (New York: Vintage Books, 1994), 136.

22. Richard Wright, "Fire and Cloud," in "Uncle Tom's Children," *Richard Wright: The Early Works* (New York: Library of America, 1991).

23. Hannah Arendt, "What is Authority," in *Between Past and Future: Eight Exercises in Political Thought* (New York: Penguin, 1993; orig. publ. 1961), 122.

24. Arendt, "Reflections on Little Rock," 46.

25. Hannah Arendt, "To Mary McCarthy" (December 21, 1968), in *Between Friends: The Correspondence of Arendt and Mary McCarthy, 1949–1975,* ed. Carol Brightman (New York: Harcourt, Brace, & Co., 1995), 229–30.

26. Arendt, "What is Authority?" 123. Arendt quotes from Theodor Mommsen's *Romische Geschichte,* 2nd Edition (London: Richard Bentley, 1864), vol. 1.

27. Ibid., 123 and 124.

28. Ralph Ellison, "Working Notes for *Invisible Man,*" in *Collected Essays,* 344.

29. Ralph Ellison, "The Art of Fiction: *An Interview,*" in *Collected Essays,* 223.

30. Ralph Ellison, "Living with Music," in *Collected Essays,* 229.

31. Ralph Ellison, "The World and the Jug," in *Collected Essays,* 161.

32. Ralph Ellison, "The Novel as a Function of American Democracy," in *Collected Essays,* 757. Perhaps not so coincidentally, Arendt's "What is Authority?" concludes by making recourse to the "act of foundation." See 140–41.

33. Stanley M. Elkins, ed., *Slavery: A Problem in American Institutional and Intellectual Life* (Chicago: University of Chicago Press, 1959).

Chapter 8

Ralph Ellison and the Invisibility of the Black Intellectual: Historical Reflections on *Invisible Man*

CHARLES "PETE" BANNER-HALEY

So my task was one of revealing the human universals hidden within the plight of one who was both black and American, and not only as a means of conveying my personal vision of possibility, but as a way of dealing with the sheer rhetorical challenge involved in communicating across our barriers of race and religion, class, color and region—barriers which consist of the many strategies of division that were designed, and still function, to prevent what would otherwise have been a more or less natural recognition of the reality of black and white fraternity.

Details of old photographs, rhymes, riddles, children's games, church services, college ceremonies, practical jokes and political activities observed during my prewar days in Harlem—all fell into place. I had reported the riot of 1943 for the New York Post, *had agitated earlier for the release of Angelo Herndon and the Scottsboro Boys, had marched behind Adam Clayton Powell, Jr., in his effort to desegregate the stores along 125th Street, and had been part of a throng which blocked off Fifth Avenue in protest of the role being played by Germany and Italy in the Spanish Civil War. Everything and anything appeared as grist for my fictional mill, some speaking up clearly, saying, "use me here," while others were disturbingly mysterious.*

—INTRODUCTION TO THIRTIETH ANNIVERSARY EDITION
OF *INVISIBLE MAN* (NOVEMBER 10, 1981)[1]

Thirty years after the publication of *Invisible Man,* Ralph Ellison ruminated on the historical context of his now classic novel. Despite the rise of conservatism in American politics and culture, the political atmosphere was not filled with the hysteria that had previously accompanied the anti-communism of the late 1940s and early 1950s. *Invisible Man* represented a triumph not just on literary grounds but also on political and historical grounds as well.

Ralph Ellison's achievement was to present, in fiction, a history of black people that was at once collective and individualist. The novel pointed out universal human values and the machinations of power even as it plumbed the depths of what Ellison called "our complex American underground." *Invisible Man* was an historical meditation on what it means to be an American in general and a black American in particular. It was a significant move in removing the veil of invisibility for Afro-American intellectuals. The protagonist-narrator, Ellison wrote in his working notes, "is a man born into a tragic national situation who attempts to respond to it as though it were completely logical." But that attempt is doomed to failure and Ellison tells us why as we follow the narrator who, intellectually and historically, starts out with a nineteenth-century mindset—that is, "He has accepted the definition of himself handed down by the white South and the paternalism of northern philanthropy"—and ends up in the mid-twentieth century in a basement filled with lights and trying to understand the meaning of it all and, perhaps, come to a resolution.[2]

What Ralph Ellison accomplished was a complex and richly layered historical meditation of United States history and Afro-Americans' integral role in the shaping of that history. Ellison's work afterwards, from the essays and short stories to the legendary work-in-progress, all managed in some way to elaborate on and deepen the historical context that coursed throughout *Invisible Man.* Despite the fact that *Invisible Man* appeared during the frenzy of the Cold War, the existence of the Korean War, and the cultural wars induced by anti-communism and McCarthyism, Ralph Ellison, through *Invisible Man,* was able to present a significant artistic interpretation of African-American history that ultimately was about American political transformations and reinventions. "So if the ideal of achieving a true political equality eludes us in reality—as it continues to do—" Ellison wrote in 1981,

> there is still available that fictional *vision* of an ideal democracy in which the actual combines with the ideal and gives us representations of a state of things in which the highly placed and the lowly, the black and the white, the Northerner and the Southerner, the native-born and the immigrant combine to tell us of transcendent truths and possibilities. . . .[3]

That Ralph Ellison could produce such a nuanced work in the midst of an era when historical thinking and political attitudes were undergoing seismic changes seems all the more incredible in retrospect 50 years later. The historical interpretation that Ellison brought to *Invisible Man* could be said to dovetail with the emerging Consensus School of historians who surveyed America's past and discovered (rediscovered?) a common culture and political structure rooted in the Western European Enlightenment in general and English common law in particular. The task these historians set was the continuing quest for an "objective" history of America that could also serve to inspire pride and loyalty, and provide to the world an example of democracy and freedom in action.[4]

Many of these historians were formerly Socialists in the Depression era when faith in capitalism was deeply shaken and radical alternatives were considered. But World War II and America's successful defeat of Nazism presented new possibilities for America as the nation entered the world stage. The chance to show America as a land of freedom, opportunity, and democracy—all made possible by capitalism and its extension around the globe—became a rallying cry for historians, politicians, and social commentators. "The American Century" celebrated a common American Culture that was grounded in equality, mobility, invention, and individual achievement. While some historians may have recognized the diversity that existed in the nation, the cultural pluralism or "melting pot" idea was now downplayed in favor of talking about unity. "One Out Of Many" became a mantra akin to the late twentieth century's incantation of "race, class, and gender."[5]

Invisible Man, on the surface, encompassed the Consensus School's ideas almost perfectly. But Ralph Ellison was in actuality far ahead of the Consensus School and, in a larger historical sense, anticipated the arguments of multiculturalism in the 1980s and 1990s. By choosing to set his novel from within America's "underground" he was able to speak, as his narrator put it, on the "lower frequencies" and thereby introduce an array of voices, situations, and ideas that we all continue to grapple with to this day.

Despite the accusations by scholars on the left, such as Jerry Gafio Watts, who sees Ellison as having turned his back on politics and the struggles of Afro-Americans in favor of an individualistic aesthetic approach to art, a close examination of Ellison and *Invisible Man* show this simply not to be true. Likewise those neoconservatives, such as Stanley Crouch, who have helped to appropriate Ellison for their own belief in a color-blind society, have caught only half of Ellison's very full cup. About the only writer who has understood Ellison has been James Alan McPherson. McPherson's prize-winning fiction and searching essays on African-American "double consciousness" clearly demonstrate the influence of Ellison and the kind of multilayered art that Ellison envisioned.[6]

What Watts missed in his otherwise perceptive analysis of Ellison's thought was the historical factor. Ralph Ellison's view of Black History and American History was that they were basically one and the same. While Ellison recognized that the Negro experience of slavery, Reconstruction, and the struggle for freedom marked them as unique, they were not just victims. All Americans in many ways were victimized by these events. Indeed, one of the resounding themes in Ellison's fiction and essays was how black Americans shaped America through an infusion of folk culture, adaptive Christian religiosity, and their steadfast belief in the American democratic creed. In turn, Afro-Americans were shaped by European, Asian, and Native American influences. These cross-cultural pollinations led to mixtures that created an American culture that was at one glance seemingly firm but on a closer look very fluid. Ellison's thoughts on these matters came from a number of sources, all of which spring up in *Invisible Man*. The historical context of these sources is not all that hard to discern. Why then would Watts and others fail to see the historical context either in *Invisible Man* or in Ralph Ellison's ideas about art and politics?

Ross Posnock, in his literary/intellectual history, *Color and Culture: Black Writers and the Making of the Modern Intellectual,* situates Ellison within William James's philosophical schema of pragmatism and pluralism. Posnock offers this insight with regards to the melting pot versus cultural pluralism debate: "Ellison, the allegedly apolitical elitist, intervenes to unsettle radically both terms of the melting-pot versus cultural pluralism debate. What makes his perspective radical is what makes it political: he recovers implicitly the root sense of politics as civic participation in the public world."[7]

This is all very good as far as it goes. But the history behind this "pragmatic pluralism" was that it was forged and tempered in the heat of 1930s radicalism. Ralph Ellison's thinking and some of his leftist credentials, which only very recently have been uncovered and appreciated, probably owed as much to W. E. B. Du Bois's ideological shift during the same period. Du Bois was an adherent of James's pragmatic pluralism but was also attempting to utilize Marxian analysis to interpret the role African Americans played in American history. Ellison, according to Carol Posgrove's study of black and white intellectuals from 1945 to 1964, was a member of the Communist Party as well as a strong believer in the Soviet Union.[8]

Writing to his mother from New York in 1937, Ellison commented about the Depression and the political situation: "All those years and all that work, and not even a job to bring a dollar a week. The people in Spain are fighting right now because of just this kind of thing, the people of Russia got tired of seeing the rich have everything and the poor nothing and now they are building a new system. I wish we could go live there."[9] This passage clearly shows Ellison's leftist views. Of course, it does not prove that Ellison joined the Communist Party, as Carol Posgrove suggests. Yet, it does show a progressive streak that was very sympathetic to the presence of the Soviet Union. As has been noted earlier, this was the Depression and there was a strong animus against capitalism. It will be left to Ellison's biographers to settle the question of Ellison's membership in the CPUSA. For now, from what we have learned from Ellison's later writings and *Invisible Man,* he was far more than a fellow traveler as received wisdom has held.[10]

His good friend and Communist Party member, Richard Wright, published Ellison's first book review in the *New Challenge*—a Communist-backed journal. Ellison published short stories there and in other leftist journals of the period. He was a political observer and participant in the leading issues of the day that affected African Americans, whether it was the Scottsboro case, Adam Clayton Powell, Jr.'s "Don't Buy Where You Can't Work" boycotts in Harlem, or protests against the German-Italian war against Ethiopia. Many of these activities, heavily disguised, appeared in *Invisible Man* and were often criticized then and later as, in some way, bashing the black American freedom struggle. But as has been pointed out, Ellison was writing mainly about the tragedy of the human condition; within his view of things, the most tragic human experience was that of the black experience in America.[11]

Ellison, in responding to his critics in the essay "The World and The Jug," put forth a measure of his historical interpretation of Afro-Americans that affirmed this tragic human condition: "Being Negro American has to do with the memory of slavery and the hope of emancipation and the betrayal by allies and the revenge and contempt inflicted by our former masters after the Reconstruction, and the myths, both Northern and Southern, which are propagated in justification of that betrayal."[12] This particular interpretation was a blend of the African-American historians Rayford Logan and Benjamin Quarles. Both of these historians were Vindicationists and integrationists who believed that Afro-American History was integral to American History.[13] Ellison was a firm believer in this school of thought in Afro-American history and in 1970 wrote testily to his friend, Stanley Edgar Hyman, "As you damn well know, I view my people as American and not African, and while our experience differs in unique ways from that of white Americans, it is never absolutely at variance with the dominant American mode. Diversity within unity is the confounding reality."[14]

In the late sixties and early seventies, Ellison took a fearsome drubbing from young black militants (many of whom had not even read *Invisible Man*) because of his stance on the American-ness of Afro-Americans. The strong anti-American fervor coupled with a separatist Black Nationalism that exalted black authenticity was bound to be at odds with an artistic temperament that focused on the individual's situation in a society rent with racial divisions, regional antipathies, and the tragedy of class. Ralph Ellison had been through those wars before in the thirties. The sixties, of course, were not the same. There was no Depression and the surge for civil rights for individuals transformed into a Black Power movement that spoke to group identity and enhancement. But *Invisible Man* presented a disturbing example of a repetitive cycle regarding race that could have been avoided by young black radicals who were angry and demanding "Freedom Now."

In *Invisible Man,* the narrator, having migrated from the South to Harlem, New York, joins the Brotherhood, a radical group that is a thinly disguised representation of the 1930s Communist Party. Within the Brotherhood, the narrator is given a new identity and the promise of a new way of life. The irony here, of course, is that the Brotherhood drapes the nameless protagonist behind more invisibility while intending to liberate him. Likewise, Ras the Destroyer, standing in for a militant Black Nationalism, also denies the narrator a voice of his own. For Ellison, the collectivism of the Left and the racial communalism of separatist black nationalists turned away from the fundamentals that made America: democracy, freedom, and the lyrical tension between individuality and community.

It was these fundamentals that caused the young black militants of the late 1960s and 1970s to dismiss Ellison and *Invisible Man* as being part of the problem and not the solution for black liberation. In the late 1980s and throughout the 1990s as the "Culture Wars" heated up, conservatives, who politically had the upper hand, sought to bring Ralph Ellison into their fold, while the Left once again revived critiques that Ellison was apolitical and too much of an individualist who was too far removed from the struggles of the black masses. Thus in this vein, Robert E. Washington, in his study of the ideologies of African-American literature, stated of *Invisible Man* that it "suggests that the primary struggle confronting black Americans is not political but existential, that is, the battle to realize their individuality, and to prevail over the stereotypes and abstracted categories that violate their humanity. This is the central normative message *Invisible Man* aims to affirm."[15]

While this is a fair enough assessment, it should be noted that this was also the basis on which the early part of the Civil Rights Movement was established, especially with regards to the thinking of the young people in SNCC (Student Nonviolent Coordinating Committee). In other words, Washington comes close to saying that the Civil Rights Movement was an existential movement unconcerned with politics. But existentialism is a form of politics more in tune, perhaps, with liberalism's autonomous individualism than a leftist collectivism.

Those defining Ellison as conservative have even a less easy time of it. Greg Robinson, in his study of Ralph Ellison, Albert Murray (Ellison's close friend), and journalist/social critic Stanley Crouch, projects these three as progenitors of a modern black cultural conservatism. Of Ellison, Robinson states:

> [W]hile he recognized the history of racial segregation and political disfranchisement in the United States, he insisted that the national culture was pluralistic and open to black participation, and that blacks had made substantial contributions to it.
>
> American culture, Ellison explained, was the product of the continuous interactions of the different racial and ethnic groups who came to the United States and contributed elements of their folk cultures.[16]

But then a page later, Robinson asserts: "Ellison, Murray, and Crouch are most easily characterized as cultural conservatives, both by virtue of their deeply patriotic view of American freedom and culture and a corresponding rejection of race-based views of (black) American identity, and by their dismissal of the importance of racism in American life."[17] While this contradicts Robinson's opening remarks at the beginning of his essay, it is also misleading. Certainly Ellison, Murray, and Crouch are patriotic with regards to American freedom, but so were W. E. B. Du Bois, Richard Wright, Lorraine Hansberry, and James Baldwin for most of their lives. Moreover, Ellison's second novel (and the heavily edited version, *Juneteenth,* published in 1999) is a studied look at the effects of racism on the American character.[18]

But overall, Greg Robinson and Robert E. Washington overlook or misread the historical contexts involved in the text of *Invisible Man.* Thus Robinson writes: "Ellison, writing during the postwar period, was primarily interested in opposing the 'damage' theory of liberal social science, which underlay the Supreme Court's 1954 *Brown v. Board of Education* ruling and other positive achievements in race relations."[19] This may well be true, but *Invisible Man* certainly shows some vestiges of damage that were inflicted by slavery and segregation. The actions and demeanor of the narrator's college president, Bledsoe (note the name), is a prime example. What Ellison believed and shared with today's multiculturalists is that black people transcended the afflictions of slavery and segregation and became not only the moral conscience of America but also influenced and shaped American culture. It is rather difficult to understand the cultural conservatism here.

Robinson, however, continues in his linkage of Ellison's distaste for "damage" theories and cultural conservatism by noting that:

In order to further their strategy of racial integration, liberal social scientists described blacks as self-hating and explained black culture as violent and joyless, a pathological version of mainstream (i.e., white) culture, while black writers, notably, Richard Wright, highlighted the pathological effects of racism on black life. Ellison, who declared that he had never for a moment hated *himself,* denounced the arguments of such "friends of the Negro" in his essays as patronizing and distorted.[20]

Again this is an oversimplification. It does not do justice to the complexity of either Ellison's or Wright's thought. Both men were incorporating ideas ranging from psychology to existentialism to class analysis in order to explain Afro-Americans and their integral American experience. It is not inherently conservative to critique liberal social science damage theorists. Daryl Michael Scott and Robin D. G. Kelley, rightly, come down on them, and they are on the Left.[21]

Leftist analyses of Ellison's *Invisible Man* sometimes misstepped also. Whether it was Irving Howe's demand that black writing mine the fields of oppression and protest or Robert E. Washington's suggestion that we view "*Invisible Man*'s existentialist perspective on black American life, again as a subtext, but now linked to moderate bourgeois liberalism and the American democratic creed," there is an acute misunderstanding of Ellison's purpose and historical mentality.[22]

Ellison himself in the "The World and The Jug" ably answered Howe's critique. But Robert E. Washington's analysis is more plausible than Greg Robinson's attempt to situate Ellison as a modern conservative. Ellison's shift from Marxist ideology to existential, psychological individualism certainly owed much to Cold War political influences, but there was also disillusionment with the Communist Party's enterprise. While Richard Wright left the country and Harold Cruse, the historian and former Communist Party member, turned to cultural nationalism, Ellison chose an entirely different route: that of seeing America as a fluid multicultural democracy that was fragmenting and reinventing itself continuously. As Alan Nadel aptly put it: "Throughout his career, in other words, Ellison has emphasized the extent to which he emerged from an integrated cultural heritage."[23]

Ellison's multicultural view goes beyond the pluralism that he advocated at the time of *Invisible Man*'s publication. As the years went on, Ellison's understanding of American society's abilities to transform and reinvent itself deepened and matured. This enhanced understanding is surely what preoccupied him with his work-in-progress. As Ellison noted to John Hersey in a 1982 interview about the new work:

> Its exasperating, but at the same time I've come to feel that one of the challenges for a writer who handles the kind of material I'm working with is to let people speak for themselves in whatever way they can. Then you draw upon more of the resources of American vernacular speech.[24]

A critical reflection of *Invisible Man* clearly demonstrates that the foundation for the later work-in-progress was laid even as Ellison admitted that *Invisible Man* created a life of its own. It was the measure of Ellison's maturity and growth from *Invisible Man* that his last project moved him to penetrate even further into the American social psyche to consider the effects of the racial situation upon the American vernacular speech and the democratic moral code.

That is why an historical context of *Invisible Man* is crucial to an understanding of Ralph Ellison's thinking, which moved from Marxist philosophy to existentialist thought; from a knowledge of collective behavior to a trumpeting of individuality; and finally from an understanding of the unique historical experience of Afro-Americans to an equal understanding of the complexity of American multiculturalism. The glue or bond that holds it all together is democracy, freedom, and religion. The last aspect, religion, may seem surprising to some scholars, whether they lean left or right, but it is a testament to Ellison's solid understanding of black American and American folkways that religion held a strong currency in American society.

We need only to recall for a moment the milieu of the 1950s. Fresh from the ravages of World War II and the shocking revelation of the Holocaust,

America set about to regain its moral bearings. From Norman Vincent Peale's power of positive thinking to the mesmerizing lilt of Bishop Fulton J. Sheen's anti-communist sermons and on to Billy Graham's evangelical proclamations, conveyed on that new invention of technology, television, Americans were awash in a culture that promoted prayer for familial unity and promoted church-going as a strong communal activity. Most importantly, as Ralph Ellison was well aware, it was religion which could serve as a balm against oppression and would soon become a focal point for the struggle for Afro-Americans' civil rights and democratic freedom.

Although *Invisible Man* does not explicitly feature these religious aspects in the way that Ellison's work-in-progress did, it is nonetheless deeply implicit. As Ellison's thought matured, he recognized the importance of religion and its shaping of morality in American history. In the 1982 interview with John Hersey, Ellison ruminated on religion's force in American society and politics. Given the rise of the religious Right and of conservatism in general at that time, Ellison noted "how we turn our eyes away from the role that religion has continued to play in American life." Ellison was concerned with the reemergence of religion that was a "potent and in some ways dangerous force." For Ellison, the danger lay in the fact that "we were not paying attention to its significance in all those earlier years."[25] The significance of religion for Ellison was best exemplified in Afro-American Christianity's role in the Civil Rights Movement. For Ellison:

> Negro religion has been a counterbalance to much of the inequality and imposed chaos which has been the American Negro experience. When Martin Luther King, Jr., emerged as an important American figure, it was an instance of the church making itself visible in the political and social life and fulfilling its role in the realm of morality.[26]

The main worry here was that the moral capital that religion held in America was being expended in extreme ways that threatened American democracy and freedom. That extremism came from certain elements of the religious Right and from black religious organizations, such as Louis Farrakhan's revival of the Nation of Islam. Religion, then, for Ellison, was important to America's moral health. But if there is an averting of our eyes away from religion's importance, we ultimately must confront its appearance in extremis. Ellison tried to show that, implicitly, in *Invisible Man* when the narrator joins the Brotherhood and then is confronted by Ras the Exhorter. Both the Brotherhood and Ras are "religious" extremes and the narrator is forced to see that neither of them can work towards providing humanity with freedom and dignity.

The rejection of extremism in religion and politics caused Ellison to be placed undeservedly at the margins of public intellectual discourse. In the early sixties, as we have seen, Ellison's thinking was overshadowed by the writings of James Baldwin. Later, black militants angrily dismissed Ellison and *Invisible Man* in favor of more extreme proclamations of black power, black pride, and, in some cases, black separatism. In the most peculiar irony of them all, Ellison's work and thinking were cloaked in invisibility in the sixties and seventies.[27] Nevertheless, Ralph Ellison continued to write and continued to grant interviews where he tried to uncover his ideas. That his thinking and his stance as a public intellectual reemerged in the 1980s is a testament to the truth-value of his ideas and the important function of the Afro-American intellectual to American intellectual discourse.

After 50 years, then, *Invisible Man* stands not only the test of time in a literary sense but also stands tall before the scrutiny of American intellectual history. Ralph Ellison wove a memorable tale of coming of age: a majestic quest for identity and the meaning of humanity that spoke not only to the individual but also to a nation searching for the meaning of who she is.

Part of the brilliance of *Invisible Man* was and is its ability to situate histor-ically the black experience firmly within the overall American experience— and then transcend it. In what has to be a crowning accomplishment, Ellison went from the particular (race) to the universal (America writ large) and back to the particular (the individual), demonstrating all along the way the impor-tance of race, region, class, gender, and perhaps most importantly, the past on the making of who we are. Ellison put it eloquently, and deceptively simply, when he explained:

> [Y]ou just write for your own time, while trying to write in terms of the density of experience, knowing perfectly well that life repeats itself. Even in this rapidly changing United States it repeats itself. The mystery is that while repeating itself it always manages slightly to change the mask. To be able to grasp a little of that change within continuity and to communicate it across all divisions of background and individual expectations seems enough for me.[28]

Ralph Waldo Ellison's *Invisible Man*, after 50 years, has succeeded in changing the mask: The veil of invisibility for the Afro-American intellectual has been lifted.

ENDNOTES

1. These excerpts are from Ralph Ellison's "Introduction to the Thirtieth Anniver-sary Edition of *Invisible Man*," in *The Collected Essays of Ralph Ellison,* ed. John F. Callahan (New York: Modern Library, 1995), 484 and 479–80. Hereinafter referred to as *Collected Essays.*

2. Ralph Ellison, "Introduction to Thirtieth Anniversary Edition of *Invisible Man*," 480; "Working Notes for *Invisible Man*," *Collected Essays,* 344.

3. "Introduction to Thirtieth Anniversary Edition of *Invisible Man*," 482–83.

4. See James M. McPherson, ed., *To the Best of My Ability: The American Presidents* (New York: Dorsley Kinderly, 2000), "Introduction," 3–10; Peter Novick, *That Noble Dream: The Objectivity Question and the American Historical Profession* (New York: Cambridge University Press, 1988), Chapter 3; Harold Evans, *In Defense of History* (New York: Penguin, 1998), Chapters 11 for excellent historiographical analyses.

5. Richard Hofstader is a good example of an historian who was a Socialist who became a leader in the Consensus School. Others include Daniel Boorstin and Arthur Schlesinger, Jr. See Novick, *That Noble Dream,* Chapters 10 and 11.

6. Jerry Gafio Watts, *Heroism and the Black Intellectual: Ralph Ellison, Politics, and Afro-American Intellectual Life* (Chapel Hill: University of North Carolina Press, 1994). For analyses of Stanley Crouch, see Greg Robinson, "Ralph Ellison, Albert Murray, Stanley Crouch, and Modern Black Cultural Conservatism," Peter Eisenstadt, ed., *Black Conservatism: Essays in Intellectual and Political History* (New York: Garland Publishing, Inc., 1999), 151–67. Hereinafter cited as "Ralph Ellison." James Alan McPherson's interview with Ralph Ellison can be found in "Indivisible Man," *Collected Essays,* 353–95. McPherson's collection of fiction, *Hue and Cry* and *Elbow Room,* are in the Ellisonian tradition. For McPherson's understanding of "double consciousness," see "Junior and John Doe," Gerald Early, ed., *Lure and Loathing: Essays on Race, Identity, and the Ambivalence of* Assimilation (New York: Allen Lane, The Penguin Press, 1993), 175–93.

7. Ross Posnock, *Color and Culture: Black Writers and the Making of the Modern Intellectual* (Cambridge, Mass.: Harvard University Press, 1998), 187. See also Louis Menand, *The Metaphysicians Club* (New York: Knopf, 2001), Chapter 3, for background on William James.

8. Carol Posgrove, *Divided Minds: American Intellectuals and the Civil Rights Movement* (New York: W.W. Norton, 2001), 66–72; David Levering Lewis, *W. E. B. Du Bois: The Fight for Equality and the American Century, 1919–1963* (New York: Henry Holt & Co., 2000), Chapter 9, 305–10.

9. Ellison letter to his mother (August 30, 1937) in John F. Callahan, "'American Culture is of a Whole': From the Letters of Ralph Ellison," *The New Republic* (March 1, 1999), 36.

10. Arnold Rampersad is currently writing the authorized biography of Ralph Ellison. But see also Lawrence Jackson, *Ralph Ellison: Emergence of a Genius* (New York: John Wiley & Sons, 2002), 184–86. Jackson maintains that Ellison was a close fellow traveler but never really committed to joining the Party.

11. On criticisms of Ellison and *Invisible Man,* see Irving Howe, "Review of *Invisible Man*," *The Nation,* May 10, 1952. On John O. Killen's' criticism of Ellison and *Invisible Man,* see Harold Cruse, *The Crisis of the Negro Intellectual* (New York: Quill, 1967, reissued 1983), 506–10.

12. Ralph Ellison, "The World and The Jug," *Shadow and Act* (New York: Random House, 1953, 1964; reprinted 1994), 131.

13. See Kenneth Robert Janken, *Rayford W. Logan and the Dilemma of the African American Intellectual* (Amherst: University of Massachusetts Press, 1993). Benjamin Quarles's historical thought is summarized by Bernard Weisberger in *American Legacy* (February 2001), 25–26. "Vindicationist" is Wilson J. Moses's term. See his *Afrotopia: The Roots of African American Popular History* (New York: Cambridge University Press, 1998) for further elaboration.

14. Letter to S. E. Hyman, May 29, 1970, "American Culture is of a Whole," *New Republic* (March 1, 1999), 41.

15. Robert E. Washington, *The Ideologies of African American Literature: From the Harlem Renaissance to the Black Nationalist Revolt* (New York: Rowman & Littlefield, 2001), 205.

16. Robinson, "Ralph Ellison," 151.

17. Robinson, "Ralph Ellison," 152.

18. See Ralph Ellison, *Juneteenth: A Novel,* ed. John F. Callahan (New York: Random House, 2000). Murray could be considered a cultural conservative given his Tuskegee education and military background. But again he does not shy away from recognizing racism or race-based identity. He simply criticizes the uses to which they are put. For recent examples of Murray's thinking, see *From the Briarpatch File: On Context, Procedure, and American Identity* (New York: Pantheon Books, 2001). Crouch is a dissenter with iconoclastic views that make him very difficult to label. For examples of Crouch's thought, see two recent books of essays, *The All-American Skin Game, Or, The Decoy of Race: The Long and Short of It, 1990–1994* (New York: Vintage, 1997) and *Always in Pursuit: Fresh American Perspectives, 1995–1997* (New York: Pantheon Books, 1998).

19. Robinson, "Ralph Ellison," 154–55.

20. Robinson, "Ralph Ellison," 156–57.

21. Daryl Michael Scott, *Contempt and Pity: Social Policy and the Image of the Damaged Black Psyche, 1880–1996* (Chapel Hill: University of North Carolina Press, 1997), Chapters 5–7, and Robin D. G. Kelley, *Yo' Mama's Disfunktional: Fighting the Culture Wars in Urban America* (Boston: Beacon Press, 1998).

22. Howe, "Review of *Invisible Man*"; Washington, *Ideologies of African American Literature,* 202.

23. Ralph Ellison, "The World and The Jug," *Shadow and Act,* 107–143. On Richard Wright, see the standard biography by Michel Fabre, *The Unfinished Quest of Richard Wright* (Urbana: University of Illinois Press, 1973; second edition, 1993). See also Hazel Rowley, *Richard Wright: The Life and Times* (New York: Henry Holt, 2001). Alan Nadel, "Ralph Ellison and the American Canon," *American Literary History* 13, 2 (Summer 2001), 393.

24. Ralph Ellison, "A Completion of Personality," *Collected Essays,* 815.

25. Ralph Ellison, "A Completion of Personality," *Collected Essays,* 813.

26. Ibid.

27. On public intellectuals see Richard A. Posner, *Public Intellectuals: A Study in Decline* (Cambridge, Mass.: Harvard University Press, 2001). Posner's interesting analysis does not deal directly with Afro-American intellectuals but he does recognize that they can serve different and important functions (10–11).

28. Ralph Ellison, "A Completion of Personality," *Collected Essays,* 806.

Chapter 9

The Litany of Things: Sacrament and History in *Invisible Man*

MARC C. CONNER

The past is hidden somewhere outside the realm, beyond the reach of intellect, in some material object (in the sensation which that material object will give us) of which we have no inkling. And it depends on chance whether or not we come upon this object before we ourselves must die.

—MARCEL PROUST, *REMEMBRANCE OF THINGS PAST*[1]

All my work is grounded in a concern with the hidden aspects of American history.

—RALPH ELLISON[2]

Near the end of "The Little Man at Chehaw Station," his magnificent essay on the mysterious cultural possibilities of America, Ralph Ellison comments that "if I had been more mature or perceptive back when I first heard of the little man behind the stove, an object that lay atop Miss Harrison's piano would have been most enlightening." Ellison then describes this potentially enlightening object, and its surprising significance, in evocative detail:

It was a signed Prokofiev manuscript that had been presented to her by the composer. Except for the signature, it looked like countless other manuscripts. Yet I suspect that to anyone who possessed a conventional notion of cultural and hierarchal order, its presence in such a setting would have been as incongruous as a Gutenberg Bible on the altar of a black sharecropper's church or a dashiki worn with a Homburg hat. Still, there it was: an artifact of contemporary music, a folio whose signs and symbols resonated in that setting with the intricate harmonies of friendship, admiration, and shared ideals through which it had found its way from Berlin to Tuskegee. Once there, and the arrangement of society beyond the campus notwithstanding, it spoke eloquently of the unstructured possibilities of culture in this pluralistic democracy. Yet despite its meticulous artistic form, in certain conventional minds its presence could arouse intimations of the irrational—of cultural, if not social, chaos.[3]

In this famous passage, Ellison views the material object as transformative, able to alter conventional ideas of time, history, politics, social hierarchy, and both self and group identity. This material object possesses an almost enchanting force, a power that far exceeds that of a merely material thing.

Such attention to objects is of great relevance to the African-American literary tradition, where the material world has long played a prominent role. Booker T. Washington famously pronounced, "I have great faith in the power and influence of *facts*. It is seldom that anything is permanently gained by holding back a *fact*."[4] African-American literature, in all its variety, is pervaded by this facticity, the "whatness" of the material world: Jacobs's detailed rendering of her nine-by-seven-by-three-foot garret; Douglass's repeated emphasis on the bodily conditions of slavery; Du Bois's anatomy of the economic and material structures of the post-Reconstruction rural South; Wright's naturalistic focus on the material determinants of Bigger's character and fate; Morrison's scrupulous attention to the cultural products of nineteenth- and early twentieth-century African-American life. The material quality of the world is always present in the African-American text.[5]

One of Ralph Ellison's remarkable traits is his awareness of the traditions that precede him—what Tony Tanner has called "Ellison's extremely literate memory"[6]—and in the presence of material objects this is quite apparent. For *Invisible Man* is dominated by a sustained litany of things, a procession of tangible, material objects that move in and out of the text, sometimes appearing only once and briefly, sometimes reappearing at crucial times: the leg chain, the briefcase, the letters, the grinning minstrel figure, the statue of the Founder, Trueblood's cabin, the blueprints, the paint, the hospital machine, Mary's cabbage, the dancing Sambo doll, Rinehart's hat and glasses, and many others. *Invisible Man* is a textual world seething with material things that unite the entire narrative, propel the narrator on his multiple journeys, and force him to his most crucial realizations. Careful attention to the objects he encounters determines the Invisible Man's destiny, and Ellison takes extraordinary care in his use and rendering of these objects. Indeed, the novel's most vivid moments cluster about these material things, which rise up to dominate the story. We might say of Ellison, as Walter Benjamin said of Proust, "there has never been anyone else with [his] ability to show us things."[7]

But these objects, as a careful attention to the text reveals, are not *merely* material. The things in *Invisible Man* do not simply exist in present time and space; rather, they are portals to a larger concept of time, history, and identity than is otherwise available to the Invisible Man. In short, they are sacramental: visible and material signs for the invisible and immaterial realm beyond.[8] The

Christian sacraments are seen as both signs of that greater world, and the very cause of that greater world—as Edward Schillebeeckx explains, "sacraments are symbols *that cause through signifying.*"[9] Similarly, Ellison's objects do not merely point the Invisible Man towards a larger universe—they create that universe, and make it exist in the present moment. Furthermore, the sacramental brings the individual out of his isolation, and into a larger sense of the present (an expanded notion of *communitas*) as well as an expanded idea of the past. The sacrament enacts, as Sarah Beckwith argues, "a ritual of remembrance."[10] Such a movement toward an expanded sense of time and of one's identity with the past is at the very heart of the Invisible Man's quest.

Ellison's sacramental use of the material world parallels Walter Benjamin's concept of the extraordinary revelatory power contained in objects—what Benjamin terms the "dialectical image." This concept is at the heart of Benjamin's aesthetics as well as his philosophy of history. Throughout his work, Benjamin argues that certain images from the past contain a revelatory power, which, if seen aright, unveils an astonishing correspondence between the past and the present—a correspondence that transcends mere historical chronology:

> The past does not throw its light onto the present, nor does the present illumine the past, but an image is formed when that which has been and the Now come together in a flash as a constellation. In other words, image is dialectic at a standstill. For while the relationship of the present to the past is a purely temporal one, the relationship of that which has been to the Now is a dialectical one.[11]

The perceptions of these objects (what Benjamin terms "the image"), as Michael Jennings explains the process, "provide an essential revelation of the true historical character of the past," as well as "reveal to the reader the only possible accurate understanding of the present."[12] In the presence of these objects, one has an experience of time that is dialectical, a back-and-forth oscillation between a new sense of the past and a new sense of the present, both happening simultaneously, caused by the revelatory action of perceiving the object. The moment of seeing this dialectical correspondence Benjamin describes as "rapturous," a "shock of rejuvenation." The perceiver beholds time anew, in a moment of seeing that is independent of one's will or agency— what Benjamin terms *memoire involontaire,* the "involuntary recollection."[13] This process, Benjamin argues, is at the very heart of Proust's aesthetic.

It is also at the very heart of Ellison's novel. Like Proust, Ellison is what Benjamin evocatively describes as "the remembering author,"[14] an author whose central obsession is the elusive, buried relation of the past to the present— "the spell of history," as John Callahan has put it.[15] Ellison's conception of history, like that of Benjamin and Proust, transcends temporal chronology, what Ellison dismisses as "official history." Ellison seeks throughout his writings to explore those "realities of American historical experience ruled out officially," that "stream of history . . . tightly connected with folklore and the oral tradition."[16] Ellison works to resurrect the past for the very purpose of seeing it anew, to reevaluate and reconsider its meaning both for the past and for the present. In this, too, Ellison parallels Benjamin, whose historical project is "redemptive," an effort to resurrect past images "from the burial ground of history," "so that some few images might reveal the fragments of truth scattered amidst the dross."[17] "Official history" for Ellison is limited to mere fact, to necessity; but his notion of history, as Callahan argues, is "comic in the sense that it opens up the field of possibility." Ellison is therefore what Callahan terms "a moral historian," one who

> prevents official history from imposing too false an order on American life. To put it positively, the pursuit of history provides a form and a frame for self-discovery. For Ellison the crucial point is that time and chronology offer cover to the historian, whereas the novelist, as he sees the craft, has nowhere to hide from the requirements of the moral imagination.[18]

Similarly, Benjamin's idea of historical awareness, as he expresses it in his "Theses on the Philosophy of History," consists in liberating historical truth from the "conformism" of the official historiographers: "For every image of the past that is not recognized by the present as one of its own concerns threatens to disappear irretrievably." Consequently, "to articulate the past historically . . . means to seize hold of a memory as it flashes up at a moment of danger. Historical materialism wishes to retain that image of the past which unexpectedly appears to man singled out by history at a moment of danger."[19] This is precisely how the potent material objects function throughout *Invisible Man:* Arising indeed at moments of danger, they explode the conventional story of history, and show instead the imaginative, even metaphysical, possibilities embedded within any cultural object. Far from being merely materialistic, Ellison's objects are phenomenological, emphasizing the revelatory power contained within the present moment of being. Or put differently, his use of history is mythic: Ellison shows how the present moment manifests an eternal, recurring archetype.

One of the most significant examples of this dialectical revelation provided by material objects is the Yam scene. This chapter, the thirteenth of the novel's twenty-five, is set at the very center of the book. The previous chapter ends with the Invisible Man "long[ing] for home," and this chapter begins by emphasizing his lack of place: "At first I had turned away from the window and tried to read but my mind kept wandering back to my old problems and, unable to endure it any longer, I rushed from the house."[20] He is homeless, wandering, and has reached the greatest state of his "lostness" in the novel; at this moment, he passes a shop window and confronts the worst of material culture:

> A flash of red and gold from a window filled with religious articles caught my eye. And behind the film of frost etching the glass I saw two brashly

painted plaster images of Mary and Jesus surrounded by dream books, love powders, God-Is-Love signs, money-drawing oil and plastic dice. A black statue of a nude Nubian slave grinned out at me from beneath a turban of gold. I passed on to a window decorated with switches of wiry false hair, ointments guaranteed to produce the miracle of whitening black skin. (262)

This is the material with nothing sacramental beyond it; here identity consists in mere surface appearance, suggesting to the Invisible Man that he is self-less—indeed everyone is self-less—and there is nothing beneath his surface appearance to be made visible. This parallels what he learns in the Rinehart section, where identity is defined as all-too-fluid possibility, with no essential self beneath the hat and the glasses—what Ellison describes elsewhere as "the personification of chaos."[21] This threat to the Invisible Man's very notion of the integrity of the self brings him to the edge of madness, as he "becom[es] aware that I was muttering to myself again" (262).

"Then," he states, "I saw an old man warming his hands against the sides of an odd-looking wagon, from which a stove pipe reeled off a thin spiral of smoke that drifted the odor of baking yams slowly to me, bringing a stab of swift nostalgia" (262). The scene that unfolds after the sight of this ancestor-figure is astonishingly sensual, invoking (literally, as the spiral of smoke suggests) all the senses: the sound of the man's cry ("Get yo' hot, baked Car'lina yam"), the "odor of baking yams," the "flash of warmth" he feels from the "glowing coals," the taste of the yam itself ("as sweet and hot as any I'd ever had"), and particularly the sight of it. He states, "I can look at it and see it's good" (263–64)—this is no longer the deceptive world of appearances, but *reality*, a physical domain that is tangible, even digestible.

When he bites into the yam, he is "overcome with such a surge of home-sickness," and at the same time "just as suddenly overcome by an intense feeling of freedom" (264). His sense of both the past and the present shift as he chews the yam; he recalls his past, and is suddenly aware that "time seemed endlessly expanded" (263). This contact with a sacramental material object not only alters his sense of time, but also brings about a sudden awareness of identity—both his own, and that of the people from whom he emerges: "I stopped as though struck by a shot, deeply inhaling, remembering, my mind surging back, back. *At home we'd bake them . . .*" (262–63; emphasis added). And he suddenly identifies with, and (crucially) laughs at, his community—"what a group of people we were," he muses, as he imagines a rollicking folk insult he could spew at Bledsoe ("it would be worse than if I had accused him of raping an old woman of ninety-nine years, weighing ninety pounds . . . blind in one eye and lame in the hip" [264–65]). His identification with the past brings about what Callahan terms "a comic perspective," in astonishing contrast with the grim madness with which the chapter begins.[22] Most important of all, the experience brings him to his first true assertion of selfhood: "'They're my birthmark,' he proudly proclaims. 'I yam what I yam' " (266).

This moment is clearly meant to parallel the *madeleine* scene in Proust's *Remembrance of Things Past,* with the delightful American difference of which Ellison is so aware: no dainty French pastry here, but *yams.*[23] For Marcel, too, the scene of remembrance begins with thoughts of home and of his mother, and only at the physical touch of the tea and cake does he realize the "extraordinary thing that was happening to me. An exquisite pleasure had invaded my senses, something isolated, detached, with no suggestion of its origin."[24] He describes the resulting "unremembered state" as a rising-up of that which had long been lost—not merely forgotten (which would make it accessible to what Proust terms "voluntary memory") but *lost,* and hence retrievable only by contact with an extraordinary material thing:

> I feel something start within me, something that leaves its resting-place and attempts to rise, something that has been embedded like an anchor at a great depth; I do not know yet what it is, but I can feel it mounting slowly; I can measure the resistance, I can hear the echo of great spaces traversed.
>
> Undoubtedly what is thus palpitating in the depths of my being must be the image, the visual memory which, being linked to that taste, is trying to follow it into my conscious mind.[25]

When the past event finally arises, when "suddenly the memory revealed itself," Marcel sees again the world of his childhood: "the old grey house" and "with the house the town . . . the Square where I used to be sent before lunch, the streets along which I used to run errands, the country roads. . . .'" Such an evocation of what is no longer remembered, "so long abandoned and put out of mind," can occur only involuntarily, only through the sensual contact with the material thing:

> [W]hen from a long-distant past nothing subsists, after the people are dead, after the things are broken and scattered, taste and smell alone, more fragile but more enduring, more unsubstantial, more persistent, more faithful, remain poised a long time, like souls, remembering, waiting, hoping, amid the ruins of all the rest; and bear unflinchingly, in the tiny and almost impalpable drop of their essence, the vast structure of recollection.[26]

Furthermore, just as Proust's work is a monumental coming-of-age tale, so too Ellison's protagonist here takes his first positive step towards self-determination. It is time, he realizes, to grapple with the "problem of choice," time to "weigh many things carefully before deciding," time to "[form] a personal attitude toward so much" (266–67).

Indeed this moment, for both Proust and Ellison, is more than mere maturation—it is a spiritual rebirth. The madeleine and the tea for Proust figure as the sacramental wafer and wine, and the moment of Marcel's remembrance is also a spiritual death and resurrection.[27] For the Invisible Man, too, this is a moment of spiritual rebirth, as he begins to move from death to life, and from blindness to insight. He signals this revelation in the Prologue, when he states that before "I lived in the darkness into which I was chased, but now I see" (13). The allusion to "Amazing Grace" further suggests the spiritual element in this rebirth that contrasts with the false rebirth in the hospital machine, in which the narrator emerges from a mechanical womb into a meaningless world. Consequently, the material object enables the Invisible Man to begin to *see*—and, of course, blindness is his real problem, not invisibility. (That's the problem of those who cannot see him, like the "poor blind fool" of the Prologue, whom the Invisible Man nearly kills, before realizing that "the man had not *seen* me, actually" [4]. Hence at the novel's end he claims, "I'm invisible, not blind" [576].) This is the crucial opening to experience, the lifting of the scales from his eyes, that the Invisible Man must have for the episode that follows: the great Eviction scene.

The Eviction scene is the pivot of the entire novel, and presents its defining metaphor: the plight of the evicted, the homeless, the dispossessed. In his early essay, "Harlem is Nowhere" (a crucial background study for *Invisible Man*), Ellison evokes this condition as a peculiar disintegration of any sense of self or belonging: "One 'is' literally, but one is nowhere; one wanders dazed in a ghetto maze, a 'displaced person' of American democracy."[28] Or, as the woman phrases it in another Harlem essay, "The Way It Is," "Anybody's liable to get dispossessed."[29] Although he sees this as a particularly pressing condition for the African American—"In our society it is not unusual for a Negro to experience a sensation that he does not exist in the real world at all"[30]—nevertheless for Ellison this condition is an archetypal experience. It reaches as far back as the Book of Exodus (perhaps even to Genesis 3) and as far forward as the anxiety adumbrated by Heidegger and Sartre. Ellison views it not merely as the quintessential American condition, but as the defining human condition, what he terms "the 'harlemness' of the national human predicament."[31]

This scene, too, begins with the Invisible Man walking through a cloud of smoke, but here it is not the upward-spiraling smoke of invocation, but the slow burning of a packing box on the street—a more infernal burning. Again, his vision begins with an intimation of home, as he sees "a motherly-looking old woman" in the chair being lugged by the trustees. This woman singles out the Invisible Man from the crowd of onlookers, and focuses his attention on the material things before him: "The old woman sobbed, pointing to the stuff piled along the curb. 'Just look what they doing to us. Just look,' looking straight at me. And I realized that what I'd taken for junk was actually worn household furnishings" (267–68).

Then, just as in the Yam scene, a procession of memories begins to stir in him, in response to the objects he beholds: "The old woman's sobbing was having a strange effect upon me—as when a child, seeing the tears of its parents, is moved by both fear and sympathy to cry. I turned away, feeling myself being drawn to the old couple by a warm, dark, rising whirlpool of emotion which I feared" (270). He fears what might emerge from this primal pool of emotion and memory, but also realizes that he is seeing his own identity before him, that he "was rapidly becoming too much a part of it to leave." He tries to turns aside, only to be confronted again by "the clutter of household objects," which directs him to the image of the old couple looking back at him: "I looked down to see looking out of an oval frame a portrait of the old couple when young, seeing the sad, stiff dignity of the faces there; feeling strange memories awakening that began an echoing in my head" (271). His own gaze is returned by the old couple, now young, in the picture, as the past and the present moment begin to merge both in the object before him and within his own consciousness.

Here, the astonishing litany of things begins: the knocking bones (evoking the history of the minstrel tradition); the suggestions of home and family in the "God Bless Our Home" card; the "High John the Conqueror" stone (with its connection to folk legends); the Lincoln portrait and the Ethiopian flag (richly suggesting a whole century of political strife); the evidence of the mother, children, and grandchildren in the child's greeting card and the old breast pump; the faded baseball scoring card (pointing to the then-unwritten history of the Negro Leagues). Story after story is embedded within these objects, which constitute what one scholar calls "the evoking of the entire Black tradition."[32] Then comes the most powerful object of all, the freedom papers. At this moment the Invisible Man feels himself jarred loose from the present, as past and present collapse into a single experience. With trembling hands and labored breath, he thinks, "*It has been longer than that, further removed in time,* I told myself, and yet I knew that it hadn't been" (271–72). This jarring re-vision of the relation of the past to the present produces a nausea in the Invisible Man, but he is unable to vomit; he cannot so easily purge himself of what he is seeing.

Instead, the Invisible Man looks beyond the objects themselves, to what they point towards, which is precisely his very past, and he experiences both an individual and a communal recollection:

> I turned and stared again at the jumble, no longer looking at what was before my eyes, but inwardly-outwardly, around a corner into the dark, far-away-and-long-ago, not so much of my own memory as of remembered words, of linked verbal echoes, images, heard even when not listening at home. And it was as though I myself was being dispossessed of some painful yet precious thing which I could not bear to lose. . . . And with this sense of dispossession came a pang of vague recognition. (273)

What gives this experience such revelatory power for the Invisible Man is not the mere objects themselves—in truth, he sees nothing he has not seen before, as his quick recognition of each object confirms—but rather the shock with which they force him to re-see the past.[33] Or put differently, and to use Benjamin's terms, it is not the finite experience that matters, but rather the infinite world of memory that it opens up. "For an experienced event is finite," argues Benjamin, "confined to one sphere of experience; a remembered event is infinite, because it is only a key to everything that happened before it and after it."[34] The act of involuntary recollection is infinite in that it transforms one's sense of the past, the present, and the future. This is precisely what happens in this pivotal scene. Indeed, this is *why* this scene is so pivotal, and why the narrator remarks that "this junk" "throbbed within me *with more meaning than there should have been*" (273; emphasis added).

But more remains to be accomplished. So far, the recollection is tame enough; he feels a stronger identification with his past community, a stirring of a sense of self—all elements that we see elsewhere in the novel. But what follows is simply extraordinary, a unique event in this book:

> *And why did I, standing in the crowd, see like a vision my mother hanging wash on a cold windy day, so cold that the warm clothes froze even before the vapor thinned and hung stiff on the line, and her hands white and raw in the skirt-swirling wind and her gray head bare to the darkened sky—why were they causing me discomfort* so far beyond their intrinsic meaning as objects? *And why did I see them now, as behind a veil that threatened to lift, stirred by the cold wind in the narrow street?* (273; emphasis added)

For the first time the Invisible Man senses what might cure the disease that pervades the novel, the sickness of dispossession and homelessness that the eviction scene epitomizes. This sickness is the very antithesis of Ellison's ethical ideal, what he calls "being at home in the world."[35] This is why, at the furthest depth of recollection, he sees the image of his mother. In a novel dominated by the struggle with fathers, from Bledsoe to the mad Vet to Jack to the enigmatic grandfather, we have a rare emergence of the mother. Ellison is thinking once again in mythic terms: the struggle with the father is the signal event in the establishment of the hero's identity, which is the overt quest of this novel; but the figure of the mother establishes *home,* the starting point from which the hero begins his journey towards identity and fulfillment, and to which he returns when his quest is complete.[36] One way to understand the Invisible Man's existential plight is that of the hero without origin and without destination—the motherless man. Consequently the Invisible Man now feels the "discomfort" that so far exceeds the mere objects before him: He beholds what he lacks, a lack that precedes and underlies his lack of identity and of name.

Indeed, he was not even aware of this lack, until it was made known to him through the crucial figure of Mary Rambo, who succors the Invisible

Man in the chapter that precedes the Eviction scene. When the Invisible Man leaves the factory hospital at the end of Chapter 11, he has been evacuated of self, and only his refusal to relinquish his folk heritage has kept him from the full lobotomizing that the doctors plan for him.[37] Chapter 12 opens with him emerging from the subway onto Lenox Avenue, fainting, and being rescued by Mary, the "big dark woman" who asks him repeatedly, "*Boy, is you all right?*" When he says he needs to get to Men's House, Mary rejects the destination, exclaiming, "*shucks that ain't no place for nobody in your condition what's weak and needs a woman to keep an eye on you awhile.*" Mary knows the community of Harlem, where she functions as a kind of mother of mercy—"*I'll take care of you like I done a heap of others*"—and she offers the narrator his first lesson in ethics:

> *I don't care what you think about me but you weak and caint hardly walk and all and you look what's more like you hungry, so just come on and let me do something for you like I hope you'd do something for ole Mary in case she needed it.* (251–52)

The lesson, and its timing, is crucial. For all its emphasis on Emersonian self-reliance (a value Ellison held quite dear), the novel here claims that self-reliance alone is not sufficient. One must depend upon, and contribute to, the good of others, without any hope for payment other than that of the Golden Rule: "all things whatsoever ye would that men should do to you, do ye even so to them" (Matthew 7:12). This ethical lesson he learns from Mary is the very opposite of the ruthless selfishness preached by Bledsoe: "Well, that's the way it is. It's a nasty deal and I don't always like it myself. But you listen to me: I didn't make it, and I know that I can't change it. But I've made my place in it and I'll have every Negro in the country hanging on tree limbs by morning if it means staying where I am" (143). Furthermore, Mary's communal ethic also contrasts with the solipsistic advice of the mad Vet, of Jack, of Dupre, and of virtually every other father-figure in the novel. The fathers urge the Invisible Man to "be your own father" (156), to assume creation to himself and isolate himself from all others. Mary is the first figure who urges the Invisible Man to turn towards others to find his own self-fulfillment.

This is the oft-overlooked complement to the Invisible Man's search for self-identity: He must insert that identity into a larger community for it to be whole and healthy. As he states at the end, "we had to take the responsibility for all of it" (574). Indeed, this is the very basis of Emerson's *full* definition of self-reliance (of which Ellison was surely aware): "It is easy in the world to live after the world's opinion; it is easy in solitude to live after our own; but the great man is he who in the midst of the crowd keeps with perfect sweetness the independence of solitude."[38] I can think of no better gloss on the Invisible Man's trajectory: His error through the first half of the novel is to live after the world's opinion; His error as he approaches the novel's conclusion is to isolate himself after his own; but the harmony between self and society, which is the ideal of both Emerson and Ellison, is the position towards which Mary would guide him.[39] This ethical teaching constitutes Ellison's true attitude towards Emerson: The novel offers not merely a satire of Emerson, as many have argued, and not merely an apology for Emerson; rather, Ellison (characteristically) both affirms and denies the Emersonian heritage, insisting on the autonomy of the self, but also on the self's need to enter into the community. In James Albrecht's words, Ellison seeks to "revise Emerson's individualism as [he extends] it, adding a more political notion of social responsibility to Emerson's ethic of self-expressive activity."[40]

The pivotal effect of Mary in the Invisible Man's development is indicated by the much larger role she plays in what Ellison terms "the original version" of the novel. Ellison published this extract from the manuscripts in 1963, as a long story in which Mary rescues the Invisible Man from the factory hospital. Ellison stated that he "found it quite pleasurable to discover . . . that it was Mary, a woman of the folk, who helped release the hero from the machine." He also said that Mary "deserved more space in the novel and would, I think, have made it a better book."[41] Of particular importance in the unpublished excerpt is the way in which Mary rescues the Invisible Man: She renames him, she recalls him to his family and his past, she feeds him, and she heals him through a "home remedy" that connects him to a much deeper concept of the American past.

Upon discovering the Invisible Man in his machine-like coffin in the hospital, Mary exclaims that he must be "Jack the Bear or John Henry"—conferring upon him the status of a hero who will survive his hibernation and emerge as a great folk leader. The Invisible Man wonders at "this feeling that I had known her for a long time"; he senses that "her voice was strangely familiar," and wonders if she is "a lost relative, a member of my forgotten family." Mary senses that his real problem is not physical, but spiritual: "Shucks, boy," she exclaims, "I ain't one of them doctors. You don't have to tell me that stuff. How long you been from down home?" She feeds him a pork sandwich piece by piece, "as though actually feeding a baby." She then returns with "a little home remedy, something I got from my mama." The Invisible Man is astonished—"You have a mother?" he exclaims—and Mary's response suggests what she will offer him: "Sure, haven't you? Everybody got a mother." When she tells him that her mother is going on 104, and that the cure itself was known to "her mama's mama," we realize that the medicine goes back to at least the early eighteenth century, and perhaps to African origins.[42] This fascinating excerpt suggests that, in Ellison's thinking, Mary provides not only a link to the Invisible Man's immediate past, but also to a deeper origin that arises at least partly in the mythic African past.

O'Meally states that Mary's "inextinguishable love and faith in the hero's sanity and manhood rescue him from destruction in the tomblike machine."[43] Her role as savior is dramatically clear in the excerpt, but this only amplifies what is evident in the novel as published. As Claudia Tate argues, Mary is more than just another of the important folk-figures delineated by George Kent and Robert O'Meally; she functions as the crucial figure who begins his ascent towards self-realization: "she is . . . the vehicle by which he departs from the world of 'Keep this Nigger-Boy Running' and arrives at the threshold of a new region of consciousness where he moves towards realizing his adult, heroic potential."[44] Mary offers to the Invisible Man the mother-figure that he so desperately needs. She gives him the first nurturing, the first sense of "home," he experiences in the novel. This experience of literal *caritas* intimates to the Invisible Man what he lacks, and thereby opens him—prepares the spiritual ground—for what he will experience in the Yam scene and the Eviction scene. His lack is all the more acute due to his sense of its potential fulfillment through Mary, and this provides much of the pathos and transformative power of the Eviction scene.

That this process of involuntary recollection should bring the Invisible Man back to the figure of the mother and the original home is no accident; such is the fundamental impulse behind the involuntary memory. "The preserve of memory," writes Benjamin, contains "the eternal repetition, the eternal restoration of the original, the first happiness."[45] This "first happiness" lies hidden beneath layers of forgetting, but through the proper constellation of material objects, and the presence of enabling figures, it is stirred. Each of the crucial characters who appear in these pivotal scenes—Mary Rambo, the Yam vendor, and the Provos—functions as what Toni Morrison terms "the ancestor figure." Morrison describes this figure as the "advising, benevolent, protective, wise Black ancestor" who is generally absent from the city, surviving only in the village. The African-American writer, transplanted from the country to the city, from the south to the north, yearns for this figure: "The Black American writer," Morrison argues, desires "to touch the ancestor," who promises restoration to the mythic past, and constitutes what she calls "the matrix of his yearning."[46] Mary Rambo functions in this manner, as does the Blueprint Man, the Yam man, and particularly this old couple, "Primus Provo"—the first, the originary figure. Through his contact with these figures, the Invisible Man begins to awaken to where he has come from and what he has left behind.[47]

Crucially, the Invisible Man's most powerful confrontation with the dialectical aspect of the material object occurs in relation to something written—the freedom papers, whose very description conveys their tactile quality: "my fingers closed upon something resting in a frozen footstep: a fragile paper, coming apart with age, written in black ink grown yellow. I read . . ." (272). The act of reading, according to Jennings, is "that most dangerous of activities," in which "the present moment recognizes itself as prefigured in that past image and only thus discovers its true nature."[48] The physical fact of the freedom papers thrusts upon the narrator's consciousness the reality of slavery, and its proximity to his own present ("*It has been longer than that, further removed in time,* I told myself, and yet I knew that it hadn't been"). He senses, as in a shock, that his own status in the present is more akin to the slave status of the past than to the ideology of freedom that he has embraced, but never achieved. This realization of the American Contradiction is at the heart of Ellison's critique of American political history. Throughout his essays, Ellison emphasizes the tragic disjunction between "the ideal morality of the American Creed" and "the practical morality" of America's "anti-Negro practices"—what he describes as the "split in America's moral identity."[49] This collapsing of past and present occurs through the contact with the written word, suggesting that the most potent material object in this novel is the novel itself, the text as object—but again, not as merely material object, but as luminous object, charged with a special relationship to time past and time present, and ultimately, to time future.

Ellison's and Benjamin's shared emphasis on the written word as revelatory object shows their similarity to another major twentieth-century thinker, Martin Heidegger.[50] Heidegger held that within the present material word we can see traces of ancient meanings; indeed, for Heidegger this constitutes the very definition of philosophy: the "source" we find within the "Greek word" that is a "path" back to the origins of thought, but also forward to our own thought and that which is to come. "We can ask the question, 'What is philosophy?'" he argues, "only if we enter into a discussion with the thinking of the Greek world."[51] Hence philosophy for Heidegger—like the dialectical moment in Benjamin, and the confrontation of past and present in Ellison—is a "dialogue" or "reply," what he calls "co-respondence." The moment in which we sense this co-respondence, Heidegger states, is one of "astonishment," of "passion"—what Benjamin calls "rapture."[52] For Ellison, the equivalent term is the "boomerang" of history, and the narrator's description of that boomerang could well be used to illustrate Benjamin's theory of history: "that (by contradiction, I mean) is how the world moves: Not like an arrow, but a boomerang. (Beware of those who speak of the *spiral* of history; they are preparing a boomerang. Keep a steel helmet handy.)" (6).[53]

For Heidegger, too, this is a specifically *historical* experience, not in a chronological or empirical sense, but in a phenomenological sense. In our co-respondence to the meanings hidden within words, our false sense of the past is dismantled, and we see in a liberated manner the true relations of past and present:

> This path to the answer to our question is not a break with history, no repudiation of history, but is an adoption and transformation of what has been handed down to us. Such an adoption of history is what is meant by the term "destruction." . . . Destruction does not mean destroying but dismantling, liquidating, putting to one side the merely historical assertions about the history of philosophy. Destruction means—to open

our ears, to make ourselves free for what speaks to us in tradition as the Being of being. By listening to this interpellation we attain the correspondence.[54]

"Correspondence" is the same term Benjamin uses to describe the dialectical experience in the images of Proust.[55] In this moment, the object we behold in the present corresponds with (in Heidegger's sense, converses with) an object in the past, thereby shocking us into a reevaluation of the past and a new understanding of the present—precisely what happens to the Invisible Man within the extraordinary moment of the eviction scene. At the start of this chapter, he is wandering, homeless, isolated; by its end, he has found his vocation as an orator, he has asserted his relation to his community, he has claimed his identity with his past, and he has begun what will be a long journey towards self-fulfillment.[56]

The material objects before him have shattered the various worldviews in which he had been imprisoned. For Benjamin (as for Heidegger) such a destructive effect is the very aim of the dialectical image. It is synonymous with what he terms "the destructive character," a style of "comedy, not humor" that "does not toss the world up but flings it down—at the risk that it will be smashed to pieces."[57] For Benjamin, destruction is the goal of this revision of history. As Jennings describes his theory, it reflects "an urge—the manifestation of his nihilism—to fragment the cultural object and reduce it to a discontinuous series of images, to mortify the text, as Benjamin calls it."[58]

To be sure, the Invisible Man's worldview needs a good deal of smashing and fragmenting, for, like the machine in the hospital, it is a prison within which he is suffocating. However, at this point the parallels between Benjamin and Ellison diverge; here the novelist goes beyond the philosopher, for ultimately Ellison is not a destructive writer. Ellison's concern is simultaneously with clearing away *and* building anew—a far more difficult project than merely destroying. In the entire range of his writings, he seeks to outline and give some form to his idea of a redeemed American reality. The conclusion of the novel, in which "the principle" is affirmed over and above the fallible men who corrupt it, is the first step in this constructive process—as is the Invisible Man's determination to end the hibernation in favor of "a socially responsible role" (574–75, 581). In his essays, Ellison offers even more pronounced and forceful visions of the integrative possibilities of America. He defines "the ideal American character" as "a delicately poised unity of divergencies," what he describes as "the mystery of American identity (our unity-within-diversity)."[59] But such a revision of the American character requires a courageous and bold revision of our past and our present, and demands what Ellison terms "a tragicomic attitude toward the universe."[60] Through such a courageous revision, one might attain what is surely the desire of the Invisible Man: "that condition of man's being at home in the world, which is called love, and which we term democracy."[61]

This requires not merely a rethinking of American values, but a powerful healing of the wounds, fears, anxieties, and scars of nearly two hundred years of history. Near the end of the prologue (which is also in many ways the novel's conclusion—"the end was in the beginning" (571), another formulation of the dialectics of past and present), Ellison hints that healing is the very core of his project. In a reference that occurs "on the lower frequencies," he states, "All sickness is not unto death, neither is invisibility" (14). The words, of course, echo those of Kierkegaard, who famously states that "the sickness unto death is despair," then pronounces, "the opposite to being in despair is to have faith."[62] I think Ellison would provide the same answer. Ellison is not a religious writer—indeed, I am often surprised at the overwhelmingly secular nature of *Invisible Man,* something it does not share with the *Flying Home* stories[63]—but he does have a certain profession of faith, the "principles we all hold sacred" that he describes in the National Book Award speech. This state of love, of "being at home in the world," constitutes the sacred vision towards which Ellison strives in *Invisible Man.* But before we can conceive this, we must first be shaken out of our inaccurate, despairing sense of existence. As Kierkegaard puts it, in a formulation Ellison would certainly approve (for it describes the very path of the Invisible Man), "the self must be broken in order to become itself."[64]

As several scholars have noted, the novel proper imitates the *Inferno,* while the epilogue (and prologue) constitute the *Purgatorio;* but we do not see the *Paradiso.*[65] Ellison suggests that paradise is what we as Americans are tasked to build.[66] He envisions the ongoing work of building the sacred within human history, which will be possible only if we see beyond the material, and attend to the transforming, revelatory power of the images that are all around us. As Ellison states, "The work of art is, after all, an act of faith in our ability to communicate symbolically."[67] His vision is, ironically and yet logically (he might say, tragi-comically), akin to that of John Winthrop, who said of the original Americans, "we shall be as a city upon a hill." Ellison's own ideal—artistic, historical, religious—is similar: "a manifestation of the idealistic action of the American Word as it goads its users toward a perfection of our revolutionary ideals."[68]

ENDNOTES

1. Marcel Proust, *Remembrance of Things Past, Volume I: Swann's Way,* trans. C. K. Scott Moncrieff and Terence Kilmartin (New York: Random House, 1981) 49.

2. Ralph Ellison, Interview with John Hersey, quoted in Robert O'Meally, "Introduction," *New Essays on* Invisible Man, ed. Robert O'Meally (Cambridge: Cambridge UP, 1988) 7.

3. Ralph Ellison, "The Little Man at Chehaw Station," in *The Collected Essays of Ralph Ellison,* ed. John F. Callahan (New York: Random House, 1995) 512–13.

4. Booker T. Washington, *Up From Slavery* (New York: Oxford UP, 1995) 19.

5. Donald Petesch notes also this emphasis on the "thingy world of the black experience" in African-American literature. *A Spy in the Enemy's Country: The Emergence of Modern Black Literature* (Iowa City: U of Iowa P, 1989) 38–39.

6. Tony Tanner, *City of Words: American Fiction 1950–1970* (London: Jonathan Cape, 1971) 50.

7. Walter Benjamin, "The Image of Proust," in *Illuminations: Essays and Reflections,* ed. Hannah Arendt (New York: Schocken, 1968) 212.

8. The traditional Christian definition of "sacrament" is a visible and material sign, symbol, or ceremony of the invisible divine grace (*The Catholic Encyclopedia,* volume XIII (Robert Appleton Co., 1912) 295–96). Of course, this corresponds richly with the very heart of Ellison's project: to make visible the Invisible Man.

9. Edward Schillebeeckx, *Christ: The Sacrament of the Encounter with God* (London: Sheed and Ward, 1963); emphasis added. Quoted in Sarah Beckwith, *Signifying God: Social Relation and Symbolic Act in the York Corpus Christi Plays* (Chicago: U of Chicago P, 2001) 70. See also *The Catholic Encyclopedia:* "The sacraments of the Christian dispensation are not mere signs; they do not merely signify Divine grace, but in virtue of their Divine institution, they cause that grace in the souls of men" (296).

10. Beckwith, 3. See also p. 17, where Beckwith asserts that in sacramental ritual, "*communitas* is conjured, dreamed, sought for, embraced." The Greek term for sacrament, *mustêrion* or *mysterion,* is perhaps more adequate for this sense of sacrament as "the sign of something sacred and hidden" (*Catholic Encyclopedia* 295). *Mysterion* also connotes the time quality implied in sacrament: an ancient secret now revealed, embracing past, present, and future.

11. Walter Benjamin, *Gesammelte Schriften,* volume V, folio 3, 1. Quoted in Michael Jennings, *Dialectical Images: Walter Benjamin's Theory of Literary Criticism* (Ithaca: Cornell UP, 1987) 36.

12. Jennings, 36.

13. Benjamin, "The Image of Proust," 210–11.

14. Benajmin, "The Image of Proust," 202.

15. John F. Callahan, "Chaos, Complexity, and Possibility: The Historical Frequencies of Ralph Waldo Ellison," in *Speaking for You: The Vision of Ralph Ellison,* ed. Kimberly Benston (Washington, D.C.: Howard UP, 1987) 125.

16. Callahan, 126.

17. Jennings, 38.

18. Callahan, 130.

19. Walter Benjamin, "Theses on the Philosophy of History," in *Illuminations* 255.

20. Ralph Ellison, *Invisible Man* (New York: Vintage, 1981) 260–61. All subsequent citations will be noted parenthetically in the text by page number.

21. Ralph Ellison, "The Art of Fiction: An Interview," in *The Collected Essays of Ralph Ellison* 223. Tanner argues that "to emulate Rinehart would be to submit to chaos," for Rinehart "represents the ultimate diffusion and loss of self" (57). Harold Bloom's characterization of Rinehart is equally appropriate to my argument: Rinehart is "chaos verging upon entropy that negates any new origin *out of which a fresh creation might come*" ("Introduction," *Modern Critical Views: Ralph Ellison,* ed. Harold Bloom (New York: Chelsea, 1986) 4; emphasis added).

22. Callahan, 126.

23. There seems to be no published scholarship on the affinities between Ellison and Proust, either in regard to this particular scene, or in more general correspondences. But Lawrence Jackson notes that Ellison would have encountered Proust's work in the pages of *Vanity Fair* and *Literary Digest* that his mother would bring home from the apartments where she worked as a maid. In 1933, when Ellison's literary education was becoming his main passion, the retired English teacher Bess Bolden Walcott acquainted Ellison with *Remembrance of Things Past.* Jackson also remarks that when Ellison was establishing his own literary and aesthetic concepts in the late 1930s, he "further explored the works of the popular modernist writers that the elite of the [New York Writers] Project's young intellectual crowd were reading—Proust, Eliot, Mann, Malraux, Joyce, Gide" (*Ralph Ellison: Emergence of Genius* (New York: John Wiley & Sons, Inc., 2002) 39, 105–6, 205). In his essays Ellison most emphasizes the influence of Eliot and Malraux on his thought; but he certainly would have read carefully so prominent a modernist as Proust.

24. Proust, 47.

25. Proust, 48–49.

26. Proust, 50–51.

27. Barbara Bucknall, *The Religion of Art in Proust* (Urbana: U of Illinois P, 1969) 155–56. See also Elliott Coleman's "Religious Imagery" in *Proust: A Collection of Critical Essays,* ed. Rene Girard (Englewood Cliffs, NJ: Prentice-Hall, 1962) 92–96.

28. Ralph Ellison, "Harlem is Nowhere," in *The Collected Essays of Ralph Ellison* 325.

29. Ralph Ellison, "The Way it Is," in *The Collected Essays of Ralph Ellison* 312.

30. Ralph Ellison, "*An American Dilemma*: A Review," in *The Collected Essays of Ralph Ellison* 328.

31. Ralph Ellison, "The Art of Romare Bearden," in *The Collected Essays of Ralph Ellison* 688. Similarly, Nathan A. Scott, Jr. argues that the Invisible Man's alienation "is related not merely to the disinherited Afro-American but, far more basically, to that 'disintegrated' or 'alienated' consciousness which . . . in the modern period, is not simply here or there—but everywhere" ("Ellison's Vision

of Communitas," 18 *Callaloo* 2 (Spring 1995): 314. See also Callahan, who argues that Ellison is "unwilling to restrict the . . . dispossessed condition to one point in time," because he aims for an "archetypal projection" (134). Ellison wrote to Albert Murray in 1957 that "there is a metaphysical restless built into the American and mose is just another form of it" (*Trading Twelves: The Selected Letters of Ralph Ellison and Albert Murray,* eds. Albert Murray and John F. Callahan (New York: Modern Library, 2000) 166).

32. George Kent, "Ralph Ellison and the Afro-American Folk and Cultural Tradition," in *Ralph Ellison: A Collection of Critical Essays,* ed. John Hersey (Englewood Cliffs, N.J.: Prentice-Hall, 1974) 167. Petesch also notes that this "listing of things" takes on a ritualistic quality, as "history tends to sacrament" (39–40). But whereas Petesch quickly explains this as "the loving evocation of a world," I see in this action a far greater philosophical purpose.

33. Callahan argues that "the Provos' belongings become *a succession of images evoking ancestral kinship ties*" through which "Invisible Man's public consciousness is heightened *by the past merging with present moments*" (137; emphasis added).

34. Benjamin, "The Image of Proust," 202.

35. Ralph Ellison, "Brave Words for a Startling Occasion," in *The Collected Essays of Ralph Ellison* 154.

36. William Schafer elaborates on these mythic elements in the novel in his "Ralph Ellison and the Birth of the Anti-Hero," in Hersey, 115–26. For a more comprehensive discussion of these mythic roles, see Joseph Campbell, *The Hero With A Thousand Faces,* 2nd edition (Princeton: Princeton UP, 1968) 245–46. Schafer's interpretation is largely based on Campbell's theories of myth. Hortense Spillers also invokes Campbell's thought in her "Ellison's 'Usable Past': Toward a Theory of Myth," in Benston, 155.

37. Robert O'Meally convincingly argues that the Invisible Man "is rescued by his stubborn memory of folk forms" from the Factory Doctors' "attempt to sever the hero's sense of identity." *The Craft of Ralph Ellison* (Cambridge: Harvard UP, 1980) 95.

38. Ralph Waldo Emerson, "Self-Reliance," in *Ralph Waldo Emerson: Essays and Poems* (New York: Library of America, 1996) 263.

39. Ellison himself gives a similar definition of self-reliance within a group when he defines "true jazz" as "an art of individual assertion within and against the group." In the jazz performance, the artist produces "a definition of his identity: as individual, as member of the collectivity and as a link in the chain of tradition." See "The Charlie Christian Story," in *The Collected Essays of Ralph Ellison* 267. For a fascinating discussion of jazz music as "a compelling suggestion about what a revitalized Emersonian liberalism could be like," see Cyrus R. K. Patell, *Negative Liberties: Morrison, Pynchon, and the Problem of Liberal Ideology* (Durham: Duke UP, 2001) 174. Patell's efforts to negotiate the tension between the individual and the community in Morrison and Pynchon are quite applicable to Ellison's writings, as well.

40. For the argument that Ellison merely satirizes Emerson's thought, see Earl Rovit, "Ralph Ellison and the American Comic Tradition," Hersey, 151–59, and William Nichols, "Ralph Ellison's Black American Scholar," *Phylon* 31 (1970): 70–75. For a more pro-Emersonian reading of Ellison's thought, see Leonard Deutsch, "Ralph Waldo Ellison and Ralph Waldo Emerson: A Shared Moral Vision," *CLA Journal* 16 (1972): 159–178. Kun Jong Lee has argued that Ellison's revision of Emerson is due to Emerson's racist categories and his "xenophobic Saxonism": "Emerson's racism, which complicates, limits, and ultimately undoes his liberationist project, is at the heart of Ellison's critique of Emerson in *Invisible Man*" ("Ellison's *Invisible Man*: Emersonianism Revised," *PMLA* 107:2 (March 1992): 334–336). While Lee's argument raises some intriguing questions about Emerson's racial attitudes, I think Ellison's main objection to Emerson's thought is the way it has been mis-read by the Nortons and "Emersons" of the twentieth century. Ellison works in his novel and essays to return to Emerson's emphasis on the healthy wedding of self and society. As James Albrecht convincingly argues: "*Invisible Man*'s parody of Emerson is best read . . . as a dual gesture of critique and affiliation: Ellison rejects canonical Emersonianism, as well as the political blindnesses commonly associated with it, in order to appropriate the ethical possibilities of a more pragmatic Emersonian individualism" ("Saying Yes and Saying No: Individualist Ethics in Ellison, Burke, and Emerson," *PMLA* 114:1 (January 1999): 47).

41. "Author's Note" to Ralph Ellison, "Out of the Hospital and Under the Bar" in *Soon, One Morning: New Writing by American Negroes, 1940–1962*, ed. Herbert Hill (New York: Knopf, 1963) 242–90. See also the other excerpt from the *Invisible Man* manuscript that treats further of Mary: "Did You Ever Dream Lucky?" in *New World Writing* (New York: New American Library, 1954) 134–45.

42. Ellison, "Out of the Hospital," 244–62.

43. O'Meally, *The Craft of Ralph Ellison* 109.

44. Claudia Tate, "Notes on the Invisible Women in Ralph Ellison's *Invisible Man*," in *Speaking for You*, 163–72. For Mary as one of the key folk figures in the novel, see O'Meally, *The Craft of Ralph Ellison* 78–104; Kent, 160–70. See also Susan Blake, "Ritual and Rationalization: Black Folklore in the Works of Ralph Ellison," *PMLA* 94:1 (1979): 121–36. Clearly Allen Guttmann's view of Mary as "an Aunt Jemima figure who offers sanctuary rather than a possible identity" radically reduces her importance; so too his link of her to "Calypso" is in error, since she enables, rather than restricts, the hero's quest ("American Nightmare," in Bloom, 32). Robert Butler's view of Mary as "a character always associated with generosity and love," comparable "in certain ways with Dante's Beatrice," is much more accurate in its sense of Mary's rich function in the novel ("Dante's *Inferno* and Ellison's *Invisible Man*: A Study in Literary Continuity"(*CLA Journal* 28:1 (1984): 72).

45. Benjamin, "The Image of Proust," 204.

46. Toni Morrison, "City Limits, Village Values: Concepts of the Neighborhood in Black Fiction," in *Literature and the Urban Experience: Essays on the City and Literature,* ed. Michael C. Jaye and Ann Chalmers Watts (New Brunswick: Rutgers

UP, 1981) 35–43. See also my essay discussing the ancestor figure in Morrison's 1992 novel, *Jazz:* "Wild Women and Graceful Girls: Toni Morrison's Winter's Tale," in *Nature, Woman, and the Art of Politics,* ed. Eduardo Velasquez (Lanham: Rowman and Littlefield, 2000) 341–69. There I briefly discuss Morrison's concept in the light of both Ellison's eviction scene and Benjamin's essay, "The Storyteller." As I remark in that essay, the connections and influences between Morrison and Ellison have not been adequately explored.

47. The mother-figure is oddly elusive throughout *Invisible Man,* and clearly, as the later published pieces on Mary Rambo prove, Ellison was not quite able to resolve his feelings about this figure. In a moving letter to Richard Wright, less than two weeks after his mother's sudden death in 1937, Ellison states that this loss "is real, and the most final thing I've ever encountered"(Jackson, 191). Callahan has argued that the loss of his mother marked what Ellison himself called the "end of childhood" and inaugurated his vocation as a writer ("Introduction" to Ellison's *Flying Home and Other Stories* (New York: Vintage, 1996) xi–xii). In the hospital scene, the Invisible Man enacts the loss of the mother that was so powerful for Ellison himself: "*Mother, who was my mother?* Mother, the one who screams when you suffer—but who? This was stupid, you always knew your mother's name. Who was it that screamed? Mother? But the scream came from the machine. A machine my mother? . . . Clearly I was out of my head" (240). I suspect that Ellison was unable in this first novel to grapple adequately with his complex feelings about his own mother. The novel is therefore primarily a novel of fathers and sons, though Ellison gestures towards the mother-figure through Mary's character.

48. Jennings, 208.

49. Ralph Ellison, "An American Dilemma," 330; "The Shadow and the Act," 304; and "Perspective of Literature," 776 in *The Collected Essays of Ralph Ellison.* See also "Going to the Territory" in the same volume, where he eloquently describes the "two basic versions of American history: one which is written and as neatly stylized as ancient myth, and the other unwritten and as chaotic and full of contradictions, changes of pace, and surprises as life itself" (594).

50. Hannah Arendt argues that Benjamin's true intellectual kindred are in the Heideggerian tradition, rather than in the Marxist-oriented Frankfurt thinkers with whom he is generally associated. See her "Introduction: Walter Benjamin, 1892–1940," in *Illuminations,* 46–47.

51. Martin Heidegger, *What is Philosophy?,* trans. Jean T. Wilde and William Kluback (Schenectady, NY: The New College and University Press, 1955) 29, 35.

52. Heidegger, 49–51, 69, 77.

53. This idea could well serve as a gloss on Toni Morrison's concept of "rememory" in *Beloved.*

54. Heidegger, 71–73.

55. Heidegger's word is "die Entsprechung," with its medieval connotations of answering or responding. Benjamin's word is the Latinate "die Korrespondenzen,"

which Zohn oddly translates as the French *"correspondances."* Its original meaning is to exchange letters or messages. Though the terms are nearly synonymous—hence each is translated as "correspondence"—it is typical of Heidegger to employ the much older, and more native, word form. See Benjamin's *Gesammelte Schriften,* volume II (Frankfurt: Suhrkamp Verlag, 1977) 320. I am grateful to Kirk Follo for his help with these terms.

56. Obviously I read the novel as showing the purposeful, progressive, and meaningful development of the Invisible Man—what I term the "teleological reading," what O'Meally describes as "the Invisible Man's archetypal movement from darkness to light" (*The Craft of Ralph Ellison,* 80). I reject the reading of the novel as ultimately purposeless, such as Marcus Klein's argument that "the novel has no real progress. . . . [it] doesn't finally go anywhere" (*After Alienation: American Novels in Mid-Century* (Cleveland: World Publishing, 1964) 108–9), and Roger Rosenblatt's claim that the hero's beliefs and assertions all "ended in nothing" (*Black Fiction* (Cambridge: Harvard UP, 1974) 197). As I argue below, only the teleological reading fits with the narrator's claims for hope, survival, and love in the Epilogue; and the negative reading is jarringly at odds with virtually all of Ellison's nonfiction writings, as well as his comments on the novel itself. Callahan argues convincingly that the hero's rebirth and ascent towards self-hood begins with his speech at the eviction. His prior ideas of oratory all "shut the gates of the self," but here he "hears a call" and "resumes his earlier attempt to tell the story of African-American history by breathing significance into the inanimate personal effects and household possessions strewn along the curb" ("Frequencies of Eloquence: The Performance and Composition of *Invisible Man,*" in O'Meally, *New Essays on* Invisible Man, 66–72). Similarly, Valerie Smith argues that the narrator's "quest for an appropriate identity" is ultimately his quest for artistic expression, which he achieves by "end[ing] at a point where he is palpably wiser than he was before" (*Self-Discovery and Authority in Afro-American Narrative* (Cambridge: Harvard UP, 1987) 90, 120). For a balanced discussion of the novel's direction and conclusion, see Per Winther, "The Ending of Ralph Ellison's *Invisible Man,*" *CLA Journal* 25:3 (1982): 267–87.

57. Benjamin, "The Image of Proust," 207. See also Benjamin's powerful, brief essay, "The Destructive Character," in *Reflections: Essays, Aphorisms, Autobiographical Writings,* ed. Peter Demetz (New York: Schocken, 1986) 301–4.

58. Jennings, 38.

59. Ralph Ellison, "Twentieth-Century Fiction and the Black Mask of Humanity," 83; and "The Little Man at Chehaw Station," 508 in *The Collected Essays of Ralph Ellison.*

60. Ralph Ellison, "The World and the Jug," in *The Collected Essays of Ralph Ellison* 177.

61. Ralph Ellison, "Brave Words for a Startling Occasion," in *The Collected Essays of Ralph Ellison* 154.

62. Soren Kierkegaard, *The Sickness Unto Death: A Christian Psychological Exposition for Upbuilding and Awakening,* ed. and trans. Howard V. Hong and Edna H. Hong (Princeton: Princeton UP, 1980) 17, 49.

63. See, for example, the fascinating "A Coupla Scalped Indians" in Ralph Ellison, *Flying Home and Other Stories,* ed. John F. Callahan (New York: Random House, 1996) 63–81, with its encounter with a mysterious, magical wise woman and its subsequent expansion of what Callahan terms "the mystery and possibility of life and the world" ("Introduction" to *Flying Home,* xxxi). Ralph Ellison's *Juneteenth: A Novel* (ed. John F. Callahan [New York: Random House, 1999]) also intimates a broader notion of the spiritual than does *Invisible Man.*

64. Kierkegaard, 65. Like so many correspondences in Ellison's work—one thinks of Ellison and Dostoevsky or Ellison and Hemingway, which have been treated only in a few essays, or Ellison and Eliot, an influence often mentioned but rarely analyzed—the Ellison/Kierkegaard relation has been only fleetingly explored. Yet, Kierkegaard's book, specifically referred to in the Prologue, also begins in the effort to heal: "it must never be forgotten," he states in his own prologue, "that the situation is the bedside of a sick person" (5). Furthermore, Kierkegaard's entire argument, like Ellison's, treats of the inauthenticity of the self, its inability to locate itself in relation to its source and its meaning: "To despair over oneself, in despair to will to be rid of oneself—this is the formula for all despair. . . . The self that he despairingly wants to be is a self that he is not . . . [H]e wants to tear his self away from the power that established it" (20). I would suggest that the projects of Kierkegaard and Ellison are strikingly parallel. Spillers briefly links the two figures in her essay, "Ellison's 'Usable Past.'"

65. See Butler's fine essay, "Dante's *Inferno* and Ellison's *Invisible Man.*"

66. Of all the American writers with whom Ellison might claim kinship (and there are many such "ancestors"), F. Scott Fitzgerald most closely shares Ellison's view that material objects are sacramental, the portals to a much larger universe of meaning and implication. The neo-Platonic structure of *The Great Gatsby,* in which the world is "material without being real," depicts a similar dialectic between the visible and the invisible, the tangible and the ineffable, to that expressed in *Invisible Man.* By the novel's end, Gatsby's "unutterable visions" and "enchanted objects" have been reduced to a crude materiality, claimed by the wasteland figure of his killer and the "hard malice" of the Buchanans. But the transcendent dream is now located in the enduring vision with which the novel closes, when "the inessential houses began to melt away" and we behold again "this island that once flowered for Dutch sailor's eyes," "the last and greatest of all human dreams" (*The Great Gatsby* (New York: Charles Scribner's Sons, 1925) 94, 112, 162, 182). Like Fitzgerald, Ellison at the end of his novel enshrines America as the final transcendent object, as the sacred possibility that he will not reduce to the merely material world.

67. Ralph Ellison, "The Little Man at Chehaw Station," in *The Collected Essays of Ralph Ellison* 15.

68. Ralph Ellison, "The Little Man at Chehaw Station," in *The Collected Essays of Ralph Ellison* 7–8.

Chapter 10

Documenting Turbulence: The Dialectics of Chaos in *Invisible Man*[*]

HERMAN BEAVERS

And the mind that has conceived a plan of living must never lose sight of the chaos against which that pattern was conceived. That goes for societies as well as individuals.

—RALPH ELLISON, EPILOGUE, *INVISIBLE MAN*

The Big E is still making up/Complexity.

—MICHAEL S. HARPER, "THE PEN"

By the time we reach the end of *Invisible Man,* Ralph Ellison's hero/narrator comes to embody a political consciousness whose energies are directed toward dialectical, as opposed to simply rhetorical, ends.[1] In light of this, it might be worthwhile to recall Stanley Fish's distinction between rhetorical and dialectical forms of literary presentation, especially his point that a presentation

is rhetorical if it satisfies the needs of its readers. The word "satisfies" is meant literally here; for it is characteristic of a rhetorical form to mirror and present for approval the opinions its readers hold. . . . A dialectical presentation, on the other hand, is disturbing, for it requires of its readers

[*] This essay was researched and written during my time as a visiting fellow in African American studies at Princeton University during the 2001–02 academic year. I wish to thank the administrators and staff of the African American studies program and the staff of the Firestone Library for their support during that time.

a searching and rigorous scrutiny of everything they believe in and live by. It is didactic in a special sense, it does not preach the truth, but asks that its readers discover the truth for themselves, and this discovery is made at the expense not only of a reader's opinions and values but of his self-esteem.[2]

This sums up the predicament of Ellison's hero, who confirms that if "the experience of a rhetorical form is flattering, the experience of a dialectical form is humiliating."[3] We know this because the hero speaks to us in the Prologue and Epilogue, where he finds that "a man's feelings are more rational than his mind and it is precisely in that area that his will was pulled this way and that. . . ."[4]

As evidenced by his essays on American literature and culture, Ellison saw himself as someone engaged in the task of rendering America's cultural complexity. So if Ellison's novel has a political agenda, it may have to do with the way *Invisible Man* dramatizes the politics of interpretation through a series of escalating calamities. And though the arguments concerning the central role literacy plays in the African-American literary canon are familiar at this point,[5] I want to insist nonetheless that Ellison's juxtaposition of the written and the spoken, history and memory, invokes the recurrent trope of textual unreliability, reminding us of Robert Stepto's observation that African-American literature "has developed as much because of the culture's distrust of literacy as its abiding faith in it."[6]

With this dialectic of literacy in mind, I began work on this essay with the intention of looking at Ellison's use of maps, documents, and blueprints to assert the importance of abandoning one form of literacy, which fails to emphasize the importance of "reading between the lines," in favor of one that has a healthy distrust of rhetorical surfaces and thus seeks the subterranean aspects of public discourse.[7] Initially, I wanted to examine these "texts" in order to understand how *Invisible Man* posits public documents as "fictions" performing cultural (and in many instances, political) work.

This function notwithstanding, it is important to remember documents, maps, and blueprints are each, in their way, vehicles of representation meant to convey information. Hence, the problem for the narrator, is how to ascertain whether the information he encounters over the course of the novel can adequately enunciate his story. This dilemma comes immediately to the fore in the form of the briefcase containing the narrator's scholarship.

Though his public eloquence has brought him to the Smoker, the narrator quickly discovers that his participation in the Battle Royal is the prerequisite to any rewards his eloquence might provide. The narrator finds himself in a circumstance where no matter how much he may wish to avoid it, he is first and foremost a physical presence whose task is to provide a rhetorical presentation. The blond dancer with the American flag tattooed on her belly, coupled with the Battle Royal, interposed between the triumph of his commencement speech and the bestowal of the scholarship, undermine his power as a speaker and reinforce his inferior status. Receiving the scholarship means that the narrator has a place in the entering class at the state college for negroes, but it also insures that he and those he wishes to lead will remain in their "place" at the bottom of the Southern social hierarchy. Though he sees himself as a figure apart from the other black boys in the ring, he has limited potential in the eyes of the town fathers. The violence of the boxing ring and the dilemma of the blond, where the boys are threatened if they look at her body and threatened if they do not, insist that "progress" and exploitation are synonymous terms.

But the Battle Royal and the blond also suggest the ways the American body politic is a site of both opportunity and inaccessibility. The joke here is that said body politic completes a circuit of desire and shame that intimates the ways "democracy" is constituted as an object of desire that men can defile and degrade. It is significant, then, that the speech the hero delivers is Washington's "Atlanta Exposition Speech," for it represents a moment in American history when nostalgia and hucksterism come together in a rhetorical constellation the narrator fails to discern.[8] As an instance where Washington's rhetorical sleight-of-hand diminished, if not denied, the brutality of Jim Crow, the narrator's use of the speech to gain a social advantage suggests the ways he is willing to impale himself on Southern race rituals that serve prescriptive ends. The Smoker confirms that the narrator's "place" is contingent on white men's whim. Nonetheless, the narrator continues to hold fast to his agenda, fighting—literally—with "hopeless desperation" for the opportunity to deliver his speech. In his estimation, the speech will serve a dual function: reverse the nullifying effect of the random violence taking place in the boxing ring and verify his standing at the apex of black achievement. "I wanted to deliver my speech more than anything in the world," he states, "because I felt that only these men could judge truly my ability . . ." (25). But if this be so, such an assessment also demands that he remain silent about racial injustice. As the Oxford English Dictionary makes clear, document functions as both noun and verb. As the former, the word is associated with access and authenticity; as the latter, it indicates inscription and disciplinarity.

With regards to maps, the novel eschews their conventional meaning as representations of the physical landscape. Rather, maps function in *Invisible Man* as a way to suggest that while physical landscapes can be plotted in terms of geographical scale and navigational coordinates, they can just as easily articulate the relationship that inheres between physical space and ideology. In its way, of course, the Grandfather's deathbed command to "agree 'em to death and destruction" is a map, especially when it is coupled with the narrator's recurring dream of being at the circus with the old man, who commands him to read an engraved document that reads, "To Whom It May Concern, Keep This Nigger-Boy Running." We also have the confluence of signs the narrator follows on his way to the eviction, where the Provos's possessions (which include a set of manumission papers), discarded on the street, lead him towards the realization that it is their status as historical subjects, not tenants, that is at stake. But these can be juxtaposed against the College campus, with its manicured lawns and bell tower, its school buildings and powerhouse. Though it does not constitute an actual map, it persists as an image in the narrator's mind. But it is reverie that renders this mapping significant. Examining the narrator's description, we can see that for all the nostalgia to be found there, it turns out that nostalgia cannot hold the scandal of the College at bay. The narrator sees the "forbidden road that winds past the girls' dormitories," "the bridge of rustic logs, made for trysting, but virginal and untested by lovers," which is not far from the road that turns off to the insane asylum. Mentally retracing his steps, he comes back to the "winding road past the hospital, where at night in certain wards the gay student nurses dispensed a far more precious thing than pills to lucky boys in the know" (35). He finds himself coming to a stop in front of the chapel and listening to "A Mighty Fortress Is Our God," but ironically what he sees in his mind's eye are the roads leading to the cabins, and beyond that, the railroad crossing where the Vets are visited by whores.

The panorama the narrator creates is one where the locations on the map are significant because they represent spaces where physical desire can be consummated.[9] Consider also that the narrator undertakes to map the campus in the same chapter where we find Trueblood's narrative and the debacle at The Golden Day. As a product of memory, the "cartography" informing the narrator's figurative mapping destabilizes the physical landscape as a thing unto itself, highlighting instead the College as a site of rhetorical presentation. It is important that the hero remembers the roads leading to the cabins and the insane asylum and their proximity to the campus, for it demonstrates the pervasiveness of Bledsoe's management of the campus's reality. As a site where he can exercise total control, the campus appears to be a site of both racial and social progress, a thing unto itself.

But maps also have value because of the way they can render relationships between physical sites located in time and space; thus, viewed in relation to Trueblood's shack, The Golden Day, and the insane asylum, the College can be read as one more site of violation, psychic injury, and disfranchisement. Indeed, the narrator's act of situating these "forbidden" sites on his map serves the purpose of undermining the rhetorical and ideological illusion Bledsoe has created. If, as Mark Monmonier suggests, all maps are distortions, the narrator's act of reimagining the campus trumps Bledsoe's declaration, "We take these white folks where we want them to go, we show them what we want them to see" (102). As a mnemonic "text," the hero's map—as a distortion of a distortion—articulates the campus and its surroundings as a conceptual matrix. We can understand, then, why the narrator's reverie takes him to the "circle where three roads converge near the [Founder's] statue" (36). For it is here that we can take the statue into account (with the image of the Founder standing over a freed slave and either lifting or lowering the veil of ignorance), as the "cold Father symbol" that divulges the corruption of Bledsoe's project.[10] Moreover, the "map" links the College's "higher purpose," which ostensibly concerns an educational institution designed to produce a "useful" form of black citizenship. But the narrator's "map" proposes that institutionalization has a great deal to do with the sublimation of desire, where the rhetoric of racial uplift demands that the black body be disciplined in a regime of individual power.[11]

In terms of blueprints, the novel provides a number of detailed plans of action at work; the narrator serves as the recipient of a number of blueprints (including his Grandfather's deathbed directive and the Brotherhood Program in Harlem), but he also proves to be a prolific architect of his own schemes and plots. Focusing on Petie Wheatstraw's cart, one sees the blueprints he hauls represent distortion of a different sort. When the hero asks Wheatstraw what the blueprints are for, he replies, "Damn, if I know—everything. Cities, towns, country clubs. Some just buildings and houses" (175). If this is the case, the blueprints represent, rhetorically at least, the power (albeit unrealized perhaps) to create a metropolis and its surroundings. It is telling, though, that Wheatstraw adds, "Here I got 'bout a hundred pounds of blueprints and I couldn't build nothing!" (175). Moreover, he notes that while some of the plans have been realized, plenty of them have never been used at all. Though he never sets out to "read" the blueprints, the narrator misses what they are communicating nonetheless. Though Wheatstraw tells him, "Folks is always making plans and changing them," the narrator concludes that to do so is a mistake, stating, "You have to stick with the plan" (175). But at that moment, he is carrying Bledsoe's letters in his briefcase, which represent nothing less than the derailment of his plans. As the textualization of the future, blueprints represent the contingent nature of information; it can be rendered useless by ideological or political whim that can overload channels of discourse to the point of meaninglessness.

Juxtaposed against the abstract potential of the blueprints, however, is Harlem, which Wheatstraw describes as a "bear's den." Though this would be cause for alarm within the world represented by the blueprints, a world driven after all by speculation and leverage, where contingency is the order of the day, Wheatstraw tells the narrator that Harlem is "the best place for you and me" (174). The difference between the designed spaces of the blueprints and Harlem is that the latter is apprehended through tangible experience. It is also a space associated with agency. Thus, Wheatstraw can state, ". . . if times don't get no better soon I'm going to grab that bear and turn him every way but loose!" (174). In a city where he knows no one, the hero should be comforted by Wheatstraw's presence, whose arrival on the scene is signaled by the blues. The effect of this, at least initially, is that the narrator's thoughts turn toward home. But rather than concluding that "home" represents both geographical location and spatial coordinates that extend beyond physical space to encompass memory, creativity, and improvisation in the face of trouble, the narrator places his faith in Dr. Bledsoe's letters in his briefcase.

If the hero were able to perform an act of reading that privileged the use of analogy and inference, he might be able to link Wheatstraw's discarded blueprints and Bledsoe's letters in an altogether different system of signification. Were he able to remember the Vet's advice, "Be your own father" (156), he might curb his determination to "stick to the plan"; he might conclude that his destiny is not contained in the briefcase. He might see that circumstances call for a healthy skepticism toward anything that attempts to fix the future in place.

It is for this reason that I have always found Rinehart to be among the most compelling characters in Ellison's novel. Without ever making a physical appearance in the novel, he is nonetheless present because the narrator, having donned a pair of green sunglasses and a wide-brimmed hat, is taken for Rinehart in all his various community roles: preacher, numbers runner, hustler, and briber. Rinehart represents an important epiphany for the narrator because he lives a life of total freedom and possibility; his different guises work to complicate such concepts as "morals" and "values," allowing him to move through the world in a state of randomized grace.

Like that penultimate African-American trickster, Brer Rabbit, Rinehart is most at home in a "vast, seething hot world of fluidity" (498). Living in an endless state of transition where he embodies both the margin and the center, Rinehart moves smoothly through a network of overlapping discursive systems where he is as comfortable using the language of the sacred as he is among those who embrace the profane. But here, we need to pay close attention to what gives Ellison's hero his power, however briefly, as he impersonates Rinehart: the sunglasses. In his pocket with Tarp's chain link and Clifton's doll, the sunglasses constitute interstitiality: both/and rather than either/or. The hero puts on the glasses and stumbles into the persona of Rinehart. Seeing "through a glass darkly," he thus comes face to face with what distinguishes Rinehart's existence from his own. Rinehart is a figure so purely of the moment, so much a part of where he is at any particular moment, that he can embody the "blackness of blackness" without any trace of cognitive dissonance and thus achieve a level of freedom that stretches the boundaries of its meaning.

But Rinehart also intimates the value of embracing risk. When the narrator informs us that he has been "boomeranged" by fate, he relates that the path to self-knowledge is anything but linear. Because linearity suggests proportionality, one might expect that the suffering Ellison's hero endures functions on a scale where small predicaments require small solutions. But self-knowledge owes as much to injury as it does insight, which is why exploring the maps, documents, and signs of *Invisible Man* are inadequate as an interpretive end in itself. In his journey toward public importance, Ellison's hero relies so heavily upon them because these sorts of texts nullify complexity and render the figure in the carpet both legible and navigable. His reliance on talismans points to his deepest fear: being overwhelmed by chaos.

From the narrator's perspective, chaos represents the ultimate state of disempowerment. As a man of Southern origins, he sees no way to advance without some form of documentation. The problem, of course, is that protection assumes such conventional forms—the briefcase given to him to "hold all the important papers that will help shape the destiny of [his] people," Dr. Bledsoe's letters of introduction, the slip containing his new name from The Brotherhood—that his failures produce chaos in progressively greater degrees. It is only when he learns how to implement his own system of signs, which leads him to seek and value radically different kinds of texts (Tarp's chain link, the record containing Louis Armstrong's "What Did I Do to Be So Black and Blue?" and his dreams) that he comes to understand that his path leads him to be a writer, to "set invisibility down in black and white."

We might say, then, that Ellison's hero has the task of eschewing those things that direct him to a predetermined location in favor of innovation and improvisation, leaping toward uncertainty rather than avoiding it. This challenge is made difficult by the narrator's deep-seated desire to affirm the desires and agendas of others. We might therefore consider it sufficient to say that Ellison's narrator must embrace the idea of risk. But in looking at the journey the narrator must take before he can make such an assertion, it may be more precise to suggest that he comes to realize that the only source of safety—at least as it pertains to his self-concept—is to be found by taking his chances in the heart of the abyss. It is here, however, that we find the proverbial rub, for the very concept of "risk" indicates not only moral uncertainty, but spatial disruption as well. Indeed, risk assumes the existence of a social contract; it cannot exist in a vacuum, for its significance emerges from a social context. Hence, those circumstances we deem most risky often have to do with the intentional and overt transgression of well-established conventions. As Pamela Caughie observes, "risk is internal."[12] It occurs when randomness invades the space of the familiar, where the light cast upon the unknown is sufficient to make it an attractive, and alternative, space.

By the novel's end, the narrator internalizes Rinehart's example and realizes that risk is inescapable and losing an eventuality. Thus, he can state, "It's 'winner take nothing' that is the great truth of this country. Life is to be lived, not controlled; humanity is won by continuing to play in face of certain defeat" (577). But herein lies the dialectic of chaos: To be able to embrace his invisibility, he must cast off his desire to be a public speaker in favor of what chaos theory refers to as stochastics—the turbulent conditions caused by chance and randomness. This leads him to adopt a life of bifurcation, which chaos theory describes as "the sudden change from a stable system to an unstable one, the change from equilibrium to [being] far-from-equilibrium."[13] Descending into the turbulence of remembering, writing allows the narrator to contextualize his movement between establishment and anti-establishment. In Hegelian terms, he has to discover a way to synthesize order and chaos into a viable narrative pattern.

But after locating examples from the text where the narrator might fall prey to the dangers of following plans to the letter, the failure to ascertain and read against the rhetoric of maps, and the hazards of believing in documents as singularly constituted texts, there is something more at work in Ellison's novel. The attempt to reconcile the overt and covert deployment of documents, signs, and maps throughout the whole of *Invisible Man* with Ellison's ruminations about the novel in American culture should lead one to think about Ellison's deeper intention: to highlight the role of chaos in the performance of American culture.

Though my interest in Ellison's use of maps, documents, and blueprints as figurations of circumscribed literacy continues, I have begun to think about *Invisible Man* as a novel that revels in chaos—what N. Katherine Hayles would insist is "orderly disorder," which calls for us to discern the deep structures in play.[14] In her book, *Chaos Bound,* Hayles asserts that chaos has undergone a transmogrification from its beginnings in antiquity as an absence or a void, a negative quantity, into a positive force.[15] She points to the nineteenth century as a moment when chaos and order come to exist as dialectic. Hayles understands that the shifting nature of chaos was being worked out in a "cultural field" that encompasses both scientific and cultural discourse. Thus, we see the chaos/order dialectic worked out in the fictions of Twain, Melville, and Poe (one thinks, for example, of "The Fall of the House of Usher" or "Benito Cereno" as texts that bring order and chaos into a productive nexus because each equates clarity of vision with tragic circumstance).

Hayles posits chaos theory as a "wide-ranging interdisciplinary research front that includes work in such fields as nonlinear dynamics, irreversible thermodynamics, meteorology, and epidemiology," and she notes that it "can be generally understood as the study of complex systems."[16] She also points out that chaos theory contains two general emphases. "In the first," she insists, "chaos is seen as order's precursor and partner, rather than as its opposite." The second emphasis, known as the "strange attractor" thesis, envisions the hidden order embedded within chaotic systems. Whereas the former equates chaos with randomness, the latter views chaos in terms of the deep structures of order, which call for an analysis of the complex patterns being articulated.[17] Hayles argues that between 1960 and 1980, "cultural fields were configured so as to energize questions about how stochastic variations in complex systems affected systemic evolution and stability." She continues:

> It is easy to see how the political movements of the 1960s contributed to this interest. Also important was the growing realization that the world

had become (or already was) a complex system economically, technologically, environmentally. Along with the information capabilities of modern communication systems came the awareness that small fluctuations on the microscale could, under appropriate conditions, quickly propagate through the system, resulting in large-scale instabilities or reorganizations.[18]

Though *Invisible Man* was written during a period running from 1944 to 1951, it achieved canonical status in the 1960s and so *Invisible Man* could productively be read as a work resonating in the space of both approaches to chaos. On the one hand, it is clear that turbulence quickly becomes synonymous with assertions of public voice during the Civil Rights Movement. But it is also an instance where, with the collapse of colonial power in Africa and the Pacific basin, we witnessed the rise of a new kind of political pattern that required innovative acts of interpretation to contextualize them in "the New World Order."

But as it emerges from mathematics, engineering, and thermodynamics, chaos theory demonstrates an abiding concern with entropy, which is best defined as the "measure of the heat lost for useful purposes."[19] As chaos theory develops, entropy becomes increasingly associated with randomness, which has allowed researchers to extend its meaning beyond the realm of machines or thermodynamic systems to other types of systems. My use of the term partakes of the heuristic project whereby entropy comes to exist in relation to information. What this means for my discussion of Ellison is simply that I can project his repeated uses and invocations of "chaos" against the rhetorical formations that have grown out of scientists' attempts to theorize disorder. As William Demastes has observed, Western cultures, following in the footsteps of non-Western cultures, are beginning "to see chaos as a place of opportunity, a site of interactive disorder generating new orders or transforming order to regenerative disorder."[20] Rather than a binary opposition between order and random nonbeing, he suggests that chaos is a site of "becoming" rather than degeneration.

In the book *Beautiful Chaos,* Gordon Slethaug asserts that writers "about chaos theory and literature often base their arguments and positions on metaphor" and he cites numerous examples of critical studies of literary texts ranging from Milton and John Barth to Thomas Pynchon and Don DeLillo. His book treats Barth, Pynchon, and DeLillo, along with Cormac McCarthy, Toni Morrison, and Norman MacLean, as writers whose works demonstrate an affinity for chaos, either as a way to structure plot or as a self-reflexive feature of the text itself, where chaos is used self-consciously.[21] On this reading, chaos theory may provide a critical framework to talk about Ralph Ellison's fiction.[22]

Of course, this means that we need to set aside, if only momentarily, the mythopoeic notion of chaos that critics are most comfortable using to discuss Ellison's work. Though this has the potential to be a move fraught with the critical slippages that accompany the use of a new theoretical apparatus, the infusion of terms from chaos and information theory leads us to consider Ellison's novel as a work devoted to exploring the ways the hero moves between open and closed systems, where energy is released and work is done (or not). Furthermore, chaos theory allows us to bring terms like entropy, bifurcation, turbulence, blockage, flow, and recursion to bear on a reading of *Invisible Man*.[23] Ellison's novel can be read as a work dealing with entropic crisis, which means we can also understand the novel's valuation of noise within the space of information theory.[24]

Ellison's fiction and essays show his use of chaos as a conceptual pivot that predates the *Invisible Man's* publication. In some instances, his rhetoric is best understood through the lens of information theory; in others, he posits turbulence as the animating force of American cultural production, particularly as it manifests itself in jazz music. In many ways, Ellison's vision of chaos anticipates the present state of affairs Demastes describes, which John Wright understood to comprise four major impulses in Ellison's work as a writer: the *"syncretic"* impulse "to link together all [he] loved within the [African American] community and all those things [he] felt in the world which lay beyond;" the "celebratory" impulse "to explore the full range of [what he refers to as] American Negro humanity," which affirms "the attitudes and values which render it bearable and human . . . and desirable;" a *"dialectical"* impulse that led him to question "those formulas" that historians, politicians, and sociologists used to describe the predicament of the black community; and finally, the *"demiurgic"* impulse that led him "to seek cultural power and personal freedom through art, to propose 'an idea of human versatility and possibility. . . .' "[25]

In Ellison's acceptance speech for the 1952 National Book Award, which he published in *Shadow and Act* under the title "Brave Words for a Startling Occasion," as well as several essays on the cultural importance of the novel in *Going to the Territory,* one finds Ellison insisting that his theory of the novel emerged from a sensibility attuned to turbulence. Thus, in "Brave Words," Ellison states, ". . . I became gradually aware that the forms of so many of the works which impressed me were too restricted to contain the experience which I knew."[26] Turning away from the "hard-boiled novel" favored by one of his "literary ancestors," Ernest Hemingway, he notes:

> For despite the notion that its rhythms were those of everyday speech, I found that when compared with *the rich Babel of idiomatic expression* around me, a language full of imagery and gesture and rhetorical canniness, it was embarrassingly austere. Our speech I found resounding with an *alive language swirling* with over three hundred years of American living, a mixture of the folk, the Biblical, the scientific and the political. Slangy in one stance, academic in another, loaded poetically with imagery at one moment, mathematically bare of imagery in the next.[27]

What Ellison describes, in talking about the American idiom, can also be understood as an assertion that the American novelist must be prepared to accept the ever-shifting nature of American speech, not to contain it, but as a way to transcend the narrow categories imposed on American life and thus come in contact with the chaotic nature of American culture itself. What makes Ellison's example so instructive, certainly, is that he saw this dialectically, in terms of art to be sure, but also in terms of the artist's duty as a citizen. Thus, in creating a narrator who could give voice to the struggle for self-awareness, Ellison was also interested in dramatizing the notion that democracy was anything but a simple, linear process. Furthermore, his use of Proteus as a metaphor for the rigors of managing novelistic form is equally useful in its insistence that the novelist must embrace chaos if she is to fashion a unique vision, flexible and mobile enough to avoid reducing American experience to a set of static binaries.[28]

But there are other manifestations of this thinking to be found in his writing. For example, in "The Little Man at Chehaw Station," published in 1977 in *The American Scholar,* we find Ellison sounding a cautionary note against American artists who imagine their audiences too narrowly. In his view American culture is a system whose open-endedness sustains it and insures that it will be in a constant state of transformation and revision, largely due to its "fluid, pluralistic turbulence." Even more intriguing is Ellison's argument that the American cultural scene

> is always in *cacophonic motion.* Constantly changing its mode, it appears as *a vortex of discordant ways* of living and tastes, values and traditions; *a whirlpool of odds and ends* in which the past courses in *uneasy juxtaposition* with those bright, futuristic principles and promises to which we, as a nation, are politically committed.[29]

As Ellison advocates, the "little man behind the stove" can serve as a guide to a deeper appreciation of American culture's propensity to move in fits and starts. And by insisting that there is indeed a "melting pot," Ellison privileges "the mystery of American identity" as a product of the "antagonistic cooperation" to be found in all aspects of American culture.[30] He reaches toward a politics of culture whose main characteristic is that in spite of our secular politics, it thoroughly obliterates boundaries, reaches for a higher matrix, even as matters of locality prevent us, like the proverbial ant traveling on the elephant, from understanding the ways we embody the whole.

In addition to these assertions, there is Ellison's rebuttal of Irving Howe's "Of Black Boys and Native Sons" in the essay, "The World and the Jug." Ellison refuses to close himself off from complexity, unwilling to let Howe force him into a conceptual box defined solely by racial animus or racial ancestry. Ellison stands against and apart from the "rationality" of Howe's argument, opting for a more "irrational" posture that insists that he can, in spite of his racial heritage, select his literary "ancestors" based on factors other than race or ethnicity. What Howe would propose as an essential move in determining the course of an African-American contribution to American letters—racial affiliation alongside the notion that "protest" is a consensual project rather than individually determined—Ellison dismisses as Howe's failure to ruminate on the deep structure residing in the unspoken. Here, the "raw, uncharted" aspects of American literature are shown by Ellison to be the result of a critical practice beset by a conceptual entropy, where the closed-mindedness of white critics leads to circumscribed mappings of the literary scene. And as John Callahan suggests, Ellison's propensity to view history and fiction, not as opposites, but as similar projects, points to his awareness that to view them as projects separate and distinct runs the risk of limiting the terms Americans have available to them in the process of self-discovery.[31]

Turning back to Ellison's fiction, several passages in the much-anthologized short story, "King of the Bingo Game," show Ellison drawing strong linkages between possibility and random chance. The protagonist, who like Ellison's hero in *Invisible Man* is nameless, seeks to resist the entropy threatening his existence by winning a bingo game that will grant him an opportunity to spin a wheel for the weekly jackpot of $36.90, which he needs for his ailing wife, Laura. Significantly, the protagonist is also a Southern migrant who, because he lacks a birth certificate, cannot find work in the North. Lacking the documentation necessary to authenticate his existence, his only chance lies in winning the money.

In what is surely a gesture meant to highlight the liberating potential of random force, Ellison sets the story in a movie house, where a movie featuring a scene with a young woman tied up on a bed, waiting to be rescued by her lover, plays on the screen. With his ailing wife on his mind, the character looks up at the projection room, where he notices that "the beam always landed right on the screen and didn't mess up and fall somewhere else."[32] Here, we see technology's power to manifest the illusion of certainty, a control over outcome that can hold chance at bay. The protagonist looks at the light and concludes, "Everything was fixed."

In what stands as a poignant treatment of the systematicity that dominates urban space, the character discovers possibility when he wins an opportunity to spin the wheel by pushing a button that controls the wheel's movement. But in a twist that anticipates the events in Charles Johnson's story, "Exchange Value," he cannot convert the potential energy of the wheel into a concrete reward. "He felt vaguely that his whole life was determined by the bingo wheel; not only that which would happen now that he was at last before it, but all that had gone before. . . ."[33] His only hope lies in keeping the wheel going by continuing to press the button. "And then he knew, even as he wondered, that as long as he pressed the button, he could control the jackpot. He and only he could determine whether or not it was to be his."[34] The story has assumed by this point a surrealism that leads the character to equate the button with deification. What should be a game of random chance becomes much more: The character enters a world separate and distinct from the one driven by cinematic titillation.

Ellison's story evinces a stochastic concern with the ways that local events can manifest influence on a global scale. Though Ellison's belief in the universality of human experience does not jibe with the critical vision that arises out of a poststructuralist ethos, his thinking remained remarkably consistent over a long period of years. Indeed, we can see notions of entropy creep into his assessment of America during the Civil Rights Movement. In an interview with Robert Penn Warren, Ellison insists that the social and political life in America can be likened to a system whose adherence to a reductionist approach to identity politics causes a loss of energy. Believing in what he refers to as "national values," Ellison asserts, "There is a basic strength in this country, but so much of it is being sapped away and no one seems to be much interested in it."[35] And later, he observes with regard to the South, "Thus a great loss of human energy goes into maintaining our stylized identities. In fact, much of the energy of the imagination—much of the *psychic* energy of the South, among both whites and blacks, has gone, I think, into this particular negative art form."[36]

Ellison's critical intervention rests on his deeply held belief in pluralistic identity. In his view, what makes the "melting pot" such a powerful symbol is that it is synonymous with chaos; it marks that site where we find a confluence of sensibilities so complete that race is an inadequate instrument for the measurement of what constitutes an American character. "And if we're going to accept [Negro claims on American-ness] as true," Ellison insisted, "then the identity of Negroes is bound up intricately, irrevocably, with the identities of white Americans. . . ."[37]

Though it did not win him many supporters among the black nationalists who would come to dominate racial discourse in the 1960s and 1970s, Ellison was unyielding in his belief that African Americans could—and should—lay claim to the whole of American culture. And so we can read his resistance to racial identity politics as an assertion that American culture represents a channel of discourse so rife with information that it could not easily be deciphered. For him, the metaphor of the melting pot allowed him to hold fast to the hope that one day African Americans would be valued for their ability to resist dehumanization because the chaos of American culture would come to be interpreted for what it was: a site of cultural exchange so constant as to render racial difference superfluous.

Chaos theory allows us to view the scenes treated at the beginning of this essay as struggles to maintain equilibrium and to deter randomness. According to the second law of thermodynamics, all systems are dissipative, losing available energy. Ellison's hero, fortunately and unfortunately, too often finds himself caught between systems struggling either to effect or resist change.

The Battle Royal sequence is an example in the text where the notion of equilibrium is explored. In many ways, Ellison's hero is the random element in the sequence; through his grandfather, who has declared himself a "spy in the enemy's country," he has been privy to a way of thinking completely foreign to the town fathers at the Smoker. Although he rejects it, his adherence to an accommodationist philosophy can be understood as a by-product of a system spinning perilously toward failure. Recognizing that the hero possesses the potential to become a catalyst of change by exposing the town elite as the purveyors of cynicism and exploitation, the white men he deems as the "judges" of his ability employ the Battle Royal as a way to direct that energy back against itself in what constitutes a negative feedback loop. The release of "heat," in the form of intraracial violence and sexual humiliation (of both the black boys and the white female dancer), is entertaining, but it also maintains the constancy of white superiority.

The feedback loop also helps us to understand the manner in which Dr. Bledsoe maintains his power. Recognizing that he has more to gain by leaving white supremacy unchallenged, Bledsoe creates a system designed to project the illusion of open-ended possibility, though it is predicated on the notion that black achievement should remain circumscribed. In order to remain a vital system, the College needs for white supremacy to exist; thus, it calls for Bledsoe to generate an illusion to justify the expenditures from the military-industrial complex supporting it. The problem, of course, is that Bledsoe is forced to recognize that as a consequence, his "system"—or if you will, his "machine"—is dependent on very careful management of his position vis-à-vis the status quo.

Hence, Bledsoe can laugh when the narrator threatens to make his corruption public. "True they *support* it," he intones, "but *I* control it" (142). Using the rhetoric of equilibrium, Bledsoe states, "Power doesn't have to show off. Power is confident, self-assuring, self-starting and self-stopping, self-warming and self-justifying. When you have it, you know it. . . . This is a power set-up son, and I'm at the controls." But this points at the ways that Bledsoe himself is caught up in a dangerous delusion. Bledsoe's notion that power is "self-starting and self-stopping" ignores the fact that "all systems must change in order to continue."[38] Perhaps most striking, then, is Bledsoe's insistence that "If there weren't men like me running schools like this, there'd be no South. Nor North either. No, and there'd be no country—not as it is today" (142).

What is inherent in Bledsoe's rhetoric is his belief that a political system's raison d'etre is to accumulate power. Moreover, his understanding of how the system works means that he sees himself as one who benefits from the negative feedback loop that constitutes the status quo. Thus, he says, "The white folk tell everybody what to think—except men like me. I tell *them;* that's my life, telling white folk how to think about the things I know about" (143). But the accumulation of power means that the risk of dissipation increases, for it requires greater effort to maintain equilibrium and stave off randomness. In light of this, Bledsoe's "vision" is corrupted by the fact that he must expend energy to keep the illusion of white superiority in place; opting against the imperative to use the College as a catalyst that might spur a different transaction between black and white, North and South, he elects to remain in his place in the cycle of expenditure that undermines the potential for black self-determination. Thus, he can conclude, ". . . I didn't make it, and I know that I can't change it. But I've made my place in it and I'll have every Negro in the country hanging on tree limbs by morning if it means staying where I am" (143).

Bledsoe's place in the wider political field illustrates the way Ellison juxtaposes notions of local and global as analogies for blockage and flow throughout the narrative. But it also urges us to see the ways that Ellison deploys turbulence as the alternative. Thus, when we look back at the Trueblood and the Golden Day sequences, we can understand them as his insistence that totalitarianism, as a kind of blockage, often creates the conditions for its transformation because, as fluid dynamic models insist, "the flow of liquid around an obstacle is, at a slow speed, nearly steady, regular, and orderly."[39] However, as time progresses, the speed of the liquid increases until turbulence intensifies and creates what is referred to as "turbulent flow," which approximates a new form of order.

We get a glimpse of this when the men from the insane asylum attack Supercargo and accost Mr. Norton. The Golden Day exists as a brothel and beer garden in spite of the College's attempt to make it a "respectable" venue because, as the narrator relates, "the local white folk had a hand in it," and prevent it from becoming so. Mr. Norton's presence effectively changes the "flow" of their visit from one where they can seek sexual release to one where they have a target against which to direct their anger. The men, it turns out, have all, in previous lives, achieved a measure of middle-class respectability. "Many of the men," the narrator informs us, "had been doctors, lawyers, teachers, Civil Service workers; there were several cooks, a preacher, a politician, and an artist" (74). Presumably, these are all men who—if the surgeon is any indication—performed tasks that allowed the status quo to maintain its equilibrium. But here we see the way Ellison uses the dialectics of chaos to highlight its potential as possibility. In what stands as one of a series of ironic reversals meant to intimate the liberating power of invisibility, the chaos is set in motion when the ruthless attendant Supercargo shouts, "I want order" (83).

Though he looks at the hero's devotion to Norton and feels disgust, the surgeon nonetheless serves as the spiritual guide who appears on the scene to assist him in his quest. In such a role, the surgeon articulates the narrator's relationship to Mr. Norton. It is he who proposes that Norton functions as "a God, a force" and that the hero is an "automaton," a "mechanical man" (95, 94). What he suggests is that white supremacy is able to stave off entropic crisis precisely because there are black men who believe in white men's power to shape their destiny. Recall that, earlier, Norton equates the hero's destiny with his own: "*You* are important because if you fail *I* have failed by one individual, one defective cog; it didn't matter so much before, but now I'm growing old and it has become very important . . ." (45). In the novel, this sentence ends in an ellipsis, which intimates that what appears to be a closed system is, in fact, nothing of the sort. Thus, when Norton tells the narrator, "I am dependent upon you to learn my fate," he points to the manner in which the local and global are not binary opposites; rather, they are indicative of the ways that systems spinning toward entropy often locate other systems whose energies they can appropriate for their own ends.

In Mr. Norton's presence, we can understand that the surgeon is committed to the asylum because he forgets the fundamentals of life for black men in the United States. Looking at the narrator, he sees himself and he recognizes Norton for who he is: "To some, you are the great white father, to others the lyncher of souls, but for all, you are confusion . . ." (93). As a man who once believed "my knowledge could bring me dignity," the vet understands that the narrator "believes in [Norton] . . . as he believes in the beat of his heart" (95), suggesting that the very blood flowing through his body is powered by white men's authority alone.

Ellison's hero can be thought of within the dual contexts of stochastic processes and recursion. In the former, "flow, turbulence, and randomness are said to set in whenever an obstacle presents itself, fragmenting and dispersing the previously unified flow into stable and unstable forces."[40] Whenever the hero "maps" out a course of action, he runs into obstacles that completely alter his path. Because he fails to embrace improvisation, here, a willingness to see turbulence and randomness as opportunities to create something unique, the hero remains trapped in what Slethaug would refer to as a recursive loop. The narrator who speaks to us in the Prologue and Epilogue has come to understand, through his many humiliations and failures, that he is invisible and thus he, too, is a system in a state of dissipation and so, he must see turbulence as possibility of a nonlinear sort. What this means can best be understood through an essay Ellison includes in *Shadow and Act,* "The Charlie Christian Story," where he talks about jazz as "a cruel contradiction," where the jazzman must lose himself in the group, even as he discovers his own individual voice,[41] what he refers to as "antagonistic cooperation."[42]

Jazz, as Ellison's controlling metaphor for all things American, is in the terms of chaos theory, recursive: a repetition of a complex structure, referring to "the replication of acts, occasions, and patterns within a given system."[43] Ellison's decision to structure *Invisible Man* along a ritualistic pattern running from "purpose to passion to perception"[44] turns on the injunction placed on the hero that insists that his adversaries "Keep This Nigger Boy Running." As suggested previously, what makes this possible is the narrator's belief in the status quo, his desire to be part of it, and to achieve a place at the forefront of his race, even if this places him at the bottom of the social hierarchy. Accepting

Mr. Norton's claim that their destinies are linked, the narrator moves from one entanglement to another, moving from a chaotic event—the explosion at Liberty Paints, the eviction—into the hospital's lobotomizing machine, into the Brotherhood. The challenge, of course, is for the hero to break the pattern, to move from equilibrium to see the full potential of disequilibrium.

Alongside a reading of Ellison's novel as a work of fiction deeply interested in chaos and turbulence, as it takes the form of entropic crisis and randomness, one can also situate it within the context of information theory, working from the notion that noise is a form of chaos. In other words, *Invisible Man* ruminates upon the nature of noise and aurality. There are practical reasons for such an interpretation. In the introduction to the Thirtieth Anniversary Edition of *Invisible Man,* Ellison talks about supporting himself as a writer by building hifidelity stereo systems and amplifiers. This means he had an implicit understanding of the way sound travels, as well as the importance of establishing and maintaining clear frequencies. We can understand his narrator's decision to wire his "hole" for sound, then, not simply because he wants to be entertained but rather because, having developed the ability to descend into a piece of music, he can "hear around corners." Thus, he announces:

> There is a certain acoustical deadness in my hole, and when I have music I want to *feel* its vibration, not only with my ear but also with my whole body. I'd like to hear five recordings of Louis Armstrong playing "What Did I Do to Be so Black and Blue"—all at the same time (8).

But this begs the question: What would this sound like? If the records were played simultaneously, it would mimic the effects of a chorus. However, because we are talking about machines that have the potential to malfunction, the slightest drop in speed on the turntable would mean, thinking about stochastics here, that the "system" would eventually become a cacophony. With "What Did I Do to Be so Black and Blue" playing at different speeds, its lyrics—which constitute the narrator's ability to engage in a perpetual act of signifying— would no longer be discernible. It would become, in other words, white noise.

As Gordon Slethaug observes, "Generally speaking, noise is unwanted sound, auditory turbulence . . . or a 'wide range of disturbances that might affect a signal anywhere between the encoder and the decoder.' It can apply 'to any unwanted fluctuation in the signal level. . . .' "[45] As the equivalent of turbulence, white noise is information-rich, so much so that our propensity is to tune it out as a useless tangle of undecipherable sound. The presence of white noise demands, however, that we invent new ways to decode information that comes to us in fragmented forms (one thinks here of musical technology like the synthesizer and the equalizer, both of which take disparate sounds and render it an audible "whole").

The problem, though, is that culturally coherent sound like music or television, when considered against the drone we are conditioned to "tune out," signals detachment rather than focus. As information theorist Claude Shannon argues, "white noise can be an important part of the process of communication and production of meaning."[46] But in light of this, the manner in which Ellison's hero aspires to make his hole into a site of white noise becomes important, and not only because we find ourselves listening with the narrator to a sermon intoning the virtues of "The Blackness of Blackness." Ellison also wants to use noise as a way to signify on our propensity as both listeners and readers to take in only a partial amount of information; we are culturally conditioned to "filter" out that which does not seem relevant. But the body of the novel teaches us that this is a mistake of grand proportions. Literacy is not only discerning legible codes, but those that are illegible, as well.

Hence, when we arrive at the novel's last words, "Who knows but that, on the lower frequencies, I speak for you?" (581), when read against the constancy of Louis Armstrong's trumpet, which he bends into "a beam of lyrical sound" in order to make "poetry out of being invisible" (8), we are invited to ponder yet again the fall into turbulence that marks the hero's transformation from "ranter to writer." For along with the narrator's decision to take up the pen, his transformation can be understood as his discovery of a new way to "make noise." But what this means for us, having been confronted with the possibility that the narrator's calamitous life is also an enunciation of our own experience, is that we must engage in an act of suture in order to close the gap between our experience outside the text and that of the narrator within. It is here, however, that we must remember how deeply Ellison's insistence that the blues are a liberatory form resonates here. If we think of experience as a closed system, the blues can be thought of as rejuvenating because it represents the manner in which the blues metaphorical "heat" keeps us from spinning into entropy. It involves a "leap" toward meaning and possibility because it documents the ways crisis and creativity come together in a matrix whose purpose is not resolution but reflection.[47]

There are numerous instances in the novel where Ellison calls our attention to the way sound is delivered and received—for example, the microphone the hero uses during his first speech for the Brotherhood (341–46)—as well as the discursive blockages that serve to disrupt channels of communication—for example, the narrator's detachment from Petie Wheatstraw's blues denotes his detachment from his own cultural past (172–77). But there are also instances where reception is a matter of positionality. When he gives the Brotherhood speech, the hero, unable to see the audience because of the bright light shining on the podium, focuses on a lone voice, developing a channel of discourse characterized by antiphony rather than the scientific discipline favored by the Brotherhood, which privileges the notion that "discipline" is what the masses need to understand their plight. In the midst of a phenomenon that belies the Brotherhood's practice, Brother Jack cautions the hero against becoming "obsolete" as an orator. In this instance, a tried and true African-American rhetorical strategy is viewed by one of the members as "wild, hysterical, politi-cally irresponsible, and dangerous" (349). He offers this critique: "Ours is a rea-sonable point of view. We are champions of a scientific approach to society and such a speech as we've identified ourselves with tonight destroys everything that has been said before. *The audience isn't thinking, it's yelling its head off*" (350; emphasis added). Because the hero's oratorical style falls outside the province of Brotherhood doctrine, his speech—and the response—is dismissed as noise, the audience transformed from an "intelligent" body to a "mob." Interestingly, Jack resists this interpretation, calling the speech, "The *initial* step, the release of energy" (350). But he insists, nonetheless, that the hero "stay completely out of Harlem" (351). The enthusiasm generated by the speech, as latent energy, needs to be guided "into channels where it will do the most good" (352).

Though he has reservations about the response, the narrator feels that his life is "all pattern and discipline" (382). This has to be juxtaposed against the experiences he has when he is mistaken for Rinehart. Significantly, the hero gains access to Rinehart's world, not through aural equipment, but the sun-glasses and hat he purchases while trying to flee from Ras's men. Though we could map what happens on a visual grid, where the narrator, as the object of a shifting communal gaze, moves from reverend to runner to lover to briber to hipster, the hero's experience is accompanied by his inclusion in conversations from which he has been previously excluded and which he has considered to be outside the purview of his upwardly mobile aspirations.

Arriving at Rinehart's church, he sees a woman "in a rusty black robe play[ing] passionate boogie woogie on an upright piano along with a young man wearing a skull cap who struck righteous riffs from an electric guitar . . ." (497). Irrespective of Rinehart's exploitative guise, we must nonetheless note the manner in which the music, gospel music, is "authentic" because it drama-tizes the uneasy melding of musical styles, a fact that may be lost on the unini-tiated and whose hybridity resists easy appropriation (as contrasted with the drunken parody of a work song sung by one of the Brotherhood members at the Chthonian Hotel).[48] The manner in which gospel music blends the blues and the spirituals, the sacred and the secular, is nothing short of a revelation for it is as much a "document" as the pieces of paper in the hero's briefcase.

Indeed, gospel "documents" nothing if not the hybridity and syncretic nature of American culture. If we consider the fact that the purpose of docu-ments is to authenticate, to provide evidence, the gospel music documents, certainly, Rinehart's ability to manipulate form in order to sustain his power of illusion.[49] Additionally, though, it "documents" the narrator's sense of place, his proximity to a channel of discourse he could barely imagine. After he leaves the church, he realizes, "I had heard of it before but I'd never come so close" (498).

When we reach the Epilogue, the narrator is well aware that his tale can be dismissed as so much noise or "buggy jiving" (581). His final words, then, are meant to provide the reader with a strategy that will allow the tale to be interpreted, for it to move from "noise" to usable information in the process of suturing described previously. If he "speaks for" us "on the lower frequencies," the narrator has identified a place inside our biases and habits from where we obscure our true nature as wounded, incomplete beings. Here, though, he has tricked us into revisiting our own experience in order to view it as chaos. What makes this so dangerous, so irresponsible, in the words of the narrator, is that our experience undergoes a recoding. The process of trying to reconcile our experiences with those of the narrator insists upon the act of destabilizing the boundary between local and global. As a dialectical phenomenon, this is unsettling, for in its way, it suggests that the process of making ourselves is always already heuristic, involving a leap of the imagination.

In 2002, which commemorated the fiftieth anniversary of Ralph Ellison's *Invisible Man,* we found ourselves in a position to assess his influence on American cultural thought.[50] Ellison's comments to the contrary, perhaps we must conclude, after all, that *Invisible Man* is a political treatise. As such, however, it takes a particularly difficult tack, for it insists that we can best document our place as citizens in the American body politic by embracing synthesis over a particular grammar and syntax. Indeed, as a man for whom the best analogy for democracy was jazz, Ellison understood that being an American was a matter of *parataxis,* which, like jazz, "maps the chaotic and diverse elements of experience" and places them "side by side in a sequential 'democracy of lateral coexistence.' "[51]

This certainly leads us to ponder this in terms of the ways American literary and cultural studies have come to value notions of the local in contrast against notions of global collectivism. Indeed, one might argue that Ellison's novel marked an instance when African-American literature, up to that point dismissed out of hand as a set of parochial texts incapable of rendering the "universality" of human experience, collapsed the hierarchy existing between local and global. This novel, which ends with a riot in Harlem, aspired to render African-American experience on an epic grid that said, "All of it is part of me." I agree with Hayles's insistence that poststructuralism marks that instance when critical work shunned the global, interpreting everything cultural as local phenomena. Having gotten out from under the aegis of the New Criticism, poststructuralism rendered static formulations like "history" and "aesthetics" as extrinsic.[52]

In the ongoing projects of canon formation, the situating of texts and methodologies in an ever-shifting constellation of approaches, program building—the institution of coherent enterprises meant to trouble the rigid boundaries of thought and action that plague us—and theorizing the volatility of the episteme, there is sometimes a tendency to forget that we can, in fact, revel in the use of language, embrace authorial purpose, see words— indeed, The Word—as the harbinger of change. We must not forget—as Louis

Armstrong understood—that neither the music nor the dance is binding, and that in keeping with Henry James's notion that being an American is a complex fate, holding chaos at bay nonetheless demands that we pay attention to the small scraps of wisdom rattling in the midst of all the noise.

ENDNOTES

1. I am grateful to Elliot Butler-Evans's essay "The Politics of Carnival and Heteroglossia in Toni Morrison's *Song of Solomon* and Ralph Ellison's *Invisible Man: Dialogic Criticism and African American Literature," The Ethnic Canon: Histories, Institutions, and Interventions,* ed. David Palumbo-Liu (Minneapolis: University of Minnesota Press, 1995), 117–39. Butler-Evans's use of Fish's study of seventeenth-century literature pointed me to a distinction that has proved to be pivotal to my argument. See also Stanley E. Fish, *Self-Consuming Artifacts: The Experience of Seventeenth-Century Literature* (Berkeley: University of California Press, 1972), 1–4.

2. Fish, *Self-Consuming Artifacts,* 1–2.

3. Fish, *Self-Consuming Artifacts,* 2.

4. Ralph Ellison, *Invisible Man* (New York.: Vintage Books, 1982), 573. All subsequent citations will be noted parenthetically in the text by page number, and emphases in original unless otherwise noted.

5. Robert Stepto's *From Behind the Veil: A Study of Afro-American Narrative* (Urbana: University of Illinois Press, 1979) remains the best source of arguments in this regard.

6. Robert Stepto, "Distrust of the Reader in Afro-American Narratives," *Reconstructing American Literary History,* ed. Sacvan Bercovitch (Cambridge, Mass.: Harvard University Press, 1986); reprinted as an Afterward in *From Behind the Veil,* 196.

7. I find myself returning to Robert Stepto's arguments regarding Ellison's novel, particularly where he notes that the hero's challenge in *Invisible Man* is to become both articulate kinsman and articulate survivor. See Stepto, 163–94.

8. Ellison has commented that part of what motivated him to write *Invisible Man* was the ineffectiveness of Black leaders. Washington's case is instructive because in order to energize the Tuskegee machine, he has to draw power from the assumptions undergirding racial separatism and black denigration.

9. But as Mark Monmonier observes in *How to Lie with Maps* (Chicago: University of Chicago Press, 1991), maps involve three attributes: scale, projection, and symbolization, each of which "is a source of distortion" (5). Indeed, Monmonier insists, mapmaking is often done by people who lack competence in cartography, which means that map users are often unable to "appreciate the map's power as a tool of deliberate falsification or subtle propaganda" (1).

10. Readers will remember the statue, drawn from the statue of Booker T. Washington on the Tuskegee campus, as one that depicts Washington lifting the "veil of ignorance" off of a kneeling slave. The narrator looks at the statue and remembers his original ambivalence about the statue, wondering if "the veil is really being lifted, or lowered more firmly in place" (36).

11. As numerous commentators have noted, Washington's *Up From Slavery* is distinguished by his repeated assertions that Tuskegee students are instructed in the value of the bath and the toothbrush. The trope Washington employs here has much to do with making the black body vanish, that is, making it inoffensive. Invisibility in this instance has to do with a rhetorical strategy intended to counter the characterization of blackness as soiled or as a contaminant. We might also juxtapose the "illicit" sexual activity on the campus against Trueblood's incestual act; in the former, we have secret activity—which, as the narrator discovers when he visits Bledsoe's office, is activated by coded language—while in the latter, Trueblood's "sin" results from the overwhelming power of a dream.

12. Pamela Caughie, *Passing & Pedagogy: The Dynamics of Responsibility* (Urbana: University of Illinois Press, 1999), 66–67.

13. Gordon Slethaug, *Beautiful Chaos: Chaos Theory and Metachaotics in Recent American Fiction* (Albany: State University of New York Press, 2000), 5.

14. Though she is one of many literary scholars who apply chaos theory to readings of literary texts, Hayles is unique among scholars because she holds advanced degrees in both Chemistry and English. What this means is that she is adept at holding scientific and literary theory in a creative tension.

15. N. Katherine Hayles, *Chaos Bound: Orderly Disorder in Contemporary Literature and Science* (Ithaca: Cornell University Press, 1990), 3.

16. Hayles, *Chaos Bound,* 9.

17. Hayles, *Chaos Bound,* 9–10.

18. Hayles, *Chaos Bound,* 5.

19. Hayles, *Chaos Bound,* 38.

20. William W. Demastes, *Theatre of Chaos: Beyond Absurdism, into Orderly Disorder* (Cambridge: Cambridge University Press, 1998), xii.

21. Slethaug, *Beautiful Chaos,* 15.

22. Starting his discussion with a treatment of the representation of orderly systems in literature, Slethaug proceeds to discuss literature in terms of entropic crisis, noise and information systems, and recursion, along with other aspects of complexity theory.

23. I want to insist that, far from appropriating piecemeal a discourse that might be considered ill-suited to a discussion on literature because it runs the risk of sealing Ellison's novel in an ahistorical amber, there are strong merits for subjecting *Invisible Man* to such an analysis. In the "Complex Dynamics in Literature and

Science," the Introduction to her edited volume, *Chaos and Disorder* (Chicago: University of Chicago Press, 1991), N. Katherine Hayles asserts:

> But the context that made disorder appear as complex information is not combined to scientific inquiry alone. It is part of a cultural milieu that included World War II, which among other things was an object lesson in the importance of information; consolidation of power by multinational corporations and the accompanying sense that the world was growing at once more chaotic and more totalized. . . . All of these factors, and more, contributed to the cultural matrix out of which the science of chaos grew (7).

What I want to suggest is that, as a novel begun during World War II, *Invisible Man* can be located in the cultural milieu Hayles describes.

24. Let me make clear that I am not attempting to elide the differences between these two distinct scientific fields of inquiry. I am, as is often the case when literary critics attempt to utilize scientific discourse as the source of critical terms, using the terms from these fields to generate fresh metaphors through which to understand Ellison's aesthetic and political inclinations.

25. John Wright, "Dedicated Dreamer, Consecrated Acts: Shadowing Ellison," *The Carleton Miscellany* (Winter 1980), 154; emphasis in original.

26. Ralph Ellison, "Brave Words for a Startling Occasion," *Shadow and Act* (New York: Vintage Books, 1964; rpt. 1972), 103.

27. Ellison, "Brave Words for a Startling Occasion," 103–4; emphasis added.

28. In "Dedicated Dreamer, Consecrated Acts: Shadowing Ellison," John Wright characterizes Ralph Ellison's career as novelist and cultural critic as one that exemplifies resistance "in the face of radical despair." As such, Ellison does not celebrate "the material, technological, or institutional achievements of American civilization—its ordering forces—but rather the qualities that most closely approximate chaos and disorder, formlessness, the fluidity, the instability, and the diversity of American life," not because he is attracted to anarchy, but because he is "an artist for whom chaos is possibility in life as in literature" (177). The dialectics of chaos Ellison embeds in his novel, then, has much to do with arguing for the workings of "ordering, stabilizing, controlling qualities" in African American life: namely, style, discipline, technique, abstractive and assimilative powers, and will even when the African American subject is beset by chaos on all sides.

29. Ralph Ellison, "The Little Man at Chehaw Station," *Going to the Territory* (New York: Vintage Books, 1985; rpt. 1987), 20; emphasis added.

30. Ellison, "The Little Man at Chehaw Station," 38, 21, 25, and 7.

31. John Callahan reminds us in his essay, "Chaos, Complexity, and Possibility: The Historical Frequencies of Ralph Waldo Ellison," *Speaking for You: The Vision of Ralph Ellison,* ed. Kimberly W. Benston (Washington, D.C.: Howard University

Press, 1987), there is Ellison's propensity to view history as "artificial," as a form of literature (126). In his view, chaos, what he characterizes as "a name for raw, uncharted experience," is juxtaposed against the making of history, "the forms we come up with when consciousness goes to work on what's happened and what's happening."

32. Ralph Ellison, "King of the Bingo Game," *Flying Home and Other Stories,* ed. John F. Callahan (New York: Random House, 1996), 124.

33. Ellison, "King of the Bingo Game," 128.

34. Ellison, "King of the Bingo Game," 130.

35. Ellison makes these comments in an interview with Robert Penn Warren in his book *Who Speaks for the Negro?* (New York: Random House, 1965), 340.

36. Ellison cited in Warren, *Who Speaks for the Negro?* 344–45; emphasis in original.

37. Ellison cited in Warren, *Who Speaks for the Negro?* 347.

38. Slethaug, *Beautiful Chaos,* 46.

39. Slethaug, *Beautiful Chaos,* 48.

40. Slethaug, *Beautiful Chaos,* 64.

41. Ralph Ellison, "The Charlie Christian Story," *Shadow and Act* (New York: Vintage Books, 1964; rpt. 1972), 234.

42. Ellison, "The Little Man at Chehaw Station," 7.

43. Slethaug, *Beautiful Chaos,* 98.

44. Ralph Ellison, "The Art of Fiction: An Interview," *Shadow and Act,* 176–77.

45. Slethaug, *Beautiful Chaos,* 80.

46. Cited in Slethaug, *Beautiful Chaos,* 81.

47. Sherley A. Williams notes that the "internal strategy of the blues is action, rather than contemplation, for the song itself is the creation of reflection." "The Blues Roots of Contemporary Afro-American Poetry," *Chant of Saints: A Gathering of Afro-American Literature, Art, and Scholarship,* ed. Michael S. Harper and Robert B. Stepto (Urbana: University of Illinois Press, 1979), 125.

48. In his pathbreaking book, *The Spirituals and the Blues* (New York: Seabury Press, 1972), theologian James H. Cone describes the blues as a "secular spiritual," and notes, "The blues tell us about black people's attempt to carve out a significant existence in a very trying situation. The purpose of the blues is to give structure to black existence in a context where color means rejection and humiliation" (123). The implication of Cone's work is that gospel music would have been the likely result since the blues and the spirituals work toward similar ends.

49. We might also think about the word "document," which can be either a noun or a verb. As noun, the word denotes a public text. It need not be public in the sense that all have access to it, but it can—in the way of a birth certificate, death certificate, or diploma—mark significant events in time and space. Moreover, the

word suggests the relationship between subjectivity and textuality within the polis. As a verb, the act of documentation is likewise necessary to fix the subject in time and space.

50. In "Ellison Unbound," *The Nation* (4 March 2002), David Yaffe talks about the various sites in American expressive culture—ranging from jazz to the Du Bois Institute at Harvard—where Ellison's influence can be felt.

51. Wright, "Dedicated Dreamer, Consecrated Acts: Shadowing Ellison," 184.

52. Hayles, *Chaos Bound,* 231.

The Lingering Question of Personality and Nation in *Invisible Man:* "And could politics ever be an expression of love?"

JOHN F. CALLAHAN

A literary executor has many responsibilities, most of them conventional and customary, if occasionally irritating and interminable. A few are unexpected and come at you out of the blue. But none caught me more flat-footed than learning recently that I was charged with keeping track of the health of Ralph Ellison's prodigal son, Invisible Man. I should have remembered that some forty-five years ago when Invisible Man was a lad of just five summers, Ellison wrote to Albert Murray that he had "picked up a book of criticism published in England under the title, *Catastrophe and the Imagination,* which gives *Invisible* lots of space and picks it for a short list of novels which that wild stud thinks will be of interest a century from now. Surely the man must be on the weed."[1] But I remembered none of this.

It happened this way. A Federal Express truck pulled up in front of my house. The driver rang the doorbell, handed me an envelope, tipped his cap, and left. I walked back into my study and opened the glossy, red-white-and-blue envelope. Inside was another envelope, inside of which was a document inside a plastic cover whose title page read simply: Invisible Man, 1952–2002. My heart skipped a beat. Good God, I thought, is the bastard dead, or is this more of his "buggy jiving"?[2] Fortunately, there was another envelope resting on top of the title page. I opened it and found a cover letter signed by a team of doctors who had examined Invisible Man. The letter explained that in 1953 the National Book Award Foundation had issued an elaborate health insurance policy stipulating periodic check-ups culminating in an exhaustive physical to be performed by specialists and a distinguished internist no later than the end of Invisible Man's fiftieth year.

I had vaguely known about the policy—Ralph had joked about it from time to time. But I thought it had expired around the time of the prodigal's thirtieth birthday. Back then in 1981 Ellison proclaimed *Invisible Man* "a most willful, self-generating novel," and in so doing seemed to wash his hands of his character's fate—content, in print at least, to let his descendant go his own way.

Turning to the report, I found it contained a lengthy evaluation of Invisible Man's health based on tests and examinations by an impressive array of doctors. On the team were a cardiologist, an oncologist, an ophthalmologist, an ear-nose-and-throat man, a psychiatrist (not an electro-shock therapist), and a specialist in internal medicine who coordinated the tests and exams, and wrote the report. I hasten to assure you that I came by the report only after the envelope addressed to Invisible Man came back to the post office marked "Addressee Unknown/Return to Sender." Despite my best efforts, said Invisible Man was nowhere to be found; his telephone was disconnected and his apartment abandoned, though apparently still brightly illuminated.

Here's the gist of what the doctors said. For a 50-year-old man whose body was kept running and sedentary by turns, not to mention chemically stimulated, his heart is remarkably strong, his pulse that of an athlete, his blood flow regular and fluid, without a hint of the eerie whistling sound that accompanies the early stages of arterial blockage. Invisible Man's lungs, too, are remarkably healthy. Despite signs of scarring similar to those found in coal miners, his lungs' capacity to hold and rapidly expel large drafts of air resembles that of a singer or perhaps a politician accustomed to giving long speeches. Even more than the other physicians, the oncologist was fascinated by what ultrasound and blood tests revealed about Invisible Man's cellular make-up. At first, he was worried because the cells tended to divide chaotically in unpredictable patterns. But, instead of turning against each other in a civil war of the body, his chaotic, idiosyncratic cellular gestalt proved over the years to be conducive to excellent health and longevity. The ophthalmologist found that the patient's former condition of extreme nearsightedness and astigmatism had corrected to one approximating 20/20 vision.

To his colleagues' findings the internist added a concern about a mysterious, on-again/off-again malady of the liver. Uncertain whether the cause was physical or emotional and psychological, or whether to treat the condition by tinkering with various medicinal chemical combinations or to advise intensive psychotherapy, he consulted the journals of a nineteenth-century Russian specialist on the liver, one F. M. Dostoevsky. But before he and the psychiatrist could confer with the entire medical team and meet with the patient, Invisible Man slipped away. Since then he has been sighted only indirectly and by second, third, and fourth hand report. But, like Elvis, he has been sighted. Traces of his existence and his voice have repeatedly turned up in more than seventy countries and twenty languages. This visibility argues for his ability to forge human connections of a strong, persisting nature with almost all of those with whom he comes in contact, regardless of race, gender, religion, political affiliation, or geographical origin.

Remembering Invisible Man's harrowing experience in the Liberty Paints factory hospital, I understand why he might have chosen to become invisible again. He would not have wanted anyone speaking for him; there was too much of that during his previous adventures "in the loud, clamoring semi-visible world" (574). Besides, he left abundant clues as to why his personality and state of mind might be full of terror and complexity some fifty years after he emerged to play a socially responsible role.

As I brood over his quest and the quest of those who pursue him in the briar patch of America, I remember the "brave words" spoken by his guardian, Ralph Waldo Ellison, on the "startling occasion" of his christening in 1953. "The way home we seek is that condition of man's being at home in the world, which is called love, and which we term democracy."[3] Ellison's connection between love and democracy was no lightly tossed off remark. His characterization of what we Americans seek urges readers once more through the pages of his novel all the way back to the guiding spirit of the American Revolution and the experiment in government, society, and culture for which it stands. Writing from Rome in 1957, Br'er Ellison told his friend Albert Murray "democracy is, or should be, the most disinterested form of love."[4]

Ellison's post–*Invisible Man* statements are essayistic answers to the question Invisible Man posed in one of the most painful, moving, and mysterious public and private moments in the novel. Left to his own devices by the Brotherhood Committee after Brother Tod Clifton's murder by a New York cop in midtown Manhattan, Invisible Man returns in shock to the Harlem district. Seeking to comfort and be comforted by the grieving brothers and sisters, he organizes a public funeral in Mount Morris Park on whose dingy benches, incidentally, the down-and-out, unemployed Ralph Ellison occasionally slept during the late thirties. The crowd is enormous beyond expectations, yet Invisible Man feels lost and alone. As he tends to do when he feels his moorings slipping away, his mind reels off one unuttered question after another. "Why were they here?" Is their presence an affirming response to Brotherhood and a posthumous expression of fraternity, or is it simply a protest against the racial violence and injustice typified by Clifton's murder? "Was either explanation adequate?" Invisible Man muses silently. "Did [their presence] signify love or politicized hate? And could politics ever be an expression of love?" (452).

Having posed questions, which Irving Howe in his infamous "Black Boys and Native Sons," calls "more portentous than profound," Invisible Man leaves the questions up in the humid summer air during the hiatus before the outdoor funeral service. But his nexus between politics and love is not an idle one, nor was it ever so for Ralph Ellison. And love in the scene that follows is exactly "that condition of being at home in the world" to which Ellison refers. Love has to do with that most elusive of the inalienable rights, the pursuit of happiness: what John Adams called "public happiness" and Martin Luther King renamed democratic *agape*.[5] In Ellison's novel, Invisible Man experiences alienation from what should be inalienable in his personality and in the world to which he belongs. He has summoned the people of Harlem— and beyond—to pay a ceremonial, last homage to Brother Tod Clifton. Questioning why thousands of others have showed up, he is really questioning his own politics and personality.

The novel's action soon provides an answer to his questions, and perhaps also to Ellison's persistent questions about American democracy. At first Invisible Man sees the crowd as exactly that—a mass of undifferentiated faces. He is uncomfortable, and his nervous questions both conceal and reveal a free-floating anxiety; whatever else he is, he is not at home in the world before him. Soon however, without prompting from him or anyone else, "an old, plaintive, masculine voice arose in a song, wavering, stumbling in the silence at first alone, until in the band a euphonium horn fumbled for the key and took up the air, one catching and rising above the other and the other pursuing, two black pigeons rising above a skull-white barn to tumble and rise through still, blue air" (452). At first, Invisible Man hears but does not see the performers of the song, "There's Many a Thousand Gone." Soon the crowd joins in, and "wet-eyed," Invisible Man "felt a wonder at the singing mass. It was as though the song had been there all the time and he knew it and aroused it; and I knew that I had known it too and had failed to release it out of a vague, nameless shame or fear. But he had known it and aroused it" (453).

Invisible Man's reflections spiral back toward the question he has just posed about politics and love. Without love, without a sense of "being at home in the world" and a corresponding sense of anger at the injustice in the violent betrayal of "what we term democracy" exemplified by Clifton's murder, the old man would not have been able to arouse the song. Nor would the man on the euphonium horn or the others, first black, then white, have been able to respond to the call. The old black man knows who he is and how the world goes; in the travail and sorrow and joy of his life, his pursuit of "that condition of being at home in the world" is the pursuit of true brotherhood as opposed to the false version embodied by the organization of that name.

In the event "all were touched; the song had aroused us all"; as often happens, Invisible Man goes abruptly from separation and alienation from the people around him, especially black folks, to a sense of integration and connection.

Yet it "was not the words." Rather, it was because the old man had "changed the emotion beneath the words while yet the old longing, resigned, transcendent emotion still sounded above, now deepened by that something for which the theory of Brotherhood had given me no name" (453). But that *something*—the feeling stirred into being by the song's performance—is less politics "as an expression of love" than love as an expression of politics.

It is important to remember that, whatever his difficulties with Brother Jack and the Committee, Invisible Man is still very much a true believer in Brotherhood, an acolyte of the organization and its ideology even as he is held at arm's length by its leaders. It should also be noted that love is as antithetical to the politics of Brotherhood as "social equality" was to the politics of white supremacy governing the Battle Royal of Invisible Man's youth. But, in the moment, instead of yielding to the emotion summoned by the song, Invisible Man "stood there trying to contain it" (453). His resistance halts the flow of his language, and when it comes time for him to speak to the assembled people, he "had no words."

Gazing down at the thousands of mourners who have come in response to his appeal, Invisible Man feels "a futility about [the scene] and an anger." When he does speak, his words sound harsh, as if hostile to an impulse to respond to the individual and communal call of the song. But his ironic, bitter refrain—"Go home"—does not fool the people; listening to him, they know from his tone that something else is happening. And they listen to his denials of love and eloquence in an anticipatory, open-ended way. "They were listening intently, and as though looking not at me, but at the pattern of my voice upon the air" (454). What matters is the rising and falling, fluid pattern of his voice—his halting, inarticulate/articulate struggle to form connections between his identity and theirs. "Go home," he repeats over and over, but, really, they are home at this moment in their park. Still, "they gave no sign," so he tells them Clifton's story in broad strokes, in an aggressive, almost tabloid, comic book style. Perhaps his staccato, deliberately ineloquent style allows him twice to utter the words, "we who loved him." The words are true to the public occasion but also true to Invisible Man's unspoken urge to atone for his unwitting but terribly consequential betrayal of Clifton and the people of Harlem in favor of an allegiance and obedience to the Brotherhood Committee and his personal ambition. "It wasn't political," he thinks, measuring his speech against the Brotherhood Committee's narrow, ideological definition of politics. But a different sense of politics is emerging in the intuitive, subterranean regions of Invisible Man's mind. Toward the end of his speech he presumes and dares to speak for Tod Clifton in a way that anticipates his last words in the book. " 'Tell them to get out of the box,' that's what he would say if you could hear him. 'Tell them to get out of the box and go teach the cops to forget that rhyme. Tell them to teach them that when they call you *nigger* to make a rhyme with *trigger* it makes the gun backfire' " (458). Finally able to reconstruct and project his fraternal closeness with Clifton, he can speak of his love and grief not in the plural but the singular—not *we* but *I* in the simple, moving, telling words: "I only know the ache that I feel in my heart, my sense of loss" (459). Invisible Man's sudden, almost parenthetical descent into the deep waters of feeling is a brief departure from the apparent despair of his text. "Forget him," he tells the crowd, before shifting once more into first person plural. "When he was alive he was our hope, but why worry over a hope that's dead? So there's only one thing left to tell and I've already told it. His name was Tod Clifton, he believed in Brotherhood, he aroused our hopes and he died" (459).

These abrupt, foreshortened words bring Invisible Man's funeral oration to a fitting conclusion. Their rhythm recapitulates Clifton's sudden violent end. But still caught in the web of Brotherhood ideology, Invisible Man "stood looking at the crowd with a sense of failure." "I had let it get away from me," he muses self-accusingly, "had been unable to bring in the political issues" (459). Once again his mind's logic lags behind the energy of his words. Granted, he does not leave the people in a fighting mood according to the precepts of classical oratory. Better perhaps, for his and their emerging political purposes, he leaves them with smoldering thoughts of how closely they (and he) are bound up with Clifton's "plunge outside history." Something is happening, nudged forward by Invisible Man's speech, in which he integrates the rhetorical techniques of a black preacher with the moves of a hip, contemporary, urban storyteller. Silenced by his on-again/off-again performance as well as by the audience's inscrutable response, he sees, for the first time, those listening to him in their reality, distinct from his identity, and from his and the Brotherhood's agenda. Most of all, "as I took one last look, I saw not a crowd but the set faces of individual men and women" (459).

If the Brotherhood had its way, Invisible Man would see those who hear him as a mere collectivity whose fitting and proper fate is to be manipulated according to the necessities of the Committee's political program. Invisible Man's nascent awareness of the crowd as discrete individuals is the first indication of a different sense of politics. Until now the "plunge outside history" by Clifton and others frightens him much more than the tight, totalitarian politics of the Brotherhood. The prospect of chaos terrifies him more than repression of personality under the rigid conformity enforced by organization and ideology. Unexpectedly, his mind is opened by the epiphany of song that issues, as do so many epiphanies in this novel, from suddenly visible characters like the old man and the horn player who step out from the mass and show themselves as individuals. Their individual actions compel others to join and form a community for the duration of the song and maybe beyond.

And this is the pattern of the novel: There are countless articulate but invisible men and women who profess "a certain necessary faith in human possibility before the next unknown."[6] Over and over again—from the Vet in the Golden Day and on the bus ride north, to Peter Wheatstraw, Mary Rambo, and the yam vendor on the streets of Harlem to Tod Clifton and

Brother Tarp in the Harlem office of the Brotherhood to Dupre and Scofield during the Harlem riot—those who make common cause with Invisible Man through language or action do so on the grounds of fraternity and love—that public, intimate impulse of personality "which we term democracy."

To the extent that Invisible Man reverses things, and projects the possibility of politics "as an expression of love," he does so in the epilogue. The epilogue stands as his personal testament after he has experienced and told his story; it is in the epilogue that Invisible Man implies that his career as rabble-rouser and orator has yielded to a new vocation as writer. The sequence and form of Ellison's novel affirm the principle of Invisible Man's life and memoir: "the end is in the beginning and lies far ahead" (6). The prologue is a kind of epilogue to the story he's experienced but not yet told and is about to tell—a way of getting the juices going before he writes. And the epilogue is a kind of prologue to the life he's about to choose—the life of a writer, and perhaps an artist. In it Invisible Man concludes, more indirectly, more elliptically than Ellison did as an American man of letters, that a writer has responsibilities as a citizen, too. Perhaps that's what he meant when he says that "even an invisible man has a socially responsible role to play" (581). That line—and Invisible Man's resolve to emerge—has been interpreted too narrowly as evidence that he will reenter the fray as a leader, a public speaker. More likely, I think, is the possibility that he first embraces the writer's calling—specifically, the calling of an American writer, who, as Ellison suggested, bears "responsibility for the condition of democracy."[7]

At the time he poses it, Invisible Man's question, "And could politics ever be an expression of love?" (452), is a plaintive one, whose source lies within his vacillating personality. Its profundity and power come later and follow from his willingness to think and act on the basis of his experience. When in the prologue Invisible Man declares, "But I am an orator, a rabble-rouser—Am? I *was,* and perhaps shall be again. Who knows?" (14), he is describing his future options before he has reexperienced his life in the act of writing down his story. By the time of the epilogue, he finds himself a moral kinsman of the old man who raised the song at Clifton's funeral: "And I defend because in spite of all I find that I love. In order to get some of it down I *have* to love" (580). No, he has not yet achieved "that condition of being at home in the world which is called love and which we term democracy,"[8] anymore than those exercising their inalienable right to *pursue* happiness achieve that condition, but his quest has advanced from a politics of personal ambition to one which he now believes should be—not "could" be but should be—an expression of love.

And love in the Ellisonian sense of democracy, as the "most disinterested form of love," is what Invisible Man brings to his rhetorical attempt, again in the epilogue, to understand the riddle of his grandfather's deathbed advice. In his long-in-coming response, Invisible Man speculates that in saying "yes" his grandfather "*must* have meant the principle, that we were to affirm the principle on which the country was built and not the men, or at least not the men who did the violence" (574). Once, responding to a young critic, who with fear and trembling characterized him as a patriotic writer, Ellison replied in terms reminiscent of Invisible Man's riff in the epilogue: "It ain't the theory which bothers me, it's the practice: My problem is to affirm while resisting."[9] And that is exactly the complex patriotic creed Invisible Man embraces when, speculating on the meaning of his grandfather's riddle, he propounds as riveting and profound a series of questions as have ever been posed about the American experiment.

Weaving back and forth between white Americans and those whom Ellison would years later name as "that vanished tribe into which I was born: The American Negroes,"[10] Invisible Man asks whether "we had to take the responsibility for all of it, for the men as well as the principle, because we were the heirs who must use the principle because no other fitted our needs" (574). Paying homage on the twin frequencies of love and politics to his grandfather, "an old slave" who "accepted his humanity just as he accepted the principle" (580), Invisible Man extends the frame of reference to African-American experience and the American reality since his grandfather's time.

Was it that we of all, we, most of all, had to affirm the principle, the plan in whose name we had been brutalized and sacrificed—not because we would always be weak nor because we were afraid or opportunistic, but because we were older than they, in the sense of what it took to live in the world with others and because they had exhausted in us, some—not much, but some—of the human greed and smallness, yes, and the fear and superstition that had kept them running. (574)

The passage touches the continuing willingness of political parties and organizations like the Brotherhood to sacrifice black people (and all vulnerable groups of people) and "take advantage of them in" what Brother Hambro arrogantly calls "their own best interest" (504) without democratic reciprocity. In an act of rhetorical transcendence, words that begin as a question modulate into a subtle, unequivocal affirmation of the ground occupied since slavery by African Americans. It is verbal high ground soon to become a redemptive, national battlefield through the mix of love and politics expressed by the Reverend Martin Luther King, Jr. and his brothers and sisters who fused politics with love in the nonviolent, heroically active, passive resistance of the Civil Rights Movement. Moreover, Invisible Man claims an advantage for African Americans in what he calls "what it took to live in the world with others," and Ellison in "Brave Words for a Startling Occasion" names as "that condition of being at home in the world."[11]

Ellison's and Invisible Man's affirmation of "politics as an expression of love" puts humane flesh on the skeleton of the American dream promised by the Declaration of Independence and the Bill of Rights. At the same time, Invisible Man's last question to his readers is prefaced by a comment, added to the final typescript in 1951, that acknowledges the difficulty of fraternity across the American spectrum. "And it is this which frightens me:" he declares, choosing a colon for punctuation to suggest a pause but not a break before his famous last question: "Who knows but that, on the lower frequencies, I speak for you?" (581). Indeed, Ellison calls attention to the complexity of his narrator's closing words by taking the unusual step of going directly from the colon to a new paragraph—the one sentence question that ends the novel. Before he asks the question that implies fraternity, that implies he does speak for his readers, Invisible Man calls this affinity a state of affairs that frightens him.

Why?

Could he mean, I might ask in paraphrase of his question about his grandfather—hell, he must have meant we are to affirm his speaking for us only if we say yes to the proposition that politics become an expression of love in America. That of course is a frightening as well as an exhilarating prospect— exhilarating in Walt Whitman's sense of a nation of free individuals working and singing together, frightening because of the obstacles in the way of bringing about "that condition of being at home in the world." Invisible Man knows the difficulty of the quest, and he knows, too, that those who put him in touch with his heart's capacity to love are African American individuals whose faces and personalities have been invisible to his readers, or, at least, to most of his white readers. Doubtless, Invisible Man's use of "frightens" conjures up a nation of individuals who, like him, have "a bottomless capacity for being a fool," and who also "have been hurt to the point of abysmal pain" (558–559, 579). The word "frightens" also suggests that in speaking truly for us, he is prepared to take fraternal responsibility for us as he earlier declared African Americans responsible for the Founding Fathers as well as for the principle those same Founders (and their descendants) "had violated and compromised to the point of absurdity even in their own corrupt minds" (574).

There is more to be said about love and politics, personality and nation. Invisible Man leaves these questions up in the air to reverberate in the ears of readers, and disappears. But Ralph Ellison does not. Invisible Man's questions remain buzzing in Ellison's ears for the rest of his life. In *Juneteenth* he voices them in the person of Senator Adam Sunraider, formerly "a little boy of indefinite race,"[12] midwifed and raised as a black child and preacher by Daddy Hickman, before he runs away, passes for white, and becomes a race-baiting United States Senator from a New England state. In one of his delirious, hallucinatory reveries while he is dying from wounds inflicted in an assassination on the Senate floor by his unacknowledged part-black son, Adam Sunraider asks Invisible Man's question all over again:

HOW THE HELL DO YOU GET LOVE INTO POLITICS OR COMPASSION INTO HISTORY?[13]

The Senator's tone is one of impatient despair, as well it should be, for in turning his back on the black folks who raised him and on the black and Indian woman in Oklahoma who bears his child, he sets in motion the betrayal of love that fuels his politics of calculation and cynicism. The Senator's joining of love and politics is expressive of his crisis and also, in Ellison's fable, the nation's. Ellison was explicit about locating "time present" in *Juneteenth:* "Roughly from 1954 to 1956 or 1957."[14] He explains why in a revealing note: "Action takes place on the eve of the Rights movement but it forecasts the chaos which would come later."[15]

Invisible Man is a novel of segregation that ends anticipating an America on the cusp of the leap from segregation to integration. *Juneteenth* is a sequel to *Invisible Man* in which Ellison projects the chaos and possibility that would follow the Supreme Court's *Brown v. Board* decision of 1954. Listen to the delirious, prophetic interior monologue of the dying Senator: "Nine owls have squawked out the rules and the hawks will talk, so soon they'll come marching out of the woodpile and the woodwork—sorehead, sorefoot, right up close, one-butt-shuffling into history but demanding praise and kind treatment for deeds undone, for lessons unlearned. But studying war once more . . ." (344–345). Certainly the owls are the nine Supreme Court justices whose rulings the Senator imagines summoning a procession of those black Americans who plunged outside history in *Invisible Man* but now barge back in with various, insistent demands. Like many black power militants from the late 1960s, these imaginary African Americans reverse the nonviolence practiced by Martin Luther King. Instead of the old shout—"Gonna study war no more"—their new refrain is "studying war once more" (345). Instead of "we shall overcome," they taunt the Reverend King, in the words of Charles Johnson's narrator in *Dreamer,* with shouts of "we shall overrun."[16]

Juneteenth ends with a chillingly concrete and surreal hallucination in which three black men, each of whom speaks a different variation of African-American idiom, menace the dying Senator. Their weapon of choice is a car—"no ordinary automobile" but what Sunraider calls "a bastard creation of black bastards— . . . an improvisation of vast arrogance and subversive and malicious defiance which they had designed to outrage and destroy everything in its path, a rolling time bomb launched in the streets" (347).

In the Senator's apparition of these men, Ellison ups the ante from *Invisible Man,* where the dispossessed burn down their tenement and become "capable of their own action," their own sacrifice. There the protest led by Dupre and Scofield, though outside the official political process, still seems a desperate expression of the desire for politics to be an expression of love. But the three black men who issue out of Sunraider's consciousness are driven by "politicized hate" (*Invisible Man,* 452). Through Sunraider's vision Ellison asks not if politics could ever be an expression of love but if, in fact, politics has become an expression of irrevocable hate? In *Juneteenth,* Bliss/Sunraider's flight from love sets in motion his and his society's chaos; the brilliant, nihilistic black men spring from his imagination. But they are also Ellison's image of the chaos of American society with which he had more than a passing acquaintance during the 1960s and early 1970s.

On his variable vernacular frequency, Ellison turns the mythical boatman of the River Lethe into three cold, cunning, implacable black men about to ferry the Senator across his American river of forgetfulness, perhaps the Potomac. Unlike Hickman and the members of his "vanished tribe," these African Americans are militant members of the party of nemesis determined to exact revenge for all the injustice and invisibility—the hubris—visited upon them by the Sunraiders of America. To the last, Ellison is true to the ambiguity, complexity, and possibility of his characters and his (and his nation's) story. For in the midst of his and his society's chaos, the dying Senator once more hears "the sound of Hickman's consoling voice, calling from somewhere above" (348). As readers, we are left to imagine that voice, perhaps as the better angel of all our natures raising a freedom song to guide the struggle for the soul of America.

Ten years ago Charles Johnson, who has spoken so eloquently about *Invisible Man*'s continuing presence in our lives and literature,[17] dedicated his National Book Award acceptance speech to Ralph Ellison in homage to his achievement and his inspiration. Looking back to *Invisible Man,* Johnson also looked forward—"the end is in the beginning and lies far ahead"—to "the emergence of a black American fiction that is Ellisonesque in spirit, a fiction of increasing intellectual and artistic generosity, one that enables us as a people—as a culture—to move from narrow complaint to broad celebration."[18] Like Ellison, Johnson anticipates novels to come. So do I. And may these novels answer *Invisible Man*'s lingering question about love and politics in such a way that the special covenant Ellison imagined between novelist and nation is fleshed out and realized in the lives and art of the American people.

ENDNOTES

1. Ralph Ellison, "Letter to Albert Murray" (April 4, 1957), *Trading Twelves: The Selected Letters of Ralph Ellison and Albert Murray,* ed. Albert Murray and John F. Callahan (New York: The Modern Library, 2000), 157–58.

2. Ralph Ellison, *Invisible Man,* (New York: Random House, 1952; reprint, New York: Vintage Books, 1995), 581. All subsequent citations will be noted parenthetically in the text by page number, and emphases in original unless otherwise noted.

3. Ralph Ellison, "Brave Words for a Startling Occasion" (January 27, 1953), *The Collected Essays of Ralph Ellison,* ed. John F. Callahan (New York: The Modern Library, 1995), 154.

4. Ralph Ellison, "Letter to Albert Murray" (August 17, 1957), *Trading Twelves*, 175.

5. For examples of "public happiness" and government as a means to the "safety, prosperity, and happiness of the people," see John Adams, "Fourth Annual Address" (November 22, 1800), and the Massachusetts Bill of Rights (1780). For democratic *agape*, see Martin Luther King, Jr., "The Power of Nonviolence," *I Have a Dream: Writings and Speeches That Changed the World*, ed. James M. Washington (New York: HarperCollins Publishers), 31–32.

6. Ralph Ellison, "The Novel as a Function of Democracy" (June 1967), *Collected Essays*, 764.

7. Ralph Ellison, "Brave Words for a Startling Occasion" (January 27, 1953), *Collected Essays*, 153.

8. Ralph Ellison, "Brave Words for a Startling Occasion" (January 27, 1953), *Collected Essays*, 154.

9. Letter to the author, August 12, 1983.

10. Ralph Ellison, Dedication, *Juneteenth: A Novel*, ed. John F. Callahan (New York: Random House, 1999).

11. Ralph Ellison, "Brave Words for a Startling Occasion" (January 27, 1953), *Collected Essays*, 154.

12. Ralph Ellison, "A Completion of Personality" (1974), *Collected Essays*, 814.

13. Ralph Ellison, *Juneteenth*, 264.

14. Ralph Ellison, "A Completion of Personality" (1974), *Collected Essays*, 816.

15. Ralph Ellison, *Juneteenth*, "Notes," 352.

16. Charles Johnson, *Dreamer* (New York: Scribner, 1998), 17.

17. Charles Johnson, "Novel Genius," *Crisis* (March/April 2002), 17–20.

18. Charles Johnson, "National Book Award Acceptance Speech," *Tri-Quarterly* 82 (Fall 1991), 209.

Works Cited

WORKS BY RALPH ELLISON

"'American Culture is of a Whole': From the Letters of Ralph Ellison." *New Republic.* Introduction by John F. Callahan. March 1, 1999. 34–49.

"Cadillac Flambé." 16 *American Review* (February 1973):249–69.

The Collected Essays of Ralph Ellison. Edited by John F. Callahan. New York: Modern Library, 1995.

———. "Address to the Harvard College Alumni, Class of 1949" (June 12, 1974):415–26.

———. "Address at the Whiting Foundation" (October 23, 1992):849–56.

———. "*An American Dilemma:* A Review" (1944):328–40.

———. "The Art of Fiction: *An Interview*" (Spring 1955):210–24.

———. "The Art of Romare Bearden" (November 25, 1968):684–93.

———. "Blues People" (February 6, 1964):278–87.

———. "Brave Words for a Startling Occasion" (January 27, 1953):151–54.

———. "Change the Joke and Slip the Yoke" (Spring 1958):100–112.

———. "The Charlie Christian Story" (May 17, 1958):266–72.

———. "Commencement Address at the College of William and Mary" (1972):405–13.

———. "'A Completion of Personality': A Talk with Ralph Ellison" (1974 and 1982): 783–817.

————. "An Extravagance of Laughter" (1985):613–58.

————. "Foreword to *The Beer Can by the Highway*" (1987):843–48.

————. "Going to the Territory" (September 20, 1979):591–612.

————. "Harlem is Nowhere" (1948):320–27.

————. "Haverford Statement" (May 30–31, 1969):427–32.

————. "Hidden Name and Complex Fate: A Writer's Experience in the United States" (January 6, 1964):189–209.

————. "Homage to Duke Ellington on His Birthday" (April 27, 1969):676–83.

————. "If the Twain Shall Meet" (November 8, 1964):563–76.

————. "Indivisible Man" (December 1970):353–95.

————. "Introduction to *Shadow and Act*" (May 1964):47–60.

————. "Introduction to the Thirtieth-Anniversary Edition of *Invisible Man*" (November 10, 1981):469–85.

————. "The Little Man at Chehaw Station: The American Artist and His Audience" (1977/1978):489–519.

————. "Living with Music" (December 1955):227–36.

————. "The Myth of the Flawed White Southerner" (1968):552–62.

————. "Notes for Class Day Talk at Columbia University" (1990):837–41.

————. "The Novel as a Function of American Democracy" (March 23, 1967):755–65.

————. "On Being the Target of Discrimination" (April 16, 1989):819–28.

————. "On Initiation Rites and Power: A Lecture at West Point" (March 26, 1969): 520–41.

————. "Perspective of Literature" (April 27–30, 1976):766–81.

————. "Presentation to Bernard Malamud of the Gold Medal for Fiction" (1983):461–67.

————. "Remembering Richard Wright" (July 18, 1971):659–75.

————. "Roscoe Dunjee and the American Language" (May 14, 1972):449–60.

————. "Society, Morality and the Novel" (1957):694–725.

————. "Some Questions and Some Answers" (May 1958):291–301.

————. "A Special Message to Subscribers" (1979):347–51.

————. " 'Tell It Like It Is, Baby' " (June 1965):27–46.

————. "That Same Pain, That Same Pleasure: An Interview" (Winter 1961):63–80.

————. "Twentieth-Century Fiction and the Black Mask of Humanity" (1946):81–99.

————. " 'A Very Stern Discipline' " (March 1967):726–54.

————. "The Way It Is" (October 20, 1942):310–19.

————. "What America Would Be Like Without Blacks" (April 6, 1970):577–84.

————. "What These Children Are Like" (September 1963):542–51.

————. "Working Notes for *Invisible Man*" (c. 1945-51):341–45.

————. "The World and the Jug" (December 9, 1963 and February 3, 1964):155–88.

"Did You Ever Dream Lucky?" *New World Writing*. New York: New American Library, 1954. 134–45.

"Eddie's Bar" (1939). *A Renaissance in Harlem: Lost Voices of an American Community.* Edited by Lionel C. Bascom. New York: Avon Books, Inc., 1999. 36–38.

"Ellison's Library Speech" (June 21, 1975). Handwritten transcript in folder entitled "June 21, 1975—Dedication Ellison Branch Library." Box 171, Ralph Ellison Papers, Library of Congress. 1–12.

Flying Home and Other Stories. Edited by John F. Callahan. New York: Random House, 1996.

Going to the Territory. New York: Vintage Books, 1985; reprinted in 1987.

"Harlem's America." *The New Leader* (September 26, 1966):22–35.

"Interview with WKY-TV, Oklahoma, 1976" (August 22, 1976). *Living With Music: Ralph Ellison's Jazz Writings.* Edited by Robert G. O'Meally. New York: The Modern Library, 2001. 255–64.

"An Interview with Ralph Ellison" (October 25, 1963). *Conversations with Ralph Ellison.* Edited by Maryemma Graham and Amritjit Singh. Jackson: University Press of Mississippi, 1995. 70–86. Reprinted from *Tamarack Review* (Summer 1964):221–27.

"An Interview with Ralph Ellison: Visible Man." 2 *Pulp* 2 (Summer 1976):10–12.

Invisible Man. New York: Random House, 1952; reprint, New York: Vintage Books, 1995.

Juneteenth: A Novel. Edited by John F. Callahan. New York: Random House, 1999.

"Letter to Charles Davidson" (July 10, 1971). *Living With Music: Ralph Ellison's Jazz Writings.* Edited by Robert G. O'Meally. New York: The Modern Library House, 2001. 250–54.

"Letter to John H. Sengstacke." January 15, 1953. Box 213, Ralph Ellison Papers, Library of Congress.

"Letter to Robert O'Meally" (April 17, 1989), "'American Culture is of a Whole': From the Letters of Ralph Ellison." *New Republic.* Introduction by John F. Callahan (March 1, 1999):47.

"Letter to Stanley Edgar Hyman" (May 29, 1970), "'American Culture is of a Whole': From the Letters of Ralph Ellison." *New Republic.* Introduction by John F. Callahan (March 1, 1999):41–42.

"My Life and Yours" (n.d.). Corrected, typed transcript ("excerpts") of University of Chicago lecture. Box 174, Ralph Ellison Papers, Library of Congress, 1–37.

"'My Strength Comes from Louis Armstrong': Interview with Robert G. O'Meally, 1976" (May 1976). *Living With Music: Ralph Ellison's Jazz Writings.* Edited by Robert G. O'Meally. New York: The Modern Library, 2001. 265–88.

"Out of the Hospital and Under the Bar." *Soon, One Morning: New Writing by American Negroes, 1940–1962.* Edited by Herbert Hill. New York: Alfred A. Knopf, 1963. 242–90.

"Ralph Ellison's Territorial Advantage" (1976). *Living With Music: Ralph Ellison's Jazz Writings.* Edited by Robert G. O'Meally. New York: The Modern Library, 2001. 15–33.

"Remarks at The American Academy of Arts and Sciences Conference on the Negro American, 1965." May 14–15, 1965. *New Black Voices: An Anthology of Contemporary Afro-American Literature.* Edited by Abraham Chapman. New York: New American Library, 1972. Originally published in 95 *Daedalus* 1 (Winter 1966):406–7.

Reply to a questionnaire (dated June 27, 1952) from the *Denver Post,* Box 174, Ralph Ellison Papers, Library of Congress, 1–10 [page 9 missing].

Shadow and Act. New York: Vintage Books, 1964; reprinted in 1972.

"Study and Experience: An Interview with Ralph Ellison" (March 8, 1976). *Conversations with Ralph Ellison.* Edited by Maryemma Graham and Amritjit Singh. Jackson: University Press of Mississippi, 1995. 319–41. Reprinted from *Massachusetts Review* 18 (1977):417–35.

"The Uses of History in Fiction." 1 *The Southern Literary Journal* 2 (Spring 1969):57–90.

OTHER WORKS CITED

Albrecht, James. "Saying Yes and Saying No: Individualist Ethics in Ellison, Burke, and Emerson." 114 *PMLA* 1 (January 1999):46–63.

Allen, Danielle S. "Law's Necessary Forcefulness: Ralph Ellison vs. Hannah Arendt on the Battle of Little Rock." 26 *Oklahoma City University Law Review* 3 (Fall 2001):857–900.

———. *Talking to Strangers: On Little Rock and Political Friendship.* Chicago: University of Chicago Press, 2004.

———. *World of Prometheus: The Politics of Punishing in Democratic Athens.* Princeton: Princeton University Press, 2000.

Arendt, Hannah. "Reflections on Little Rock." 6 *Dissent* 1 (Winter 1959):45–56.

———. "To Mary McCarthy" (December 21, 1968). *Between Friends: The Correspondence of Arendt and Mary McCarthy, 1949–1975.* Edited by Carol Brightman. New York: Harcourt, Brace, & Co., 1995. 229–30.

———. "A Reply to Critics." 6 *Dissent* 2 (Spring 1959):179–81.

———. "What is Authority." *Between Past and Future: Eight Exercises in Political Thought.* New York: Penguin, 1993; originally published in 1961.

Aristotle. *Politics.* Translated by Carnes Lord. Chicago: University of Chicago Press, 1984.

Baker, Houston A., Jr. *Blues, Ideology, and Afro-American Literature: A Vernacular Theory.* Chicago: University of Chicago Press, 1984.

———. "Failed Prophet and Falling Stock: Why Ralph Ellison was Never Avant-Garde." 7 *Stanford Humanities Review* 1 (1999):4–11.

———. "To Move Without Moving: An Analysis of Creativity and Commerce in Ralph Ellison's Trueblood Episode." 98 *PMLA* 5 (October 1983):828–45. Reprinted in *The Critical Response to Ralph Ellison.* Edited by Robert J. Butler. Westport, Conn.: Greenwood Press, 2000. 73–93.

Balkin, Jack M., ed. *What Brown v. Board of Education Should Have Said: The Nation's Top Legal Experts Rewrite America's Landmark Civil Rights Decision.* New York: New York University Press, 2001.

Barthes, Roland. "The Death of the Author." *Image/Music/Text.* Edited and translated by Stephen Heath. New York: Hill and Wang, 1977. 142–48.

Beckwith, Sarah. *Signifying God: Social Relation and Symbolic Act in the York Corpus Christi Plays.* Chicago: University of Chicago Press, 2001.

Benhabib, Seyla. *Critique, Norm, and Utopia: A Study of the Foundations of Critical Theory.* New York: Columbia University Press, 1986.

Benjamin, Walter. "The Destructive Character." *Reflections: Essays, Aphorisms, Autobiographical Writings.* Edited by Peter Demetz. New York: Schocken, 1986. 301–4.

———. *Gesammelte Schriften.* Vols. II and V. Frankfurt: Suhrkamp Verlag, 1977.

————. *Illuminations: Essays and Reflections.* Edited by Hannah Arendt. New York: Schocken, 1968.

Benston, Kimberly. *Speaking for You: The Vision of Ralph Ellison.* Washington: Howard University Press, 1987.

Bergson, Henri. *Laughter: An Essay on the Meaning of the Comic.* Translation by Cloudesley Brereton and Fred Rothwell. New York: Macmillan, 1911.

Black Dispatch. "An Inflammatory Appeal" (October 15, 1920):4.

————. "The Negro Before the Law" (January 28, 1921):4.

————. "Oklahoma's Rotten Educational Law" (January 21, 1921):4.

————. "Senseless Negroes" (July 9, 1920):4.

————. "Terrible Lessons" (August 22, 1919):4.

————. "Upright Men Shall be Astonished" (August 15, 1919):4.

————. "White Justice Likened Unto White Sepulchers" (June 4, 1920):4.

Blake, Susan. "Ritual and Rationalization: Black Folklore in the Works of Ralph Ellison." 94 *PMLA* 1 (1979):121–36.

Bloom, Harold, ed. *Modern Critical Views: Ralph Ellison.* New York: Chelsea, 1986.

Bone, Robert. "Ralph Ellison and the Uses of Imagination." *Ralph Ellison: A Collection of Critical Essays.* Edited by John Hersey. Englewood Cliffs, N.J.: Prentice-Hall, Inc., 1974. 95–114. Originally published in *Anger and Beyond.* Edited by Herbert Hill. New York: Harper & Row Publishers, 1966. 86–111.

Boyd, Mary Patillo. *Warriors Don't Cry: A Searing Memoir of the Battle to Integrate Little Rock's Central High.* New York: Pocket Books, 1994.

Braithwaite, John. "Survey Article: Repentance Rituals and Restorative Justice." 8 *Journal of Political Philosophy* 1 (2000):115–31.

Branch, Taylor. *Parting the Waters: America in the King Years, 1954–63.* New York: Simon and Schuster, 1988.

Brennan, Timothy. "Ellison and Ellison: The Solipsism of *Invisible Man*." *CLA Journal* 25 (December 1981). 162–81.

Brophy, Alfred L. "Humanity, Utility, and Logic in Southern Legal Thought: Harriet Beecher Stowe's View in *Dred: A Tale of the Great Dismal Swamp*." 78 *Boston University Law Review* (1998):1113–61.

————. *Reconstructing the Dreamland: The Tulsa Riot of 1921—Race, Reparations, and Reconciliation.* New York: Oxford University Press, 2002.

Brophy, Alfred L., ed. "Ralph Ellison and the Law." 26 *Oklahoma City University Law Review* 3 (Fall 2001).

Brown, Lloyd L. "The Deep Pit." *Twentieth Century Interpretations of* Invisible Man: *A Collection of Critical Essays.* Edited by John M. Reilly. Englewood Cliffs, N.J.: Prentice-Hall, Inc., 1970. 97–99. Originally published in *Masses and Mainstream* V (June 1952):62–64.

Bucknall, Barbara. *The Religion of Art in Proust.* Urbana: University of Illinois Press, 1969.

Burke, Bob and Denyvetta Davis. *Ralph Ellison: A Biography.* Oklahoma City: Oklahoma Heritage Association, 2003.

Butler, Robert. "Dante's *Inferno* and Ellison's *Invisible Man*: A Study in Literary Continuity." 28 *CLA Journal* 1 (September 1984):57–77.

Butler-Evans, Elliot. "The Politics of Carnival and Heteroglossia in Toni Morrison's *Song of Solomon* and Ralph Ellison's *Invisible Man:* Dialogic Criticism and African American Literature." *The Ethnic Canon: Histories, Institutions, and Interventions.* Edited by David Palumbo-Liu. Minneapolis: University of Minnesota Press, 1995.

Callahan, John F. "Chaos, Complexity, and Possibility: The Historical Frequencies of Ralph Waldo Ellison." *Speaking for You: The Vision of Ralph Ellison.* Edited by Kimberly Benston. Washington: Howard University Press, 1987. 125–43.

———. "Frequencies of Eloquence: The Performance and Composition of *Invisible Man.*" *In the African-American Grain: Call-and-Response in Twentieth-Century Black Fiction.* Urbana: University of Illinois Press, 2001; originally published 1988. 150–88.

———. "Frequencies of Memory: A Eulogy for Ralph Waldo Ellison." 18 *Callaloo* 2 (1995):298–309. Reprinted in *The Critical Response to Ralph Ellison.* Edited by Robert J. Butler. Westport, Conn.: Greenwood Press, 2000. 199–209.

Campbell, Joseph. *The Hero with a Thousand Faces.* 2nd edition. Princeton: Princeton University Press, 1968.

Case, Richard. "A Novel is a Novel." *The Critical Response to Ralph Ellison.* Edited by Robert J. Butler. Westport, Connecticut: Greenwood Press, 2000. 35–38. Reprinted from 14 *Kenyon Review* (1952):678–84.

The Catholic Encyclopedia: An International Work of Reference on the Constitution, Doctrine, Discipline, and History of the Catholic Church. Volume XIII. Edited by Charles G. Herbermann et al. New York: Robert Appleton Co., 1912.

Caughie, Pamela. *Passing and Pedagogy: The Dynamics of Responsibility.* Urbana: University of Illinois Press, 1999.

Chambers, Simone. "Discourse and Democratic Practices." *The Cambridge Companion to Habermas.* Edited by Stephen K. White. Cambridge: Cambridge University Press, 1995. 233–62.

Chicago Defender award program. "49th Year of Progress: 1953 Seventh Annual Robert S. Abbott Memorial Award Presentation." May 16, 1953. Box 213, Ralph Ellison Papers, Library of Congress.

Childers, Joseph and Gary Hentzi, eds. *The Columbia Dictionary of Modern Literary and Cultural Criticism.* New York: Columbia University Press, 1995.

Coleman, Elliott. "Religious Imagery." *Proust: A Collection of Critical Essays.* Edited by Rene Girard. Englewood Cliffs, N.J.: Prentice-Hall, 1962.

Cone, James H. *The Spirituals and the Blues.* New York: Seabury Press, 1972.

Conner, Marc C. "Wild Women and Graceful Girls: Toni Morrison's Winter's Tale." *Nature, Woman, and the Art of Politics.* Edited by Eduardo Velasquez. Lanham, Md.: Rowman and Littlefield, 2000. 341–69.

Connolly, William. *Identity/Difference: Democratic Negotiations of Political Paradox.* Ithaca: Cornell University Press, 1991.

Crouch, Stanley. *The All-American Skin Game, Or, The Decoy of Race: The Long and Short of It, 1990–1994.* New York: Vintage, 1997.

———. *Always in Pursuit: Fresh American Perspectives, 1995–1997.* New York: Pantheon Books, 1998.

Cruse, Harold. *The Crisis of the Negro Intellectual: From Its Origins to the Present.* New York: William Morrow & Company, Inc., 1971; originally published in 1967.

Demastes, William W. *Theatre of Chaos: Beyond Absurdism, into Orderly Disorder.* Cambridge: Cambridge University Press, 1998.

de Tocqueville, Alexis. *Democracy in America.* Introduction by Sanford Kessler and translated by Stephen D. Grant. Indianapolis: Hackett Publishing Company, Inc., 2000.

de Tocqueville, Alexis. *Democracy in America.* Edited and translated by Harvey C. Mansfield and Delba Winthrop. Chicago: The University of Chicago Press, 2000.

Deutsch, Leonard. "Ralph Waldo Ellison and Ralph Waldo Emerson: A Shared Moral Vision." *CLA Journal* 16 (1972):159–78.

Dickson, Del, ed. *The Supreme Court in Conference, 1940–1985: The Private Discussions Behind Nearly 300 Supreme Court Decisions.* New York: Oxford University Press, 2001.

Dickstein, Morris. "Ralph Ellison, Race, and American Culture." 18 *Raritan* 4 (Spring 1999):30–50.

Dissent Editors. Untitled Note. 6 *Dissent* 1 (Winter 1959):45.

Du Bois, W. E. B. *The Souls of Black Folk: Authoritative Text, Contexts, Criticism.* Edited by Henry Louis Gates Jr. and Terri Hume Oliver. New York: W.W. Norton & Company, 1999.

Eddy, Beth. "The Rites of Identity: The Religious Naturalism and Cultural Criticism of Kenneth Burke and Ralph Ellison." Unpublished Dissertation. Department of Religion. Princeton University, 1998.

Eichelberger, Julia. *Prophets of Recognition: Ideology and the Individual in Novels by Ralph Ellison, Toni Morrison, Saul Bellow, and Eudora Welty.* Baton Rouge: Louisiana State University Press, 1999.

Elkins, Stanley M., ed. *Slavery: A Problem in American Institutional and Intellectual Life.* Chicago: University of Chicago Press, 1959.

Emerson, Ralph Waldo. "The Conservative" (December 9, 1841). *Ralph Waldo Emerson: Essays and Lectures.* Edited by Joel Porte. New York: Library of America, 1983.

———. "Fate" (1860). *Selections from Ralph Waldo Emerson.* Edited by Stephen E. Whicher. Boston: Houghton Mifflin Company, 1957. 330–52.

———. "Nature" (1837). *Selections from Ralph Waldo Emerson.* Edited by Stephen E. Whicher. Boston: Houghton Mifflin Company, 1957. 21–56.

———. "Self-Reliance" (1841). *Ralph Waldo Emerson: Essays and Poems.* New York: Library of America, 1996.

Evans, Harold. *In Defense of History.* New York: Penguin, 1998.

Fabre, Michel. "From *Native Son* to *Invisible Man:* Some Notes on Ralph Ellison's Evolution in the 1950s." *Speaking for You: The Vision of Ralph Ellison.* Edited by Kimberly Benston. Washington: Howard University Press, 1987. 199–216.

———. *The Unfinished Quest of Richard Wright.* Urbana: University of Illinois Press, 1973; second edition, 1993.

Fish, Stanley. *Self-Consuming Artifacts: The Experience of Seventeenth-Century Literature.* Berkeley: University of California Press, 1972.

Fitzgerald, F. Scott. *The Great Gatsby.* New York: Charles Scribner's Sons, 1925.

Foley, Barbara. "Reading Redness: Politics and Audience in Ralph Ellison's Early Short Fiction." 29 *Journal of Narrative Theory* 3 (Fall 1999):323–39.

———. "The Rhetoric of Anticommunism in *Invisible Man.*" 59 *College English* 5 (September 1997):530–47.

Foucault, Michel. "What is an Author?" *Textual Strategies: Perspectives in Post-Structuralist Criticism.* Edited by Josué V. Harari. Ithaca, New York: Cornell University Press, 1979. 141–60.

Franklin, Jimmie Lewis. *Journey Toward Hope: A History of Blacks in Oklahoma.* Norman: University of Oklahoma Press, 1982.

Friedman, Lawrence M. "*Brown* in Context." *Race, Law, and Culture: Reflections on* Brown v. Board of Education. Edited by Austin Sarat. New York: Oxford University Press, 1997. 49–73.

Fullinwider, S. P. *The Mind and Mood of Black America.* Homewood, Ill.: The Dorsey Press, 1969.

Gates, Henry Louis, Jr. *The Signifying Monkey: A Theory of Afro-American Literary Criticism.* New York: Oxford University Press, 1988.

Gayle, Addison, Jr., "Cultural Strangulation: Black Literature and the White Aesthetic." *Within the Circle: An Anthology of African American Literary Criticism from the Harlem Renaissance to the Present.* Edited by Angelyn Mitchell. Durham: Duke University Press, 1994. 207–12. Originally published in *The Black Aesthetic.* Edited by Addison Gayle. New York: Doubleday, 1971.

———. *The Way of the New World: The Black Novel in America.* New York: Doubleday, 1976.

Gibson, Donald B. *The Politics of Literary Expression: A Study of Major Black Writers.* Westport, Conn.: Greenwood Press, 1981.

Graham, Maryemma and Amritjit Singh, eds. *Conversations with Ralph Ellison.* Jackson: University Press of Mississippi, 1995.

Guttmann, Allen. "American Nightmare." *Modern Critical Views: Ralph Ellison.* Edited by Harold Bloom. New York: Chelsea, 1986. 29–35.

Habermas, Jurgen. *Moral Consciousness and Communicative Action.* Translated by Christian Lenhardt and Shierry Weber Nicholsen. Cambridge, Mass.: MIT University Press, 1990.

Harper, Michael S. and Robert B. Stepto. *Chant of Saints: A Gathering of Afro-American Literature, Art, and Scholarship.* Urbana: University of Illinois Press, 1979.

Hayles, N. Katherine. *Chaos Bound: Orderly Disorder in Contemporary Literature and Science.* Ithaca: Cornell University Press, 1990.

———, ed. *Chaos and Order: Complex Dynamics in Literature and Science.* Chicago: University of Chicago Press, 1991.

Heidegger, Martin. *What is Philosophy?* Translated by Jean T. Wilde and William Kluback. Schenectady, N. Y.: The New College and University Press, 1955.

Hersey, John, ed. *Ralph Ellison: A Collection of Critical Essays.* Englewood Cliffs, N. J.: Prentice-Hall, 1974.

Hirsch, E. D., Jr. *Validity in Interpretation.* New Haven: Yale University Press, 1967.

Honig, Bonnie. *Political Theory and the Displacement of Politics.* Ithaca: Cornell University Press, 1993.

Honneth, Axel. "The Other of Justice: Habermas and the Ethical Challenge of Postmodernism." *The Cambridge Companion to Habermas.* Edited by Stephen K. White. Cambridge: Cambridge University Press, 1995. 289–324.

Horwitz, Morton J. *The Transformation of American Law, 1870–1960: Crisis of Legal Orthodoxy.* Cambridge: Harvard University Press, 1992.

————. *The Warren Court and the Pursuit of Justice: A Critical Issue*. New York: Hill and Wang, 1998.

Howe, Irving. "Black Boys and Native Sons." *A World More Attractive: A View of Modern Literature and Politics*. New York: Horizon Press, 1970; originally published by *Dissent* in 1963. 98–122.

————. "Review of *Invisible Man*." *The Nation* (May 10, 1952).

Hughes, Langston. "To Certain Negro Leaders." *The Collected Poems of Langston Hughes*. Edited by Arnold Rampersad. New York: Vintage Books, 1994.

————. "The Negro and the Racial Mountain." *Nation* (June 23, 1926). *Crossing the Danger Water: Three Hundred Years of African-American Writing*. Edited by Deirdre Mullane. New York: Anchor Books, 1993. 504–507.

Hyman, Stanley Edgar. "Ralph Ellison in Our Time." *Ralph Ellison: A Collection of Critical Essays*. Edited by John Hersey. N.J.: Prentice Hall, 1974. 39–42; reprinted from 47 *The New Leader* 22 (October 26, 1964):21–22.

"Investigation of Lynching of Claude Chandler." Attorney General File 1017. Oklahoma State Archives, Oklahoma City.

"Investigation of Lynching of Roy Belton." Attorney General File 1018. Oklahoma State Archives, Oklahoma City.

Jackson, Lawrence. *Ralph Ellison: Emergence of Genius*. New York: John Wiley & Sons, 2002.

————. "Ralph Ellison, Sharpies, Rinehart, and Politics in *Invisible Man*." 40 *The Massachusetts Review* 1 (Spring 1999):71–85.

Jackson, Walter A. *Gunnar Myrdal and America's Conscience: Social Engineering and Racial Liberalism*. Chapel Hill: University of North Carolina Press, 1990.

Jaffa, Harry V. *A New Birth of Freedom: Abraham Lincoln and the Coming of the Civil War*. Lanham, Md.: Rowman and Littlefield Publishers, Inc., 2000.

Janken, Kenneth Robert. *Rayford W. Logan and the Dilemma of the African American Intellectual*. Amherst: University of Massachusetts Press, 1993.

Jennings, Michael. *Dialectical Images: Walter Benjamin's Theory of Literary Criticism*. Ithaca: Cornell University Press, 1987.

Johnson, Charles. *Dreamer: A Novel*. New York: Scribner, 1998.

————. "National Book Award Acceptance Speech." *Tri-Quarterly* 82 (Fall 1991):208–209.

————. "Novel Genius." *Crisis* (March/April 2002):17–20.

Kaiser, Ernest. "A Critical Look at Ellison's Fiction and at Social and Literary Criticism by and about the Author." 20 *Black World* 2 (December 1970):53–59, 81–97.

Kelley, Robin D. G. *Yo' Mama's Disfunktional: Fighting the Culture Wars in Urban America*. Boston: Beacon Press, 1998.

Kent, George E. "Ralph Ellison and the Afro-American Folk and Cultural Tradition." *CLA Journal*. 13:3 (March 1969):265–76. Reprinted in *The Critical Response to Ralph Ellison*. Edited by Robert J. Butler. Westport, Conn.: Greenwood Press, 2000. 51–57.

Kierkegaard, Soren. *The Sickness Unto Death: A Christian Psychological Exposition for Upbuilding and Awakening*. Edited and translated by Howard V. Hong and Edna H. Hong. Princeton: Princeton University Press, 1980.

King, Martin Luther, Jr. "The Power of Nonviolence." *I Have a Dream: Writings and Speeches That Changed the World*. Edited by James M. Washington. New York: HarperCollins Publishers. 29–33.

————. "I See the Promised Land" (1968). *I Have A Dream: Writings and Speeches that Changed the World.* Edited by James M. Washington. San Francisco: HarperSanFrancisco, 1992. 193–203.

————. *Stride Toward Freedom: The Montgomery Story.* New York: Harper & Row, Publishers, 1958.

Klarman, Michael. "Rethinking the Civil Rights and Civil Liberties Revolutions." 82 *Virginia Law Review* (1996):1–67.

Klein, Marcus. "Ralph Ellison." *After Alienation.* Cleveland: World Publishing, 1964.

Kostelanetz, Richard. "Ralph Ellison: Brown Skinned Aristocrat." 20 *Shenandoah* 4 (Summer 1969):56–77.

Kousser, J. Morgan. *Dead End: The Development of Nineteenth-Century Litigation on Racial Discrimination in Schools.* New York: Oxford University Press, 1986.

Landauer, Carl. "Deliberating Speed: Totalitarian Anxieties and Postwar Legal Thought." 12 *Yale Journal of Law and the Humanities* 2 (Summer 2000):171–248.

Lee, Kun Jong. "Ellison's *Invisible Man:* Emersonianism Revised." 107 *PMLA* 2 (March 1992):331–44.

Lewis, David Levering. *W. E. B. Du Bois: The Fight for Equality and the American Century, 1919–1963.* New York: Henry Holt & Co., 2000.

Lincoln, Abraham. "Address Delivered at the Dedication of the Cemetery at Gettysburg—Final Text" (November 19, 1863). *Collected Works of Abraham Lincoln.* Edited by Roy P. Basler. New Brunswick: Rutgers University Press, 1955. 7:23.

————. "First Debate with Stephen A. Douglas at Ottawa, Illinois" (August 21, 1858). *Collected Works of Abraham Lincoln.* Edited by Roy P. Basler. New Brunswick: Rutgers University Press, 1955. 3:1–37.

————. "Message to Congress in Special Session" (July 4, 1861). *Collected Works of Abraham Lincoln.* Edited by Roy P. Basler. New Brunswick: Rutgers University Press, 1955. 4:421–41.

Madison, James. *The Federalist.* Edited by Jacob E. Cooke. Middletown, Conn.: Wesleyan University Press, 1961. No. 63.

Margolies, Edward. *Native Sons: A Critical Study of Twentieth-Century Black American Authors.* Philadelphia: J. B. Lippincott Company, 1968.

Maxwell, William J. *New Negro, Old Left: African-American Writing and Communism Between the Wars.* New York: Columbia University Press, 1999.

McCormick, John. *Catastrophe and Imagination: An Interpretation of the Recent English and American Novel.* London: Longmans, Green and Co., 1957.

McPherson, James Alan. "Junior and John Doe." *Lure and Loathing: Essays on Race, Identity, and the Ambivalence of Assimilation.* Edited by Gerald Early. New York: Allen Lane, The Penguin Press, 1993. 175–93.

McPherson, James M., ed. *To the Best of My Ability: The American Presidents.* New York: Dorsley Kinderly, 2000.

McSweeney, Kerry. *Invisible Man: Race and Identity.* Boston: Twayne Publishers, 1988.

Menand, Louis. *The Metaphysicians Club.* New York: Knopf, 2001.

Mommsen, Theodor. *Romische Geschichte,* 2nd Edition. London: Richard Bentley, 1864. Vol. 1.

Monmonier, Mark. *How to Lie with Maps.* Chicago: University of Chicago Press, 1991.

Montgomery, Maxine Lavon. *The Apocalypse in African-American Fiction.* Gainesville: University Press of Florida, 1996.

Morel, Lucas E. "America's Racial Divide: Of Debts Spoken and Unspoken." 9 *On Principle* 3 (June 2001):1, 3–4.

———. "Ellison's 'Invisible' Still Walk Among Us." *Los Angeles Times* (April 14, 2002):M1.

———. "Ennobled by Jazz: Ralph Ellison and the Music of American Possibility." *Books & Culture: A Christian Review* (May/June 2002):9–10.

———. "Juneteenth: American Democracy in Theory and Practice." *Christian Science Monitor* (June 19, 2000):9.

———. "On Becoming Visible: Race and the *Imago Dei.*" *Books & Culture: A Christian Review* (September/October 2000):24–26.

Morrison, Toni. "City Limits, Village Values: Concepts of the Neighborhood in Black Fiction." *Literature and the Urban Experience: Essays on the City and Literature.* Edited by Michael C. Jaye and Ann Chalmers Watts. New Brunswick: Rutgers University Press, 1981. 35–43.

Moses, Wilson J. *Afrotopia: The Roots of African American Popular History.* New York: Cambridge University Press, 1998.

Murray, Albert. *From the Briarpatch File: On Context, Procedure, and American Identity.* New York: Pantheon Books, 2001.

Murray, Albert and John F. Callahan, eds. *Trading Twelves: The Selected Letters of Ralph Ellison and Albert Murray.* New York: The Modern Library, 2000.

Nadel, Alan. *Invisible Criticism: Ralph Ellison and the American Canon.* Iowa City: University of Iowa Press, 1988.

———. "Ralph Ellison and the American Canon." 13 *American Literary History* 2 (Summer 2001):393–404.

Naison, Mark. *Communists in Harlem during the Depression.* Urbana: University of Illinois Press, 1983.

Neal, Larry. "Ellison's Zoot Suit." *Ralph Ellison: A Collection of Critical Essays.* Edited by John Hersey. Englewood Cliffs, N.J.: Prentice-Hall, 1974. 58–79; originally published in 20 *Black World* 2 (December 1970):31–50.

Nichols, William. "Ralph Ellison's Black American Scholar." *Phylon* 31 (1970):70–75.

Nietzsche, Friedrich. *Zarathustra. Collected Works of Friedrich Nietzsche.* Edited by Walter Kaufmann. New York: Viking/Penguin, 1982.

Novick, Peter. *That Noble Dream: The Objectivity Question and the American Historical Profession.* New York: Cambridge University Press, 1988.

Nussbaum, Martha. "Invisibility and Recognition: Sophocles' *Philoctetes* and Ellison's *Invisible Man.*" *Philosophy and Literature* 23 (1999):257–83.

O'Meally, Robert G. *The Craft of Ralph Ellison.* Cambridge: Harvard University Press, 1980.

———, ed. *Living With Music: Ralph Ellison's Jazz Writings.* New York: The Modern Library, 2001.

———, ed. *New Essays on Invisible Man.* New York: Cambridge University Press, 1988.

Ostendorf, Berndt. "Anthropology, Modernism, and Jazz." *Ralph Ellison: Modern Critical Views.* Edited and introduced by Harold Bloom. New York: Chelsea House Publishers, 1986. 145–72.

Palumbo-Liu, David, ed. *The Ethnic Canon: Histories, Institutions, and Interventions.* Minneapolis: University of Minnesota Press, 1995.

Park, Robert E., and Ernest W. Burgess. *Introduction to the Science of Sociology.* Chicago: University of Chicago Press, 1921.

Parrish, Timothy L. "Ralph Ellison, Kenneth Burke, and the Form of Democracy." 51 *Arizona Quarterly* 3 (Autumn 1995):117–48.

Patell, Cyrus R. K. *Negative Liberties: Morrison, Pynchon, and the Problem of Liberal Ideology.* Durham: Duke University Press, 2001.

Patterson, James T. Brown v. Board of Education*: A Civil Rights Milestone and Its Troubled Legacy.* New York: Oxford University Press, 2001.

Petesch, Donald. *A Spy in the Enemy's Country: The Emergence of Modern Black Literature.* Iowa City: University of Iowa Press, 1989.

Porter, Horace A. *Jazz Country: Ralph Ellison in America.* Iowa City: University of Iowa Press, 2001.

Posgrove, Carol. *Divided Minds: American Intellectuals and the Civil Rights Movement.* New York: W. W. Norton, 2001.

Posner, Richard A. *Public Intellectuals: A Study in Decline.* Cambridge: Harvard University Press, 2001.

Posnock, Ross. *Color and Culture: Black Writers and the Making of the Modern Intellectual.* Cambridge: Harvard University Press, 1998.

Proust, Marcel. *Remembrance of Things Past, Volume I: Swann's Way.* Translated by C. K. Scott Moncrieff and Terence Kilmartin. New York: Random House, 1981.

Random House. Press release (March 25, 1952), Box 154, Ralph Ellison Papers, Library of Congress.

Rawls, John. *Political Liberalism.* New York: Columbia University Press, 1993.

Reed, T. V. *Fifteen Jugglers, Five Believers: Literary Politics and the Poetics of American Social Movements.* Berkeley: University of California, 1992.

Reilly, John. "The Testament of Ralph Ellison." *Speaking for You: The Vision of Ralph Ellison.* Edited by Kimberly Benston. Washington: Howard University Press, 1987. 49–62.

Rice, H. William. *Ralph Ellison and the Politics of the Novel.* Lanham, Md.: Lexington Books, 2003.

Robinson, Greg. "Ralph Ellison, Albert Murray, Stanley Crouch, and Modern Black Cultural Conservatism." *Black Conservatism: Essays in Intellectual and Political History.* Edited by Peter Eisenstadt. New York: Garland Publishing, Inc., 1999. 151–67.

Rosenblatt, Roger. *Black Fiction.* Cambridge: Harvard University Press, 1974.

Rovit, Earl. "Ralph Ellison and the American Comic Tradition." *Ralph Ellison: A Collection of Critical Essays.* Edited by John Hersey. Englewood Cliffs, N.J.: Prentice-Hall, 1974. 151–59.

Rowley, Hazel. *Richard Wright: The Life and Times.* New York: Henry Holt, 2001.

Schafer, William. "Ralph Ellison and the Birth of the Anti-Hero." *Ralph Ellison: A Collection of Critical Essays.* Edited by John Hersey. Englewood Cliffs, N.J.: Prentice-Hall, Inc., 1974. 115–26.

Schaub, Thomas Hill. "From Ranter to Writer: Ellison's *Invisible Man* and the New Liberalism." *American Fiction in the Cold War.* Madison: The University of Wisconsin Press, 1991. 91–115.

Schillebeeckx, Edward. *Christ: The Sacrament of the Encounter with God.* London: Sheed and Ward, 1963.

Scott, Daryl Michael. *Contempt and Pity: Social Policy and the Image of the Damaged Black Psyche, 1880–1996.* Chapel Hill: University of North Carolina Press, 1997.

Scott, Nathan A., Jr. "Ellison's Vision of Communitas." 18 *Callaloo* 2 (Spring 1995):310–18.

Slethaug, Gordon. *Beautiful Chaos: Chaos Theory and Metachaotics in Recent American Fiction.* Albany: State University of New York Press, 2000.

Smith, Valerie. *Self-Discovery and Authority in Afro-American Narrative.* Cambridge: Harvard University Press, 1987.

Southern, David W. *Gunnar Myrdal and Black-White Relations: The Use and Abuse of An American Dilemma, 1944–1969.* Baton Rouge: Louisiana State University Press, 1987.

Spillers, Hortense. "Ellison's 'Usable Past': Toward a Theory of Myth." *Speaking for You: The Vision of Ralph Ellison.* Edited by Kimberly Benston. Washington: Howard University Press, 1987. 144–58.

Steele, Miele. "Arendt versus Ellison on Little Rock: The Role of Language in Political Judgment." *Constellations* 9 (1996):184–206.

———. "Democratic Interpretation and the Politics of Difference." *Comparative Literature* 48 (2002):326–42.

———. "Metatheory and the Subject of Democracy in the Work of Ralph Ellison." 27 *New Literary History* 3 (1996):473–502.

Stephens, Gregory. *On Racial Frontiers: The New Culture of Frederick Douglass, Ralph Ellison, and Bob Marley.* Cambridge, U. K.: Cambridge University Press, 1999.

Stepto, Robert B. "Literacy and Hibernation: Ralph Ellison's *Invisible Man.*" *From Behind the Veil: A Study of Afro-American Narrative.* Urbana: University of Illinois Press, 1979. 163–94.

Stowe, Harriet Beecher. *Uncle Tom's Cabin.* New York: Penguin, 1983.

Strout, Cushing. "'An American Negro Idiom': *Invisible Man* and the Politics of Culture." *Approaches to Teaching* Invisible Man. Edited by Susan Resneck Parr and Pancho Savery. New York: The Modern Language Association of America, 1989. 79–85.

Tanner, Tony. *City of Words: American Fiction 1950–1970.* London: Jonathan Cape, 1971.

Tate, Claudia. "Notes on the Invisible Women in Ralph Ellison's *Invisible Man.*" *Speaking for You: The Vision of Ralph Ellison.* Edited by Kimberly W. Benston. Washington, D.C.: Howard University Press, 1987. 163–72.

Tulsa Star. "The Facts Remain the Same" (September 18, 1920):8.

Unsigned letter to the *Chicago Defender.* Newbern, Ala. *Journal of Negro History* (April 7, 1917):420.

Vogler, Thomas A. "*Invisible Man:* Somebody's Protest Novel." *Ralph Ellison: A Collection of Critical Essays.* Edited by Hersey, John. Englewood Cliffs, N.J.: Prentice-Hall, Inc., 1974. Originally published in *Iowa Review* I (Spring 1970):64–82.

Wald, Alan M. *Exiles from a Future Time: The Forging of the Mid-Twentieth-Century Literary Left.* Chapel Hill: The University of North Carolina Press, 2002.

———. "As White as Anybody: Race and the Politics of Counting as Black." *New Literary History* 31 (2000):709–26.

Warren, Kenneth W. "Ralph Ellison and the Reconfiguration of Black Cultural Politics." 11 *Yearbook of Research in English and American Literature.* Edited by Winfried Fluck. Tubigen: Gunter Narr Verlag, 1995. 139–57.

Warren, Robert Penn. *Who Speaks for the Negro?* New York: Random House, 1965.

Washington, Booker T. *Up From Slavery*. Edited with an introduction by William L. Andrews. New York: Oxford University Press, 1995.

Washington, Booker T. *Up From Slavery: An Autobiography*. Introduction by Langston Hughes. New York: Dodd, Mead & Company, 1965.

Washington, Robert E. *The Ideologies of African American Literature: From the Harlem Renaissance to the Black Nationalist Revolt*. New York: Rowman & Littlefield, 2001.

Watts, Jerry Gafio. *Heroism and the Black Intellectual: Ralph Ellison, Politics, and Afro-American Intellectual Life*. Chapel Hill: The University of North Carolina Press, 1994.

Weisberger, Bernard. "History Maker." *American Legacy* (February 2001):25–26.

Whalen-Bridge, John. *Political Fiction and the American Self*. Urbana: University of Illinois Press, 1998.

Williams, Melissa S. *Voice, Trust, and Memory: Marginalized Groups and the Failings of Liberal Representation*. Princeton: Princeton University Press, 1988.

Williams, Sherley A. "The Blues Roots of Contemporary Afro-American Poetry." *Chant of Saints: A Gathering of Afro-American Literature, Art, and Scholarship*. Edited by Michael S. Harper and Robert B. Stepto. Urbana: University of Illinois Press, 1979. 123–35.

Winther, Per. "The Ending of Ralph Ellison's *Invisible Man*." 25 *CLA Journal* 3 (1982):267–87.

Wright, John. "Dedicated Dreamer, Consecrated Acts: Shadowing Ellison." *The Carleton Miscellany*. Winter 1980. 142–98.

———. "Shadowing Ellison." *Speaking for You: The Vision of Ralph Ellison*. Edited by Kimberly Benston. Washington: Howard University Press, 1987. 63–88.

Wright, Richard. *Black Boy (American Hunger): A Record of Childhood and Youth*. Introduction by Jerry Ward Jr. New York: Perennial Classics/HarperCollins Publishers, 1998; originally published by Harper & Brothers, 1945.

———. "Fire and Cloud." "Uncle Tom's Children." *Richard Wright: The Early Works*. New York: Library of America, 1991.

X, Malcolm. "The Ballot or the Bullet" (April 3, 1964). *Malcolm X Speaks: Selected Speeches and Statements*. Edited by George Breitman. New York: Grove Weidenfeld, 1965. 23–44.

Yaffe, David. "Ellison Unbound." *The Nation* (March 4, 2002).

Young-Bruehl, Elisabeth. *Hannah Arendt: For Love of the World*. New Haven: Yale University Press, 1982.

Index